RURAL RUSSIA

UNDER

THE OLD RÉGIME

CASUALTIES OF A RECURRENT REVOLUTION

Stenka Razin and Pugachev (*above*) were leaders of revolts of the Cossacks and the peasants in the seventeenth and eighteenth centuries, and were executed by the government. The Tsars Alexander II and Nicholas II granted certain reforms, agrarian and other, particularly in the eighteen-sixties and in 1905, but were killed by the revolutionists

GEROID TANQUARY ROBINSON

RURAL RUSSIA
UNDER
THE OLD RÉGIME

*A History of the Landlord-Peasant World
and a Prologue to the Peasant Revolution of 1917*

UNIVERSITY OF CALIFORNIA PRESS
BERKELEY AND LOS ANGELES

California Paper-bound Edition

Third printing, 1972

This edition is published by arrangement with
The Macmillan Company

Printed in the United States of America

ISBN: 0-520-01075-2

To C.

THE WILLIAM A. DUNNING FUND

In the preparation of this book the author has received assistance from the fund for the encouragement of historical studies bequeathed to Columbia University by Professor William A. Dunning.

IN PLACE OF A PREFACE

OCCASIONALLY a Russian writer heads a preface as this one is headed, in the hope, no doubt, of getting it read. Such, at any rate, is my own reason for following this Russian precedent — for I should like very much to entice the reader into examining these few sentences of explanation and acknowledgment before he begins the reading of the history itself.

Perhaps I may best begin by calling attention to the fact that certain of the matters treated in the text are somewhat elaborated in the notes at the end of the volume. The citations in the notes are given with all possible brevity, but the books and articles referred to are fully identified in the bibliography, and the titles are there translated for the benefit of those readers who do not have command of the Russian language but may still wish to know the nature of the materials employed in the writing of this book. Throughout the volume, dates are given in "old style" — that is, in accordance with the Julian calendar, which was in use in Russia until 1918. In forming the plurals of the few Russian terms employed in the text, I have as a rule treated them as English words. It is hoped that when each of these terms first appears, the context will make its meaning sufficiently clear; nevertheless, those words that are repeatedly employed have been given a brief explanation in the glossary at the end of the volume.

I was occupied for several years with the preparation of this volume and with the study of the peasants in the Revolution of 1917. Up to date, the work has involved a protracted study of printed materials both here and in Russia, as well as three periods of travel in Russia, in 1925–27, 1937, and 1958, and the better part of two years spent in the examination, in Russia, of private and public collections of documents pertaining to the Revolution of 1917. The most important of these documents are those of the Provisional Government of 1917, now assembled in the central archives in Moscow.

I am most sincerely grateful for the generous assistance granted, in one stage or another of my work, by Mr. and Mrs. Francis Neilson of Chicago, by the Social Science Research Council, and by Columbia University (from the William Bayard Cutting and the William A. Dunning funds). From first to last the work has gone forward with the unfailing sympathy and encouragement of Professor Carlton J. H. Hayes. To him and to many other members of the staff of Columbia University (in particular to Professors Robert E. Chaddock, Austin P. Evans, Charles Downer Hazen, Vladimir G. Simkhovitch, Lynn Thorndike, and William Linn Westermann, and to Dr. John H. Wuorinen), I am deeply indebted for their many criticisms and suggestions. The same grateful acknowledgment is due likewise to Professor James T. Shotwell as general editor of the *Economic and Social History of the World War,* and to Dr. Michael T. Florinsky as associate editor of the *Russian Series* of that history, for permission to examine in manuscript several of the volumes on Russia at a time when my own work was still in its earliest stage.

Of the scholars and the agrarians with whom I came in contact in the Soviet Union, I have not words enough to say all that should be said. Intensely preoccupied, of necessity, with the demands and distractions of their own contemporary life, they still opened their private libraries to me; they admitted me to public and private collections of documents; they even offered the use of manuscripts which they themselves had written but had not yet published. I do not know why they should have done so much, and I have given up trying to find a way of thanking them; but from these Russians I learned the lengths of generosity to which scholarship may go.

In closing, let me express my deepest appreciation to my wife Clemens, for her unfailing inspiration and encouragement.

GEROID TANQUARY ROBINSON

Columbia University

CONTENTS

LIST OF ILLUSTRATIONS

RURAL RUSSIA
UNDER THE OLD RÉGIME

CHAPTER I

SERFDOM AND THE EARLIER SERVILE WARS

VOYAGING the south-central *step* of Russia in the Autumn of 1926, the writer came quite unexpectedly upon a monument to those historic events which it is the chief purpose of this history to describe — and in so far as may be, to explain. Against a horizon of rolling fields, banded black, green, and yellow with strips of fresh-plowed earth, sprouting winter grain, and fallowed stubble, there appeared a formal block of tree-tops; then, eventually, a keeper's lodge, and the wide gateway of a park. Walled off here from the casual *step*, was a deliberately conventional grove, now very much bedraggled; and beyond, facing upon a broad crescent of brambles, stood the wreck of a manor-house — one of those classical structures that speak so clearly of the wealth and the self-conscious culture of the nobility of the old régime. Against thick walls of plastered brick, stood four substantial columns supporting a balcony at the level of the second floor, and a low pediment above. The frames of the doors and windows gaped empty now; and except for two rooms where the district agronomist was quartered, the interior had been peeled long ago of every scrap of woodwork. The brick vaulting which had supported the upper floors was exposed to view, and some of the stoves — of brick and tile — had been mined away to their foundations.

Prowling among these architectural bones, one could imagine anything: *troikas* at the door; bearded servants bowing and scraping; harpsichords and hunting feasts; the gossip of St. Petersburg and Paris; hoopskirts, silks and sabres; medalled dignitaries with powdered wigs, or the mutton-chop whiskers of a later day;

1

daughters in French gowns, home from the Riviera; sons in the Guards' uniform of the Napoleonic Wars or the Great War — all musty and remote, buried more deeply by these last ten years than by the ten decades that went before. . .

To the rear of the house, a columned gallery looked out upon another brambly garden, penetrated here by a footpath which opened presently upon a carefully-tended orchard and led on through the trees to a shelter of poles and branches — the temporary home of the peasants who had come up to harvest the fruit. A generous gift of apples was offered us, and accepted; but when we made petition for a newspaper, lying at hand, to be used in wrapping up the fruit, the peasants were embarrassed: if this paper were carried off, how, then, would one prepare a cigarette? To make the need more evident, each of the fruit-gatherers rolled a scrap of newspaper into a slender cone, bent the end upward like the bowl of a pipe, filled it with tobacco, and set the tip alight. And there on the ground in front of their primitive shelter, the three shaggy, bark-shod peasants sat smoking, as we climbed back through the orchard and the wreckage of the garden, toward the empty mansion of the cavaliers.

LIVING along from year to year in a world of warm breakfasts and trains-on-time, it is easy to believe that history has no place, nowadays, for catastrophic change; and yet it was no ordinary ten years' evolution that emptied this mansion of its masters, and brought in the peasants to possess the land. The rural society of Old Russia has been turned upside-down with a resounding crash; if it is altogther too early, as yet, to attempt to appraise the *results* of this great revolution, still there can be no mistaking the historic importance and the compelling interest of the *process;* and toward the description and analysis of that process, something may even now be done.

To assert that the change came with appalling suddenness does not mean, of course, that it came unprepared. The prologue reaches far back into the past of the Russian people — back to the time when the mounted nomads of Asia were still careering through the *step,* and comparatively few of the ancestral Russians themselves had yet emerged, as settlers, beyond the southern boundary of their forests.

If the history is a long one, in the scale of time, it is vast in the extent of its theatre of action. Whether the inquirer trusts to the map, or himself pushes out by rail or river-boat across the Great Eurasian Plain, the one impression that dominates all others is the impression of the vastness and the unity of this land-ocean. In all the expanse from the Baltic shore and the Carpathians to the mountains of eastern Siberia, and from the Arctic Ocean to the Central Asian highland, there is no important natural frontier. The Ural range is easily crossed, in the latitude of Moscow, at levels of fifteen hundred or two thousand feet, while farther south, between the extremity of the Urals and the Caspian Sea there is no barrier of any sort; in this open *step* the sheep wander from Asia into Europe, and the Kirgiz shepherd drives them back again into Asia without knowing that he has crossed a geographer's frontier.

The great plain has its differentiated regions, but these are set off one from another, not by geographic barriers, but by natural characteristics which melt and mingle along the borders of the four great zones. A traveller who lands at the arctic port of Murmansk, in the extreme north-west, and pushes down in a general south-easterly direction, through Leningrad and Moscow, then across the middle Volga at Samara, and on to Tashkent and the Afghan frontier, will traverse in the course of this journey each of the longitudinal zones into which nature has divided the great plain: the frozen desert of the North, the forest region, the arable *step*, and the sun-baked desert of the South.

Along the shores of Kola Bay, north of Murmansk, this traveller will see something of the arctic *tundra*, a forbidding landscape even in mid-July, when the sun, "a golden ball almost without heat," has already hung for weeks unremittingly in the sky. However favorable the other natural conditions in the *tundra* might be, the severity of the climate, with its growing season of only six or eight weeks, would alone prevent the development of any considerable vegetation. The clayish sub-soil is covered with only a very thin vegetable deposit, and a real soil can hardly be said to exist; and then, too, great areas are occupied by swamps which never melt to the depth of more than a few inches. The form of vegetation most significant for animal life is the moss which serves as the chief food of the reindeer, and the reindeer are in turn the main economic dependence of the inhabitants. Arctic foxes, white bear, and certain fish and birds are found in this region the year round, and in Spring the life of earth, air, and water is enriched by the arrival of wolves, geese, salmon, and other seasonal migrants from farther south or from the open sea. The *tundra* thus offers certain resources for a semi-nomadic existence of hunting, fishing, and reindeer-herding; but whatever may be said in behalf of "the friendly Arctic," it seems that historically this environment has proved hostile to the development of the more advanced and complex forms of human life.

Along an irregular line that lies sometimes far north of the Arctic Circle and sometimes several degrees to the south of it, the open *tundra* merges by slow degrees into the forest. In this zone, which includes more than half of the entire Eurasian Plain, the precipitation diminishes toward the east, but is in general at least adequate for agriculture, while heat and cold show the wide seasonal variation which is characteristic of a continental climate. In January and in July, the temperature at Moscow, near the southern border of the forest zone, is about the same as that of northern Michigan. Farther eastward, the districts in the latitude of Moscow have approximately the same Summer temperature as the capital, but the Winters become progressively colder, and the difference between Summer and Winter therefore increases in a marked degree as one moves from west to east. At Verkhoiansk, within the Arctic Circle in Siberia, a temperature of 93.6 degrees below zero, Fahrenheit, has been recorded, and at the opposite end of the scale a Summer heat of 92.7 — a range of variation and a degree of cold which for a time exceeded, and perhaps still exceed, anything of the kind ever recorded in any other part of the world.

In the forest zone the soil varies in character from place to place, but is predominantly coarse in grain and either clayish or sandy in composition. This soil has no great capacity for absorbing moisture, and in most areas the organic deposit is comparatively small. Evergreens are found throughout the zone, and to the south and west of a line running from Leningrad to Nizhnii Novgorod the somber blue-green of the northern forest is enlivened by an intermixture of silver birches and other Spring-leafing trees. There are myriads of lakes in the North-west, and great areas of bog and swampland, especially in the North, while the country is threaded everywhere with slow-moving, navigable streams. In early times the forest offered large resources to the fisherman and the hunter, but the northern portion of the zone lies beyond the limit of cultivation for even such hardy grains as rye and barley; and elsewhere, by reason of the severity of the climate, the comparative infertility of the soil, the inadequate drainage, and the difficulty of clearing the land, the natural environment of this zone is, at its worst, posi-

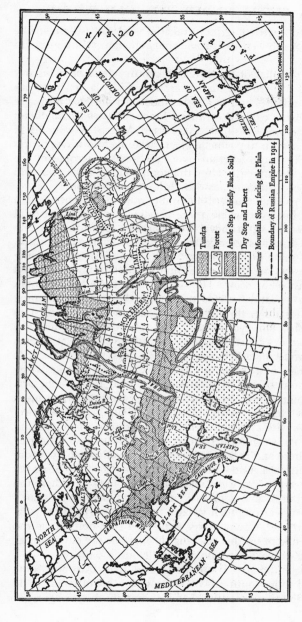

THE NATURAL ZONES OF THE GREAT EURASIAN PLAIN

As a result of natural causes, the four great zones blend and interpenetrate along their borders, and this map therefore presents an extreme simplification of nature's work. Further than this, it must be remembered that within the boundaries here indicated for the natural forest, large areas west of the Urals have been artificially cleared for cultivation.

This map is based in part upon the map compiled by Professor Banjamin Semenov-Tian-Shansky; see *The Geographical Review*, October 1928, p. 619.

tively hostile to a settled agricultural life, while at its best, in the West and the South-west, it is somewhat reluctantly responsive to the plow.

An English traveller of the sixteenth century describes Muscovy as "a countrie . . . full of marish ground, and plaine, in woods and riuers abundant," and in another book dating from the same period and relating to the *North-East Frostie Seas and Kingdomes Lying that Way*, one reads that "there are in Moscouia, wooddes of exceedyng bygnesse in the whiche blacke woolues and whyte beares are hunted. The cause whereof may bee thextreme colde of the North, whiche doth greatly alter the complexions of beastes, and is the mother of whitenesse, as the Philosophers affirme."

With time's passing, much of the timber of the west-central plain was cut away, but everywhere there remain scattered forests and even great stretches of primeval wilderness to remind the traveller that Old Russia was essentially a forest land, and its folk a forest people. In some degree typical of this zone is a region lying along the course of an old imperial highway, about three hundred miles north-east of Moscow. The writer once travelled this road — a strip of grass-land perhaps two hundred feet wide, running straight away for miles through the forest, and turning occasionally with the slow surveyor's curve of a railroad track. There was no formal roadway; instead, the continuous belt of grass was marked by wandering wheel-tracks, which converged at intervals to take advantage of a stretch of "corduroy" bridging some boggy spot. For an hour or two at a time there would be no sight of a house or a human being, and then the forest would open out upon a wide, brown clearing, with its peasant village — a dozen two-storeyed houses with closely huddled outbuildings, all of logs and thatched with straw, the walls and roofs weathered to a slate-grey tone relieved here and there by a spot of pale yellow where a roof had been repaired or a new thatch recently laid on; the fields deserted, the harvest in, a drift of smoke from the log kilns where the grain was drying, a sound of axes at work on the winter's fuel. From the forest near one such village, there came a peculiar ringing sound, and the peasant driver explained that hereabouts the herdsmen often kept up this clacking throughout the day in order to frighten the wolves away from the cattle out at pasture.

The region of the *step* is another world than this, and some three hundred miles south-east of Moscow is a bit of countryside with many of the characteristics that are common to other parts of this third great zone. Through this particular region the writer once drove in late Autumn, over half-roads of black mud that usually followed a rectangular pattern but sometimes rambled off at an odd angle across the strips of plow-land. Wherever the track was fairly passable, the driver of the *troika* kept the middle horse trotting smartly under his high yoke, while the smaller flank-horses cantered along with their manes flying and their hoofs throwing up jets of mud and water. The *step*-wind blew as steadily as the wind that sets against the prow of a liner at sea, and the long, slow roll of the fields recalled the comparison so often made, of the *step* with the open ocean. There were a few peasants at work in the fields, but the *step* was too big for them; it reduced them to complete inconsequence.

Finally a landmark floated up into view — the wings of a windmill, then the onion-shaped dome of a church — and soon the road dropped into a narrow valley, its slopes lined with young birches, and along its bottom a double row of peasant houses standing close together beside a street that followed the irregular course of a stream. The houses were much smaller than those of the North, and most of them were not built of horizontal logs but of poles set vertically in the earth and plastered over with yellow clay. This land of little wood is also a land of few watercourses, and more than two hundred houses were clustered together beside this single stream.

For centuries the line where the natural forest breaks up and melts gradually into the *step* was the frontier between two profoundly different types of human life — between the farmer-hunter of the forest and the pastoral nomad of the grass-lands; and even after the arable *step* was brought under the plow, the old frontier still marked such a change of natural environment that the farm-life of the open plain was, and still is, different in many ways from that of the forest zone. For one thing, the soil is of a very different quality from that farther north. The region of the "black earth" occupies nearly the whole of the western *step*, down to the Black Sea and the Caucasus, and extends east of the Urals in a narrower belt which reaches into central Siberia. This black soil absorbs moisture readily, is rich in humus, and is easily worked, and these qualities combine to make it exceptionally productive. In this region agriculture is favored, too, by a climate somewhat milder than that of the forest, but toward the south-east the rainfall becomes progressively lighter and more fitful, while the winds which blow out of Central Asia sometimes parch the fields in Summer, and in Winter sweep them clean of the snow which protects the germinating seed. Thus, if the peasant of the forest may expect to receive with some regularity the limited return which his land brings in, the peasant of the black-soil *step* has his fat years and his lean years — lean sometimes to the point of famine.

As the black soil fades and the moisture diminishes, the arable *step* merges by slow degrees into the desert which extends from the region of the lower Volga through the whole of the Central Asian plain to the great highland which rises toward the frontier of Persia, Afghanistan, and the Chinese domain. In this zone the soil is for the most part sandy, and impregnated with salt, the rainfall is slight, and the heat in Summer extreme. The grass which covers the plain in Spring is usually burned to a crisp by the end of June, and the nomadic inhabitants drive their flocks northward toward greener pastures, and southward again in Autumn. In some of the valleys of the desert zone, the soil is very productive when brought under irrigation, and has for many centuries supported a complex and highly developed civilization, but only in very recent times have the Russians come into close contact with the people of these oases.

As far as written history is concerned, Russian colonization has no beginning, and as yet no end: no beginning, because long before they learned to make any adequate record of their doings, the Slavs entered upon their great Eastward Movement across the Eurasian plain: [1] no end, because from year to year the stream of Slavonic colonization still moves on, with the persistence of some force of inanimate nature. This Eastward Movement is no less important in the history of Russia than is the Westward Movement in the annals of the United States; and each year these two currents bring the civilizations of Eastern Europe and Western Europe, transmitted respectively by Russia and by America, into closer contact upon the shores of the Pacific — civilizations which have from remote times confronted each other on the opposite side of the world in the region of the Baltic Sea.

From the Carpathian region,[2] or perhaps from the marshes of the Pripet,[3] certain of the Slavs began about the second quarter of the seventh century A. D. a movement toward the east.[4] In the forests along the old Græco-Scandinavian river-road from the Black Sea to the Gulf of Finland and the Baltic, important towns grew up, Scandinavian warrior-traders came to mix their blood with that of the Slavic colonists, and under the influence of a flourishing trade with the imperial city of Constantinople, Russian life received once for all the impress of the Græco-Roman-Christian civilization in its Eastern form.[5] The Russians learned their lessons from the New Rome on the Bosphorus, as the Europeans of the West (and with them the Poles and the other Western Slavs) learned theirs from the Old Rome of the Cæsars and the Popes; and this difference in nurture helped to lay down across the map of Europe a cultural frontier which even today cannot escape the notice of the most casual traveller.

At the time when the Kievan cities were flourishing most promisingly along the Old-Russian water-road, Slavic explorers and settlers still continued their eastward advance,[6] and most active of all were the men from Great Novgorod (near the Gulf of Finland), who probably reached the north-westernmost corner of Asia before the year 1100.[7] With the decline of Kievan civilization in the basin of the Dnepr during the succeeding century, there came however a much more numerous exodus, both westward and north-eastward, which had gone far toward depopulating the old South-west, even before the destroying Tatar hordes came in the thirteenth century to complete its desolation.[8] This exodus carried the bulk of the Russian population into the forest lands centering about the Oka and the upper Volga,[9] and here in a region, cold, inhospitable and remote, draining not toward Byzantium or the Baltic but toward the ancient East, the Russians lived for more than two centuries under the lax overlordship of the Tatars, and took from Asia some part of that second cultural impress which has helped to mark them off from the Occidental world. Here, then, in the Volga forest, we may venture to begin the study of the historical processes which were eventually to empty that southern manor-house of its masters, and open its windows to the storm.

ALONG the rivers and through the swamps and forests of the central plain, the Russian colonists advanced, not with the panoply of conquest and the drawing out of definite frontiers, but by a slow and casual percolation, dealing for the most part peacefully with the sprinkling of Finnish forest-dwellers who had already settled here, and pushing them gradually northward, or amalgamating with them.[10] Open spots sufficiently high and dry to form attractive dwelling-sites were widely scattered and often very small in area; and then, too, it was hard to find lands which were not immoderately difficult to clear for cultivation. Under such conditions, the individual house-yards either stood alone, or were grouped by two's, three's and four's in favored spots, and until the end of the seventeenth century these small settlements still predominated in the northern region,[11] though larger villages were growing up by this time along the widely-separated water-courses of the southern *step*.

In the center and the North, where climate, soil, and forestation made the land so generally inhospitable to agriculture, the settlers usually plowed only a narrow area, and gave much of their time to hunting, fishing, and the gathering of honey and wax, and to the practice of household industries.[12] Their exploitation of the streams and forests, like their primitive and soil-exhausting agriculture, prescribed a sparse and broadcast population; but to say no more than this, is to give an impression of dispersion, isolation, and individualism which runs far beyond the fact.

Ordinarily these Russian colonists did not live the lonely life of an American frontier family. In the number and in the close inter-relationship of its inhabitants, the smallest Russian settlement had usually the double character of a village and a family. With its numerous population, a single "court" or house-yard standing alone in the forest might still quite properly be called a "village," and often was so called by the Russians of the time.[13] The dwellers in such a house-yard made up a "complex" or patriarchal family which usually included not only the children and grandchildren of the head of the household, but other relatives by blood and by marriage, and frequently also a number of unrelated persons who had been absorbed into the economic and social organization of the group. As a result of the natural expansion of the complex family, new "simple" families were sometimes set up in adjoining dwellings, but it appears that during the earlier centuries of Russian history, such a change did not ordinarily involve a dissolution of the patriarchal group; whether they occupied a single dwelling or several adjoining ones, the members seem in early times to have held their lands and performed their labors collectively, and it is also possible that they regarded the products of their work as common property.[14] Before the sixteenth century, there had begun in Little Russia (then under Polish-Lithuanian rule), and in the northern stretches of Great Russia, a progressive loosening of patriarchal ties,[15] while from the sixteenth century onward, the emigration of junior members to the *step* was operating to reduce the size of the peasant families of the central forest-plain.[16] Sometimes, in spite of all this, the patriarchal order still survived, while from this time onward there is increasing evidence of economic interconnections among peasant families not known to be of a common ancestry — connections which may or may not have been in part an outgrowth of the earlier patriarchal system.

In the sixteenth century the plow-land around the village was sometimes divided into three open fields which were seeded according to a regular rotation: that is, the second of the fields was each year one step ahead of the first, and the third field one step ahead of the second, in the three-year crop-cycle of Winter grain, Spring grain, and fallowing. But instead of holding consistently to this rotation, most of the peasants followed the more primitive custom of permitting large stretches of land to lie unseeded for several years on end, and even to fall permanently out of cultivation.[17]

Where the village included several households, each customarily held one or more strips of land in each of the several fields, and in each of these fields all the households followed, of necessity, the same cycle of cropping and fallowing. It was the custom to re-divide the meadows each year before the mowing, while the pasture-lands and forests were generally used in common; and sometimes a forest was used not only by the households of a single village, but by those of a group of neighboring villages.[18]

United in communes which combined a number of households, the peasants of central and northern Russia held folk-meetings, elected elders, and collectively exercised important fiscal and land-administrative functions.[19] The registered householders of the communes were held to a joint responsibility for taxes, and the apportionment among them of this burden, in accordance with the extent and quality of the land in occupation, was left to their elected chiefs.[20] Again, as early as the fifteenth century, instances are recorded of the allotment by the *volost*-commune of unoccupied lands within its territory.[21] In the North the *volost*-communes, each uniting a number of villages, exercised in the seventeenth century important functions of local self-government, bore a joint responsibility for the preservation of order and the discharge of fiscal obligations, and made reallotments of abandoned farms; and often these organizations figured also as the common holders and collective exploiters of meadows and of fisheries.[22] In central Russia the *volosts* were during the sixteenth century in process of dissolution into smaller village-communes, which also had their folk-meetings, their elected chiefs, and their joint responsibility for taxes to be apportioned among themselves; and it is from this central region that there come the first reports, dating from this same century, of a practice which was eventually to have a profound importance in Russian agrarian history — the redistribution, within the commune, of the landholdings of its members.[23]

Such, then, was the general character of the two basic institutions of Old-Muscovite peasant society: the *family*, which united its members not only for the common holding of land, but for the everyday business of getting a living from the narrow clearings and the forests that hemmed them in; and the *commune*, a tax-apportioning and tax-responsible organization with certain functions of land-control which are by no means clearly defined by the records of the time, but had either grown out of, or would eventually develop into, that wide community of interest in the land which — at least in later times — was so characteristic of Russian peasant life.[24]

Turning from the internal relationships of peasant society to the external contacts of the peasantry with the members of other social orders, one discovers marked differences between village and village; and these differences depend primarily upon the character of the over-rights which lay, in each specific case, upon the village lands. In the preceding discussion, the peasants have been referred to not as owners, but as holders, of land — and the importance of this distinction will now become apparent. By long and complex historical processes, non-peasant over-rights of one sort or another were extended to wide territories in advance of their settlement, as well as to the lands previously appropriated by the peasant colonists. In the sixteenth and seventeenth centuries, there were certain regions (including the extreme North, almost in its entirety) where no landholder stood between the peasants and the Tsar; but elsewhere intervening rights were still being extended to cover wider and wider areas, and upon the basis of the absence or presence of these rights a major distinction may be drawn between the lands of the State and the seigniorial lands — lay and ecclesiastical, and between the corresponding categories of the village population — the State peasants, on the one hand, and the seigniorial peasants on the other.[25]

During the thirteenth and fourteenth centuries, most of the peasants were still able to discharge the economic obligations laid upon them by this expanding system of overlordships, and thus to exercise their right as free men to move on from one place to another, when and if they chose;[26] but by the end of the sixteenth century their obligations had been so increased and their freedom so restricted that they were already partly or completely bound in fact, though not yet definitively so in law. The peasants on the State lands bore a tax, and — at least in some instances — additional dues which were payable to the State in money, in kind,[27] or in labor,[28] and resembled the obligations of the peasants on the private estates to their overlords. Joint responsibility for taxes had existed among them at an earlier time, but this alone had not prevented the removal of those who could discharge their obligations.[29] However, by the early years of the seventeenth century, or perhaps even before this time, it had apparently become the general official practice to permit the registered and tax-responsible heads-of-households on the State domains to leave their communes only if they provided substitutes to fill their places.[30] Obviously it was the peasants with the poorest lands and the heaviest tax who would be most likely to wish to remove from their villages, and it was precisely these peasants who would find it most difficult to discover others who would take over their allotments and assume their share of the fiscal burden.

At least as early as the fifteenth century, the peasants on the estates of the landlords and of the Church were also held jointly responsible for any taxes levied by the State upon the lands which they cultivated;[31] but in the "binding" of the peasants of this class, there were other factors of much greater importance than the tax-union. During the course of the sixteenth century the lands directly administered by the State decreased considerably in area, especially in the central region of Old Muscovy, while the monasteries, the great lords or *boiare,* and the lesser gentry in the service of the Tsar, continued to extend their holdings.[32] Within the limits of these holdings, the nobles and the clergy enjoyed wide immunities which wholly or in part exempted their peasants from taxation, and bound them over to the private jurisdiction of the landlord[33] except in the most serious offenses.[34] The dues and services which the peasant-householder rendered in return for the use of the land, were defined by a contract between himself and the landlord.[35] In the sixteenth century these obligations were often so heavy, and the average land-allotment was so small and so rapidly diminishing in size, that in many villages the peasantry were loaded to the breaking point. This, of course, helped to open the way for the multiplication of landlords' loans,[36] and as the burden of indebtedness increased and the economic strength of the peasantry declined, the practical value of the right of removal also ebbed away. The householder might lawfully exercise this right only when his obligations had been discharged or transferred, and by the end of the century the right itself had therefore become, for the great majority of the householders, simply a legal fiction.[37] Some notion of what the peasants thought of the conditions under which they lived, may be gathered from the fact that many of them voluntarily gave up their place on the land and sold themselves into personal bondage, rather than attempt any longer to carry the burdens laid upon them as men still free before the law.[38]

During this same century — the sixteenth — there began a great movement of population which one might have expected to bring prosperity to the Russian plowman. The main tide of colonization had hitherto moved eastward and northward, through the forest region, but now with the conquest of the Tatar khanates of Kazan (1552) and Astrakhan (1556), Russian colonists emerged for the first time in large numbers upon the *step*.[39] Here was a world so different from the ancestral forest of the Russians, that one may almost see them blinking in the sunshine of these open plains; and certainly they must have been astonished at the easy turning of the rich black soil before the plow, and the manifold reward of the harvest. If with the opening of these new lands, the villagers had a better reason than before to try to keep alive the right of free removal, the landlords of the forest, threatened with the abandonment and consequent ruin of their estates, became all the more active in their attempts to establish and maintain control over the valued person of the peasant. Into the competition for the command of labor, there now entered, too, a swarm of Tsar's grantees whose new estates along the southern border would be valueless until colonists could be found to till their soil. Had the factors in this situation been purely economic, the peasantry could hardly have failed to prosper, either through their own direct exploitation of the southern *step*, or through the competitive bidding of the landlords for their labor. But if the peasant ran away to the nearer borderland, he found the landlord already in control; and how could the peasant profit through the contest for labor between the old landlords and the new, when the contestants resorted not so much to competitive inducements, as to contractual or forcible restrictions of movement, on the one hand, and to forcible captures and removals, on the other ? [40] Thus there arose this apparent contradiction: that during the first century of expansion into the richest region ever opened to Russian colonization,[41] the mass of the Russian peasantry were in process of decline toward serfdom. The success of this progressive encroachment upon the economic and personal status of the peasant can hardly be explained without some reference to the fact that the Russian State was also in process of formation. The separate principalities had been united under Muscovite rule; and through the destruction of a considerable part of the old nobility, the extension of royal land-grants to new retainers, and the establishment of a State-service obligation for the nobles,[42] a compromise of interests was effected, and upon this basis there was gradually built up a political and military organization powerful enough to control, by force, both the land and the labor of the country. The development of this organization is often described as the growth of autocracy — of the power of one over all; and certainly it did involve a diminution of the liberties which had belonged to the Russian nobility of the fourteenth century. But even more conspicuous than the extension of the Tsar's power over the landlords, was the extension of the landlords' power over the peasantry. For the nobles who stood between the sovereign and the peasant, there was involved a loss on the one hand, and a gain on the other — and unquestionably the first change, with the accompanying integration of the State, helped to make the second possible. But unlike their lords, the peasants could not shift the burden; upon them, by and large, there fell the final incidence of autocracy.

Under this system of increasing obligations and restrictions, the peasants who lived on the private estates maintained themselves by cultivating the lands conditionally allotted to them, and rendered dues and services regularly to their landlords — perhaps such and so many shocks of grain, to be set aside at the harvest, a certain area of land to be cultivated directly for the landlord's benefit, or certain appointed tasks to be performed in or about the manorial courtyard. Besides these villagers, there existed also on the estates certain special groups of bondsmen, some full-bound in heredity, others under specific contracts which were frequently drawn to run only for the lifetime of the master.[43] These bound people were employed for the most part in the domestic service of the manor, but by the latter half of the sixteenth century the landlords had here and there provided them with allotments, and set them up as cultivators on their own account, with current obligations resembling those of their peasant neighbors on the same estates.[44] As these bondsmen became divorced from day-to-day dependence upon the master, and took on the responsibilities of householding and cultivation, they approached, by that much, the status of free peasants; while at the same time the peasants, still self-supporting householders and small farmers, were by their progressive loss of freedom approaching the status of chattel slaves.[45] The process of elevation on the one hand and degradation on the other, was at once juridical and practical: on the legal side, it would result at a later time in the assimilation of the whole working population of the estates in a medial level of bondage, uniform before the law; but even then, there would still remain an all-important practical distinction between the small minority who lived in complete economic dependence upon their masters, and those who got a livelihood for themselves out of the lands allotted for their use.

In the history of the Polish-Lithuanian State, which in the sixteenth century included territories extending from the Baltic Sea far down toward the Black, there was much that paralleled the contemporary developments in Muscovy. In Poland, the institution of serfdom was established, in fact and in law, at an earlier time than in Russia,[46] while the southeastward movement of colonization was also of earlier origin and in the late sixteenth century had already reached considerable proportions.[47] It was this movement that repeopled Ukraina, the region which had been before the Mongol invasions the chief center of Kievan civilization; and it is probable that most of the new colonists were descendants of those Russians who had migrated *westward* at the time of the original exodus from the Kievan region, when the majority of the populace had moved *northeastward,* to form a new center between the Oka and the upper Volga.[48]

Against the encroachments of serfdom, many of the peasants of Russia and of Poland tried to find remedy in a transfer to some new master, or in escape beyond the last frontier into the open *step,*[49] and as a result of removals legal and illegal, many villages in the older-settled regions of both countries were depopulated [50] — a state of affairs described graphically enough by Giles Fletcher, who visited Muscovy toward the end of the sixteenth century, and reported that ". . . many villages and townes of halfe a mile and a mile long, stande all unhabited: the people being fled all into other places, by reason of the extreme usage and exactions done upon them." [51]

It is, however, a mistake to think that the whole extent of the *step* was easily or quickly overspread with Polish and Russian serf estates. The Tatars still swarmed periodically across the plains from their towns near the Black Sea, and there was hardly the security needed for a settled life even within the lines of Polish and Russian military posts, joined together along the Russian frontier by ramparts stretching for hundreds of miles through the open country [52] — a kind of European Chinese Wall. The advance of the fortified frontier meant the advance of servile agriculture, digging itself into the *step;* but beyond the last stockade, there was a no-man's-land that drew out to itself many a free-hearted peasant who had no taste for the obligations of the serf. Here, with an admixture of Tatar nomads, these adventurers formed the wild self-governing communities of the Don, the Dnepr and the Volga, and attacked with almost equally good will the manorial estates to the northward and the Tatar towns on the south. [53] It is here among these Cossacks of the open border that one must look for the Daniel Boones and the Davy Crocketts of Russian history, and the reckless heroes of many a Russian folk-song. In one of the Russian "Robber Songs," the Tsar questions a Cossack prisoner about his companions, and the frontiersman answers:

> I will tell thee, O source of hope, Orthodox Tsar,
> All the truth will I tell to thee, the whole truth.
> The number of my companions was four.
> My first companion — the dark night,
> My second companion — a knife of steel,
> My third companion — my good steed,
> My fourth companion — a tough bow,
> And my messengers were keen arrows.

The Orthodox Tsar then promises the Cossack "a lofty dwelling in the midst of the plain, with two pillars and a cross-beam"; that is — in the fashion of the time — a gallows. [54]

Thus far it has been the object of this sketch to show how the Russian peasantry were schooled in collective action by the internal organization of village society; how the burdens laid upon this society from without were progressively increasing; and how there had grown up in the *step* a class of free-roving men whose very existence was a threat to the established order of things in the

Polish and Muscovite States. That the Cossacks should resist the extension of the servile agricultural system into the *step*, was just as natural as that the Sioux and Apaches should attack the wagon-trains of the American frontier; but in Eastern Europe there was one factor for which no important counterpart is to be found in American history: the peasants on the estates of Russia and Poland became the natural allies of the Cossacks, and the great social wars, when they came, were destined to take essentially the form of a double attack upon serfdom — an attack from below, and an attack from beyond the border. If the Indians of the American West could have formed an effective alliance with the Negro slaves of the South, the earlier social uprisings of Russia and Poland might have been in some measure duplicated in the United States.

While the institution of serfdom was still in process of establishment, the first of the great revolts took place — during the period known in Russian history as the Time of Troubles (1598–1613).[55] The way was prepared by two special circumstances, one of negative, and one of positive significance. The ancient dynasty of the Muscovite Tsars faded out at the end of the sixteenth century, and the subsequent feuds and outright contests of force among the nobles and the gentry resulted in a pretty complete disintegration of the organized power which had held the peasants in subjection. Then, in the second place, there came a failure of the harvest for three years in succession (1601–1603), and famine brought to an unbearable crisis a life already hard enough to bear. Attempting somehow to escape starvation, masses of peasants voluntarily became the slaves of masters who they hoped would feed them,[56] while others fled to the open *step*, or went out upon "the great road" to form robber-bands and prey upon the rich and the great who passed that way. The time was ripe for large events, and when the first Pretender to the throne appeared, hordes of Cossacks, peasants and desperate people of every sort swarmed to his assistance.[57] After the overthrow and dispatch of this Pretender by the Moscow mob and the *boiare* or greater nobles, the mass-movement took on a more distinctly revolutionary character, under the leadership of a bold ex-slave named Bolotnikov who issued proclamations calling upon the peasants to plunder and slay their masters. "Robbing the *boiare* of their lives," destroying their dwellings, and taking captive their wives and children, the horde of have-not's advanced from the southern frontier almost to the gates of Moscow.[58] After these early successes, Bolotnikov's forces were defeated and dispersed, and the leader himself disappeard from sight in the whirlpool of the time; but before long, the same Cossack-peasant elements reappeared under the leadership of a new Pretender to the throne, the "Thief of Tushino," who established a vast entrenched camp near the capital.[59] For the nobles, the situation had become so desperate that some among them invited foreign intervention, first by the Swedes and then by the Poles; "everywhere 'good,' opulent citizens said [so reports a contemporary] that it were better to serve the son of the [Polish] King than to be murdered by their own slaves, or to suffer in perpetual bondage to them." [60] In the end, after a fury of blood-letting, the foreigners were expelled,[61] the provinces were pacified, and the house of Romanov was established on the throne.[62] The economic, social and political structure of Russia had been more rudely shaken than it was to be again until three centuries had passed — and then would come another "time of troubles," when this same house of Romanov would be finally engulfed.

Although the higher circle of the old nobility had been destroyed in the period of factional war and mass revolt, the accession of the Romanovs was in its essence a restoration; that is, it marked a resumption of the progressive enserfment of the peasantry,[63] and of the building — on the basis of a compromise of interests — of a consolidated ruling class.[64] Some of the Cossacks fled beyond the reach of Muscovy, toward the Caspian, while those who remained on the Don preserved their institutions of self-government and served the Tsardom in the capacity of a frontier guard against the Turks and the Tatars.[65] In central Muscovy, the land was sewn more thickly than ever with brush-grown fields and abandoned villages, and after years of feud and famine, the peasants were hungrier and more ragged than before the Troubled Times.[66] As before, those on the domains of the State were permitted to quit their tax-unions only if they could find substitutes to fill their places.[67] The relations of the private landlords with their peasants were still subject to contractual arrangement, but this usage was in process of self-destruction: instead of providing some means through which the peasant might hope eventually to discharge his obligations and set himself free (long a mere legal fiction in most cases, inasmuch as the peasant was usually without power of fulfilment), the loan-contracts came generally to embody a final surrender of freedom, without provision for its recovery; and toward the middle of the century these agreements began to be so extended as to bind explicitly the family of the contracting householder, as well as the man himself.[68] Side by side with such private contracts, operated the public registrations of the taxable peasantry, designed to fix each man permanently in his village.[69] The effect of the Code of 1649 was to sanction the binding of the registered private peasant to the land and to the landlord's authority, the second bond being stronger than the first, in that the landlord might even go so far as to separate his peasants from the land upon which they had been settled — and this without their own consent.[70] The possibility of the peasant's retreat into the non-tax-responsible status of slavery was eliminated,[71] and at the same time the landlord's right to act for the recovery of an absconding peasant, formerly exercisable only during a limited term after the flight, was extended to perpetuity.[72] Saying so much, the Code also left many things unsaid, and in general the peasant's interests remained undefined and unprotected — in the matter of forced labor,[73] for example; and also in respect to the status of movable goods, where the times seemed to recognize concurrently the factual possession of the peasant and the superior property-right of the master.[74] By its omissions, then, as well as by its commissions, the Code of 1649 contributed generously to the degradation of the peasants.

Besides exercising extensive rights and privileges in his own behalf, the seventeenth-century landlord represented within the confines of the manor the higher authority of the State. He exercised important functions of justice and police; he represented his peasants in certain processes in the public courts; he collected, and was held responsible for, the taxes of those who lived upon his lands.[75]

All this showed the trend of social change, as it affected the once-free peasantry; and now, as before the Time of Troubles, the slave continued to approach, from below, the status of serfdom, as did the peasant from above. More and more, the courtyard slaves — of course far less numerous than the peasants — were settled on the land,[76] and from 1678, those so provided for were held to the same tax-liability as their peasant neighbors.[77] The slave and the peasant had already proceeded very far toward their ultimate amalgamation.

In a sphere of Russian life remote from the log huts of the plowmen and the log mansions of the proprietors, there began, less than a half-century after the Time of Troubles, a movement which was eventually to have a profound effect upon the relations of the peasants with their masters. At least in part as a result of the poor education of the Russian clergy and the comparative isolation of the Russian Church from its Orthodox neighbors, the centuries had accumulated in its ritual-books and practices a number of variants which had come to differentiate the Russian rites from those of the other Churches of the Eastern Orthodox communion.[78] About the middle of the seventeenth century, an attempt was made to eliminate these variants; the Russians were now required, for example, to make the sign of the cross, not with two fingers, but with three, and to repeat the alleluia not twice only, but three times.[79] The revisionist movement was directed by the Patriarch of Moscow, and supported by the Council of the Russian Church, the *Boiarskaia Duma,* and the Tsar,[80] but some of the clergy set themselves against it, and soon the opposition gathered strength among the merchantry and the peasants. In their obstinate refusal to alter one single peculiarity of the Russian service — one gesture or one word of the rites which they had been taught to venerate, the "Old Ritualists" may have elevated a question of form to the dignity of a question of doctrine; but in this they were hardly alone, for the revisionists excommunicated as heretics all who declined to accept their emendations,[81] and the government undertook in 1685 to torture the recalcitrants into a recognition of the truth (as revised), or else to burn them.[82]

This crisis in the history of the Russian Church has two aspects which are deserving of special emphasis in any history of the peasants and their lords. First, the revision was sponsored by the dignitaries of Church and State and accepted, if not welcomed, by the nobility, while in the rural districts, the Old Ritualist opposition found support, not in the manor-house, but among the peasants.[83] In the second place, Old Ritualism was essentially conservative, refusing to surrender the old for the new. The question naturally arises, whether there is any organic connection between the peasantism and the conservatism of the movement. Was this the conservatism of simple men who clung to every word and letter of the formulæ which they believed had served them well; or did this conservatism arise out of a natural peasant distrust of *any* change sponsored by the class which had been engaged in reducing the village to serfdom; or again, did there linger among the villagers a tradition of a better time, when men, now everywhere in chains, were free, and did the peasants cling to everything that was old — even to old religious observances — because nearly everything that was new had fallen upon them as a burden? The early social history of Old Ritualism has been so little explored [84] that a definite answer can hardly be given to such questions as these; but even where so much is in obscurity, this at least is clear: Old Ritualism was, in the rural districts, almost purely a peasant movement, and as such, it served to increase the cultural difference between the peasants whom it affected — only a small part, to be sure, of all the peasantry of Russia — and the proprietors; and whether or not the movement arose in part out of a previous antagonism of master and man, it can hardly have failed, as time went on, to sharpen this hostility.

While these changes were taking place in the internal life of Muscovy, the march of colonization was still advancing along the Polish and Muscovite frontiers. [85] In Siberia, the Russian State did not grant away its lands to large private holders, and the colonists who settled there retained the character of State peasants; [86] in the European *step*, on the other hand, the advance of the frontier meant, sooner or later, the advance of private landholding and of servile agriculture — and now, as before, neither the intensive nor the extensive development of this institution went unopposed. In the region where the serf estates were already well established, there were occasional minor disturbances, [87] and it was a common thing for a peasant to run away, with as much of his master's goods as he could get his hands on — and perhaps then to be pursued with hunting-dogs and dragged home again. [88] For those who escaped, the most tempting refuge was still the "wild fields" out beyond the fortified frontier. But here the trading and marauding activities of the Cossack plainsmen were increasingly hampered by the presence of Polish, Turco-Tatar and Russian outposts near the sea-outlets of the Dnepr, the Don, and the Volga. [89] Among the plainsmen there was also becoming increasingly evident a division of interest between the new refugees, and the "old Cossacks" who had begun to live a more settled life and to make compromises of one sort and another with the Russian and Polish governments. [90]

Among the "beggar" Cossacks of the Muscovite frontier, there was eventually ignited the prairie-fire of another uprising. Led by a certain Stenka Razin, the "beggars" took control of the region of the Don, and then raised the populace against officialdom and the landlords in a revolt which spread eight hundred miles through the Volga basin, from Astrakhan to the neighborhood of Nizhnii Novgorod. At Nizhnii, the conflagration had reached within two hundred and fifty miles of Moscow; but now there were in the upper levels of Russian society no such weakening feuds as had marked the Time of Troubles, and the rising was suppressed in less than two years. In 1671, Stenka Razin was executed in the Red Square of Moscow [91] — a ceremony which closes the last act of a post-revolutionary opera composed in Razin's honor, and first performed in 1926 in a theatre which stands a few blocks from the spot where the execution itself took place.

In Poland, disturbances by peasants and Cossacks were frequent, but the social wars of Russia are most closely paralleled by the great uprising which took place in the middle of the seventeenth century. In the Ukraina or "borderland," the cleavage was sharpened and the situation complicated by national and religious differences: the chief nobles were Polish or Polanized, and Roman Catholic; the peasantry were generally Ukrainian (or "Little Russian") in nationality and Orthodox in religion; while the Cossacks figured usually as enemies of the Poles, and sometimes also as champions of the Orthodox Church.[92] After a series of Cossack-peasant risings, the Poles made in 1638 a systematic attempt to deprive the landed Cossacks of their hereditary holdings, to bring under the control of Polish officers those Cossacks (usually the best-off economically) whom they had long been trying to organize as a frontier guard, and to reduce the rest to serfdom.[93] After a few years of grumbling, there began in 1648 the great Cossack rising led by Bogdan Khmelnitskii and supported in the beginning by the Tatars of Crimea; but even before the Cossacks marched into the region of the Ukrainian serf-estates, the "dark people" there had already begun to rise against their landlords.[94] A furious *jacquerie* swept through the southeastern Polish *step*, but Khmelnitskii presently signed with the Poles a treaty which promised favors to the Cossacks and to the Orthodox Church, but offered nothing to the serfs as such.[95] In fact the Cossack leader even ordered the bondaged people to submit themselves once more to their masters — and thus he sacrificed the possibility of peasant support for any enterprise of his in the future.[96]

An extraordinary tangle of domestic and international relations marked the next half-century, sooner or later involving in the Ukrainian question the governments of Crimea, Russia, Sweden, and Turkey; and in the end, Poland lost the territory on the east bank of the Dnepr to the Tsar, and a part of that on the west bank to the Sultan.[97] In the west-Ukrainian lands which remained to Poland, a restoration of the old social and economic system was effected with little difficulty,[98] but on the eastern side of the Dnepr, in the region ceded to Muscovy, the developments were much more complex. Here the fury of Cossack raids and peasant risings had cleared the country of most of the old nobility and gentry, freed the mass of the peasants, and opened much of the land to the use of anyone who wished to plow it.[99] There still survived, however, the estates of the Orthodox Church, and some of those of the gentry, and with these examples before them, the Cossack aristocracy very shortly began to extend over-rights to the lands occupied by the peasantry, and even to those held by the lower ranks of their own Cossackdom.[100] Here serfdom was once more in the making, and the government at Moscow, progressively restricting the freedom of the Cossack "elders" and the autonomy of the Cossacks as a whole, gave its sympathy and support to the downward extension of the elders' powers and privileges at the expense of the poorer folk of the borderland.[101] The social change here under way therefore resembles that already observed in the older territories of Muscovy — a compromise between autocrat and aristocrat, at the cost, in larger part, of the plowman.

CHAPTER II

THE TRIUMPH OF THE SERVILE SYSTEM [1]

IN THE eighteenth century, the Russian court-circle undertook to do itself over in the mode of Versailles, and along with the paint and powder, the furnishings and fashions, the manners and morals of the West, it imported some of those liberal ideas to which the Enlightenment was giving currency. Great Catherine even convoked in 1766 a commission representing most of the social classes of Russia (though not the private serfs, who, of course, were most in need of redress), and assigned to this body the task of preparing a project for a new code of law, on the basis of her own liberal but vague "Instruction" — a document which "contained enough maxims to knock a wall down." However, after some two years of discoursing up and down, the commission passed quietly into oblivion; [2] the major accomplishments of the period were effected by other means than these.

Of these chief accomplishments, there are two that touch most intimately upon this history: the further consolidation of the ruling class (with the subsequent "emancipation" of the nobility), and the continued intensive and extensive development of serfdom.[3] In the State-serving nobility of the time of Peter the Great, it is difficult to recognize the successors of the petty princes and free-roving retainers of the fourteenth century. Under Peter the process of regimentation reached its climax. The service of the State was made obligatory for the nobles for the whole period of competent adult life (an obligation not always successfully enforced, however),[4] and State service so far superseded family as a gauge of rank, that even a youth of highest birth was required to begin his duties in the lowest civil or military grade (though he usually entered the privileged "Guards"). Beginning so, the noble was thereafter rated officially according to his position in the service, while on the other hand, a commoner might rise through

25

the same official hierarchy to a grade that would give him and his heirs a full hereditary membership in the nobility.[5]

With the progressive increase in the obligations which the State service laid upon the nobles, there had come, on the other hand, an increasingly effective control, by the nobility, of the land and the peasants who cultivated it; and with Peter's recognition of the nobles' tenure of their serf-estates as everywhere hereditary, the last trace of the old system of temporary land-grants disappeared from the law.[6] In law and in fact the noble landlord was at once an hereditary serf-master, and an hereditary State-servant, and the double process of enserfing the peasantry and consolidating the ruling class appeared complete. But in history there seem to be no points of equilibrium and rest; at any rate, there is no pause in these two parallel streams of change, one of which continued now to flow on much as before, while the other altered, even in a sense reversed, the direction of its movement. The coming decades were to make the peasant more than ever a serf, but the same period was to bring an "emancipation of the nobility" — a process finally completed by the imperial manifesto of 1762 which declared that, except in the presence of some public emergency, the nobles were free to serve the State or not, as they might choose.[7] Thus toward the middle of the eighteenth century the obligations of the nobility diminished, while its privileges still increased.[8]

This "emancipation" of the nobility did not accompany or produce a dissolution of the ruling class into conflicting groups. It is true, a number of factional disturbances took place in the capital during the decades which followed the death of Peter the Great, but after 1762 such difficulties diminished, rather than increased.[9] The service of the State had schooled the nobles in co-ordinate action, and by this time they had apparently become more conscious than before of those bonds of interest which united them one to another, and to the autocracy. At any rate, the "Golden Age of the Russian Nobility," now begun, is characterized, as far as the nobles are concerned, neither by feudal disorders nor by compulsory co-ordination, but rather by a decline of factionalism and a widespread loyalty to the Empress Catherine, sometimes called "the Great."

However, for the peasants in the possession of these noblemen, the story of this period is not one of interests served and loyalty inspired, but of oppression and revolt. The proportion between the total numbers of private serfs and of State peasants was some-what altered by the secularization, beginning in 1762, of the Church lands, and the conversion of the serfs on these lands into State peasants.[10] When the century is considered as a whole, the secularizations are approximately balanced, however, by transfers of State lands and State peasants to private lay grantees.

The bondaged plowmen and courtyard people on the estates of the nobles outnumbered the Church serfs nearly four to one (in the 'sixties [11]), and for them the century of the Enlightenment was a century of abysmal darkness and depression. Through develop-ments extending from the time of Peter the Great into the reign of Catherine II, the once clear distinction between the chattel slaves and the free peasantry of the estates was finally submerged in a bondage uniform before the law and increasing in its sever-ity.[12] Besides sharing with the peasants on the State lands the obli-gation to pay taxes and to furnish recruits for the army,[13] the private peasants bore a number of special burdens and disabilities. By custom, most of the peasants on the estates lived on from gen-eration to generation in the same huts; got their living out of the cultivation of their allotments; sometimes, in a good year, added to the household wealth a heifer, or a plow, or a sheepskin coat; joined regularly in the debates and decisions of the village assem-bly; and rendered certain dues and services to the lord of the manor. But in no one of these activities did they enjoy any real security. The landlord might add to or reduce the amount of land allotted to the village as a whole or to any single householder; [14] he might leave to the peasants' assembly the matter of distributing and redistributing the allotment-land, or he might interfere as he saw fit; [15] he might increase the dues and services required,[16] seize the peasant's movable goods,[17] restrict his economic relations with persons beyond the borders of the estate (in such matters as wage-work, the leasing of land, the contracting of loans [18]), remove him entirely from the soil for a lifetime of domestic service,[19] com-mand or prevent his marriage,[20] sell him with or apart from the land and with or without the other members of his family.[21]

Where the masters took their returns from the peasants in the form of money-dues or *obrok,* the average weight of this obligation seems to have increased considerably between the 'sixties and the 'nineties — perhaps even as much as one hundred per cent.[22] In the forest region, where the bulk of the population still lived, these dues per acre amounted in the 'eighties to two or more times the average rentals paid in the same regions in the early years of the twentieth century.[23] On the estates where the principal exaction was in the form of forced labor or *barshchina*, three days' work per week was the amount usually required of adult peasants of both sexes, but four or five days' work was sometimes exacted, and not infrequently the peasant was forced to work continuously for a considerable period in the manorial fields, while his own plot waited for seeding, or his own harvest rotted on the ground. Furthermore, it was customary to require of the forced-labor peasants certain payments in kind — poultry, eggs, meat, honey, homespun cloth, and the like.[24] Again, it was this century that witnessed the first considerable development of mining and manufacturing in Russia, and numbers of private serfs were put to forced labor in these industries.[25] Sick and aged peasants who were unable to render the dues and services required by their masters might be "liberated" — that is to say, expelled from their villages to go where they could.[26] As a final guarantee of authority, the landlord held an ill-defined prerogative of manorial justice, which, however, he sometimes exercised with the advice of his serfs, or in part relinquished to them. Brigandage and murder were under the jurisdiction of the public courts, but in the exercise of his judicial power over other offenses, the landlord might have his people beaten, send them into military service, or exile them to hard labor in Siberia.[27] He was obligated, in law at least, to feed his peasants in famine-years and to provide them with seed in case of a failure of the harvest,[28] and was forbidden to ruin them or to deal cruelly with them;[29] but the real force of this protective legislation may in a measure be judged from the fact that the law did not even go so far as to provide a specific punishment for a landlord who tortured a peasant to death — a thing by no means unheard of in this enlightened time. History abounds in stories of the landlords' cruelties, but the chief authority on peasant life during the period discovers only twenty instances in which the landlords were punished for actions of this kind during the thirty-four years of Great Catherine's reign.[30] The serfs on their part were expressly forbidden by law to make complaint to the authorities against their lords, under penalty of punishment with the knout and banishment to hard labor in Siberia.[31] Thus, for all practical purposes the bound people were in person and in property at their masters' disposition.[32] Whether his serfs numbered a score, or a score of thousands (in 1767 the greatest proprietor of the day owned 44,561 male "souls," and perhaps as many females [33]), the landlord ruled a little monarchy within the great one, and the central government utilized him as its viceroy, or (in the phrase of the Emperor Paul) its "gratuitous chief-of-police." [34]

To most of the State peasants, as well as to those of the landlords, the eighteenth century brought unfavorable changes of circumstance.[35] The "black-plowing peasants" of the North lived on lands which had long been claimed as State property, but only during this century was the title of the State fully established by the imposition of a rent or *obrok* in addition to the poll-tax,[36] and by the official attempts to put a stop to the mortgaging and selling of these lands by the peasants.[37] This check on peasant sales tended of course to eliminate the old possibility of separation from the tax-union through a transfer of land to a substitute tax-payer, while a law of 1797 prohibited even the temporary absence of a State peasant from his village without the permission of the elected authorities of his *volost* or district.[38]

Somewhat less numerous than the "black-plowing" peasants were the *odnodvortsy* or freeholders, counting in 1762 about half a million registered males. They had originally received small individual grants along the southern border under a military-service tenure; but unlike those nobles who had held their lands in a similar tenure, the *odnodvortsy* were not made full proprietors by Peter the Great, but were subjected to the peasant poll-tax and to the system of joint responsibility. Later, in 1727, they were forbidden to alienate their holdings, and in the end, as a result of changes which culminated only in the 'thirties of the nineteenth century, most of their special land-rights were lost, and as a class they were assimilated to the peasantry of the State.[39] The obligation to pay the poll-tax and to furnish recruits was, with minor exceptions, borne by the State peasants as well as by those on the proprietary lands,[40] and the *obrok* assessed against them was from five to seven times as heavy in 1797 as it had been three-quarters of a century earlier.[41] The State peasants exercised limited functions of self-government, through their assemblies and their elected officers, but the appointees who managed the affairs of the State domains possessed large and arbitrary powers resembling those of the landlords.[42] The interference and extortion of the officials in charge of the State lands sometimes went to such lengths that certain contemporaries even regarded their administration as more oppressive than that of the private proprietors themselves.[43]

A partial substitution of *obrok* for forced labor brought some improvement in the status of the special group of peasants, numbering in 1796 some half-million males, who were bondaged to the estates of the Imperial court.[44] On the other hand, the system of forced labor was extended to approximately the same number of State peasants of other categories, who were allotted to service in the admiralty forests and in the mines and factories of the State and of private persons.[45] Industry, developing with considerable vigor from the time of Peter the Great,[46] was dependent upon compulsion for the recruitment of the bulk of its labor supply. It was the original intention that the State peasants ascribed to the industrial establishments should devote a part of their time each year to the cultivation of their own fields, and a part to industrial labor; but often the mine or factory was so far distant from the village (even hundreds of miles away), the exactions of the new work were so heavy, and the treatment so cruel, that the ascribed peasant was ruined as an agriculturist, and driven into a mood for any kind of desperate adventure.[47]

During this century there was a huge shifting of lands and peasants from private to public control, and from public to private. The secularization of the lands of the Church involved the conversion of some two millions of serfs of both sexes into State peasants, with an accompanying substitution of money dues for labor.[48] This change was, however, in a considerable degree offset by the gifts of populated State lands with which Catherine II and Paul I rewarded their favorites. As a result of the lavish donations of these two rulers, more than 1,300,000 State peasants were transferred to private bondage, while such gifts for the whole century probably totalled about 2,000,000 persons of both sexes.[49]

Again, this century saw a further extension of the servile system into the new lands along the southern border, through the restriction of the rights of the earlier settlers,[50] and the colonization of the *step* with serfs imported from central Russia. It has already been shown that during the decades which followed the uprisings of the mid-seventeenth century, the Cossacks of eastern Ukraina [51] were in process of absorption into the Muscovite system; that is, the "elders" were being assimilated to the Russian gentry, while the lesser Cossacks were declining, with the peasantry of the same region, toward serfdom. This change continued into the eighteenth century; but farther to the east, where other groups of Cossacks had the endless *step* behind them, the Russian system of privilege and obligation advanced more slowly. The great revolt of Stenka Razin had been finally suppressed, but in 1707 an attempt by the Russian Government to round up the recent run-aways to the Don, resulted in another rising of the poorer Cossacks. Their bands of "thieves" (as the Russians called all who took part in such revolts) roamed through four hundred miles of *step* from the Sea of Azov to Tambov, fought with and defeated the wealthier Cossacks and the Muscovite troops, and were finally subdued only when heavy military forces were sent against them by Peter the Great. This defeat put an end to the semi-independence of the Don Cossacks; [52] but their old free life, founded, so to say, on flight, was now preserved by flight, and many of the more adventurous spirits settled in the remote regions along the courses of the Kuban and the Terek (north of the Caucasus) and on the Ural River (beyond the lower Volga).[53] The country had not yet seen the last of Cossackdom as an explosive force in Russian society.

During the first half of the eighteenth century, there occurred sporadic local outbreaks of the agricultural peasants against their masters, while from the 'fifties onward these disturbances increased in frequency,[54] and eruptions also occurred among the State peasants ascribed to the metal-works in the Urals.[55] As before, whole droves of peasants ran away to the *step,* where detachments of soldiery hunted them like wild game.[56] Behind the peasants and the Cossacks, there followed always — somewhat ponderously — the Muscovite system; and with the establishment of fortified posts at such remote places as Orenburg and Iletsk, south of the Ural Mountains, the increasing friction finally kindled the last great uprising in which Cossacks and peasants fought as allies.

In 1773 there appeared in Ural Cossackdom a certain Pugachev, an illiterate Cossack of the Don, who had been confined for a time in a prison at Kazan. Declaring himself to be Peter III, the rightful Tsar,[57] he assembled a considerable force of Cossacks (many of them Old Ritualists), together with numbers of Asiatic tribesmen and of ascribed peasants from the mines and metal works of the Ural Mountains, and with these he defeated the Imperial troops first sent against him (many of whom deserted to his side). He then gathered a swarm of peasants from the estates along the Volga, and in 1774 captured and burned the important city of Kazan. In his role of Tsar, Pugachev condemned the landholding nobility as "opponents of our power, traitors to the empire, despoilers of the peasants," and ordered the villagers to seize these landlords and put them to death.[58] Whether the Cossacks and the peasants could have agreed upon a constructive program for the future, is a question which has remained unanswered; but with a furious destroying rage they joined in a *jacquerie* which spread through the length of eastern Russia. There was a headlong flight of the landlords to the cities — even to Moscow; an orgy of robbery and burning; a great man-hunt, with gibbets raised everywhere by the rebels and hundreds of persons put to death.[59] "In some villages," reported the chief pacifier sent out by the government, "these murders have so completely exterminated the proprietorial families that it is not yet known to whom the villages ought legally to pass." [60] The fury of the revolt was succeeded by a fury of repression, with breaking-wheels, gibbets, and gallows erected around the rebellious villages; [61] and Pugachev himself was brought to Moscow in an iron cage and there publicly quartered for the instruction of the populace. When the work was finished, serfdom stood restored on the estates, and the Cossacks along the Ural, Terek, and Kuban rivers had been forced into service as a frontier guard.[62] But even the Terror could not induce a feeling of contentment in the peasants, and at the accession of Paul I, in 1796, disturbances occurred once more in many provinces.[63]

The extension of the Russian frontiers southward to the Black Sea, at the expense of the Turks and Tatars, opened the way for the further expansion of Russian agriculture into the *step*,[64] and led to the final dissolution of the historic Cossack community at the rapids of the Dnepr.[65] The Cossack "elders" of the southwestern frontier had become the proprietors of estates — a Little Russian nobility; on the other hand, many of the lesser Cossacks were being deprived upon minor pretexts of all that distinguished them from the peasantry, while at the same time a series of official acts dating from 1765, 1783, and 1796, formally and finally abolished the peasants' freedom of movement throughout the new lands of the South, from the Dnepr valley to the Caucasus.[66] With the Cossack communities now either dissolved into conflicting elements, or made subject to a special military service, it appeared likely that in the future the wind from the *step* would carry no more firebrands into the villages farther north; the fire had been put out at its source.

Thus the eighteenth century saw a progressive degradation of the peasantry, an intensive and extensive development of the servile system which brought it to a place of vast importance in Russian life.[67] The peasants had resisted these changes by the only means they knew: they had fled by hundreds of thousands to the open *step* — but after the middle of the century, escape had become more and more difficult, and the frontiers of law and order had caught up with the earlier refugees; [68] they had risen against officialdom and the landlords, in one huge revolt and in a long series of minor disturbances [69] — but violence had been drowned in violence, and the Cossack allies had been beaten or bought off. Not in the absence of opposition, but in spite of it, about nineteen and one-half millions of persons stood bondaged to the landlords in 1797, while the State peasantry, subject to such burdens as have been described, numbered about fourteen and one-half millions — some thirty-four millions altogether, in a total population of thirty-six. The peasant millions were hardly likely to forget the "Golden Age of the Russian Nobility" — but they would perhaps remember it by some other name.

CHAPTER III

THE PEASANTS IN THE LAST DECADES
OF SERFDOM

FROM the Golden Age of the Russian Nobility, with lace cuffs at court and iron-weighted flogging whips here and there in the villages, the proprietorial peasants came forth with the heavy tread of men in bondage, while most of their brothers on the State domains were also more severely burdened than before. But it was not only in the external relations of the peasantry with the lords of the land that important changes had taken place; the internal life of the village had also been profoundly altered through a further development of collectivism. It has already been pointed out that in Old Muscovy, before the Time of Troubles, a number of neighboring households often held and cultivated strips of land in each of several adjacent fields, and at the same time made common use of pasture-lands and forests. For the conduct of their collective affairs, these groups of households held folk-meetings and elected elders who governed the land-relation of the members, and apportioned among them the tax-assessments laid against the commune as a unit. All this was important enough, but from the sixteenth century come the first records of a still more significant manifestation of collectivism — the *redistribution* of lands among the members of the commune.[1]

Throughout the seventeenth, eighteenth, and nineteenth centuries, down to the Emancipation of the 'sixties, the practice of making periodically an equalizing redistribution of lands among neighboring peasants was spreading more and more widely through the country. It was in the old central-forest region that this practice first became general, both on the lands of the State and on those of the nobility.[2] Nearer the frontiers, it was of a later growth, and among the peasants on the State lands of the North and of the nearer *step,* this kind of redistribution came to be widely practised only in the later decades of the eighteenth century or the first half of the nineteenth — and then in part at least as a result of official sponsorship.[3] In the southern and southeastern areas, most recently colonized, redistribution was only beginning to appear on the eve of the Emancipation,[4] and among the peasants of Lithuania, White Russia, and Little Russia or Ukraina, equalization by repartition was little known.[5]

Some idea of the significance of the commune as a landholding and land-distributing body may be gained from the fact that in the general survey of Catherine's time, the lands used by the State peasants were laid off village by village, with no official attempt at a more minute division.[6] In the actual conduct of a redistribution, the peasants were sometimes left quite to themselves, sometimes subjected to interference or control by officials on the State domains, or more especially by the landlords on those estates where the forced-labor system was maintained.[7] The land was often apportioned by lot, sometimes in accordance with the number of workers of both sexes, sometimes in proportion to the number of males of all ages in each household (children included) who had been registered in the most recent census.[8] Besides being a collective holder and partitioner of the peasant lands, the commune continued to be the collective bearer, and — in so far as the proprietors and the officials did not choose to interfere — the distributor, of assessments due to the landlords and to the State.[9]

The periodic readjustment of landholdings, to keep pace with the procession of birth and death, maturity and decline, tended naturally toward the preservation of economic equality as between man and man within the commune.[10] Further than this, through the employment of the communal authority in such fundamentally important matters as the apportionment of land and of taxes,[11] there was provided for the peasant a continuous training in collective action, and this was naturally conducive to group activity in other directions. Sometimes, instead of distributing all the land, the village cultivated a certain area in common, and devoted the yield to a common purpose — perhaps to the relief of dependent members of the group, or to the payment of the tax-assessment. Sometimes the commune leased additional land from the State or from a neighboring proprietor, or even undertook to purchase land for the members' use, with the master's permission and in his name. Again it might build or lease a grist-mill, or make a common purchase of some such necessity as salt.[12] Where the landlords maintained the system of *corvée* or forced labor, they often interfered in the affairs of the commune, but on the estates where dues were collected in kind or in money, and on the public domain, the peasants were left somewhat more to themselves.[13] In the case of the State peasants, the village assemblies and their elective officers were given recognition in the laws of 1760 and 1761 and in a number of subsequent enactments, but in spite of all this, the local appointees of the government continued to interfere more or less as they pleased in the affairs of the State villages.[14] Thus the commune was wide open to attack, whether proprietorial or official, from above; it acted only on sufferance, or — worse still — under duress; and yet the very existence of this collective apparatus with its collective functions, could not fail to be of profound importance in peasant life.

Somewhat less closely supervised than the proprietary peasants, the villagers on the State domains were also in a more favorable situation economically. Some of the State peasants were still attached to factories operated by the government, and were forced to work out their obligations there, but these formed in the nineteenth century only a minor group.[15] In the 'forties, the new Ministry of State Property undertook an elaborate land-reform which was extended in the course of nearly twenty years' work to most of the *guberniias* or provinces of European Russia. By increasing the smaller allotments at the expense of the larger ones, and in some instances by the apportionment of additional State lands and by colonization, the cadastral commissions in some degree improved the situation of the poorer villagers on the State lands, but in 1866 the allotments of the State peasants still varied widely in size, from an average of about fifteen *desiatinas* of non-waste land for each registered male in the northern *guberniias,* to one *desiatina* in the Little Russian *guberniia* of Poltava.[16]

The amount of the dues assessed against the State peasants was proportioned to their total income, and therefore included a charge upon the proceeds of wage-work and of craft-industry as well as upon those of agriculture. However, these dues were distinctly more moderate than those which the private proprietors assessed against their serfs,[17] and the more favorable situation of the State peasants, in respect to both the weight of their obligations and the size of their allotments, was destined to put its mark quite definitely upon the future of Russian agrarian history.

Geographically, the State domains and the lands of the private proprietors were intermingled, the former predominating toward the North, the latter in the South; [18] and it was upon the serfs of the private estates that the age laid its heaviest burdens. The first half of the nineteenth century was marked by a number of regulatory measures which improved the position of these serfs, as far as the letter of the law was concerned, and seem in retrospect to indicate a reversal of the earlier official policy, and an advance toward emancipation; but in spite of all this, the peasants' allotments diminished, their obligations were increased, and the material weight of the servile system rested upon them even more heavily than before.

Before the opening of the century an important step had been taken toward defining the relation of the private peasantry with the soil: a regulation of 1798, applying to Little Russia only, prohibited the sale of serfs apart from the land.[19] In 1827 the subject was approached from the opposite side by a law of general application, which required the landlords to allot to their village serfs at least four and one-half *desiatinas* of land for each registered male, and prohibited any sale of land which would reduce below this minimum the allotments of the serfs remaining on the estate.[20] Again, in 1841, nobles who were themselves landless were forbidden to buy serfs otherwise than with land.[21] In the White Russian, Lithuanian and Little Russian territories which had been secured through the partitions of Poland (nine *guberniias,* extending from Kovno and Vitebsk to Kiev and Podolsk), the earlier Polish-Lithuanian law had required the maintenance of "inventories" defining the allotments and the obligations of the serfs, and from the year 1844 onwards, the Russian authorities made some attempt to regulate the preparation and observance of these schedules.[22] These various laws and regulations appeared to attribute to the peasant a right to the use of the soil — even to a certain minimum acreage; but side by side with this right, if there were such, there existed until 1858 another which constituted its negation — the right of the landlord to convert the serf, who normally supported himself by his own part-time labor on his own allotment, into a wholly dependent landless man, employed in continuous compulsory service about the manor-house or in the fields cultivated wholly for the provisioning and profit of that establishment.[23] The great majority of the peasants were not subjected to this conversion; but even so, the laws which appeared to recognize their land-right remained almost entirely without effect, for the reason that there was no proper supervision to secure the observance of the inventory-schedules,[24] and no serious attempt to enforce the all-important laws of 1827 and 1841.[25] These measures may have prepared the way for those reformers who later maintained that when the serf was emancipated, he should receive a part of the land which he had previously occupied and cultivated; but the immediate effect in guaranteeing the serf a sufficient allotment was practically nil.

Actually the landlords cultivated directly an increasing proportion of the area of their estates, while the proportion allotted to the serfs for their own self-support declined.[26] Partly on this account, and partly because of the growth (up to 1835) of the servile population, the mean area of the serf-allotments was diminished. The data on this subject are fragmentary in the extreme, but they seem to indicate a very considerable shrinkage in the size of the allotments.[27] In most of the non-black-soil *guberniias,* the average plot would no more than suffice for the provisioning of the peasant family, and in a number of black-soil *guberniias,* the situation was still more desperate.[28] Where, then, was the serf to find the means of meeting his obligations to the landlord and to the State ?

Partly from choice and in part from bitterest necessity, many of the serfs not only cultivated their narrowing acres, but employed other means of supporting themselves and meeting their heavy dues; and like the private serfs, the peasants on the State domains also had their supplementary occupations. In the central-forest region, great numbers of villagers were engaged in part-time handicraft production, not simply to meet their household needs, but for exchange with their neighbors, and increasingly — with the development of the "domestic system" — for the account of merchants who disposed of the products in a widening market.[29] With the permission of their stewards or owners, many thousands of the peasants of this same region left their villages for at least a part of the year to engage in wage-work or in trade in the towns.[30] In the *step,* the peasants' chief source of supplementary income was not craft-production, urban wage-work, or trade, but agricultural work-for-wages on some nearby estate, or even at the end of a long seasonal pilgrimage into the labor-short *guberniias* toward the frontier.[31]

Out of their earnings from such sources as these, or by laboring without payment in the fields under manorial cultivation, the serfs discharged their obligations to the proprietors. Here, as in the matter of the allotments, there appeared something in the way of a regulatory legislation: in 1797 an Imperial manifesto stated, apparently more as a pious maxim than as a law, that three days' forced labor each week was enough to satisfy the landlord's needs.[32] This declaration was later interpreted as a prohibition against greater demands upon the peasants, but there is ample evidence that this prohibition was not everywhere enforced.[33] As far as dues in kind and money were concerned, there was no pretence at official regulation, except in the half-hearted attempt to systematize and enforce the inventories in the western and southwestern *guberniias*.[34] The Code of 1857 declared that the proprietor might lay upon his serf every kind of labor, and demand of him any sort of payment in goods and in money, with only these two restrictions of importance: that the serf should not be required to work for his master on Sunday, or on certain holidays, or for more than three days per week, and that he should not be ruined by the master's exactions.[35] Such was the law, but history is more concerned with the fact.

On the estates where the system of forced labor or *barshchina* was employed, the serfs, men and women, were usually required to work for the master three days each week, or so to arrange matters among themselves as to supply an equivalent amount of labor; but not infrequently the demand was still heavier, and sometimes the proprietor kept his people at work continuously during the harvest, leaving them to gather their own crops as best they could, at night, on holidays, or after the manorial fields had been cleared.[36] In the majority of cases, the serfs were obliged to supply not only the labor but the implements and the animals for the cultivation of the master's fields.[37] Where the serfs paid dues or *obrok*, instead of rendering *corvée*, the assessments were substantially increased between the last years of the eighteenth century and the Emancipation.[38] Nevertheless the position of the *obrok* serfs was still very much to be preferred to that of those on *barshchina*, chiefly for the reason that, in the nature of things, the former were left much more to their own devices.[39]

Toward the time of the Emancipation, the private serfs on *barshchina* out-numberd those on *obrok* by more than two to one in the forty-one *guberniias* for which data are available.[40] The two systems were not everywhere mutually exclusive, however; and as the century advanced, the proportion of peasants who rendered both dues and services materially increased.[41] In general, it may be said that the *obrok* system predominated in most of the *guber-*

niias from Moscow northward. Largely for the reason that the natural conditions here were not particularly favorable to agriculture, the proprietors of this region, instead of employing serf-labor extensively in manorial farming, preferred to lay on assessments which rested in considerable part upon the non-agricultural earnings of the villagers. Farther south, the landlords usually found it more profitable to employ their serfs in the plowing and reaping of the manorial fields.[42]

The burdens of the servile system, heavy as they were, did not rest equally upon all the peasants of the private estates, or reduce them all to one common level of misery. Even in Great Russia, where the periodic redistribution of land by the communes worked toward the maintenance of economic equality, some serf families managed to accumulate goods and animals, and to draw other serfs into their hired service. In the western and southwestern *guberniias*, where the land-commune with its levelling tendencies was rarely found, the inequalities in landholding and in general economic condition were much more pronounced than in other quarters of the country.[43] But although differentiation did exist, the well-found and prosperous peasant was to be discovered on the private estates only by exception; for most of the proprietary serfs, the half-century which preceded the Emancipation was a period not simply of static distress, but of increasing misery,[44] sinking at intervals in many districts to the level of actual famine.[45]

As long as the bound peasant had an allotment of land, and at least a part of his time free for its cultivation, and had also the responsibility for the housing, feeding and clothing of his family, he still enjoyed — whatever might be his obligations to the landlord and to the State — a certain measure of that autonomy which perhaps best serves to distinguish the daily life of the serf from that of the slave. However, as the new century advanced, a few Great Russian landlords, and a larger proportion of those of Little Russia, converted their estates almost literally into slave plantations, by merging the village fields with those of the manor and assuming at one and the same time the full direction of their peasants' labor and the full responsibility for their maintenance.[46] Some of the landlords also carried on the manufacture of cloth, and other like industrial activities, and most of the serfs whom they put to this work were landless men; the number so employed, however, was not great, and toward the middle of the century it showed a tendency to decline.[47] Large numbers of serfs were em-

ployed in the manorial apartments, kitchens, workshops, court-
yards, and stables, and sometimes the proprietors even hired out
their serfs to others, for work in factories or in the construction of
roads and canals.[48]

There is no means of determining with accuracy what proportion of the peasants had been affected by this debasement from an
autonomous serfdom into a life of near-slavery. In general, the
serfs who held allotments, and were responsible for their own self-
support, were officially registered as "bound peasants," while the
greater part of the totally dependent landless serfs were registered
as "courtyard people"; but in actual practice, many serfs who had
held allotments were detached from the land and put to full-time
work in the manorial fields, about the manor-house, or in factories, without any corresponding change in their official registration; [49] and on the other hand, many who were carried on the
registers as "courtyard people" had cattle, gardens, and separate
dwellings, which gave them some degree of economic autonomy.[50]
Hence the statistical totals drawn from the registers do not give
the true number of self-sufficient serfs on the one hand, and near-
slaves on the other. However, since it may perhaps be supposed
that these figures represent the situation with no greater inaccuracy at one time than at another, the very rapid increase in the
proportion of registered "courtyard people" among the proprietorial serfs (an increase from 4.14 per cent in 1835 to 6.79 per cent
in 1858) may probably be accepted as an indication of the growth
of landless dependency. In 1858 the further registration of transfers of "bound peasants" into the status of "courtyard people,"
and likewise of transfers in the opposite direction, was prohibited;
but during the seven years just preceding, the growth of registered
dependency had been especially pronounced.[51] If this evidence
alone were considered, it might be said that not emancipation, but
enslavement, was approaching.

In his control over the property and person of his serfs, the landlord was subject to limitations slight enough in theory, but of
even less consequence in practice. Under a law of 1848 the serf
might with the consent of his master acquire real property; but
the master might call for evidence of ability to make the necessary
payments, and then simply confiscate the peasant's savings.[52] The
proprietor was forbidden to reduce his serf to ruin, but on the
other hand the serf was prohibited by law from bringing a civil
suit against the master for his own protection, or from initiating a

civil process against an outsider without the master's full consent.[53] In sum, the serf had no property-rights which could be effectively defended against his master.[54]

In respect to the person of the serf, the proprietor's control went far beyond the mere command of labor. He was still at full liberty to sell the serf with land, and although after 1822 it was unlawful to publish advertisements offering to dispose of serfs without land, such notices continued to appear, in the guise of offers to hire rather than to sell, and no attempt was made to stop the sales themselves. The separate sale of different members of a peasant family was forbidden by laws of 1833 and 1847, but there was hardly a minimum of enforcement.[55] One enterprising landlord made a practice of purchasing orphaned serf-children, raising them on his estate, and selling the girls for marriage, and the young men to the landlords for use in meeting their quota of recruits, or to the State for settlement in Siberia.[56] The proprietor might withhold the permission without which no marriage could be made on his estate; or he might — and frequently did — take the opposite course of pairing off his peasants, and marrying them whether they would or no. It was a common thing for the master to make what use he pleased of the girls and women of his household and his villages — sometimes in all the pomp and circumstance of a manorial seraglio; and such abuses were even less likely than others to be checked by official interference or the censure of neighboring proprietors.[57]

Under the system of manorial justice, the proprietors had such wide powers to judge and to punish their serfs, that they could enforce compliance with almost any kind of extortionate demand. According to the Code of 1833, the proprietor was free to employ, for the maintenance of order and authority, any domestic means of correction which would not endanger life, or result in mutilation.[58] Confinement and beating were common forms of punishment, and a devilish cunning had been employed in perfecting a whole arsenal of flogging instruments: rods, staffs, whips, bundles of leather thongs twisted with wire — sometimes, though certainly rarely, so zealously employed that the serf was beaten to death.[59] The punishments permitted by the law of 1845 were still severe enough, since the proprietor might, for example, sentence a serf to four months' detention, or to forty blows with rods.[60] The landlords might also dispose of offenders by sending them into the military service, or banishing them to Siberia; and in case of banishment, the wife and younger children were to accompany the husband, but boys over five years of age and girls over ten might be separated from the family and retained on the estate, if the proprietor so desired.[61]

Instead of exercising the prerogative of manorial jurisdiction, the proprietor might at his option surrender the serf to public justice, but under the law of 1845 he was *compelled* to do this only where the offense, if against himself, his family, or another of his serfs, was a very serious one, or where the injured party was an outsider who preferred to carry his complaint to the public authorities.[62]

As has been said, the proprietor was forbidden to ruin his serfs or to treat them with cruelty, and the law of 1845 provided that if these principles were violated, all the estates of the offending landlord should be taken under official guardianship.[63] Enough has already been said to show that the law specifically sanctioned many practices which appear ruinous or cruel; but laxity in enforcement competed with laxity in the law itself, in contributing to peasant misery. There was really no adequate means for the discovery and punishment of the proprietors' offenses. The flow of information from its most natural source had been deliberately checked; the punishment provided for the peasant who complained against his master had been progressively ameliorated since the eighteenth century, but the law of 1845 still permitted as many as fifty blows with rods for this offense, and only in 1858 did the Minister of the Interior so far depart from the letter of the law as to make a distinction between just and unjust complaints, and to indicate that the latter might perhaps not necessitate the punishment of the complaining serf.[64] But whatever the law might say, the peasants showered the officials with petitions, and although the petitioners were often severely dealt with, their complaints were received, as time went on, with a somewhat increased attention.[65] The chief obstacle to the discovery of abuses, and to their elimination, once they were revealed, was that the enforcement of the law against a given proprietor depended so largely upon other members of the proprietorial class and upon officials under their political control or secretly in their pay.[66] During the nineteenth century, official supervision made some advances against the arbitrary rule of the landlords,[67] but these changes were so inconsiderable that, down to the era of the Emancipation, the proprietorial peasant remained without adequate means of defending such legal rights as now distinguished his bondage from full slavery.[68] It is true that most of the proprietorial peasants were suffered to enjoy on their allotments a measure of the economic autonomy which perhaps best differentiates serfdom from slavery; but this autonomy might be lost between dawn and dark, for even in the law the master was always free (at least until 1858) to detach the peasant from the soil, and convert him into a hand-to-mouth dependant of the manorial household.

Much has been said here of the trespasses of the landlords upon the narrow rights of the serfs, but there is no intention to imply in all this that the insecure frontiers of the law were never crossed in the opposite direction, by invasions of the serfs into the almost limitless domain of the manor-lord's prerogative. It will be shown hereafter that the opposition of the serfs to the law and practice of serfdom is one of the most characteristic and vital features of the manorial system; but first there remain to be considered certain other aspects of the internal life of the village.

Not only was the serf set apart from his master by a variety of economic, social, and political disabilities, but as the eighteenth century advanced, the cultural gap widened more and more. For the landlords, this was a century of education and Europeanization, carrying them farther and farther from the old Muscovy where the serfs and the peasants of the State still lived. Before the time of Peter the Great, the villagers had been almost entirely innocent of formal education, and the grandiose projects of Peter and Catherine II provided only a handful of villages with elementary schools.[69] In 1804 another ambitious project was launched, and during the decades that intervened before the Emancipation, some progress was made in establishing official primary schools among the peasants.[70] In addition to these official schools, there existed an indeterminable number of unregistered primary schools, maintained sometimes by the peasants themselves and sometimes by the landlords.[71] A beginning had thus been made, but the great mass of the serfs on the private estates and of the peasants on the State domains had hardly been touched by the cultural changes which since Peter's time had so deeply affected the nobles and the *bourgeoisie*.

Some few of the serfs, most often from among the "courtyard people," were, however, selected and trained for higher things. If the landlord maintained a school on the estate, it was likely to be devoted to the preparation of clerks and bailiffs, and perhaps to the preliminary education of other serfs who were destined to serve on the estate as barber-surgeons, surveyors, solicitors, or in some such technical capacity. Sometimes it pleased the proprietor to nurture the arts among his peasantry — to have some of them instructed in architecture, painting, poetry, music — to organize them into orchestras, ballets, opera troupes, or dramatic companies. To send a serf to a gymnasium or a university was forbidden in 1827, and again in 1843 (unless he was to be set free), but occasionally a proprietor even sent a favorite abroad to study — perhaps to become more cultivated, more European, than himself. Thus, in the matter of culture, a handful of serfs had crossed over into the masters' world — but was this likely to make them the more content with bondage? In the stories of talented and highly-trained serfs who sought liberation from their lot in flight, in drunkenness, even in suicide, there is some ground for thinking that this was hardly so.[72]

But the tendency of the time was for the aristocracy to go their separate way, leaving the peasant mind to revolve within a pre-Petrine, even in part a pre-Christian, world. Pagan sprites and spirits still haunted the black forests and grey waters that lay between the log-built village and the pseudo-classical manor-house of the landlord, and in the peasant huts young men were nurtured and old men consoled by the repetition of folk-songs and folk-tales which often bore the mark of a dual pagan-Christian faith.[73] It is true that on most of the estates, master and man still performed the same religious rites and listened to the same religious teachings, with Orthodoxy as a cultural tie between them; but sometimes even this bond had snapped, and the peasant had taken refuge in his own special "City of God."

Old Ritualism continued to flourish among the peasants and the merchantry, and religious persecution provided the adherents with a special stimulus to fly to the frontiers, where they established settlements in the northern, southeastern and southwestern borderlands, and in Poland.[74] That Old Ritualism was not purely a religious movement, is suggested by the fact that the Priestless branch proclaimed Peter the Great to be Antichrist come to earth, while the *Stranniki* or "Wanderers," an extremist group which arose among the Priestless late in the eighteenth century, were distinguished for a time by their denunciation of the Tsardom as a devil's rule, and their refusal to submit to official registration, to carry passports, or to pay taxes.[75] Many of the Priestless, and the

Stranniki in particular, refused to pray for the Tsar, and also repudiated the sacrament of matrimony, but the vast majority of these nevertheless formed family unions which were usually though not invariably permanent.[76] The strong feeling of fraternity among the Old Ritualists or *Raskolniki*, and their custom of settling all disputes among themselves without recourse to any outside tribunal,[77] gave their villages more than the usual degree of solidarity.

The propagation in the villages of a variety of evangelical and spiritualist teachings also helped to alienate the peasants from their masters. The *Dukhobortsy* or "Spirit-Wrestlers," and the *Molokane* or "Milk-Drinkers" (so-called because they drank milk on fast days, when it was forbidden to the Orthodox), first appeared in considerable numbers during the latter half of the eighteenth century. The *Khlysty* or "Flagellants," the *Skoptsy* or "Eunuchs," and a number of other sects were also propagated with some success.[78] Both the *Dukhobortsy* and the *Molokane* condemned the institution of serfdom.[79] Some of the former practised a thoroughgoing collectivism, with common flocks and herds, and "common granaries, from which each was supplied according to his needs," while a sub-sect of the *Molokane* undertook to establish ideal communes in the Caucasus and in Eastern Siberia.[80] The *Dukhobortsy*, the *Molokane*, and the *Khlysty* did not forego conjugal union, but repudiated the sacrament of matrimony; the *Skoptsy* went far beyond this, in the practice of such a mutilation of both sexes as would make generation impossible.[81] In the teachings and practices of the first two of these sects, an anti-Tsarist, or perhaps better, an anti-State tendency was clearly visible. A group of *Dukhobortsy*, imprisoned for their beliefs, prepared in 1791 a confession in which they said: "Verily the children of God have no need either of Tsars or of ruling powers or of any human laws whatever." [82] Nor is this by any means a unique case of the repudiation of all temporal authority by members of this sect.[83] Sometimes, too, they specifically refused to pay taxes or to pray for the Tsar, while the refusal to bear arms was general with them, and with the *Molokane* as well.[84] In 1826 the *Molokane* would not pay their taxes, but a severe harrying by the government forced them to give in on this point.[85] In a *Molokan* Confession of Faith printed abroad in 1865 it was declared that the members of this sect were obedient to the temporal power in all except spiritual matters, and that they regularly prayed for those in authority; nevertheless it is related that during the Crimean War, the *Molokane* had said that prayers ought to be offered for the defeat of the government which persecuted them, rather than for its success.[86]

When peasant dissent meant at the least a kind of cultural separatism, and at the most a direct hostility to the manor-lord, the bishop, and the Tsar, even sometimes an all-inclusive repudiation of life through a refusal to propagate the species, it is not surprising that the government's attitude toward the dissenters was not exactly friendly. The earlier persecutions were considerably relaxed under Peter the Great, and still more in the time of Catherine II, but the accession of Nicholas I brought a much more severe régime. In 1842 the government classified the dissidents in three groups: first, the *less pernicious* (those Old Ritualists who accepted priests), and second, the *pernicious* (the more moderate of the priestless Old Ritualists), both of which groups the officials were expected to hold in check, rather than to destroy; and third, the *most pernicious* group (the priestless Old Ritualists who repudiated marriage and refused to pray for the Tsar; and all such sects as the *Dukhobortsy* and the *Molokane*) whom the government now hoped to hunt out and extirpate completely. The ill success of the official program is however indicated by the fact that about the middle of the century there were hardly less than a million sectarians and seven millions of Old Ritualists among the country's total population of some sixty-nine million persons.[87]

Any tendency of the peasants to live their religious life apart, or with exceptional intensity — as in the mad ecstasies of the Flagellants — might perhaps be interpreted as in some sense an attempt to find refuge from a world which handled them so ill; but very often the idea of deliverance took a clearer incarnation. Shortly after Russia acquired from Persia in 1828 the region of Mt. Ararat, it was rumored about among the sectarians that Christ would soon return to inaugurate the "thousand years of glory" at the base of this holy mountain. A sectarian deserter from the army undertook to lead the peasants of Saratov on the Volga toward this land of milk and honey, and in various other *guberniias* groups of peasants took the great road toward the New Jerusalem — some, we are told, in their Sunday clothes; [88] and is it too much to believe that they marched on singing:

> Sometimes I'm up, sometimes I'm down, Oh, yes, Lord;
> Sometimes I'm almost to de groun', Oh, yes, Lord.

Although you see me goin' 'long so, Oh, yes, Lord;
I've had my trials here below, Oh, yes, Lord.
One day when I was walkin' along, Oh, yes, Lord,
De element opened, an' de Love came down, Oh, yes, Lord.

. . . . .

Oh, nobody knows de trouble I've seen,
Nobody knows but Jesus,
Nobody knows de trouble I've seen,
Glory, hallelujah! [89]

This American Negro "spiritual" seems to catch the mood of this peasant exodus — but sometimes in the Russian songs there was a cry of defiance, too:

He has destroyed us,
The evil *barin*, the seignior.
It was he, the evil one, who chose
The young men,
The young men
To be soldiers,
And us, the beautiful girls,
To be servants;
The young married women
To suckle his children,
And our fathers and our mothers
For labor.
But our young men gathered
On the steep hill —
Our young men defied
The lord-*barin*:
"Seignior, author of evil,
We will not be soldiers for you;
The beautiful girls
Shall not be your servants,
The young mothers
Shall not nurse your children,
And the fathers and mothers
Shall labor for you no more." [90]

In the ecstasy and lamentation of their "spirituals," the black slaves of America sang themselves right off the plantations and through the pearly gates — and for one who has lived long in the sound of these Southern voices, there is a haunting return of his own and his country's past in the wailing songs one hears in the forest beyond Kostroma and the *step* beyond Tambov.

In the expression of their discontent, the peasants not infrequently went far beyond the confines of song, prayer, and prophecy — sometimes to the length of a direct attack with torch and pitchfork. Where there was no major insubordination, the stubborn shirking and sabotage of the villagers sometimes so clogged the economy of an estate that the proprietor was obliged to sell it at a sacrifice, or to ask for an official guardianship.[91] But the open forms of opposition were by no means lacking: among the peasants on the State domains, there were instances of disorder on a considerable scale, with furious repression in consequence,[92] while with increasing frequency the proprietorial serfs carried their woes to the public authorities in hope of redress,[93] or undertook by some forbidden act of their own to remedy their situation. For the last thirty-five years preceding the Emancipation of 1861, there have been tabulated 1186 instances of insubordination on the private estates — instances which in almost every case involve, not individuals, but groups of peasants, whole villages, even several estates with a number of neighboring villages.[94] This tabulation is based chiefly upon the records of the Ministry of the Interior, and — at least up to 1854 — the Ministry usually received reports only of the more serious disturbances; [95] further than this, the table does not include arson, murder, or — in general — peasant flights; [96] hence the figures by no means represent the full range of the disturbances on the estates, and their principal value lies in the fact that they make possible a comparison of one period with another:

INSTANCES OF INSUBORDINATION ON THE PRIVATE ESTATES

Period	Total number	Average number per year
1826–29	88	22
1830–34	60	12
1835–39	78	16
1840–44	138	28
1845–49	207	41
1850–54	141	28
1855–61	474	68
Total	1186	

The official recording-apparatus was no doubt more sensitive during the period immediately preceding the Emancipation than during the earlier decades, but even when some allowance is made for this circumstance, there seems to be clear evidence of the presence in the villages of an increasingly active discontent.[97]

As far as the very incomplete and one-sided records show, active insubordination was connected most often with a protest against the economic conditions of the servile life, and less frequently with an attempt to effect by one means or another a complete escape from the system of serfdom.[98] Often it is not reported just what the disturbers did, but where the information is available, the most common manifestation is a refusal to work, or to pay dues, or to fulfil some other obligation to the proprietor.[99] In general these tables do not cover the more spectacular forms of attack, but it was not unheard of for the peasants to wrap a great manor-house in flames, or to devote the manor-lord to violent death in some one of its several forms. During the period 1835–1861, 30 bailiffs and 166 proprietors came thus to their end in the full climax of tragedy.[100]

Instead of trying somehow to improve matters in the village, or taking a red vengeance upon the landlord, many of the serfs simply departed between the dark and the daylight, in search of a freer and better land.[101] Sometimes a local crop-failure set them moving, but more often it was a rumor that in some distant place the bondsman could find freedom. Before the exodus from the *guberniia* of Vitebsk in 1847, it was reported there that the peasants of Great Russia had already been set free, and that all who desired freedom should hurry thither to receive it.[102] Again, during the Crimean War, there was a rumor that freedom had been promised to everyone who would volunteer for the Russian military or naval service, and it was reported, too, that the English and French armies would liberate all the serfs who fled to them in the Crimea. Many of the serfs hoped for and expected some special dispensation from the Emperor; and once it was told about, that upon the top of a mountain at the Crimean isthmus, the Tsar of All the Russias was sitting in his golden cap, dispensing freedom to all who came promptly to his royal throne.[103]

Of the number of individual flights, no serviceable estimate has ever been made; but sometimes the movement carried whole villages and groups of villages out along the road to the Promised Land. The flight from Vitebsk counted perhaps ten thousand persons; the movement at the time of the Crimean War affected ten *guberniias* in 1854, seven in 1855, and seven in 1857; from two *uezds* or counties in the *guberniia* of Ekaterinoslav, there were some nine thousand run-aways during the year 1856. And these were by no means the only mass-flights of the peasantry.[104]

During the years 1826–1854, military detachments are known to have been employed in 228 different instances to restore order and authority in the villages, and to round up and return the fugitives.[105] In the Vitebsk affair, one regiment, one battalion, and two additional companies were used, and during the Crimean War, with troops so badly needed elsewhere, there were employed to deal with the peasants in the *guberniia* of Kiev alone one full division of the army, one battalion of *chasseurs,* two companies of sappers, and sixteen squadrons of cavalry.[106] Ordinarily the arrival of a detachment was enough to bring an immediate submission, but in rare instances there was a show of resistance, and in the *guberniia* of Kiev at the time of the great exodus thirty-seven peasants were killed, and fifty-seven wounded.[107] The peasants were often brought before courts-martial — though this practice declined with the approach of the Emancipation — and flogging and exile were common forms of punishment; after the Vitebsk flights, some four thousand persons were beaten with rods.[108]

Such, then, was the servile system, as the peasant saw it, from below. If we ask to what end it all existed — all the sweating at unpaid labor, all the flights, all the flogging and herding back to work again — the answer may best be sought for, not in the peasant's hut, but first of all in the manor-house of the proprietor.

CHAPTER IV

THE MANOR-LORDS BEFORE THE GREAT REFORM

IN THAT very period when the claims of the government upon the nobles were relaxed, their emancipation consummated, these nobles were pressing their demands upon the peasants with an increasing exigence. As a result of the double change, abundance and leisure were, so to say, impounded in the manor-house — and this at the very time when closer European contacts were introducing new modes for their enjoyment. "The nobles' lack of employment, either political or economic, was the foundation upon which there was built in the second half of the eighteenth century a social life with its own peculiar relations, manners and tastes." [1] As a preparation for the service of the State, Peter the Great had attempted to enforce, for boys of noble family, a certain minimum of education.[2] When the service requirement was relaxed, and finally abolished in 1762, the nobles were still required to provide for their sons a minimum of instruction; [3] and this education, and the intercourse involved in the official service, whether compulsory or voluntary, helped to open channels through which new influences from abroad might flow.

Thus in the higher circles of Russian society "the Petrine noble — an artilleryman or a navigator, was transformed into the beau of Elizabeth's time; under Catherine this fop was re-born as an *homme de lettres*, out of whom at the end of the century there was made the philosopher-nobleman — the Freemason and Voltairian. This philosopher-nobleman was the typical representative of that social class whose task it was to carry Russian society forward along the road of progress; hence it is necessary to point out his chief characteristics. His social position was founded upon political injustice and crowned with idleness. From the hands of his teacher, the cantor and clerk of the village church, he passed into the control of a French tutor, rounded off his education in Italian theatres

or French restaurants, made use of his acquirements in the draw-
ing-rooms of St. Petersburg, and finished his days in a private
study in Moscow, or at some country place, with a volume of Vol-
taire in his hands. On *Povarskaia* [one of the finest avenues of Mos-
cow], or in the country in Tula *guberniia*, with this volume of Vol-
taire in his hands, he was a strange phenomenon. All his adopted
manners, customs, tastes, sympathies, his language itself — all were
foreign, imported; . . . he had no organic connections with his
surroundings, no sort of serious business in life. A foreigner among
his own people, he tried to make himself at home among foreigners, and in European society he was a kind of adopted child. In
Europe he was looked upon, indeed, as a re-costumed Tatar, and
at home, people saw in him a Frenchman born in Russia." [4]

In describing his father, a nobleman whose lifetime extended
from the eighteenth century well into the nineteenth, Alexander
Herzen said: "At the time of his education, European civilization
was so new in Russia that a man of culture necessarily became less
a Russian. To the end of his life he [Herzen's father] wrote French
with more ease and correctness than Russian, and he literally
never read a Russian book, not even the Bible. . . When my father heard that the Emperor Alexander was reading Karamzin's
History of the Russian Empire, he tried it himself but soon laid it
aside: 'Nothing but old Slavonic names ! Who can take an interest
in that ?' " [5]

To be French in dress and manner, even to use the language of
France in preference to one's own — this sort of thing came more
and more to be the token of gentility. The Old Muscovite manor-
houses of logs or plaster-finished brick, with their rambling roofs,
fantastic turrets and bulky ornaments,[6] (architectural transfigurations of the peasant's cabin, as the folk-tales were so often literary
transfigurations of his life) — such houses as these were no fit setting for a gentlemanly life; and accordingly the nobles began to
build colonnaded mansions, sometimes of considerable size with a
great columned reception hall and long, low wings half circling a
broad fore-court of honor. With their stately porticos, their chapels
and their theatres, their gardens, lakes, and parks, their swarming
retinues of servants (one landlord had three hundred "courtyard
people," another five hundred),[7] some of these mansions, in their
borrowed European style, were very tolerable miniatures of Versailles.[8]

It was in the theatre that this life most clearly exhibited something better than mere luxurious expenditure. Toward the end of the eighteenth century, there were counted in the city of Moscow and its environs as many as twenty private theatres of the nobility, the finest of which was that maintained by the family of Sheremetev at one of their country seats. There is good reason to believe that Moscow had no public theatre equal to this last, and it was quite naturally a matter of astonishment to a foreign visitor, who witnessed a performance there, that "the poet and the musician who wrote the opera, the architect who constructed the theatre, the painter who decorated it, the actors and actresses who played in the piece, the members of the ballet and the musicians of the orchestra were all serfs of Count Sheremetev." [9]

Not only in their modes and manners, and in the physical properties with which they surrounded themselves, but in the books which they read, the Russian aristocracy of the eighteenth century showed what enticement Western Europe held for them. The French neo-classical drama and poetry, together with the Russian imitations of the same, supplied the polite world with a considerable share of its literary ration, and the philosophers of the Enlightenment enjoyed in Russia a most impressive popularity.[10]

It was natural that these several Europeanizing influences should not affect all the nobility at one and the same moment, or in the same degree. In general these currents flowed outward and downward from the capitals, affecting first and most deeply those nobles who spent at least a part of their time in St. Petersburg or Moscow, touching next the many who maintained similar connections with the capitals of the *guberniias,* and penetrating only very slowly and much less effectively, to those petty squires who kept always near their rural "nests." [11]

During the first half of the nineteenth century, the rise of Romanticism, and then of Realism, in Russian literature, and of the Slavophil school of social philosophy, did something to recall the interest of the Russian aristocracy from its European wanderings,[12] but much more than this would have been required to undo entirely the work of the eighteenth century. Since the seventeenth-century schism in the Church, and the subsequent opening of Peter's "window on the West," the Russian landed nobility had experienced a cultural change which was qualitative as well as quantitative — a change which had unquestionably widened the gap between themselves and the people of their villages. Having replaced the mode of powdered curls and velvet breeches with side-

burns and boot-strapped pantaloons, the Russian noble was perhaps, in the view of his European neighbors, still something of a
Tatar retailored — but still certainly something of a foreigner to
the mild Russian eyes which looked up from the plow.

The cultural climate of Russia being somewhat severe, the deli-
cacies of a Europeanized gentility required to be nurtured here, as
it were, under glass, at a very considerable expense — and the very
character of this gentility was one of the things which made it so
often impossible for the Russian proprietors to expand their revenues, in proportion as their wants increased. What the serf-estates
produced under the old routine of exploitation — whether in peasant dues, or in the yield of manorial cultivation or the products
of the manorial shops — became available almost automatically,
if only discipline were maintained — a task that could with the
greatest ease be delegated. The old methods were therefore conducive to a mental if not also to a physical absenteeism, whether
on the part of the State-serving noble of the seventeenth century
or the Europeanized gentleman of the eighteenth. The new European contacts might, of course, have contributed not only to the
rarefaction of proprietorial tastes, but also to an improvement in
the technique of manorial production — and indeed new crops
and new implements did make their appearance on some of the
estates. Upon the whole, however, agricultural technique did not
profit greatly; "in the 'thirties and 'forties, the lands seeded to hay-
crops were no more than a drop in the ocean of three-field cultivation," and "on estates where the manor-house was refurnished
every two or three years, there were very often no machines for
seeding the fields, and none for threshing or winnowing" the
grain.[13] The efforts to secure a larger revenue from the estates
were directed chiefly to the extension of manorial cultivation at
the expense of the village lands, and to a more severe exploitation
of the peasantry, but even where no changes of this sort were tried,
the insubordination of the peasants was often an obstacle to manorial operations.[14] The cultural attainments of the nobility were
at times considerable, but their economic power was not extensively employed to make such a contribution as might conceivably
have been hoped for, where the mere technique of farming was
concerned.

In the eighteenth and nineteenth centuries, several factors contributed to the decline of the isolated "natural economy" of the
estates, and helped to bring the manor into the general stream of

trade.[15] The demand of the proprietors increased, for things which the estate could not produce; the growth of towns and of urban industry in Russia [16] and abroad, increased the supply of goods which the proprietors might purchase, and the demand for the agricultural surplus which the estates might offer; while at the same time the emergence of Russia upon the Baltic Sea and the Black opened easier channels for international exchange.[17]

As a means of securing an additional revenue, some of the nobles set up factories of considerable size, and tried their hand at industrial production for the general market. During the reign of Catherine II, when non-noble industrialists were for the time being prohibited from buying serfs for use in factories, the nobles enjoyed some success, but later they proved unable to compete either with peasant handicraft-production or with the factories set up by the *bourgeoisie,* and during the 'thirties and 'forties of the nineteenth century the number of their manufacturing enterprises declined both relatively and absolutely [18] — a portent of that economic decline of the nobility which was at a much later day to extend even to their own ancestral realm of agriculture.

With the development of a "money economy," and the comparative ill success of the landlord's industrial ventures, the tendency was to concentrate the manorial forces increasingly upon the production of food-stuffs and agricultural raw materials for the domestic and foreign markets.[19] The problem of transportation presented no great difficulties to the landlord, for when the snow had laid its hard roads everywhere, it cost no more than a command, to start a sled-train equipped and manned by the serfs of the estate, on a trek of hundreds of miles to some supposedly favorable market.[20]

But in spite of the proprietors' control of inherited lands and gratuitous labor, their economic condition was very often anything but prosperous. In the eighteenth century many of the landlords were in so desperate a situation that they overloaded themselves with debts which bore interest at twelve, fifteen, even twenty per cent. It was mainly with the object of providing cheaper credit for the nobility that a State loan bank was established in 1754, and from this time on, the financial resources of the government were actively employed in an attempt to prop up the manorial economy.[21] Toward the end of the era of serfdom, the indebtedness of the landlords mounted to huge proportions, and on the eve of the Emancipation two-thirds of all the private serfs had been mortgaged by their masters to State institutions for loans totalling about 400,000,000 *rubls,* or more than half the market value of these serfs at the prices then prevailing [22] — and this does not include the loans from private sources, for which the landlords paid a higher interest. In 1841, Nicholas I expressed the hope that the State loans to the landlords would not be expended for luxuries, but employed in the development of agriculture and industry on the estates. However, the general improvement which was hoped for did not materialize, and most of the loans evaporated, leaving only debts behind.[23]

The situation of the landlords being what it was, it was only natural that there should be an active discussion of its causes. In the course of this debate, it was maintained by many economists that free hired labor could be employed on the estates with greater advantage than the unproductive forced labor of serfs.[24] In the *step,* the land was rich, and the manorial income was drawn almost exclusively from the soil, either directly, through the yield of manorial farming, or indirectly, through the dues of agricultural serfs; and here, too, except in the more recently settled frontier *guberniias,* there was usually an abundance and even a surplus of bondaged peasants and therefore the prospect of a large supply of wage-labor at a low cost in case the serfs should be emancipated without land or with such small holdings that they could not support themselves by independent cultivation. Hence a certain number of the more progressive landlords of this region were impressed with the possibilities of capitalistic farming, and were prepared to accept even a gratuitous emancipation of the persons of their serfs, if only they (the landlords) were left in possession of all or nearly all the land.[25]

In the forest region, there was little to support this point of view, for here the land was comparatively poor, and only a limited revenue could be hoped for from its exploitation, however efficient might be the hired laborers of the future, and however low their wages. In this region industry and trade outweighed agriculture in importance, and the major part of the landlords' income was drawn indirectly from non-agricultural sources, in the form of dues levied upon serfs engaged in independent handicraft-production, in wage-work, or in trade or transportation. Naturally there was no very strong disposition on the part of the landlord of the forest to embark upon a career of industry or trade; and how then could he continue to share in the proceeds of these activities unless he kept control of the person of the serf? Or, if the serf were to be liberated in spite of everything, it must be only at the price of a heavy ransom upon his person.[26]

In this connection, a very considerable interest attaches to the records of the purchase and sale of estates during the years 1854–1859. These records show that the price per acre of lands with serfs attached, exceeded the price of lands without serfs by a much larger margin in the forest *guberniias* than in those of the *step* (except toward the frontiers, where there was a labor-shortage); hence, inasmuch as the landlords of the *step* set a much lower value upon forced labor or *corvée,* they would obviously be much less reluctant to give it up in favor of a system of wage-work. In the central-industrial *guberniias,* the premium paid for lands with serfs attached, ran from twenty-nine to fifty-two per cent — in the central-agricultural *guberniias*, from five per cent to twenty.[27] The fact that even in the *guberniias* of the latter group, this premium was demanded and received, might be taken to indicate that the majority of the landlords had not become convinced of the economic advantages of free labor; and the same conclusion might be drawn from the fact that although some of the landlords employed hired workers to supplement their own supply of forced labor in case of need, comparatively few undertook to clear away their serfs and to reorganize their agricultural operations on the wage-work system.[28] However, a belief that free labor would be profitable, once the system were generally established, did not necessarily entail a willingness to experiment individually with this system in the midst of a sea of bondage. Again, under the régime of forced labor, the serfs supplied something more than man-power; commonly they entered the manorial fields as an army self-equipped, with their own horses or oxen, their own carts, plows, harrows, and the like. If the landlords were to become thorough-going capitalists in agriculture, they would have to equip the manorial barns and stables with all this inventory, as well as to employ hired labor; but often they lacked the ready funds to make the necessary purchases, and to advance the wages of labor, and this lack of capital was of course an obstacle to any general economic overhauling. In sum, it may be said of the rural economic conditions which affected the attitude of the nobility toward emancipation, that the estates were in general far from prosperous, that certain writers of the time laid the blame for this upon the old forced-labor system, that some of the landlords had become familiar with free labor through its supplementary employment, and that a few estates had been profitably reorganized upon a capitalistic basis.

It was however in the field of non-agricultural production that free labor first gained predominance. After earlier legal fumblings and contradictions, it had been officially ruled in 1754 that the right to own serfs belonged exclusively to the nobility,[29] but for a time there still remained a special arrangement under which non-noble factory-owners might maintain the forced-labor system in their plants. Specific permission for industrialists of the "merchant" class to purchase serfs for permanent attachment to their factories was granted in the time of Peter the Great (in 1721), withdrawn in 1762, renewed in 1798, and finally abrogated in 1816.[30] Besides the serfs purchased during the life of this permission, groups of peasants from the State domains were sometimes ascribed to the factories; and in the one case as in the other, the work-people were considered to be bound, not to the person of the manufacturer, but inseparably to the plant itself as an institution.[31]

Thus after 1816, with the nobles still free to make increasing use of forced labor in industry, the middle-class manufacturers were not permitted to expand their bondaged labor-forces through purchase. This restriction, as well as the growing recognition of the greater productivity of wage-work, may have been one of the causes for the increase in the proportion of "free hired laborers" among the factory workers — an increase from forty-eight per cent in 1804 to fifty-four per cent in 1825 and to still larger proportions during the remaining decades of serfdom.[32] These "free hired laborers," so called, were for the most part not really free men, but peasants from the State domains or serfs from the private estates, who had not broken connection with their villages, but had simply received permission to absent themselves temporarily in order to engage in wage-work. In the industrial relation they were usually free, in the sense that they made their own individual contracts with their industrial employers — but sometimes every element of freedom was lacking, and the serf-owner himself made the contract with the manufacturer and himself received the wage.[33]

If the unlimited right to employ forced labor had been an important advantage in industry, the nobles might perhaps have been expected at least to hold their own in this field (although, of course, many other factors enter here). Actually it appears that not only the proportion but the number of factories belonging to the nobility declined during the 'thirties and 'forties, when industry in general was undergoing a rapid expansion.[34] An interesting indication of the changing position of, and the changing attitude toward, bound labor in industry is to be found in the fact that under a law of 1840 which gave the owners the option of liberating serfs bound specifically to their factories, more than 15,000 males — perhaps as many as one-half of all the males of this class — were voluntarily liberated before the general emancipation.[35] By 1860, middle-class ownership and "free hired labor" had come into complete predominance in the field of industrial production — but in order that the importance of this fact may not be exaggerated, it is necessary to remember that industry itself did not bulk large in Russian life; the total force of factory workers, bond and "free" alike, was inconsiderable,[36] while in number and general influence the middle-class industrialists fell very far short of the nobility.

But besides the demonstration in industry of the profitability of free labor, and the question as to its potentialities in agriculture, brought forward so urgently by the economic difficulties of the landlords, there were other considerations which helped to carry the nobles and the government forward toward emancipation. If the strength or weakness of the economic motives for emancipation may not properly be judged by the very limited scope of voluntary manumissions on the estates, certainly the number of such liberations is even less a measure of the force of the other motives now to be mentioned. Could, for example, an individual proprietor hope by freeing his own serfs to escape the vengeance of a general peasant rising, if such should subsequently occur?

The restlessness of the peasants undoubtedly had an important effect upon their masters' attitude of mind. The proprietors could not possibly disregard the reports of flights, burnings, murders, or the rumors of judgment to come, like the one which circulated among the nobles of Smolensk *guberniia* in 1848, when it was said: "Not far away the peasants are slaughtering the landlords, and it's not at all impossible that they'll soon be doing the same right here." Such reports and rumors were made all too credible by the tradition of Pugachev's revolt, when forks and reaping-hooks had been put to fearful uses, and fire and blood had swept through great stretches of the land. The behavior of the peasants during the Crimean War was hardly reassuring, but among the nobles there were some who thought that emancipation was more likely to bring on, than to avoid, a general *jacquerie*. This however was not the prevailing view; long ago Catherine II had said, and Nicholas had repeated, that unless the system of serfdom were modified, the serfs would take matters into their own hands; and Alexander II faced the same alternative when in 1856 he said: "It were better that the emancipation came from above, than from below." [37]

The economic retardation, the social disunity, the military impotence, revealed by the Crimean War left the ruling class with self-confidence somewhat diminished, and in a mood more favorable to general reform; and all the time, before and after this sad affair, education was spreading among this class, and the ferment of liberal ideas was at work.[38] However, it hardly requires to be emphasized that the liberalism which helped to inspire the Emancipation of the 'sixties was very often a liberalism well informed by economic interest, and sensitized by lively fears of wrath to come.

Some of the motives for emancipation had only a brief significance; some of them spanned many decades, and in this resembled the emancipation itself, a century-long process finally completed only when all peasant redemption-dues still remaining unpaid were cancelled during the Revolution of 1905. More than a hundred years before this, in 1803, an important step had been taken toward "the Great Reform": an *ukaz* of this year, as confirmed and strengthened in 1807, provided that *whole villages* of serfs were not thereafter to be liberated except with land.[39] The proprietor might still liberate individuals and single families without land, nor was there anything to prevent his converting large groups of village serfs into courtyard people, and then giving them a landless manumission. The new legislation was important chiefly because it established a precedent; it embodied the principle that when village serfs were emancipated in large groups, they should not be reduced to a complete dependence upon wage-work for a living, but should be provided with holdings out of which they could produce at least a partial livelihood.[40] The proprietor was of course in a position to fix the price of land and liberty; if the serfs would not or could not meet his terms, their condition remained as before, and the actual liberations under this law (down to 1858, something more than one hundred thousand registered males,[41] and perhaps as many females) reduced only by an inconsiderable fraction the mass of those in bondage.

The next important step had been taken on the initiative of the nobility of Esthonia, who proposed in 1811 a liberation of their serfs. This was decreed in 1816; and in 1817 and 1819 similar measures were applied in Kurland and Livonia. In flat contradiction to the principle embodied in the law of 1803, the serfs of these Baltic provinces (the registered males numbered some 416,000) were liberated without land, and were at the same time forbidden to emigrate from this region, or to become citizens of the towns.[42] As a result, they were forced to compete within an artificially restricted field, as agricultural wage-workers and as renters of proprietorial lands; and in this again there was much that was prophetic of conditions which would follow the general emancipation, still to come.

In 1842 there came a general *ukaz* authorizing contractual arrangements between masters and serfs which would leave all the land of the estates in the ownership of the former, but assign a portion to the use of the serfs in return for dues and services to be fixed by agreement. This measure is generally described as one providing for emancipation by free contract, but inasmuch as the contracting peasant was not made free to leave the allotment, and was still subject to manorial justice and to corporal punishment at the order of the landlord, it would seem that in fact this law did no more than provide the means of regulating by agreement certain phases of the master-serf relation. Still, those who entered into these contracts were no longer officially registered as serfs, and in 1858 the number of males in this special status was just under thirty thousand.[43]

Emergence from the servile status might be effected not only through individual emancipation, with or without land, and through group-emancipation with land, but also in several other ways, especially through flight, through banishment, through purchase from the master by the State, or through the fulfilment of the almost interminable period of military service for which a certain proportion of the lower classes of the population were conscripted.[44] It may perhaps have also been true that the increasing hardships of bondage operated, as the era of serfdom drew toward its close, to put a check upon the natural increase of the servile population.[45] At any rate, the number of serfs diminished after 1835, while the number of State peasants, and of all classes of the population taken together, still continued to increase, as the following table will show:

	Private Serfs [46] (registered males only)	State Peasants [46] (registered males only)	Total Population of the Empire [47] (both sexes)
1796	9,790,000	7,276,000	36,000,000
1835	10,872,000	10,550,000	60,000,000
1858	10,696,000	12,800,000	74,000,000

In the Grand Duchy of Warsaw, created by Napoleon out of a part of the territory of the old Polish State, the liberation of the serfs was proclaimed in 1807, but the actual change in their condition was hardly what the word would indicate. The land remained in the possession of the masters, and in return for the use of temporary allotments, the peasants rendered dues and services in very much the same manner as before. After 1815, there was even a reestablishment of manorial jurisdiction in that part of the Grand Duchy which fell under Russian control. From 1846 onward, the Russian Government undertook to limit the freedom of the landlords in the control of allotments and in the assessment of obligations, but the reform was still far from complete, and the next important step was not taken until after the Polish uprising of 1863.[48]

In Russia proper, with a precedent set for personal liberation, and the number of serfs already in decline, a precedent was being created also for the establishment of peasant private property in land. Liberated serfs, and — under a law of 1801 — State peasants,[49] might acquire and hold landed property, and on the eve of the Emancipation there were 3,700,000 *desiatinas* in peasant ownership. This however was a mere handsbreadth as compared with some 232,000,000 *desiatinas* held by the State and the Imperial family, in European Russia, and about 105,000,000 *desiatinas* owned by the nobles, in forty-three *guberniias* alone.[50] A beginning had been made at serf reform, but only a beginning — a minor treatment of a vast epidemic of distress which, on the economic side, was nearly everywhere more intense than it had been three-quarters of a century before.

CHAPTER V

THE EMANCIPATION

As LIFE runs, the downfall of serfdom and the triumph of social revolution in Russia do not stand far separated: in 1926, nine years after the Revolution, the writer lived for some weeks in a provincial household where the soup and the samovar were brought in each day by a spry old *babushka* who had been a serf — the goose-girl on a neighboring estate. During the period of revolution and civil war, this town had been occupied and re-occupied by various groups of Reds and Whites; some of its buildings were still in ruins, a Communist Club was quartered in the House of Nobles, and on one occasion the writer happened to see a goat looking out through the empty window of a neighboring mansion; but the old *babushka* lived on in another age: she still resented, and volubly disapproved of, any attempt of the mistress of the house to lend a hand in the kitchen — to those old eyes this was still a thing most unbecoming and unseemly.

But the Emancipation and the Revolution are joined by much more than mere proximity in time. One September day in the fateful year 1917, by a roadside in the south-central *step,* a man climbed a telephone pole, and cut the minute thread of communication which joined a manor-house on the northern horizon with the towns, the police-offices, and the barracks along the railway line to the southward. In one sense, this manor-house now stood quite alone; but not really so, for within sight of its groves there were several peasant villages. Thus the two elements — peasant and proprietorial, were left momentarily to react upon each other in isolation; and within a few hours the estate had been looted, the mansion was in flames, and somewhere within the fiery circle the master of the house lay dead.[1]

From the day when the servile system was still in the making, fire had smouldered in the Russian village, and several times a hurricane of fire had raged through the country, never sweeping the

64

manors clean, but never quite extinguished. On the eve of the Emancipation, the smell of smoke was strong enough to alarm the Tsar-Liberator himself, and the air was by no means cleared by his "Great Reform." In very much that it preserved, even in much that it created, the Emancipation of the 'sixties contributed powerfully to the making of the Revolution of 1917; the meaning of the Proclamation of 1861 did not become altogether clear until it was illuminated by the glare of that great conflagration.

If the reader will consider the peasant reforms of the 'sixties in terms not of law but of life — if he will think of an individual peasant in his long coat, his feet in plaited bark slippers and his legs wrapped to the knee with strips of linen; of his crowded log house, the whitewashed interior and the great brick stove, the cluster of outbuildings around the court, and the scattered strips of plow-land; of the village with its grass-grown street as wide as a field, where wheel-tracks wander in deliberate confusion and the peasant assembly forms its triple circle of bearded householders, grave-faced women, and scooting, tumbling children — if the reader will think in such terms as these, he will be impressed by the fact that very much of the old life survived the changes of the time.[2]

The peasants on the lands of the State and of the Imperial family were made the subject of special legislation, but it was the bound people on the private estates who were most deeply affected by the reform. "The right of bondage over the peasants settled upon the landlords' estates, and over the courtyard people, is forever abolished" — so declared the first article of the General Statute of Emancipation. Among the private bondsmen, it will be convenient to deal first with the plowmen of the villages, and to leave the non-agricultural bondsmen for later consideration. The Statutes of 19 February 1861 provided not only for the emancipation of these millions, but for their endowment with land, and for their social-economic organization. These laws of 1861 were so verbose, so full of variables, so loaded down with qualifications and exceptions, and in general so astonishingly involved and complicated, that it is difficult to understand how any serf could ever by any possibility have known what rights might be hidden in this legislative haystack. As late as 1906, the Ministry of the Interior could still quite properly report to the Council of Ministers that the provisions of the peasant land-laws were "incomplete, inexact, and in some instances even contradictory."[3] In certain respects, the regulations for the three Little Russian *guberniias* of Chernigov, Poltava and Kharkov, and for the western *guberniias* from Kiev and Podolsk to Kovno and Vitebsk, differed from those about to be described. No attempt will be made here to deal with the peculiarities of the former Emancipation-settlement, but in the case of the more numerous western *guberniias* several important points of variation will be indicated hereafter.

Under the Statutes of Emancipation, the former serf was not simply offered an allotment; he was required to accept it, in one form or another, at least for the time being. Because of the obligations attaching to it, he might think this allotment a liability rather than an asset, and might therefore wish to renounce it outright; but it will presently be shown that there were serious obstacles to such a renunciation — obstacles which were quite often insuperable. If instead of wishing to "throw away" his allotment, the former serf desired rather to transfer it, and perhaps to receive some sort of compensation for his land-right and for his improvements, he was faced with difficulties which varied with the character of his tenure (either hereditary or repartitional), and will presently be discussed. The point to be made here is that there were important obstacles to the sale of the allotment — even to its being "thrown away"; and this fact is inseparably bound up not only with the subject of peasant organization under the reform, but also with the question (to be considered later) of the economics of the Emancipation.

The Great Reform did not effect a revolutionary change in the internal organization of the peasantry on the private estates: on the contrary, for the purpose in part of securing the payment of the excessive charges laid upon the emancipated serfs, the government shored up and strengthened with legal guarantees those basic institutions of peasant life — the household and the commune. Even a glance at the Statutes of Emancipation will show that they deal primarily in terms, not of individuals, but of groups and group-functions.

The question as to the character of the property-relations *within* the peasant household is one of the most vexed problems in Russian agrarian history. Between the claims of the household as a group, and those of the head of the household as an individual, neither the law of the Emancipation nor the custom of the village gave always and everywhere the same decision, but the weight of peasant practice and of legal interpretation is on the side of the

opinion that the allotment was assigned to the household as a collective, and that each member had the right to share the common
use of this allotment and of the implements and animals necessary
for its cultivation.[4] The household was subject to a joint responsibility for taxes and for redemption-dues — a responsibility so
strict, that in case of a default, any member might be put to compulsory labor.[5] The land and its agricultural equipment were to
be employed under the control of the householder, in the interest
of the group, and the members and their side-earnings were likewise under his control; but under certain conditions (and with the
approval of the commune) the juniors might divide the allotment
and establish an additional household, even against the opposition
of the original head of the house.[6] In the use, division, or alienation of the allotment, the householder was subject to many *external* restrictions, which varied with the character of the tenure,
and at the same time he himself and the other members of his
household were closely restricted in their personal right of movement. Some of the details as to all this hobbling and tethering will
be given presently, in the discussion of land-tenure and of the
commune, but the matter at issue just here is the internal constitution and the general importance of the household — and the point
to be made is that it was difficult for the householder to get rid
of the allotment if it were a burden, or to sell it if it were an asset; that the personal mobility of the peasant was also seriously
hampered; and that these restrictions upon property and person
helped to preserve and stabilize the household as a basic integer
of peasant society.

Before the Emancipation, the neighboring households on the
estates had usually been connected in various ways by common interests in the land, and the General Statute of 1861 recognized this
as a proper basis for the economic and political organization of the
emancipated peasantry when it said that "the village-community"
or *selskoe obshchestvo*, as now officially constituted, should consist
of peasants who shared in the use of one or more kinds of land,
or had "other economic interests in common." This principle was
vague enough: for example, it did not indicate what was to be the
basis of organization when, as often happened, two groups of peasants were entirely distinct, the one from the other, in respect to
their plow-lands, but were joined as common holders of lands of
some other kind — perhaps a natural pasture, or a wood-lot. What
was to be done, in other words, when an interest in *different* hold-

ings attached the same household to *different, non-coincident* groups ? It would seem that the accepted principle might have been developed quite logically by providing that the households which shared in any specific holding should be recognized as a commune *with respect to that particular holding* — and so on with respect to each other holding in which a common interest was involved. Under such an arrangement, a given household might be a shareholder in several non-coincident corporations or collectives, each with its definite sphere of activity and its recognized organ of control.

But to assume a logic in the law on this question, is to set up an insuperable obstacle to the understanding of the legislation of 1861. Instead of building upon its own recognition of the pre-existent common interests in the land, the General Statute confused and confounded this principle with two others. In the interest of those large landowners who wished to deal with all the emancipated serfs on each estate as a body, the Statute provided that the village-community should be composed of "peasants settled upon the land of a single landlord"; and under this provision, separate land-groups of peasants who had previously had no general interest in common, were in many cases joined in a single official community. Again, the Statute said that when there were no more than twenty "male revision souls" on a given estate, these peasants should be joined with others in the neighborhood to form a single community; and thus, in the interest of convenience in administration, the law created still other conglomerations of previously independent groups.[7]

Finally, quite regardless of any difference between a given official community which coincided with an old land-group, and one which included, say, two distinct groups of peasants with separate plow-lands which they had been accustomed to redistribute separately, the General Statute called all the official groups by the same name (that of *selskoe obshchestvo* or "village-community"), and constituted for each of these communities a single parliament of its householders for the governance of its economic and political affairs (the *selskii skhod* or "village-assembly"). For the land-commune as such, and for the traditional land-assembly of its householders, the Statutes of 1861 had no clear recognition and no name, and the same confusion existed under the laws which subsequently extended the reform to the State peasants.[8]

An interesting problem was now posed for practical solution:

where the official village-community did not coincide with the traditional land-commune, would the old organization be dissolved
and absorbed in the new ? The answer was given, in the long run,
by the strength of peasant custom, and the mountain weight of
peasant numbers. In most cases of non-coincidence, the villagers
preserved the identity of the separate land-communes and their
holdings, and exercised in group-assemblies the functions of land-
control which had been officially assigned to the assembly of the
village-community as a whole.[9]

In the face of this situation, the fuddling and fumbling which
had characterized the drafting of the Statute became characteristic also of its official interpretation and enforcement; and yet,
when a period of sufficient length is brought under observation,
it is evident that there was a certain tendency toward the official
recognition of peasant practice. The Ministry of the Interior, in
recording the land-census of 1877, employed as its collective unit,
not the *selskoe obshchestvo* (the official "village-community"), but
the *krestianskaia obshchina* or "peasant commune." The report of
the census defined the *krestianskaia obshchina* as a group of peasants who had received their allotments at the time of the Reform
under a single documentary grant (regardless of whether the allotments were held in heredity by the separate households under this
grant, or were subject to periodic redistribution); and the census-
report also said that in any given case the "peasant commune"
might be identical with the "village-community," or form only a
part of it.[10] In 1884, the Governing Senate (the supreme interpre-
ter of Russian law) declared that the control of each of these separately documented group-holdings belonged, not to the assembly
of the community as a whole, but to a separate assembly of the
holders. On the other hand, in examining the project for the law
(of 1893) on the partitioning of peasant families and their allotments, the State Council discarded a proposed clause which gave
to the sub-assembly (where such existed, on the basis of a documentary grant) an authority co-ordinate with that of the general
meeting of the community, in respect to this particular matter. However, a few years later, the Senate not only in effect restored this clause by interpretation, but declared that the right
of decision in this matter of family partitions belonged exclusively
to the smaller assembly.

But not only did the land-group and the official community
often fail to coincide; sometimes it happened, too, that in practice

the documentary grant was fitted neither to the one nor to the other; and accordingly, the Senate declared in 1896 that whatever the documents might say, "every settlement . . . that in fact has separate plow-lands, should be regarded as, in respect to land-holding, an independent group." And finally in 1899 there came the law which recognized, for fiscal purposes, the separate identity of the smaller holding-groups as such, and of their assemblies.[11]

Thus, in the course of four long decades, a good deal had been done to clarify the situation — but following the revolutionary crisis of 1905–1906, there appeared the famous land-decree of 9 November 1906, drawn wholly and entirely in terms of the official "village-community," the *selskoe obshchestvo* of 1861 ! And last of all, the land-laws of 14 June 1910 and 29 May 1911 recognized the authority of the separate land-groups within the community in questions having to do with the *dissolution* of existing land-relations, but failed to clarify the status and function of these groups in respect to those land-relations which were not dissolved, but were preserved intact.[12]

If this sketch properly represents the state of affairs at the center of government, what must then have been the uncertainty and confusion of the local bureaucracy and the local courts ? When the land-commune and the village-community were identical, the relationships among the households were complex enough — but that is another problem. The question here is: where, and when, and to what degree, did the land-commune exist and function apart from the official village-community ? The student interested in the realities of peasant life is hounded by a desire to assign each common interest and each collective function to the group which actually shared that interest and exercised that function; but to do this would require an interminable study, such as has never yet been made, of the actual practice of the peasants, as more or less modified and aborted by the agrarian laws, the interpretations of the Senate, the rulings of the local courts, and the actions of the local bureaucracy. It may be said that as a general rule the political functions were in the hands of the village-community as a whole, while the land-functions were exercised by separate land-communes and their assemblies wherever the basis for this arrangement existed in a holding which was factually distinct; but in any detailed discussion, the continued employment of the terms "village-community" (*selskoe obshchestvo)* and "land-commune" (*zemelnoe obshchestvo* or *pozemelnaia obshchina*) involves an ever-present obligation to draw distinctions between the one and the other — an obligation which in many circumstances cannot be fulfilled. The only honest course, in the premises, is to adopt a neutral term; and accordingly the word "commune" will be employed here to designate both the political group and the land-group, with no implication as to their coincidence or non-coincidence in any particular time or place or in respect to any particular interest or function.

The Emancipation not only preserved and strengthened the communal basis of peasant life; it also preserved the two historic forms of tenure which defined the land-relationships among the households of each commune, and still served to divide the communes themselves into two major types — first, those with the right of periodic quantitative repartition; and second, those with hereditary household tenure — a form of holding which was confined almost exclusively to the western and southwestern *guberniias*.[13]

Even in the communes with hereditary household tenure (*podvornoe polzovanie* or *vladenie*), the households were joined by varied and complex land-relationships. The lands were allotted to the commune, and a house-and-garden lot in the village, together with a share of land in the fields, was then assigned to the household in heredity and was not subject to quantitative repartition upon the order of the communal assembly. However the household allotment of plow-land did not normally consist of a single plot, but of a number of separate strips scattered among the fields around the village; and in the actual or supposed interest of the commune as a whole, the exploitation of these strips was to a certain extent controlled by the communal assembly. Under the direction of this assembly, all the householders were required to follow a common crop-cycle (that is, they all planted and harvested simultaneously their strips in each particular field), while after the harvest and in fallow years all the strips were used alike as a common pasture for the animals of the commune; and in order that there might be no artificial obstacle to the free movement of the cultivators and of their cattle, and no reduction in the area of pasturage, the holders were prohibited from building upon or enclosing their strips without the consent of the assembly. In addition to the house-and-garden lots and the open fields with their tangle of intermingled strips, there were almost always still other lands (natural pastures, and the like) which remained undivided, and were used by all the households of the commune under the regulation of its assembly. Finally, the emancipation of the lands and persons of these allotment-holders commonly involved substantial redemption-payments to the landlord — payments which might be covered either by the households acting separately, or by the commune. The law declared that from the beginning of the redemption-process, the character of the tenure would be governed by the method of redemption: that is, the redemption of hereditary allotments by the commune as a whole would involve a collective responsibility for the payments, and a conversion of the allotments into repartitional communal holdings. In the great majority of the communes with hereditary allotments, the redemption was actually undertaken by the commune as a whole, and the administration and the courts became involved in a maze of confusion and contradiction respecting the tenure of the holdings so redeemed. The prevailing tendency of officialdom was to deny in such cases a collective responsibility for redemption or a liability to repartition, and in general (though certainly not always consistently) to preserve the hereditary character of these allotments against the collectivist provisions of the redemption-law.[14] The process of redemption will be discussed in some detail below, but its effect upon the land-relation within the communes of hereditary holders is a subject that had of necessity to be mentioned here.

The next question is: how and under what conditions might the land-linkages be dissolved, in a commune of hereditary holders ? A final apportionment among the households of any land hitherto undivided might be arranged by a two-thirds' vote of the assembly, but on the other hand, the law did not specifically provide a means for making a general consolidation of the scattered strips of plowland into a unitary farm for each household and thus eliminating the common crop-cycle and the common pasture-right. In fact, the general provisions in regard to the character of the hereditary tenure were usually interpreted as prohibiting such a wholesale relocation of strips without the unanimous consent of the holders.[15]

Under certain conditions, the individual householder with an hereditary allotment might act independently to alter or terminate the land-relation with his neighbors. If he remained a member of the commune, it was theoretically possible for him to renounce the allotment with all the obligations attaching to it, but in most of the *guberniias* the statutes made prerequisite requirements (for example, the independent purchase of a given area of land) which the great majority of the peasants were economically unable to ful-

fil. If the householder withdrew from the commune, the surrender
of the allotment was not only permitted (without condition, after
1870) but required; but the personal withdrawal itself was possible
only after the fulfilment of conditions which will be described
hereafter. However, all this applied only during the period before redemption was begun in any particular case, and most of
the hereditary holders were very soon involved in the redemption-
process (for one thing, a special regulation of 1863 made redemption compulsory in nine of the western *guberniias*); and once this
process had been initiated, there could no longer be any possibility of the outright rejection of an individual allotment, but only
of its transfer to someone who would assume the debt upon it.
When the commune as a whole engaged in the redemption of the
land, with the help of a loan from the State (and this was the usual
process under hereditary tenure), the question as to who then controlled the transfer of the allotments was of course involved in the
general question as to the effect of collective redemption upon
hereditary tenure, but the prevailing tendency was apparently to
recognize in the householder the same rights of transfer or retention that he would have acquired under an entirely independent
redemption. In case of an independent redemption, it was specifically provided that after 1870, the holder who remained a member of the commune was free to transfer the allotment with any
debt upon it to anyone inside or outside the commune, without
regard to the wishes of the assembly. If the allotment were in process of separate redemption with State aid, and the householder
wished to withdraw personally from the commune, he was obliged
not only to meet the general requirements for a personal separation but either to pay off the entire debt or to find someone who
would take over the allotment with its obligations. If the separate
redemption of the allotment were completed, the withdrawing
holder might either transfer or retain the land. Such were the laws
governing the right of the holder to dispose of the allotment; but
it not seldom happened that the redemption-debt exceeded the actual value of the holding, and thus defeated any attempt to find
anyone who would accept the land together with its obligations;
and sometimes it also happened that a householder who wished to
withdraw personally from the commune was unable either to find
a taker for the allotment with its debt, or to pay off the debt himself, and was therefore unable to effect the personal separation.
If the householder wished to consolidate the scattered strips of his

allotment and thus to render his farming operations independent
of the common crop-cycle and the common pasture-right, this
change might be accomplished only with the consent of all the
other householders whose strips would be displaced — an agreement usually impossible to secure.

In general, it must be said that in the Statutes of Emancipation
and in the subsequent interpretations of the administrators and
the courts, the question of the nature of the hereditary household
tenure (*podvornoe vladenie*) and of the apportionment of rights
under this tenure between the commune and the household, was
befogged and befuddled by omissions, inconsistencies, and outright contradictions.[16] The task of describing this tenure in a few
paragraphs is therefore difficult and hazardous in the extreme; and
yet it is at least clear that under this hereditary tenure the land-
relations of the households were by no means so intimate as under
the repartitional communal tenure now to be discussed.

In the communes with repartitional tenure (*obshchinnoe polzovanie* or *vladenie*), the house-and-garden plots were assigned to
the several households in heredity, and neither their size nor their
location was subject to subsequent adjustment by the communal
assembly. On the other hand, the assembly might by a two-thirds'
vote repartition periodically among the households the other lands
allotted to the commune. The assembly itself was to decide the
rules under which each distribution should be made, and was required only to apply these general rules fairly and equably to each
of its member-households. In these communes, each household
usually held (subject to redistribution) a number of scattered strips
of plow-land and meadow; and here, as in the communes with
hereditary tenure, the intermixture of the strips of plow-land involved a common crop-cycle and a common pasture-right. And
finally there almost always remained still other lands (most often
a natural pasture) which the assembly preferred not to divide,
even temporarily, but reserved for common use under its own
immediate control. In other words, the lands of the repartitional
commune were ordinarily of three kinds: those allotted in heredity to the households, those allotted temporarily to the households and subject to repartition, and those held undivided for
common use. For the first nine years after the confirmation of the
Statutes, the commune was prohibited from disposing of land to
anyone outside its membership; and thereafter, while any part of
the redemption loan remained unpaid, the commune might make

such an alienation only with the consent of certain authorities of the *guberniia*. In the repartitional communes, as in those with hereditary tenure, the completion of the Emancipation usually required the payment of a considerable sum to the landlord, but here the land could be redeemed with State aid only if all the households of the commune acted as a unit and accepted a joint responsibility — and in a vast majority of the repartitional communes, the allotments were actually redeemed in this way.[17]

In the repartitional communes, the individual householder was strictly limited in his right to alter the land-relation. The consent of a majority in the assembly was required before a household and its holding might be divided for the purpose of establishing an additional household and providing it with an allotment. Only with the consent of the assembly might an allotment (with its obligations) be transferred by a holder who remained a member of the commune; and in any case, such a transfer was legally effective only until the time of the next general repartition, when as far as the law was concerned the rights and duties of the original holder and of the transferee were exactly what they would have been if no transfer had taken place. Before redemption was begun, the obstacles to the renunciation of the entire allotment by the householder who remained a member of the commune, or withdrew from it, were similar in a general way to those that existed under hereditary tenure and have already been described. If the holder effected a separate redemption of the house-and-garden plot only, he might then renounce the remainder of his allotment, but there were serious economic difficulties in the way of such a separate and partial redemption. During the process of collective redemption with State aid (the usual procedure), the holder who remained in the commune might renounce or transfer the allotment only with the consent of the assembly, and only temporarily (that is, until the next general repartition). If the holder undertook to withdraw from the commune while joint redemption was still in progress, he was obliged not only to meet the general conditions for a personal separation, but to pay half the debt still due on his allotment, and to surrender the land to the commune, with the doubtful privilege of knocking his buildings down and hauling them away, or of selling them either to the commune's next allottee, or to someone else for removal; and in this situation the commune on its own part might refuse to assume the balance of the debt, and thereby prevent the holder from *either* surrendering his allotment or effecting the release of his person. Where the joint redemption-loan had been repaid, or the commune had cleared its holdings without the help of such a loan, the holder who retained his membership was still subject to the restrictions already mentioned respecting the rejection or transfer of the allotment, while in case of a personal withdrawal he was required to meet the usual general conditions and to divest himself of his allotment in the manner "prescribed by local custom" — a rule under which the retiring member might control the transfer of his house-and-garden plot, but was more or less at the mercy of the commune in respect to his remaining land-rights.[18]

Speaking now in general and summary terms, it may be said that in the repartitional communes, membership and allotment-holding were inseparable. So long as the land remained in repartitional tenure, it was the duty and the right of the commune to offer the allotment — and it was the right and the duty of the householder to receive it; so it had to be, if the system of repartition were to operate when the allotment was a burden, as well as when it was an asset. If membership and allotment-holding were bound up together, just so the termination of membership and the divestment of land were interlocked, and any difficulty in the way of either of these operations was therefore at the same time an obstacle to the other. That is to say, the general restrictions upon personal withdrawal acted as an additional check upon the alienation of allotment-rights, while on the other hand, the difficulty of disposing of the allotment (the difficulty of getting rid of an overburdened allotment under any condition, or of disposing of a profitable one at a fair value) was by all odds the most important artificial barrier to the personal separation of the peasants from the commune.

All this applies to the communes with repartitional tenure; but the law also provided certain means for changing these conditions fundamentally by altering both the nature of the tenure and the physical arrangement of the holdings. If the change were to extend throughout the commune, the decision must rest with the assembly. By a two-thirds' vote, this body might divide the lands of the commune into hereditary holdings (each bearing its appropriate share of any redemption-debt which might still be outstanding); and at the same time, or thereafter, the assembly might consolidate the scattered strips and establish a unitary farm for every household. In other words, it was in the power of the assembly to convert the repartitional tenure into an hereditary household tenure identical in most particulars with that established in some of the communes at the Emancipation, and already described above; and through consolidation, the assembly might also dissolve the common crop-cycle and the other like connections associated with the physical intermixture of the allotment-strips.

Finally, in a commune where both the repartitional tenure and the physical arrangement of the holdings remained in general unaltered, it was possible, at least theoretically, for a single householder to secure, even without the consent of the assembly, a separate hereditary title to his allotment, and perhaps even its physical consolidation. The repayment of the loan incurred under joint redemption with State aid was expected to require ordinarily almost half a century, and during this period of repayment, the holder might obtain an hereditary title only if he paid off in advance the full share of the redemption-debt assignable to his allotment — a condition which the peasant was rarely able to fulfil. When the hereditary tenure of a single allotment was so established, the holder lost all rights and duties under any subsequent repartition of the other allotments in the commune, and his position and land-relations were now substantially the same as those of a peasant who had belonged from the first to a commune with hereditary tenure and had completed the separate redemption of his allotment. The member of a repartitional commune who thus through pre-redemption obtained an allotment in heredity was privileged, however, to go still farther than this in the direction of individualization: that is, he might also compel the commune to give him in exchange for the scattered strips of his allotment, a holding of the same quality and extent, but consolidated "in so far as possible" in one place. Where the repartitional commune had acquired its allotment-lands without governmental aid, or had already completed the repayment of the joint redemption-loan, the holder might demand both a separation of tenure and a physical consolidation of an allotment proportionate in size — in case there had been a redemption — to the total amount of the redemption-payments made by the household; but when some years had passed after the Emancipation and the dues (as well as the lands) had been repartitioned several times, it was usually impossible to determine the total amount which the household had paid toward redemption — and besides this, the commune had the option of retaining the land and indemnifying the claimant.[19]

Such then was the original character of the land-relation within the two types of commune (the relation of holder with allotment; of allotment with allotment; of holder with holder); and such were the obstacles to the alteration of these relations, and especially to the economic disentanglement of one allotment from another. To complete the picture, it must be added that the communes were often involved with one another, and even with private proprietors, by the common tenure or the physical intermixture of certain of their lands.[20]

Whatever might be the nature of his relation to the land, and whatever changes this relation might undergo, the ex-serf was still for political-administrative purposes a member of the commune.[21] All-inclusive as far as the peasants were concerned, the commune was closely organized and high-walled against every other class: the neighboring landlord remained an alien, even though the avenue of his park opened directly upon the village street, and the priest who often lived in a log house beside the church in the very center of the village, was still not a member of the corporation.

The affairs of the peasant commune were to be conducted by an assembly of the heads of households, and by the *starosta* or "elder" and the other officers elected by this assembly.[22] All the members bore a joint responsibility for taxes, and it was one of the functions of the assembly to apportion this burden among the households, and to levy additional assessments for its own local uses.[23] With the abolition of immediate personal subjection to the landlord, there were transferred to the peasant commune — in theory at least — the bulk of the public-law powers which the masters had formerly exercised upon their serfs.[24] For example, the peasant assembly might put to forced labor any member of a household whose public obligations were in arrears, and might even sentence to banishment any peasant whom it adjudged guilty of "vicious" conduct.[25] A passport was necessary for temporary absence at any considerable distance, and certain officials elected by the peasants had the right, not definitely limited by law, of denying passport-applications.[26] If it were a question not of a temporary absence but of a full and permanent separation from the commune, the obstacles were much more serious: if the candidate for separation were a junior member of a household, he had to have the consent of his father;[27] if any taxes charged against the household were in arrears, their payment was required;[28] as a rule the candidate for separation was required to produce evidence that some other commune had already voted to receive and register him as a member; [29] and finally, if he were a householder with an allotment, he was usually called upon to divest himself of this land under conditions which have already been described — conditions which very often could not be fulfilled and therefore made the personal separation quite impossible.

Just as a number of households formed a peasant commune, so a number of such communities formed a *volost* [30] — again a purely peasant organization, with assemblymen, judges, an "elder," and other officials, elected directly or indirectly by the householders of the *volost*.[31] The elder was answerable for the maintenance of order, while the judges had jurisdiction over minor delinquencies and might sentence an offender to a small fine, a short term of imprisonment or of hard labor, and even a flogging with as many as twenty blows with rods.[32] This same elective court also dealt with most of the civil disputes which did not involve members of other classes, and in civil matters it was to be guided by peasant custom rather than by written law.[33] Finally under a statute promulgated in 1864, but put into effect only gradually, and never in all parts of the Empire, certain all-class organs of self-government, the *zemstvo* institutions, were set up in each *uezd* and *guberniia,* with assemblies in which the peasant communes, the individual landed proprietors, and the richer townsmen were to be represented in proportion to the extent of their lands, or (in the case of the townsmen) the value of their urban property.[34]

In addition to the purely peasant institutions and to the *zemstvos,* there still existed a vast hierarchy of appointive officials, with wide and illy-defined powers, in control of the police, and answerable in the last analysis only to the central government.[35] The *zemstvos* sometimes protested against, and even tried to resist, the inroads and depredations of this bureaucratic army, but when the *volost* and the commune were attacked, resistance was impossible. The organs of peasant self-government had in practice no choice but to execute the commands delivered in the name of higher authority, by the booted and spurred police who clattered through the countryside more importantly than ever, now that the landlords' immediate power over the peasants was so much reduced.[36]

But to say that the *volost,* the commune, and the household had no really effective guarantee of independence, is not to say that they had no functions and no force. It is particularly true of the commune and the household, that however much they might be checked or driven from without, they were moved also from within; and in their actions, forced or voluntary, was embodied a large proportion of the villagers' life. So it had been in the days of serfdom, and so it continued now to be.

But how is one to interpret the great official solicitude for the preservation of the household and the commune ? Is it to be taken as a sign that the nobility (the group most influential in the government) were especially devoted to these institutions, in and for themselves ? And as for the households and the communes — were they in need of such solicitude ? Would the peasants have dissolved these bodies, if they had been entirely free to do so ? A prerequisite to any attempt to answer such inquiries, is a study of the work which these institutions had now been set to do — above all, the work of guaranteeing the redemption of the peasant's allotment at a price so high that it in fact included a redemption of his person also. Under these circumstances, the household and the commune might usually be looked upon as burden-bearing groups; and so long as they maintained this character — so long as they were employed as engines of an over-priced redemption, the circumstances were hardly favorable for a peasant plebiscite upon their value. But whether it was official solicitude, or popular desire, that was chiefly responsible for the survival and strengthening of these institutions, in any case their existence drew out and developed, or gave expression to, a capacity for collective action — for doing things in common — which helped most powerfully to shape the course of a peasant history in the catastrophic time to come.

THE SERF of the manorial village did not become, under the terms of the Emancipation, a free-moving, landless man. It has been shown that he was far from free, but it still remains to inquire more closely into the conditions under which he was given — perhaps it would be better to say, required to accept — a plot of earth. In this connection, there are three matters of first and last importance: the social apparatus of allotment and redemption, the size and quality of the holding, and the weight of the redemption-payments. The functions of the household and of the commune as recipients and payors have previously been discussed, and it is now appropriate to ask what it was that the peasantry received, and at what cost.

The Statutes of Emancipation provided that the allotments were to be assigned on the basis of the number of "revision souls" found in each commune in 1858 — that is, the number of males of all ages recorded in the census of that year.[37] Throughout the greater part of the country, local maximal and minimal norms were established for the allotment per soul, the minimum amounting in each case to one-third of the maximum. In the extreme South, as well as in the Southeast, only one statutory norm was set up for each locality.[38] The norms having been established, it was provided that the size of the allotments might be fixed by voluntary agreement between the landlord and his peasants, with this general restriction: that the old pre-reform allotments might not be diminished to less than half the maximal or statutory norm, and might not be reduced at all where they already stood below this level.[39]

Where the landlord and the peasants did *not* reach an agreement, there were certain regulations which in a measure determined the size of the allotment. In the South, the peasants were supposed to receive allotments according to the statutory norm, but on the other hand, the landlord was free to retain one-half of the non-waste land of the estate, no matter how much this might limit the area of the peasant lands.[40] In the black soil and the forest, the landlord had the choice of cutting off from the former allotments any surplus *above* the maximal norm, or leaving the surplus in the hands of the peasants, if the terms they offered were sufficiently attractive. If, on the other hand, the former allotment fell *below* the statutory minimum, the landlord might make a proportionate reduction in the dues, or (if the peasants did not object) he might increase the amount of the land to the minimal norm.[41] Where the old allotments fell *between* the norms, there was to be in general no change in their size, but special regulations deprived many of the peasants of the forests which they had been using.[42] And finally (whatever effect this might have upon the realization of the other conditions just mentioned) each landlord of the black soil and the forest was free to reduce any and all allotments as far as the minimal norm, if this were necessary in order to enable him to keep in his own hands one-third of the non-waste land of his estate.[43]

For nine years after the confirmation of the Statutes, or at any time when redemption was begun with State aid, an allotment already granted might be reduced by mutual agreement to a legal minimum fixed for the district — usually not to less than one-third of the maximal or statutory norm.[44] Under certain conditions the peasants might redeem the house-and-garden plot, or *usadba*, separately from the remainder of the allotment, but if the landlord refused to come to terms in the matter of the price, there were special financial difficulties in the way of such a fractional redemption. If the peasant did redeem the *usadba* separately, he could, after 1870, refuse to hold any longer the remainder of the allotment,[45] unless the landlord had in the meantime enforced a redemption. If the landlord exercised at any time his right to compel redemption, the peasants on their part might refuse to buy out more than the legal minimum.[46] If, on the other hand, the landlord were willing to surrender all claims for dues, services, and redemption-payments, and to make an outright gift of an allotment equal to one-fourth of the maximal or statutory norm, and the peasants were willing on their part to accept such an allotment, a final settlement might be arranged on this basis;[47] the grants offered under this provision, the "beggarly allotments," were accepted by about six per cent of the peasants as a means of avoiding the excessive charges on the larger plots. But among all these complications, the most impressive fact is that whenever during the first nine years a decision in respect to the size of the allotment was to be made not by mutual agreement but by a one-sided choice, the right to make that choice belonged to the peasants only in the case of enforced redemption; otherwise it belonged to the landlord, who would usually make his decision with an eye to the dues and services which the law would permit him to extract, in exchange for a given acreage assigned to the peasants.

The size of the allotment was not the only crucial point; its quality was also a matter of the first importance. In spite of the peasants' essential need for timber and fuel in this country of white winters, log-walled houses, and huge stoves, forest-lands were seldom included in the new allotments. The superior position and influence of the landlords, and in particular their right under the conditions already described to make "cut-offs" from the peasants' former holdings, and to demand a reallocation of the holdings in order to eliminate the intermixture of the peasants' lands with their own (the peasants on their side did not possess the latter right) — all this made it possible for the landlords to impose numerous inconveniences in the arrangement of the allotments, and even sometimes to leave the peasants without such essential elements of village economy as water-courses and meadow lands.[48]

For an indeterminate period of "temporary obligation," the whole area of the estate was to continue to be the property of the landlord, while the peasants were to hold of him their revised and officially approved allotments, and to render in return such services or payments as were mutually agreed upon, or were prescribed by the Statutes of Emancipation when no agreement was arrived at.[49] The peasants were given the option of passing from the system of labor-dues to that of money-payments or *obrok*, and — for reasons to be explained hereafter — the statutory rates for payments in this latter form affected profoundly the course and the outcome of the whole reform.

The two most conspicuous characteristics of the official rate-schedules were: first, that the charges usually exceeded the rental value of the allotments; and second, that this excess was not equitably distributed among the allotments of a given district, or among the districts of the country. For each district, the official schedule provided a maximal annual charge, to correspond with the maximal allotment per peasant soul; but in most of the districts the charge was not diminished in full proportion when the amount of land fell below the maximum, and where the allotment stood at the official minimum, the rate often amounted to double as much *per acre* as was assessed upon maximal allotments in the same locality.[50] A second method of comparison, not between small and large allotments in the same district, but between different districts as a whole, makes it apparent that the official rates were often inversely proportional to the rental value of the land, and stood at higher levels for a given acreage in some of the clay-soiled central-industrial *guberniias*, than in the rich black-soil *guberniias* farther south.[51] These apparent inconsistencies did not arise by chance; if the payments were disproportionately high when the allotments were small, it was because there went with the smallest allotment, as well as the largest, not only the house-yard but the person of the peasant; if the rates were at a maximum in the thin-soiled industrial *guberniias*, it was not because the land was here more valuable (actually it was less so), but because the person of the peasant had here a greater value, by reason of the greater development of side-earnings in the household crafts and in wage-work in the towns.[52] For the time being, the peasant was really renting not only his land but his own person from his former master.

If this condition of affairs had affected only the period of "temporary obligation," the emphasis here put upon it might be spared; but actually the weight of these current charges was of the first importance in determining what sums the peasant would have to pay in order to terminate the "temporary obligation," and free himself and his land once and for all from his former master.[53] The government had declared that it would not permit so much as a discussion of the ransoming of the persons of the serfs; but when the treasury assisted financially in the redemption process, the land had to be evaluated before the State loan could be advanced, and this basic valuation was fixed by capitalizing at six per cent the peasants' current payments, which under the official schedules commonly exceeded the rental value of the land.[54] The resultant basic redemption value was usually much in excess of the market value of the land, and included a substantial price upon the peasant's head.[55]

So far as the law was concerned, the period of temporary obligation might be prolonged indefinitely; but wherever redemption operations were actually initiated, the government stood ready to make an immediate advance to the landlord in interest-bearing bonds, and to recover from the peasants concerned the amount of this advance plus interest, ordinarily distributed in annual payments over a period of forty-nine years. If the peasants were to buy out all the land which they had held during the period of temporary obligation, the advance was to amount to eighty per cent of the basic value of this land, as determined in the manner already indicated; if the allotment were reduced in size when redemption was begun, the advance was then to amount to seventy-five per cent of its basic value.[56]

Redemption was left to be initiated locally in one of two ways: The peasants and the landlord might reach a voluntary agreement, fixing the redemption-price quite independently of all regulations if there were to be no government loan, or providing for the acceptance of the loan of an amount officially determined in the manner already described, and perhaps calling also for additional compensation to be paid by the peasants directly to the landlord. Or, until 1870, and under certain circumstances thereafter, the landlord might act alone, compelling the peasants to undertake the redemption of at least the legal minimum of land, in which case the landlord would receive the amount of the State loan as officially determined, but could not obtain any additional compensation.[57] The real significance of all this is apparent only when the steps are retraced from the beginning: the peasants' current dues under the official schedule were often in excess of the rental value of the land (and why should the landlords have voluntarily accepted less?); the official valuation of the land was based upon the dues; the amount of the State loan was based upon the valuation; and at the demand of the landlord (whatever the peasants might say) the government would advance to the landlord the scheduled amount of the loan and undertake to collect this amount willy-nilly from the peasants. Thus the law provided the possibility of enforced purchase for a specified sum, and in spite of all that was said on the subject of voluntary agreement, there was thus established a minimum price for the protection of the landlords. From the allotment of the land to the projected repayment of the last *rubl* of redemption-money sometime early in the twentieth century, the chain was complete.

The western *guberniias,* extending from Kiev and Podolsk to Kovno and Vitebsk, were in part excepted from the general system of allotment and redemption. In these *guberniias* the allotments and the obligations of the serfs had been previously defined by inventories, and in the greater part of this territory these inventories were made the basis for the Emancipation.[58] Most of the peasants of this region were Lithuanian, White Russian, or Little Russian, while the majority of the landlords were Polish either by descent or by cultural assimilation. With the special stimulus of the uprising of 1863 in Russian Poland proper and among the Poles of the neighboring Russian territories, the government revised the Emancipation arrangements at the expense of the landlords of the western *guberniias,* making substantial reductions in the peasants' obligations and directing that redemption should begin at once.[59] In Russian Poland proper, where there had been an ineffectual emancipation without land in the time of the Napoleonic Grand Duchy of Warsaw, the landlords were deep in the black books of the Russian Government, and the reform of 1864 was far more favorable to the Polish peasants than had been the Statutes of 1861 to the Russian. Under the reform of '64, the landed peasants received the full acreage which they had previously held of the landlords, and some of the landless peasants were also provided with allotments. For the compensation of the landlords, the previous dues and services (somewhat diminished for the purpose of this calculation), or the annual net revenues of the allotment-lands, were capitalized at six per cent, the capital sum was paid over in interest-bearing securities, and provision was made for recovery, not through levies on the redeemed lands alone, as had been the case in Russia, but through the taxation of all the im-movable property in Poland.[60] At the same time, manorial juris-diction was abolished and the peasants were given a form of organ-ization much like that of the Russian villagers, except that the Polish *gmina* was not to be a purely peasant institution like the Russian *volost* with which it corresponded, but was to include all persons of whatever class within a given territory; and in the elec-tions of the *gmina* all who held a certain minimum of land were to have an equal suffrage. Even more than in Russia, the elected officers were dominated by the police, but in so far as the adminis-tration of the *gmina* was directed from within, the character of the suffrage put it under the control of the peasants rather than the landlords; and in this, one sees the clearest possible evidence of the attempt of the Russian Government to ally itself with the peas-antry against the Polish nobles.[61]

In Transcaucasia the reform followed the general pattern laid down in the Statutes of 1861; but whereas in the western *guber-niias* of European Russia and in Poland, the government had shown unusual favors to the peasantry, here in Transcaucasia all its mercies were extended to the landlords, and it is probable that nowhere else in the Empire were the serfs confronted with ar-rangements so unfavorable to their interest.[62]

Such in brief was the character of the Great Emancipation; and the terms being what they were, it was hardly to be expected that the peasantry who had stormed so many manor-houses in the name of land and liberty, would be universally content with what was offered them at the price they were asked to pay. Just after the publication of the Statutes, the villages swarmed with rumors of a fuller liberation still to come, or already granted but kept hidden from the peasants by officialdom and the landlords. During the four months following the publication of the manifesto announc-ing the reform, the Ministry of the Interior recorded 647 instances of rioting among the peasants — a situation "demanding in the course of the year 1861 the employment of the military forces in 499 instances, with the killing, wounding and maiming of peas-ants, with condemnations to run the gauntlet, and above all with beatings with rods." [63]

Within a year, the more active forms of peasant opposition had been nearly everywhere suppressed, but passive opposition was more widespread and more persistent.[64] Thus in 1880, about fif-teen per cent of the ex-serfs still remained in the state of "temporary obligation"; in the forest *guberniias,* where the super-charge upon the land (that is, in reality, the personal ransom) was particularly heavy, the peasants were especially reluctant to redeem their allotments. To put a period to this situation, a law of 28 December 1881 required all peasants who had not yet begun to redeem their lands to undertake the process of redemption.[65] They had hung back for twenty years, but now they were to be fully emancipated, whether they would or no.

The Statutes of 1861 embodied so many variables, that it was impossible to predict how much and what quality of land the peasants would receive, or just what payments would be demanded of them. Within a few years, however, the application of these statutes had produced such results as to define once and for all the nature of the Emancipation on its economic side. In their arrangement and composition, many of the allotments offered serious obstacles to peasant culture. Sometimes the allotments were entirely surrounded by the lands of the former master, or divided into separate plots by his intervening holdings; but a much heavier handicap was the lack of forests, and (in a country of primitive agriculture, where natural grass was still so urgently required) the dearth of pasture and of meadow land.[66] The former master was often in a position to rent out just such lands as the peasant lacked, and the mal-arrangement and mal-assortment of the peasant holdings helped to preserve a measure of the old economic dependence upon the lord.

Data as to the total area of the allotments of the proprietary peasants before and after the Emancipation are available for forty-three *guberniias* of European Russia. According to these data the area diminished from 35,197,000 *desiatinas* before 1861, to 33,755,-700 in 1877–78 — a loss of 1,441,300 *desiatinas,* or 4.1 per cent. These general figures are, however, by no means so significant as those which deal separately with the several regions of the country; for here one discovers that the allotment area was increased in the western *guberniias* (for very special reasons which have already been discussed) and in the infertile regions of the extreme North, Northeast, and East — that is, in sixteen *guberniias* altogether. Everywhere else (except in the partly arid *guberniia* of Astrakhan), the area was reduced as a result of the Emancipation, and in a broad belt of the black soil, from Poltava and Ekaterinoslav to Kazan and Samara (where the land was especially rich, and agriculture profitable) the reduction in each *guberniia* amounted to more than twenty-five per cent of the former holdings of the serfs.[67]

If these figures are brought into connection with those for market-prices and redemption-loans, the general economic character of the Emancipation will be somewhat illuminated — for it will become apparent that (except in the western *guberniias* with their objectionable Polish squires) the government advanced to the landlords, and undertook to recover from the peasants, a sum much greater than the value at current prices of the land to be redeemed; and this over-valuation was especially conspicuous in the northern non-black-soil region, where the allotments were sometimes so generously enlarged: [68]

Region	Value at market prices of 1863–1872, of land under redemption	Original redemption-loans of Government to landlords (to be recovered by Government from peasants)	Excess (+) or shortage (—) of redemption-loans as compared with market value of land
Non-black-soil *guberniias* ..	179,900,000 R.	342,000,000 R.	+ 162,100,000 R.
Black-soil *guberniias*	283,900,000 R.	341,500,000 R.	+ 57,600,000 R.
Nine western *guberniias* ..	184,000,000 R.	183,100,000 R.	— 900,000 R.
	647,800,000 R.	866,600,000 R.	+ 218,800,000 R.

Thus in the black-soil belt, where the land was well worth keeping, the landlords cut the peasants off with reduced allotments, to be redeemed at a moderate premium; in the North, the allotments were more ample, but the price upon them was nearly doubled for redemption purposes. North and South, the scales were weighted against the peasant; he was coming forth from the Emancipation with limited rights and little land, but abundant obligations; and behind him was a history that showed him not always passive in his discontent.

This was the Great Reform, as it was applied to the plowmen of the manor-lords; but besides these, there were two other important groups of private bondsmen to whom the Emancipation was extended. It will be remembered that there were on the estates, besides the village peasants, many landless "courtyard people" who served in and around the manorial establishments, while on the eve of the Emancipation the industrial enterprises of the country were still operated in part by the forced labor of serfs whose connection with the soil was often so attenuated that they held only a minute strip of plow-land and sometimes only a house-lot and garden. As a result of the Emancipation, the industrial peasants were in general left with allotments even smaller than those of their agricultural neighbors — sometimes with none at all,[69] while the "courtyard people" became for the most part landless men and drifted away to the slums and factories of the towns — the recruiting ground of the new industrial army.[70]

OPPOSITE the mass of proprietary serfs, there stood the even more numerous peasants of the State. In 1858 the personal rights of State peasants were extended to the bound people (including about 826,000 registered males) who lived on the lands of the Imperial family.[71] Under a special statute of 1863, these Imperial peasants received allotments approximating in extent the maximal norms established for the private estates of the districts in which they lived, and were required to begin within two years a forty-nine-year cycle of redemption-payments. The effect of the reform was to place the Imperial peasants in a better position than the former proprietary serfs, in respect to both the size and the price of their allotments.[72]

Far more important, because it involved a much larger mass of humanity, was the settlement made for the other peasants of the State — a subject involved in endless complications, partly by reason of the fact that on the eve of the reform there existed more than thirty categories of these peasants, varying so widely in their rights and duties that any general statement respecting them is in danger of doing violence to the facts of history.[73] The Statute of 24 November 1866 laid down the terms of the land-reform for the great majority of these peasants, and its general principles were subsequently extended to a number of the minor groups, while still other minor groups were dealt with independently.[74]

The peasants affected by the Statute of 1866 were to receive as permanent allotments all the lands, excepting the forests, which were at the time in their continuous employment; if the area so employed had not already been definitely delimited, the peasants were to keep not more than fifteen *desiatinas* per male soul in the districts where State lands were abundant, or eight *desiatinas* per soul where there was a shortage of such lands. In return, the peasants were to pay an annual *obrok* to the State at fixed rates generally somewhat higher than those previously in force, and usually based, not alone upon the value of the land, but upon the total amount of the peasants' income, whether from agricultural or industrial sources.[75] Because they had previously had larger allotments, and because these allotments were now subject to "cut-offs" only in exceptional cases, the State peasants entered the new era more liberally provided with land than were the former serfs, while at the same time their annual dues per acre were materially lower than those of the latter group.[76] In the matter of redemption, the law provided that if the peasants would surrender interest-bearing government securities to the public treasury, their annual payments would be reduced by the amount of the interest on these securities.[77] This plan for clearing the land of obligations had little practical result, and finally in 1886 the collection of the poll-tax was stopped, and the *obrok* was replaced by an annual redemption charge, materially larger in amount, which would terminate in 1931, leaving the State peasants then in unburdened possession of their allotments.[78] As these words are written, this terminal date has just now arrived, but the redemption scheme, like many other plans of mice and men . . .

In apparent harmony with the preferential treatment which the State peasants had usually received, the average redemption-price per acre of their lands was, under this arrangement, only about one-half the average amount advanced by the government on each acre redeemed by the former serfs in *guberniias* other than those of the West.[79] This takes no account of any supplementary redemption-payments made by the former serfs directly to their masters, but on the other hand it also fails to take account of the fact that most of the land redeemed by the State peasants was situated in the north-central and northern *guberniias* where values were normally lower than they were farther south.[80]

Like the private serfs of the nine western *guberniias*, the State peasants of this region were dealt with by special legislation; the Statute of 16 May 1867 placed them in a favorable position in respect to the size and price of their allotments, and required that redemption should begin at an early date.[81] In Siberia, where almost all the land had remained the property of the State, and in the *guberniias* of Transcaucasia, the era of reform brought no fundamental change in the land-relations of the State peasants, who continued as before to occupy the State domains and to pay dues to the treasury.[82] In Poland the reform of 1864, already discussed in its application to the peasants on the private estates, was applied under approximately the same terms to the peasants on the Crown domains.[83]

Among the State peasants of Russia, just as among the emancipated serfs, the old form of organization in household and commune was preserved and strengthened. Under the law of 18 January 1866 and other enactments of the period, all the State peasants except those of the Caucasus were assimilated to the household-, commune-, and *volost*-structure prescribed for the emancipated serfs in the General Statute of 1861; and like the serfs, the State peasants were given representation in the *zemstvos*.[84] The law of 18 January carries the usual provisions for the several and joint liability of the household and of the commune, and fixes for temporary absences and for final separation approximately the same general conditions that had already been established for the former serfs.[85] In sum, it may be said that the assimilative processes of the reform produced one great class of villagers — a class marked off from the remainder of the population by special institutions and governed in part by laws quite peculiar to itself.[86]

The laws of 24 November 1866 and 16 May 1867, extending the land-reform to the great majority of the State peasants, were drawn in the familiar terms of the household and the commune, and in general they preserved that form of peasant tenure which they found already in existence — whether the hereditary or the repartitional. In the great majority of the communes affected by these laws, the land was assigned in repartitional tenure, and the land-relations among the State peasants here resembled in most respects those already described as existing in the repartitional communes of the former private serfs. The intermingling of strips, and the possibility of their periodic repartition by a two-thirds' vote; the common holding of undivided pastures; the collective redemption of the land; the communal control over the division of households; the serious obstacles to the renunciation of an allotment; the general inseparability of membership and landholding — these are some of the familiar features met with here again. One especially burdensome requirement was not repeated, however, in the case of the State communes — the requirement that the peasant who wished to withdraw from membership during the redemption process must surrender his land, pay half the outstanding debt upon it, and await the agreement of the commune to assume the other half. A member withdrawing from a repartitional commune of State peasants was nevertheless required to divest himself of his allotment in the manner "determined by local custom" — and it would seem that under such a rule, the commune might impose conditions which would make it next to impossible to transfer the land, and therefore practically impossible to effect the personal separation. For a dissolution of the land-ties throughout the commune (through the substitution of hereditary tenure for repartitional, and the assembly of scattered strips into unitary farms) a two-thirds' vote of the assembly was required, and for the separation and consolidation of a single allotment, a similar vote was necessary. That is to say, the individual State peasant did not share the right of the former private serf to compel the commune to grant him a consolidated allotment with an hereditary title, if he first advanced his full share of the redemption-dues.[87]

The Cossacks stood apart from these general arrangements, but in view of the role which they had already played and would still play in peasant history, some account must be given of the settlement made for them. The major groups of the Cossacks were called armies, each of which was divided into a number of *stanitsas;* and each of these was in turn composed of a number of villages. Both the village and the *stanitsa* had their assemblies of heads of households. Down to the end of the 'sixties, the common land of the Cossacks was regarded as the possession of the whole army, although boundaries had been established in practice between the *stanitsas,* but a law of the reform period (1869) called for the allotment of about two-thirds of all the Cossack lands to the *stanitsas,* or to the separate villages. These lands were given in communal tenure, for periodic reapportionment among the householders who were themselves to have no alienable right in the allotments. The remainder of the Cossack land was kept for the common use of the army, or held in reserve for future allotment, or assigned in full property to the Cossack administrative and military officers. In return for their unusually generous endowment of land, the Cossacks were required to perform twenty years of military duty, in active service and in the reserve, and to provide their own horses and their own arms and ammunition.[88] By a combination of generosity and compulsion the government had disciplined the whirlwind; these fighters-on-horseback who were once the terror of the landlords had now become the scourge of a discontented peasantry.

If the government had need of such retainers, it was largely because of the conditions created or perpetuated by the Great Reform. It has been the attempt of this chapter to review these conditions under which the masses of the peasantry were mobilized, marshalled and equipped for their march into the new time — the former serfs with diminished lands and exorbitant obligations, the former State peasants with more generous allotments but with burdens heavier than before, and all alike with their historic forms of organization unbroken, but with severe restrictions upon the disposition of their persons and their property. The conditions were not altogether favorable to good morale, and some of the observers who looked on, in those not-very-distant decades, must have recalled that more than once before, this peasant army had been in mutiny — not a reassuring recollection.

CHAPTER VI

THE HUNGRY VILLAGE

DURING the decades that followed the Emancipation, the Russian peasantry carried on a desperate struggle with a desperate situation — a struggle for existence which reached a preliminary crisis, but certainly was not resolved, in the great *jacquerie* of 1905 and 1906.

The fecundity of the peasant families was prodigious — and it was said that every hand that held the sickle, must hold also the wooden spoon. That is, for every new worker in the field, there had to be also a new place at the table; but too often the place could not be found. Within less than four decades after the Great Reform (during the period between 1860 and 1897), the peasant population of the fifty *guberniias* of European Russia increased from fifty millions to seventy-nine millions — that is, there were more than half again as many wooden spoons to fill.[1]

The combined area of the allotment-lands of the proprietary serfs before the Emancipation and the State peasants before the reform of 1866, was apparently something more than 113,000,000 *desiatinas*.[2] As the result of "cut-offs" at the time of the Emancipation, the area declined to 111,629,000 *desiatinas* in 1877, but by 1905 it had increased again to 123,183,000 *desiatinas*.[3] Just as the former proprietary serfs had been most injured by the cut-offs, so they were least benefited by the increase after 1877, the additional allotment-lands going for the most part to the former State peasants.[4] For the period 1877–1905, and all the more for the whole stretch of time between the Emancipation and the Revolution of 1905–06, the increase in the allotment-lands did not by any means keep pace with the growth of the peasant population,[5] and the trend of the times was reflected in the shrinkage in the average size of the household allotments from 13.2 *desiatinas* in 1877 to 10.4 in 1905.[6] In other words, there was an increasing dearth of the peasant's chief source of subsistence.

But the peasants had not only somehow to feed themselves;

even at the cost of going hungry, they had to meet their public obligations. They had to make annual payments on the lands which in very many instances they were redeeming at an excessive price; and in addition, they taxed themselves for the common purposes of the village, and were taxed still further by the *zemstvos* and the State. There are no adequate early data for the amount of self-taxation in the village, and attention must therefore be limited to the assessments of the *zemstvos* and the State. In the period 1871–75, in the fifty *guberniias*, the average annual sum of these latter assessments upon the land and person of the peasant (including the redemption-dues, where redemption had begun) amounted to one *rubl* and forty-four *kopeikas* for each *desiatina* (2.7 acres) of allotment-land.[7] According to data collected by an Imperial commission of the early 'seventies, the annual levies on the lands of the private proprietors (chiefly the estates of the nobility) amounted to only fourteen and one-half *kopeikas* per *desiatina,* or one-tenth as much as the peasants were asked to pay.[8] The two sets of figures are not properly comparable, since the total for the peasants includes not only perpetually recurrent taxes, but redemption-payments which would some day cease. Still, when all due allowance is made for this circumstance as well as for the probable inaccuracy of the estimate of the levies on the non-allotment-lands, and for the fact that the allotments were more largely made up of plow-land than were the private holdings, it is still obvious that in proportion to their agricultural resources, the public obligations of the peasants were enormously in excess of those of the private proprietors. Indeed an official investigation showed that in many cases, even in the rich black-soil *guberniias,* it was entirely impossible for the peasant to meet his obligations if he had no income other than that derived from the cultivation of his allotment.[9] The outcome was inevitable: in spite of the attempts of the peasants to draw upon every sort of supplementary resource, their arrears increased; at the end of the period 1871–75, the sum of arrears in payments due to the State, amounted to twenty-two per cent of the average annual assessment for the period; during the next five years, the average annual assessment increased, but the sum total of the arrears increased still more rapidly, and amounted at the close of the year 1880 to twenty-seven per cent.[10] So critical was the situation that in 1881 and again in 1884 the government made a reduction in the total redemption-debt charged against the former proprietary serfs;[11] in 1886 the poll-tax on all peasants was abolished; [12] and under laws of 1896 and 1899 some of the redemption-payments were deferred, and portions of the debt were cancelled outright.[13] These steps were taken by sheer necessity; but in spite of the reduction of the sum of State and *zemstvo* dues from an anual average of one *rubl* and forty-four *kopeikas* per *desiatina* in 1871–75, to an annual average of one *rubl* and twelve *kopeikas* in the period 1896–1900, the accumulation of arrears in the payments assessed by the *State* (much heavier assessments than those of the *zemstvos*), amounting in 1875 to twenty-two per cent of the average annual assessment for the period 1871–75, had increased by the end of the century to *one hundred and nineteen per cent* of the average annual assessment for the period 1896–1900. In other words, the total accumulation of arrears (118,695,000 *rubls*) in payments due to the State had finally come to exceed by a substantial margin the average amount of the current assessments (99,341,000 per year in the period 1896–1900) which the State was attempting to collect.[14]

In 1903 the annual direct charges per *desiatina* upon the allotment-lands were still greatly in excess of those upon the private non-allotment-holdings; [15] but it was one thing to assess such sums, and quite another to collect them. By 1904, the arrears in the redemption-payments alone amounted to at least 130,000,000 *rubls*,[16] and it was during this year that the government initiated a new series of financial concessions partly inspired, in the beginning, by the widespread peasant disturbances of 1902, and soon driven to unexpected lengths by the great uprising of 1905.

In all that has been said here of the peasants' obligations, no mention has been made of indirect taxation. The national revenue from this source was increasing very rapidly, and in 1899 the treasury realized from it more than three and one-half times as much as from redemption-dues and direct taxes combined. The proceeds of indirect taxation were drawn chiefly from levies on such things as *vodka*, sugar, tobacco, kerosene, and matches, and from import-duties on tea, cotton, iron, and the like. In other words, the burden rested chiefly upon articles of general consumption, and was therefore borne in considerable part by the peasant mass.[17]

If during the decades which followed the Emancipation, the growing peasant population were to be fed, and the demands of the tax-gatherer satisfied — if the standard of living were to be maintained (to say nothing of its improvement), there had to come from somewhere a very substantial increase in peasant income.

Theoretically the peasant might have found this increment in a more intensive cultivation of his allotment-land, or in an extension of his farming operations to rented or purchased fields; or through a development of animal husbandry, or of household-craft production; or through wage-work, whether agricultural or industrial; or through definite removal to the city or to some area of colonization. It will be necessary to give brief attention here to each of these theoretical possibilities, and to the extent of its actual fulfilment.

In European Russia in 1877 the average allotment of a peasant household (*dvor*) was 13.2 *desiatinas* or about thirty-five and one-half acres; in Poltava, where the allotments were smaller than in any of the remaining forty-eight *guberniias,* the average stood at sixteen and one-half acres.[18] In France in 1884, the average size of *all* holdings, great and small, was less than nine acres — far below the average for *peasant allotments alone* in Russia; and three-quarters of all the holdings in France were less than five acres in area.[19] Whatever allowance may be made for the difference between the number of human beings dependent upon the Russian household-allotment, and upon the French holding, it appears that by West-European standards the Russian peasant was not badly off, in so far as the mere extent of his acres was concerned. If he could only have made his fields produce as did those of Western Europe, these pages would have had a very different history to recount; but whatever were the possibilities of the Russian soil and the Russian climate, the peasant did not and could not realize them to full advantage. Thorough fertilization, deep plowing, a complex diversification and rotation of crops, were for the most part beyond his power — even beyond his knowledge and desire. He lacked the stimulus of a large urban market, and his individual activities and movements were to a considerable extent controlled by his commune, with a uniform crop-rotation usually necessitated by the intermixture of his strips of land with those of his peasant neighbors. In the repartitional commune, there was always the possibility, too, that any strips of land which he fertilized and improved would later be assigned to someone else. And besides all this he was very often too poor to lay out anything on new equipment, or to take the risk of trying new methods and new crops.[20]

At any rate, the fact is that at the beginning of the twentieth century, the primitive routine of cropping the land year after year to the point of exhaustion, and then leaving it unseeded for ten years or more, was still extensively employed in the far north and in the newly developing regions of the southeastern *step;* nearly everywhere else, and especially in the central black-soil region, the somewhat less primitive three-field system continued to be the prevailing one; and although the peasants succeeded in reducing somewhat the proportion of land annually left fallow, it still amounted each year, in European Russia, to about one-third of all the plow-land of the allotments (37.07 per cent in 1881, and 32.21 per cent in 1903).[21] A greater improvement was made in the productivity of the acreage actually seeded; for example, the average annual yield of grains on the peasant allotment-lands of the fifty *guberniias* of European Russia increased from twenty-nine *puds* per *desiatina* in 1861–70 to thirty-nine *puds* in 1891–1900.[22] However, the peasant was still unable to get as much wheat out of an acre of land as did the neighboring landlord,[23] and both fell far behind the cultivators of Western Europe. Even the American farmer, with his casual methods, showed a yield per acre half again as great as the general average for European Russia.[24]

According to an official calculation, in every one of forty-seven *guberniias* studied at the beginning of the twentieth century the number of workers found in the villages exceeded the number required for the cultivation of the allotment-lands under the prevailing system of tillage. The excess was greatest in the central, west-central, and southern *guberniias,* and for all forty-seven *guberniias* together it was estimated to amount perhaps to almost four-fifths of the working-strength found in the villages.[25] On the other hand (according to the same estimate) in the northwestward two-thirds of European Russia, above a line drawn roughly through Podolsk, Poltava and Nizhnii Novgorod, the supply of grains and potatoes produced by the villagers on their allotment-lands was at this time inadequate to provide for their own subsistence and for the re-seeding of their fields; in the fifty *guberniias* as a whole the production of these foods on allotment-lands appeared to fall short of these requirements by about 11.5 per cent.[26] These estimates are of dubious value, partly because they involve in the one case a norm for the day's work, and in the other a subsistence norm, both naturally somewhat theoretical in character. Nevertheless the results may be taken to indicate that the peasants did not or could not make adequate use of their labor on the allotment-lands, or draw from these lands an adequate supply of food. With a third of their plow-land still turned wild each year to recuperate, and their fields still producing but a slender harvest, they had not found in intensive agriculture an exodus from their economic Egypt. Perhaps they could not conceivably have found it there; but inasmuch as they had failed, there was a tremendous pressure upon them to seek elsewhere for relief.

Instead of applying new methods to the old allotments, it was much more natural for them to attempt to extend the old methods to new fields; and just here centered their hopes of a literal and figurative Promised Land. The conduct of farming-operations, as most of the peasants understood them, required a certain balance between plowed fields, natural hay-lands, and pastures, and of the last two there was a special dearth.[27] Thus the peasants' allotments appeared to them to have both qualitative and quantitative shortcomings; and whatever might have happened *theoretically,* what most often happened *historically,* in the black-soil region, was that the peasants swarmed across the boundary-lines of the neighboring estates. With small reserves of capital, or none at all, it was far easier for them to rent than to buy, and in the black-soil *step* their rent-holds attained a prodigious figure. There are indications that in the 'eighties, more than one-third of the peasant households of the fifty *guberniias* were renting non-allotment-lands, exclusive of pasturage; [28] and according to an official estimate, the area of all the non-allotment rent-holds of the peasants at the beginning of the twentieth century was about nineteen and one-half million *desiatinas.*[29] The peasants were therefore renting about one *desiatina* for every six in their own allotted holdings.

The chief factor in the development of non-allotment renting by the peasants appears to have been their desire somehow to make good a relative shortage of land. It is true that the poorest peasants with the smallest allotments sometimes did not rent additional land for their own use, but (partly because of their lack of animals and implements) leased their own allotments to their neighbors, and then hired themselves out as wage-workers; and it is also true that the well-to-do peasant with a large allotment sometimes rented additional land in order to extend his operations beyond the scope of mere production for a livelihood. But in general, the less land the peasants owned in a given district, the greater was the number of peasant tenants and the more land they took in rent from non-peasant holders; and further than this, the peasant rent-holds were prevailingly small in size. According to the theory of "consumption-renting" advanced by certain writers, peasant leas-ing arose chiefly out of a shortage of allotment-land in proportion to the number of "*eaters*" in the household; but there has recently been put forward a modified theory of "production-renting," the proponent of which undertakes to show that there was a direct correlation between the extent of peasant leasing on the one hand, and the number of *workers* and the amount of capital goods per household on the other.[30]

The rent-term was usually so short as to give the maximum ef-fect to competitive bidding, and in the absence of all legal, con-tractual and customary guarantees to the tenant of a return for any improvements he might make, it was naturally to his imme-diate interest to take out of the soil everything that he could get out of it, during the short period for which it was at his disposal — that is, it was to his interest to practise an "economy of devasta-tion." [31]

Not only the soil was ravished under this system, but the culti-vator also. That the desire for food operated more effectively than the desire for profits to make renters out of the peasants, would seem to be indicated by the weight of the rents themselves. Upon the basis of an odd assortment of data, gathered up from scattered periods and districts, the peasant's average net income per year from a *desiatina* of his own allotment plow-land (due allowance being made in most of the data for wages for all the labor ex-pended) appears to have been something more than four *rubls,* whereas in 1901 the average money *rental* which the peasants paid for a *desiatina* of non-allotment plow-land was nearly five and one-half *rubls* per year under long-term contracts, and above nine *rubls* where the land was taken for one year only.[32] Serious as are the shortcomings of these statistics, they hardly fail to confirm the striking statement that in a great many instances after the pay-ment of the rent "there did not remain for the renter even so much as the customary wage for the labor he had expended in the culti-vation" of the rented plot.[33] "Consumption-renting" was hardly the term appropriate here; "hunger-renting" would have been a better name.

During the decades following the Emancipation, the peasant was a buyer as well as a renter of lands. In the 'sixties, peasant pur-chases averaged 91,500 *desiatinas* a year; during the 'nineties, nearly eight times as much.[34] In 1883 the Peasants' Land Bank was founded by the government to provide credit for land-purchasing operations,[35] and although the scope of the Bank's activities fluctuated considerably, there was a marked tendency toward expansion, and in the period 1887–1903 assistance was given in the purchase by peasants of more than five and a half million *desiatinas*.[36] Whether purchased through the Bank or without its help, some of the land acquired by the peasants was of course re-sold to non-peasant buyers, but sales of this kind by no means kept up with peasant purchases, and the total amount of non-allotment-land remaining in peasant hands increased from 6,552,000 *desiatinas* in 1877 to 23,642,000 *desiatinas* in 1905.[37] It is a strange and stirring experience to examine for the first time the statistical tables which deal with this subject of the agglomeration of landed property in the possession of the villagers. The returns are confessedly incomplete, but there can hardly be a question as to the tendency they indicate: the condensed tabulations undertake to show whether the non-allotment-lands in the possession of the villagers increased or decreased in area as a result of purchase and sale, in each of forty-five *guberniias* during each ten-year period from 1863 to 1902; this means four entries for each of the forty-five *guberniias* — one hundred and eighty entries in all, and among them there are one hundred and seventy-five instances of increase, and only five instances of decline; and the detailed tabulations for the years 1903 and 1904 also present an almost unbroken record of expansion all along the line.[38] In the vast sweep of this change, there is something not quite human — something that suggests the movements of inanimate nature; but there is something very human in the thought of so many millions of men in so many thousands of villages, sweating and straining at the same laborious task.

The urge of peasant buying naturally helped to advance the price of land. For lands purchased with the help of the Peasants' Bank, the average price was 36.5 per cent higher in 1896–1900 than in 1883–1885, while the average of the prices registered by the public notaries for land-sales of every kind during the decade 1888–1897 was 60.4 per cent above the average for the preceding decade, and exceeded by 122.5 per cent the average for 1868–1877.[39] The data from these two sources do not by any means coincide, and the notarial reports are known to be neither accurate nor complete;[40] nevertheless, taken in the large, the figures leave no doubt as to the heightening of the price-wall which stood between the peasant and the land which he might wish to purchase.

Just as was the case with the redemption of the allotments, so in the purchase of non-allotment-lands, many of the peasants fell behind in their payments. Where the transactions involved the Peasants' Land Bank, the percentage of arrears decreased somewhat with the expansion of the Bank's activities, but the absolute sum in default continued to increase.[41]

It has already been shown that the increase in allotment-land did not by any means keep pace with the growth of the village population; and it is easily demonstrated that non-allotment-holdings were not added in a sufficient quantity to restore the balance. If the peasant non-allotment-holdings had been distributed pro rata, the total amount of land per peasant would still have been much smaller in 1905 than it was on the eve of the Reforms of 1861 and 1866; and even in the later decades, between 1877 and 1905, the figure would probably have diminished.[42] The point is, however, a somewhat academic one, for — as will be shown hereafter — the distribution of the non-allotment-lands held by the peasants was anything but uniform.

During the early part of this period of rising land-values, the price of the principal product of these lands was in decline. In the period 1881–1885, grain prices were high, but during the next three five-year periods, they were fairly stable, at much lower levels (except that rye advanced during the famine-period of the early 'nineties, and then returned to its former price). In the period 1901–1905, grain prices were again at higher levels, though still well below the figure for the early 'eighties.[43] In Russia, where so many peasants were buyers rather than sellers of the rye which formed their principal food, the price of this cereal was of critical importance; and this was most particularly true in the case of the poorest peasants. It is therefore a fact of very special interest that during the decade which preceded the Revolution of 1905, the price of rye increased in every region of European Russia; [44] but the significance of this fact will become fully apparent only when it is hereafter brought into connection with the data on the wages of agricultural labor.

By increasing the money-obligations of the peasants, the Emancipation had put them under an increased pressure to raise and sell those cereals which were the one great product of agriculture as traditionally understood in the villages. However, the peasant was prompted to leave the closed circle of natural economy not only by external pressure, but by external attraction, and as time passed, more and more of his wants (for clothing and shoes, for example) were satisfied through purchase in the market. The growth of exchange and of a money-economy was of course facilitated by the building of railroads,[45] but neither this nor any subsequent development placed the peasants of European Russia in a position to compete on favorable terms, in the international grain-market, with the plowmen who were now turning up fresh soils overseas, and in Siberia. If the Russian peasant had grain to sell, he was obliged to enter a market in which the prices were fixed, in the last analysis, by international competition; if, on the other hand, he wished to buy manufactured goods, he had to purchase them in a market where the prices were maintained at high levels by the increasing protectionism of the government.[46]

If the peasants of European Russia had all been producers of a grain-surplus for the market, the decline in prices would have been a hardship upon them all; but actually many millions of them did not produce enough grain for their own subsistence, and therefore appeared in the market primarily as purchasers rather than as sellers of cereals.[47] In very many cases, however, the peasants had a more intimate and active relation with the grain-market than was required by the existence of a surplus or a shortage in their own individual production. They sold wheat, and bought rye for their own consumption; or, in the pinch of need for ready cash, they often sold grain in the glutted Autumn market, only to buy back the same kind of grain later on, at a much higher price, in order to feed themselves until the succeeding harvest [48] — a practice which aggravated the surfeit of Autumn and the shortage of Spring, and so affected the seasonal swing of prices that its sweep was wider in the rural districts than in the towns.[49]

Among the many symptoms of the peasants' economic weakness, one of the most serious was the increasing dearth of domestic animals. The Russian peasant knew little of the hand-cultivation of minute plots of land; he lived chiefly by the sowing and reaping of grain-crops, and without the help of animals, the human frame can hardly drag the load of such a culture. It is, then, no mere matter of detail that in proportion to the number of peasant households, the number of their work-horses diminished, until at the end of the century there was approximately one of these work-animals for each household. In other words, for each peasant house that had two horses, there was somewhere another household that had none.[50]

Whether by choice or by necessity, the peasants were often something more than farmers — sometimes not farmers at all, for millions of them were engaged, at home or in the cities, for a part or all of their time, in self-directed non-agricultural work of some sort, or in agricultural or industrial wage-labor.[51] Among all these activities, the handicrafts of the forest *guberniias* have held a very special interest for students of peasant life, for the reason that these craft-industries belonged in a peculiar sense to the peasantry themselves. The crafts were not free from external influence, and yet in their methods and their products they were still a rich repository of peasant science and peasant art. The workers produced an endless variety of work in wood, bark, cloth, leather, felt, clay and metal, varying in quality from the crudest articles of mass-consumption (wooden snow-shovels, brooms made of twigs, unglazed milk-pots, thick felt boots, heaped up by hundreds in the village markets), to silver ornaments and religious pictures which sometimes fully merited the name of works of art. Production was carried on sometimes quite independently in the peasant's home; sometimes at the order of an *entrepreneur* who distributed the raw materials to many home-workers, paid for the labor at a piece-rate, and collected and disposed of the product; sometimes, too, in a small shop set up co-operatively by an *artel* of workers, or maintained by a master who hired other craftsmen to work under his direction. The entire household, men, women, and children, often worked through the short Winter day and well into the night, for a beggarly return; but when the brief agricultural season did not yield a living for the peasant family, then to work for less than a subsistence through the long Winter months was better than to be altogether idle — and perhaps to be buried in the Spring. Strong traditions of the village, close legal restrictions upon the mobility of the peasant, favored an attempt on his part to find a source of side-earnings in the handicrafts rather than in some distant factory. The craft-industries might still live, even though they did not produce a living; they were generally supplementary to agriculture and, in effect, subsidized by agriculture, and it was this, above all, that enabled them to maintain a footing in a country where the Industrial Revolution was now well under way. Some of the craft-industries had not yet been subjected to factory-competition, some survived in spite of competition, some collapsed and disappeared. Exactly what was happening, will never be known, in terms of statistical accuracy; the number of persons engaged in handicraft-production, though perhaps diminishing toward the turn of the century, still very much exceeded the number employed in the factories; and yet the crafts could not be called prosperous, nor did they offer opportunities of increasing promise to a peasantry hard-pressed to find help in one direction or another.[52]

Wage-work in agriculture and other rural non-industrial occupations was also an important source of peasant income, and the census of 1897 enumerated in the fifty *guberniias* 1,837,000 persons who made this work their chief occupation, and were usually engaged in it throughout the year. It is in the very nature of the highly specialized grain-production of Russia, that for brief periods it demanded whole armies of extra plowmen and especially of harvesters, but of these short-term workers, the census took no account,[53] nor does there exist a dependable estimate of their number.[54] If there were more than a million and a half of long-term laborers, those hired for the harvest alone probably counted several millions more.

The level and trend of agricultural wages was therefore a matter of vital concern to millions of the peasantry. During the harvest, when wages were at the maximum, the male day-laborer received in the period 1901–1905 an average of fifty-eight *kopeikas* a day with subsistence, or seventy *kopeikas* without,[55] and from the fact that the difference allowed for rations is twelve *kopeikas*, or about six cents, one may gather something as to the standard of living at the time. In the 'nineties, the average wage paid to male workers hired for the entire year was sixty-one and one-half *rubls* with subsistence,[56] or only about one hundred and twenty times as much as was paid during this decade for a single day's work during the harvest season. The general low level of these wages is impressive enough, but still more striking, perhaps, is the difference between the maximal daily rate and the annual rate of pay. The fact that men would work for a year for one-hundred-and-twenty days' harvest wages, indicates the highly specialized and seasonal character of Russian agriculture and the sad situation of every villager who had to work for others when the demand was slight, as well as in the height of the season.

The data on the *movement* of wages show that in the period from 1882–1905, the agricultural day-wage first declined, in the time of declining grain-prices, and then began to rise again in the early 'nineties.[57] A more detailed examination of the data will make it evident that between 1895 and the earliest years of the new century there was an increase in the money-wage in each of the thirteen regions of European Russia. During this same period, the price of rye also increased in each of these regions, but in general at a slower rate, with the result that in ten of the thirteen regions the wage increased not only in terms of money, but also in terms of the worker's principal food. For the last years of this decade, there is, however, an entirely different story to tell: in 1901 or shortly thereafter, the money-wage turned downward nearly everywhere, and in 1904 it stood below its maximum for the decade in twelve of the thirteen regions, and even below the level of 1895 in two regions. During this period, the rye-wage also declined in twelve of the thirteen regions, and generally at a more precipitate rate than the money-wage. As a result, the earlier gains were outbalanced almost everywhere, and in eleven of the thirteen regions the rye-wage of 1904 was lower than that of 1895.[58] This one grain is by no means an adequate medium for the measurement of "real wages," but on the showing of these data one is perhaps justified in saying that for the poorer peasants who produced least for themselves, and were most dependent upon wage-work and the food which they bought with their wages, the period which immediately preceded the Revolution of 1905 was one of more than usual distress.

With agricultural wages not only at a low level, but varying widely from place to place, and with a more liberal reward offered in many branches of mining and manufacturing,[59] it was only natural that many of the peasants who were looking for work should try to find it, not on the next estate, but at the end of a much longer road. The question as to what force set this great economic pilgrimage in motion, is hardly one to be separately discussed; the answer is implicit in all that has been said about the conditions of life in the village. Nevertheless it may be appropriate to quote a summary of some thousands of answers given by the peasants themselves to this question, as it was put to them by official registrars in the Trans-Volgan *guberniia* of Samara, in 1899: Why had they come (many of them from other *guberniias*) seeking work? One cause was mentioned twelve thousand times — too little land at home; ten thousand times — there had been a bad harvest; nearly eight thousand — there was not enough work to be had in their own communities; seven thousand — they were loaded with debts and obligations-in-arrears.[60]

It is impossible to determine with any degree of accuracy the number of peasants who made periodic journeys away from their villages in search of wage-work in agriculture or in industry; but that they were counted in millions there is no doubt, and the rapid increase in the number of short-term passports issued each year indicates that "going-away work" was enlisting a growing army of laborers.[61]

It was the villagers of central and northern Russia, who were most given to these labor-excursions; and the most mobile of all were the peasants of the "central-industrial region," stretching from the northern limits of the *step* to beyond the upper Volga. In this region, the periodic movement from the village sometimes included practically the entire male population of working age, with many women besides, and was directed chiefly toward the cities, and most of all toward St. Petersburg and Moscow. The second great source of the labor exodus was the broad belt of agricultural *guberniias* lying south of, and parallel with, the forest-*step* boundary, and extending from Kiev on the southwest to the middle Volga on the east; but from this source, the main stream of labor flowed, not toward the industrial centers of the country, as was the case farther north, but outward toward the more sparsely-settled lands of the south and east, where farm-work might be had.[62]

Along the muddy roads and the swollen rivers of Spring, armies of agricultural workers hurried southward to be first at hand when men were wanted for the plowing; and later there followed other armies of reinforcements for the harvest. Often almost destitute, even at the beginning of the pilgrimage (of 910 workers questioned on their way to Crimea in 1891, 260 had five *rubls* or less); frequently travelling on foot, in carts, in row-boats, directly along the lines of railways and river-steamers on which they could not pay for passage; feeding themselves sometimes "with Christ's name" (that is, by begging); following the road for a few days only, or for a month or more — after all this, these pilgrims often wandered helplessly about without finding the sacred thing they came to look for; or if they found it, they were frequently obliged to work as much as sixteen hours a day, to sleep in the open, or in quarters no better than stables, and to feed on a veritable barnyard ration.[63]

Among the masses who swarmed into the industrial centers, the desperate competition for employment kept the average wage of the workers in the mills and factories down to something like eighteen *rubls* a month (the figure is for the year 1900). It appears that toward the end of the century, not only the industrial money-wage but the real wage also was rising; but the fact that it still stood very often at the level of sheer misery, is attested by various investigations of living-conditions among the workers.[64]

When the first general census of the population was taken, in 1897, more than five million "villagers" were found in the cities of European Russia.[65] As this census was taken in the winter season, this five million probably included most of the peasants who left the village periodically for industrial wage-work, but it certainly included also many who had broken all vital connection with village life and settled permanently in the towns.

In the period just following the Emancipation, most of the peasant-workers in industry lived and labored a part of the year in their own villages, and left their families behind them when they went away in search of work. However, with the increasing mechanization of industry, and the piling up of capital investments in machinery, the employers began to demand a more regular operation of their plants, and to impose penalties to check the migratory tendency of their employees. Partly by compulsion, and no doubt partly by their own desire, the peasant-workers' connection with the village was slowly weakened, as is evidenced by the decline in the proportion of short-term passports (for from one to three months) issued in the central-industrial *guberniias* in the 'seventies and the 'eighties;[66] and by the beginning of the new century, a majority of the peasant artisans had established themselves and their families in the neighborhood of the factories, and now lived there throughout the year.[67] But this certainly did not always signify that all connection with the village had been cut: as a rule these peasants continued to carry village passports, and among some 2600 craftsmen, factory-operatives and unskilled workers of St. Petersburg whose relations with the countryside were investigated in 1900, eighteen per cent returned to the village in the Summer season, fifty-two per cent sent money to the village, and *69.4 per cent were still holders of allotment-lands.*[68] If in the case of a certain *proportion* of the peasant-workers, the connection had become very much attenuated, it is to be remembered that on the other hand the *number* of peasants working in the cities had been greatly increased. The extent to which one of these factors balanced the other, it would be difficult if not impossible to determine; but even so, there is no doubt of the persistence of a lively intercourse between the log-built villages of the Russian forest, and the tenements and factories of Russia's largest cities.

That these tenements and factories were multiplying, is one of the most conspicuous facts in the history of the time. Between 1858 and 1897 the rural population of the Empire, exclusive of Finland, increased by about two-thirds, while the urban population, reflecting the growth of industry and commerce, approximately doubled. If at the end of the period Russia was still overwhelmingly an agricultural country, with only some thirteen people in a hundred living in the towns, still the Industrial Revolution was well under way, and the village was sending both volunteers and economic conscripts into the industrial armies.[69]

It was not only by going away temporarily for agricultural or industrial work, or by settling finally in the cities, that the peasants sought to better their lot, or to find an exit from their difficulties. In increasing numbers they turned also to the colonization of the farther *step* which lay toward and beyond the Asiatic border. From the Emancipation down to 1889, colonization was hampered not only by all the general checks upon the mobility of the village population, but by special official obstacles to this particular kind of movement. However, the weight of enforcing the burdensome regulations was too much for the bureaucracy to carry; in the 'seventies and the 'eighties, the colonists who emigrated without sanction were much more numerous than those who received the official permit, and the total number of emigrants to Siberia and Turkestan during the first quarter-century after the Emancipation was about 300,000. In 1889 the official policy took a turn in the direction of assisting those colonists whose removal had been approved, and in the 'nineties the building of railways in Siberia and the granting of State lands and the State loans to settlers helped to stimulate emigration.[70] During the years 1894–1903 new settlers moved into the Asiatic domain at an average rate of nearly 115,000 per year — about three times the annual average for the preceding decade;[71] but even for the years 1897–1900, inclusive, when the stream of colonization was running higher than in any other like period between the Emancipation and the Revolution of 1905, the natural increase of the rural population of the fifty *guberniias* was nearly fourteen times as great as the net loss which these *guber-*

niias incurred through emigration to Siberia.[72] Thus the colonization movement had done, and was doing, comparatively little to solve the agrarian problem in European Russia.

These, then, are the general outlines of the peasants' situation. Almost half a century had passed since 1861, and the air still buzzed with arguments designed to prove that the free peasant was — or was not — economically better off than he or his father had been in the days before the Great Reform. But when all was said and done, the means did not exist (nor do they now exist) for determining, year by year, during the decades which preceded and followed the Emancipation, the total "real" income of the peasantry; nor is it possible even now to measure cumulatively all the changes in their economic situation. There are no all-inclusive data; the best that can be done is to select certain measurable factors, which appear to focus and reflect the general condition:

Among a poor agricultural population, where a certain degree of economic equality exists, and where the number of persons competing for supplementary wage-work is directly affected by the economic condition of the families to which they belong, the level of the local day-wage in terms of rye (the laborer's chief food) may perhaps reflect in some degree not only the condition of the laborers themselves at the moment, but the general economic situation of the community. At any rate, one may recall here, for whatever it is worth, the fact that the rye-wage was considerably higher in the early 'nineties than it had been a decade earlier, but lower in 1904 than it had been in 1895.

Or better still, in the search for an economic index, one may reconsider the question of dues and taxes. The peasant's obligations to the public treasury were a contributory cause of his distress, but the statistics as to the *amount* of these obligations are worthless, by themselves, as an index of the peasant's situation, for the reason that their total sum and all their fluctuations might conceivably have been compensated by other economic factors. On the other hand, the data regarding the *arrears* in these public payments are altogether of a different order. What then is the significance of these arrears; is the default sometimes nothing more than an indication of unwillingness to pay? The answer may be found through even the most casual inquiry into the methods of collection. The seizure of property was not the only possible procedure when the payments were not met; the peasant and his family might be put to forced labor, and sometimes the whip was employed, even against an entire village, in the attempt to "beat out" the tax.[78] An army of collectors heaved and strained at the task, but not all the king's horses and all the king's men could make the tale complete; and the methods of collection being what they were, non-payment may be considered as usually indicative of a sheer inability to pay. The arrears therefore present perhaps the best of all indices of the peasants' economic situation, and their considerable total, their wide territorial distribution, and the fact of their continual accumulation would seem to indicate a widespread and increasing distress in the villages.

IN THIS discussion of peasant life after the Great Reform, the talk has been all of averages; but the question may be raised as to the legitimacy of procreating by statistical method an "average peasant," and writing for him a statistical biography. How many of the peasants really lived this average life, rather than something better, or something worse? And is it not important to draw distinctions, not only among the peasants, group by group, but among the several regions of the country?

The first observation to be made in answer, is that the total of peasant wealth is so small, and the number of peasants so great, that there is hardly room for any sizable number of very rich peasants, unless there stand opposite them an enormously larger number of paupers. The sum of the wealth of one day-laborer and one millionaire is very considerable; and this sum divided in half, produces for these two men an "average" wealth which is quite meaningless. If the sum were one thousand times smaller, and the number of possessors one thousand times as great, the "average" might perhaps have some significance. In the case of the Russian peasantry, the sum is comparatively limited, and the system of landholding set up by the Emancipation made it certain that for a long period a vast majority of the peasants would be possessed of at least something. With millions of small peasant farmers, and an average of hardly more than one peasant work-horse to the household, it is not in the nature of things to suppose, for example, that the ownership of peasant horses was highly concentrated. The employment of averages may therefore be more defensible than at first appears.

However, the question as to differentiation is a legitimate one, and some attempt must be made to deal with it here. That economic differences existed between peasant and peasant on the eve of the Revolution of 1905, there can be no doubt; but the question as to whether these differences were diminishing or increasing has long been a bitterly controversial one.[74] One important original factor of differentiation was the granting to the State peasants of allotments much larger, on the average, than those assigned to the private serfs. It has already been indicated, too, that the Statutes of 1861 left a wide latitude for variation in the size (per male person) of the allotments finally obtained by the communes and by their households, even where the recipients were immediate neighbors and the lands were of identical quality — and this was in some degree true also of the land-reform allotments of the State peasants. After the fixing of the reform allotments, there was a further opportunity for differentiation to appear spontaneously as the individual families and communities increased or diminished in numerical strength. Only a thoroughgoing system of periodic redistribution among neighboring peasant communes and among the households of each separate commune, could have preserved between man and man the proportionate relation set up by the reform; but as a matter of fact, there was no general provision for later readjustments between communes, and where the original grants were made in hereditary household tenure, there was also no provision for any subsequent reapportionment among these households. The only mechanism of readjustment in wide use was that within the *repartitional* communes. These communes included the greater part of the peasant population and of the allotment-area of the country, but even here, the reallotment of lands was sometimes unfairly conducted under the influence of the richer members of the community, or was perhaps omitted altogether for decades at a time at the option of the peasant assembly.

Such — speaking of the allotment-lands alone — were the original factors of differentiation, the spontaneous changes which promised a further variation from the original norms, and the limited means provided for the restoration of the balance. But besides all this, there were restricted opportunities for equalization or differentiation through the purchase and sale of allotments. The original regulations of 1861 governing such transfers have already been described, but in the case of the hereditary allotments, new legal difficulties arose at a later date. After 1882, there was no means available for the official registration of the transfer of those hereditary allotments which were still under redemption, and the purchasers therefore had no real security of title. Again, it was provided in 1893 that no hereditary allotment might thereafter be sold except to someone who was already a member of the seller's own commune, or became a member at the time of the purchase.[75]

In the case of the repartitional communes, the laws and court-decisions provided that in general a household allotment might be transferred only with the consent of the communal assembly, and that any allotment so transferred must nevertheless be pooled with the other lands of the commune in the next general repartition. As a matter of fact, the holders of repartitional lands sometimes made informal "sales" which were authorized, or simply tolerated, by the commune. In case there were no general repartition thereafter, such transfers were permanently effective, and even where a general repartition was carried out, the communal assembly sometimes honored the "sale" by the assignment to the purchaser, in addition to the usual allotment, of an amount of land proportioned to his purchase. Sometimes, too, the equalitarian land-system of the repartitional commune was deranged by the withdrawal of an allotment from a household which had failed to meet its dues and taxes, or by the division of an existing family without an assignment of land to the members who withdrew to set up a new household.[76]

Finally the peasant commune as a body might alienate allotment-lands through sales to outside purchasers, but only with the permission of the local or central administrative authorities.[77] In any attempt to explain how it was that at the beginning of the twentieth century some peasants had large allotments, some had small ones, and some had none at all, it is necessary to take all these conditions and possibilities into account.

In 1905, two per cent of the peasant households with allotments belonged to communes showing an average of less than one *desiatina* of allotment-land per household; 2.9 per cent of the households belonged to communes averaging between one and two *desiatinas* per household; and altogether nearly one-quarter (23.8 per cent) of the households were included in communes with an average of five *desiatinas* or less per household — and this in a country where intensive agriculture was as yet little developed. These 2,857,000 households (the 23.8 per cent) held altogether nine million *desiatinas* of land,[78] while at the other extreme there were 25,560 households — about one-fifth of one per cent of the total number — belonging to communes with an average of more than one hundred *desiatinas* per household and total holdings of nearly 3,600,000 *desiatinas*.[79] It must be understood that in these returns there is no comparison of household with household in the terms of their *individual* status, but only of commune with commune, upon the basis of the *average* amount of allotment-land per household in each — an average obtained by dividing the total allotment-area pertaining to each commune by the number of the allotment-holding households.

In many districts, however, the *zemstvos* recorded the area of the peasant allotments, household by household, and the tabulations of these returns also show a considerable variety in the size of the holdings. For example, among the 16,043 households in one of the *uezds* in the *guberniia* of Pskov, in 1897, 573 had no allotments, while 1,169 had more than fifteen *desiatinas*. Again, in one *uezd* in the *guberniia* of Ekaterinoslav, in 1898–99, the total of 33,269 households included 2,967 without allotments, 853 with less than one *desiatina*, and 2,156 with more than fifteen *desiatinas* each.[80] Whatever allowance may be made for differences in the quality of the land and in the size of the households, these data undoubtedly indicate a certain degree of economic inequality among the peasants.

All this relates to the allotment-lands and to them alone. Whether the purchasing of non-allotment-lands by the peasants was tending to strengthen the weak, or to make the strong still stronger — to separate the extremes, or to draw them nearer together, it is perhaps impossible to determine, because of the difficulties involved in the Russian land-statistics.[81] Nevertheless there are certain possibilities of a round-about approach to this question.

In 1905 the non-allotment-holdings of the peasants of the fifty *guberniias* totalled about 24,597,000 *desiatinas*, of which 13,214,-000 *desiatinas* were personal property while 11,383,000 *desiatinas* were held by peasant collectives.[82] The villagers who joined in making collective purchases from the Peasants' Land Bank, were usually the previous possessors of small or very moderate-sized holdings; and one may perhaps be justified in drawing from this fact the conclusion that *collective* purchasing in general — whether or not it was made through the Bank — was strengthening the position of some of the poorer peasants.[83] On the other hand, the distribution of the *individual* non-allotment-holdings of the peasants in 1905 was such as to leave no doubt that, although a large majority of the purchases as such had been in small amounts, the bulk of the *acreage* had gone to the larger buyers and had contributed to the strength of those already strong.[84] In 1905, there were less than half a million of these individual non-allotment-holdings, against more than twelve million household-allotments; in other words, only a small proportion of the peasants were concerned in any way with these holdings. Almost two-thirds of the properties in question were ten *desiatinas* or less in area, but altogether these small properties included less than one-tenth of the non-allotment-land owned individually by the peasants; the remaining third of the properties included nine-tenths of all the acreage.[85] To the class of holdings above 100 *desiatinas* in size belonged 4.4 per cent of the individual holdings of non-allotment-lands, with 56 per cent of the acreage of these lands.[86] Hence, whatever may be said of the collective holding of non-allotment-lands, the individual holding of such lands was much more highly concentrated than was that of the allotments, and served as the clearest of all indications of the existence of economic differences among the peasants.

Another such indication is to be found in the data for the distribution of work-horses. The proportion of households without horses was growing; in 1893–96, 38.7 per cent of the households had two or more horses each, 29.1 per cent had one horse, and 32.2 per cent had none. In the southwestern *guberniias*, oxen were much used and the dearth of horses has little meaning; but elsewhere the percentage of peasant establishments without horses runs from 4.2 in Kurland to 40.7 in the *guberniias* of Voronezh and Nizhnii Novgorod.[87] In this grain-growing country, the existence of millions of farms without work-animals is a fact that assaults the imagination with suggestions of every sort of hardship.

That the situation of the peasantry was especially serious in certain particular regions of European Russia, was demonstrated and emphasized by the Department of Direct Taxes in the materials prepared for the Imperial Commission set up after the turn of the century to inquire into the economic condition of the peasants. The conclusion reached by the Department was that conditions were "extremely unsatisfactory" throughout a broad belt of *guberniias* stretching along and below the forest-*step* boundary from southwest to northeast and expanding in middle Russia to include the whole Central Agricultural region.[88] But this does not mean that individual differences were absent in this area of special crisis;

in the Central Agricultural *guberniia* of Tambov, for example, nearly a third of the peasant households had no work-horses, while more than a third had two or more apiece.[89]

Serfdom was gone, but poverty remained: the mark of it was stamped upon the bodies of the people. The peasants formed the bulk of the population and of course furnished the bulk of the military conscripts, and among all the youths of all classes called for military duty in the years 1899–1901, more than one-fifth were found temporarily or permanently unfit for service.[90] Again, the death-rate was higher in the villages than in the cities, and in the first years of the twentieth century the annual rate for European Russia as a whole stood at 31.2 per thousand, against 19.6 in France and 16 in England.[91] Whole masses of the peasantry were dragging along so near to the margin of subsistence that a crop-failure meant starvation — and so came the great famine of 1891 and the lesser famines of earlier and later date. Whether the general well-being of the peasantry had shown improvement or decline — whether there had been within the peasant mass a tendency to draw together or to draw apart — still, as the day of revolt approached, there was no doubt of the existence in the countryside of a morass of penury sufficiently large, an antithesis between poverty and plenty sufficiently sharp, to give rise to whatever results might legitimately be bred and born of economic misery and economic contrast.

CHAPTER VII

THE PEASANT WORLD

POPULATION and production, taxation and redemption, colonization, industrialization, equalization, differentiation — the color
has all been twisted out of such words as these; and how impa-
tiently one turns from them, sometimes, to remember a certain
stretch of *step*-land within a limitless horizon, reclaimed and hu-
manized by intricate strips of peasant cultivation; a certain village
of plaster walls and thatch, with the smell of straw-fires drifting
from the chimneys; a certain wise old man with deep eyes and the
beard and dignity of a prophet, talking of crops and pastures, asking finally whether Americans really walk, feet-upwards, on the
underside of the world.

"Not to laugh at the actions of men, nor yet to deplore or de-
test them, but simply to understand them" — that is all that the
historian may strive for, and more than he can at best accomplish.
Lines laid down upon cross-section paper will perhaps contribute
to this understanding, and in so far as they may do so, they are
good; but there is so much of truth that cannot be caught within
this net ! Historical generalization is not simply what the word
implies; it is falsification too, since the truth about the actions of
men cannot be compressed, without undergoing in the process a
qualitative change. The statistics on the death-rate in the villages
— what empty things they are, unless one remember a certain village near Tambov, a certain house with broken windows and
rotted thatch, and the sound of wailing that went on all night.

One's task is to try to tell all the truth, but the thing cannot be
done. And somehow the method of generalization seems particularly inadequate when one attempts to deal with things so much
alive as the household and the commune. More and more, in the
post-Emancipation period, the peasants were going away for wage-
work, and the conditions which attracted or compelled them to do
this were operating on the one hand to dissolve the old structure

of rural life, and on the other hand to stabilize and preserve it. So many temporary absences from the household and the village had in the nature of things a disintegrating influence, but at the same time certain counteracting forces were at work. It was generally believed that the larger households were economically more stable, that they could more easily and profitably divide their forces between farming and wage-work. The earnings of the members, present or absent, belonged to the common fund, and the head of the household would naturally be reluctant to liberate a wage-worker whose earnings contributed to the support of the household.[1] The junior worker might not leave the district without a passport, and the authorities would not issue a passport against the protest of the house-father. If the house-father desired to compel the return of an absent member of the household, the police would deprive the absentee of his passport and send him home.[2]

The government was particularly concerned with the household as a tax-responsible organization, and as the arrears piled up, the official solicitude became more manifest. Under a law of 1886, applying only to repartitional communes, the division of a family and its allotment was made contingent upon the consent of the householder in all but exceptional cases; and now the approval of a two-thirds' vote of the peasant assembly — not of a simple majority, as before — was also to be required. In addition, an attempt was made to provide for the bureaucratic review of each proposal for the division of a family with a repartitional allotment.[3]

In spite of all this, the number of dissolutions actually effected was enormous. Very often the step was taken entirely without the consent of the administrative officials, and toward the end of the century there were frequent expressions of concern over the decline of patriarchal authority and the break-up of the old household system.[4] Actually, the division of old households and the establishment of new ones was apparently running ahead of the growth of the village population: in 1870, the average number of persons in a village household was 6.4; in 1900 it was 6. The latter figure includes only the approximate number of persons actually present in the village about the end of the year 1900; if allowance were made for the number of wage-workers temporarily absent, but still maintaining full membership in rural households, the figure for 1900 would approach much more closely to that for 1870.[5] The old system had not disappeared; the household-communes, large or small (sometimes with even as many as fifty

THE LANDLORD-PEASANT WORLD IN THE SEVENTEENTH CENTURY

Above, a log village with its plow-lands; *at the left,* a group of peasants; *at the right,* a nobleman giving alms, with a church in the background; *below,* a landlord's house, which is itself hardly more than an overgrown log cabin. The pictures record the impressions of foreign travellers of the time

IN THE DAYS OF SERFDOM

Above, the interior of a peasant house; the huge brick stove, the long-handled fork for removing cooking-pots from the fire, and the cradle swung from a limber pole are still a common sight in the Russian village. *Below,* a flogging is in progress — an accepted means of punishment before, and even after, the Emancipation. The upper picture was published in 1803, the lower one in 1768

LE SEIGNEUR S'AMUSE

The upper picture had the title, "A Landlord's Harem"; the drawing below presents a gay assembly of provincial gentry and officials in the costume of the eighteen-forties — the second decade before the Emancipation

EUROPE COMES TO OLD RUSSIA

In the eighteenth century, many of the landed nobility turned European, and some of the wealthiest built neo-classical palaces which occasionally included even a private theatre; at the top of the page is a manor-house which dates from the eighteenth century. On the more modest estates, even rough boards were eventually turned to the uses of this Europeanism, as is suggested by the photograph below. Yet near each manor-house was a peasant village, and there much of the life and tradition of Old Russia was still preserved (compare photographs opposite page 208)

ATTACK AND COUNTER-ATTACK IN THE REVOLUTION OF 1905

At the left, a force of peasant revolutionists on the march; *at the right*, the Cossacks in the act of disciplining a village. In these pictures, first published during the revolution, there is something of the bitterness and fury of the conflict itself

PEASANT DWELLINGS OF THE FOREST AND THE STEP

The upper pictures are from the forest *gubernïas* of O'onets and Arkhangelsk; those below show villages in the *step gubernïas* of Poltava and Tambov

HAND-WORK IN A MACHINE-AGE

Many of the peasants earned a substantial part of their living in the practice of the handicrafts, as pictured in the two photographs above. In farming, many continued in the
twentieth century to sow and reap after the manner of their fathers, but some of the peasants
as well as many of the landlords began to make use of agricultural machinery

members), with their joint allotments, their collective enterprises, and their common funds, still continued to form, in law and in practice, the foundation of peasant society.[6]

The solicitude of the government for the maintenance of the *status quo* is shown also in a new limitation placed upon the sale of hereditary allotments: under a law of 1893, such allotments might not be sold to any except peasant purchasers.

In this period the peasant commune, like the household, was subjected to new influences, and to new regulations designed to secure its stability. The alienation of allotment-land by the commune as a body, was restricted more closely than before by a law of 1893 which specified that transactions of this kind involving more than five hundred *rubls* might be effected only with the approval of certain ministers of the central government. The question of the withdrawal of household-allotments from repartitional tenure and communal control was also revived. Under the Statutes of 1861, any household among the former private serfs might convert its share of the repartitional land into a consolidated hereditary holding, even against the wish of the assembly, if this household first paid in full its share of the redemption-dues. This possibility of acting against the vote of the assembly had never been open to the former State peasants, and from the year 1893 it was closed to the former serfs. In the repartitional communes which owed redemption-payments to the State (whether these communes were composed of State peasants or of former serfs), the separation and consolidation of an allotment hereafter required in every case the consent of the peasant meeting.[7] Inasmuch as the acts of this assembly were subject, after 1889, to review by the *zemskii* chief, a local representative of the bureaucracy who was sure to be dominated by the official solicitude for the preservation of the commune, it is apparent that permission to withdraw land was not likely to be easily secured. The path of separation, strait and narrow in the beginning, had since become still more difficult. Down to the end of the year 1906, the total number of individual householders who had pre-paid their share of the redemption-dues and had in this way converted their repartitional allotments into hereditary holdings, was only about one hundred and fifty thousand; and because of the indifference of many of these holders, and the practical obstacles set up by many of the communes, these separations of tenure were very rarely accompanied by a physical consolidation, and the separated allotment therefore still consisted almost always of a number of strips scattered among those of the repartitional holders, though no longer subject to quantitative readjustment. Further than this, the new hereditary holder usually did not receive a separate section of the natural pasture or of any other lands which had previously been in undivided use, but continued to use such lands in common with his neighbors. In other words, the individual separations of tenure here described did not usually involve a thorough-going economic disentanglement of the holding from the other lands of the repartitional commune; nor was the number of individual separations effected through preredemption, or by other means, really consequential in so vast a population.[8] However, under the circumstances, it would be difficult if not impossible to say whether the principal check upon separation and consolidation was the preference of the peasants for the old land-system, or the difficulties which stood in the way of their escaping from it.

Besides the provision for the separation of the allotments of single households, there had also been a provision that, by a two-thirds' vote, any repartitional commune might make a general division of all its lands into hereditary allotments. But that comparatively little use was made of such opportunities as existed for retail or wholesale dissolution, is suggested by the land-returns for 1877 and 1905; in 1877, in forty-nine *guberniias* 74.8 per cent of the peasants-with-allotments were listed as repartitional holders,[9] while in 1905, in fifty *guberniias*, this system included 76.7 per cent of the allotment-holding households; [10] the remainder of the allotment-holders fell in both cases under the system of hereditary household tenure. It is known that these returns are not altogether accurate and that they do not fully reflect the changes which took place during the period in view, and yet these data are at least in harmony with other evidence which goes to show that between the Emancipation and the Revolution of 1905 there was no widespread dissolution of the repartitional tenure. In 1905, in the Baltic *guberniias*, there was no repartitional tenure; in the western and southwestern regions only about one-fourth of the peasants held land under this system, and in the *step guberniias* next to the eastward, about two-thirds. Everywhere else — that is, throughout the whole North, Center, East and Southeast — the repartitional system was almost completely in control and embraced in each of the seven census-regions into which this territory was divided, not less than 96.9 per cent of the peasant households.[11]

The major distinction between repartitional tenure and hereditary tenure was the possibility in the case of the former of a periodic redistribution of the communal lands among the constituent
households. Where such redistributions were not made, the distinction lost much of its practical significance.[12] If there had been
no official interference with the repartitions, their character and
frequency would have been the best index of the innate vigor or
obsolescence of the commune; and even in the presence of a certain amount of official manipulation, this same test is still perhaps
the most informing. In a commune where repartitional tenure existed, the majority required for the ordering of a repartition was
the same as that required for a final dissolution into separate household plots. That is to say, a two-thirds' vote might bury the system
once for all by a final dissolution, or might, on the other hand,
renew that function (of periodic repartition) which showed the
commune most vigorously alive.[13] The manner and frequency of
redistribution were at first wholly within the control of the commune, but in 1893 a new law prescribed that at least twelve years
(four crop-cycles, under the three-field system) must elapse between distributions.[14] Where reallotments had been more frequent, this provision acted as a check upon the local practice; but
another section of this same law appears to have had the opposite
effect (of stimulating redistribution) in communes where it was
rarely or never initiated by the peasants on their own account.
This section gave the *zemskii* chiefs a special power over the decisions of the village in this matter; [15] and it appears that these officials very often converted the law's twelve-year limitation into a
positive command, and insisted that the peasants make a new partition where twelve years had elapsed since the last re-deal.[16] Hence
the weight of official influence was on the side of maintaining not
only the system of common holding, but, with restrictions, the
practice of redistribution also — a fundamentally important practice which tended to check the development of economic inequality among the peasants. This preventative practice was certainly
not everywhere effective, however, and toward the end of the preceding chapter, in the paragraphs on economic differentiation
among the peasantry, something is said of the special conditions
under which inequality in allotment-holding might arise even
within a repartitional commune.

Described in the peasants' phrase, the redistribution took land
from the dead, and gave it to the living — took it, that is to say,

from those households which had diminished in size since the last partition, and assigned it to those which had increased. But the peasants' estimate of the size and land-worthiness of the household had no uniform foundation; it might be based upon the number of males of any age, or the number of workers of both sexes, or the total number of "eaters" in the household, or some combination of these or other factors; and in place of a complete reallotment of the strips in the several fields, there might be simply a slicing-away here, and an addition there, or only a partition of the holdings of a family that had become extinct, or the reallocation of only a few strips to produce a qualitative, but not a quantitative, equalization; or there might even be a minor shifting of *persons* from one household to another, to produce the same equalizing effect as a reallotment of the lands.[17]

The rich variety of these customs makes a summary treatment almost impossible. Unfortunately no complete statistical record was kept of the workings of the peasant repartitions, or even of the number of communes which reapportioned their lands, in one way or another, during the decades which followed the Great Reform.[18] There are indications that toward the early 'nineties, repartition was increasingly resorted to, at least among the former State peasants in both European Russia and Siberia,[19] but certainly the practice was by no means universal.

According to an unofficial estimate, the communes which did not practise redistribution, or had made only inconsequential readjustments since the Emancipation, included toward the beginning of the new century something like one-fifth of all those peasant households of European Russia which held their lands in repartitional tenure. A later official estimate would make it appear that more than one-third of such peasant households belonged to communes which made no fundamental redistribution between the granting of their reform allotments and the Revolution of 1905.[20] The accuracy of this last estimate has been called in question,[21] but if it even loosely approximates the truth, it would indicate a considerable degree of inertia in communal life.

But where there was no repartition, even where there existed the hereditary tenure which would not permit it, the roots of the peasant households were still interlocked. The evidence of this fact lay everywhere around the villages, in the very aspect of the fields. The system under which each household held its allotment-land in many (sometimes even a hundred) scattered strips, prevailed alike under both tenures, repartitional and hereditary, and in the case of the holdings originally granted in heredity (as well as those under repartitional tenure), little was done during this period to disentangle the land-relations by means of physical consolidation. North of the forest-*step* boundary, the strips held by the household were especially numerous, while farther south where the households were gathered in large villages around the widely-separated water-courses, some of the strips often lay at a distance of many miles from the home of their cultivators. In both repartitional and hereditary communes, it was inevitable that the households should follow a common routine in the seeding, harvesting, pasturing, and fallowing of the intermingled strips in each great field, and almost everywhere they also made common use of certain lands left undivided.[22] Whatever the form of their title to the land, it was rarely that the Russian peasants knew the independence and the loneliness of living in an isolated farmhouse and cultivating an isolated farm.

The commune's functions as a holder and distributor of lands were not confined to the allotments; often, too, it acted as a corporate renter or purchaser of the lands of private proprietors or of the State. When a repartitional commune acted as lessee, the rented land was usually distributed among the households in the same proportion as the allotment-lands already held — that is, in a way more or less proportional to the size of the households concerned. Collective renting by the commune as a whole was sometimes practised even where the allotments were held in hereditary tenure; or, in the presence of either form of tenure of the allotment-lands, a number of the householders might form a separate association for the leasing of non-allotment-lands, and apportion these lands among themselves on the basis of the number of shares which each participant had taken in the enterprise.[23] Incomplete as are the data on this subject, it appears fairly well established that the village-communes and the peasant associations, taken together, leased a larger acreage of non-allotment-land than was rented by peasants acting independently.[24] This development was undoubtedly favored by the preference of private landlords and public officials for letting land in large blocks, but this alone will hardly explain the strength of collective renting.

In the matter of the outright acquisition of non-allotment-lands, it is possible to define much more exactly the activities of the peasant collectives. That they had a large and increasing importance here, is clearly indicated by the following table of peasant holdings of non-allotment-lands in 1877 and in 1905:

Peasant Holders and their Holdings of Non-Allotment-Lands [25]

	1877	1905
Individual Holders .... }	5,788,000 des.	{ 12,671,000 des.
Associations .... }		{ 7,299,000 des.
Communes	765,000 des.	3,672,000 des.
Total	6,552,000 des.	23,642,000 des.

For every five-year period from 1863 to 1897, a decreasing percentage of peasant purchases were individual, and an increasing percentage collective,[26] and the weight of evidence in respect to the purchase and holding of non-allotment-lands thus lies clearly on the side of a strengthening of collective action among the peasants.

It is not to be forgotten that the commune had also its political-administrative side, and that a personal withdrawal from membership required not only the fulfilment of a number of general conditions, but in certain cases a transfer of the allotment-land. This original interlocking of membership with landholding has already been discussed in some detail in the chapter on the Emancipation, but two new developments require to be mentioned here. For one thing, new legal difficulties were placed in the way of the sale of hereditary allotments, by the change made in 1882 in the system of sales-registration and by the law of 1893 which prohibited the purchase of such allotments by non-peasants. On the other hand, with the general increase in land-rents and land-values, and the progressive reduction of the balance due on the redemption-debt, it became somewhat less difficult, economically, to transfer the allotment, or to complete a separate redemption and thus to secure the right to keep the land in case of a personal withdrawal from the commune. Otherwise the conditions governing individual transfers under each of the two forms of tenure remained substantially unchanged, and it is safe to say that the difficulty of getting rid of an overburdened allotment or of realizing the value of a profitable one, continued to be the chief legal obstacle to the personal separation of the landholders from the commune, and helped to make these separations comparatively rare.

Thus far it has been the chief object of this chapter to outline the changes which took place between the Emancipation and the

THE PEASANT WORLD

end of the century, in the laws which dealt with the internal relations of the household and of the commune, and to show how these institutions actually changed within this legal framework. The history of the commune was characterized during this period by a comparative stability of membership, by the rarity of dissolutions of repartitional tenure, by a still greater rarity of physical consolidations, perhaps by an extension of the practice of repartition, and certainly by an increasing activity in the renting and the purchase of non-allotment-lands. How much of its life the commune derived from official sources, and how much from the desire and urge of the peasantry themselves, it will perhaps be forever impossible to say. Like the question as to whether the commune was official or popular in its origin, this question as to whether it now drew its energy chiefly from above or from below, was at this very period, and has not yet ceased to be, a matter of bitterest controversy.[27] But whatever may have been the primitive and present sources of the commune's strength, it is beyond dispute that it still played a part of the greatest importance in the life of the peasantry. Whatever the cause, whatever the result, the commune *was;* for history, that is the outstanding fact.

But collective action was not confined to the communes and land-associations, as functional groups, or to such activities as the holding, renting, purchasing and distributing of the land. Collectivism, in one form or another, also appeared, though much less commonly, in the actual labor of production. In the early 'nineties, Sergei Witte, already powerful in official circles and at that time a partisan of the repartitional commune, said: "In *artels* or co-operative groups, the peasants plow the land, and sow, harvest and thresh the grain; . . . mow hay, cut down forests and brushwood; cut reeds, rent land . . . construct enclosures, common threshing floors, grain-kilns, grist-mills, drying-rooms, baths, barns, pasture-fences, bridges, dams, roads, ponds, and ditches. In *artels* they buy horses and machines, hire blacksmiths, and so forth. Finally, the commune works as a collective group in supplementary non-agricultural enterprises: in hunting, salt-distilling, stone-breaking, lime-extracting, fishing, and so on; and in communes and *artels* the peasants build breweries, break stone, construct barriers along the rivers, and set up shelters for use when they are hunting and fishing."[28]

This rather illy-arranged enumeration by no means exhausts the scope of the villagers' collective activities. The peasants who went away to look for agricultural work, usually hired themselves collectively, in labor *artels*,[29] and peasant colonists often combined in the sending of scouts to Siberia, and later in the emigration itself and in the establishment of new settlements.[30] In fact, history cannot go back to the beginnings of peasant collectivism, or measure even approximately the variety and extent of these activities.

The co-operative movement, formally organized and called by this specific name, had its beginnings in Russia in the early 'sixties,[31] and during the period between the Emancipation and the Revolution of 1905, its development was not especially impressive. At the end of this period, there were in existence about fourteen hundred savings and credit societies, devoted chiefly to peasant needs, and nearly one thousand consumers' groups (about two-fifths of them in the villages). In addition, there were more than eight hundred rural associations organized primarily to educate the population in improved methods of agriculture, but these associations often functioned in the purchase of implements and in the sale of farm-products for the peasants; and finally there existed co-operative creameries and other such productive undertakings, the number of which it is impossible to determine.[32] The traditions and customs of village life had prepared the peasants to fall in quite naturally with these new enterprises, but as yet the co-operative movement gave hardly a hint of the huge development which was soon to follow.

THE TRAVELLER of our own day who has journeyed across-country in Russian peasant wagons; watched the plowing, harvesting, and threshing; eaten from the common bowl, heard the peasant songs, and felt the rhythm of the peasant dances, can hardly help but think of the Russian village as a world apart; and yet times have changed, and already at the end of the nineteenth century many influences were at work to break the circle of the peasants' isolation. Certainly the village had not ceased to be the chief repository of the past: there was ample evidence that this was so, in the primitive land-system; in the organization of the household and the commune; in the peasant folk-lore, with its occasional traces of a paganism officially abandoned nearly a thousand years ago; [33] in the material arts, which still created many a fine thing in the old tradition — a rich embroidery, a carved stair-rail, a door- or window-frame of skilful brick-work in excellent proportions.[34]

Some of the peasants still stood apart from the upper classes of society in religion also: the old schismatics and sectarians persisted in their activities, and the new sect of *Shtundisty* spread the dangerous doctrine that all men are equal and that the lands and goods of this world should be divided equally among them.[35] In spite of the fact that a toleration-law was published in 1883, the government still persecuted many of the dissident communities, even sometimes taking the children from the parents and prohibiting the sectarians from meeting for any kind of religious service.[36]

Still arrayed against all these separatist tendencies, was that great cultural assimilator of races and classes, the Eastern Orthodox Church. Somewhere within almost every horizon its walls and towers were seen (sometimes in the *step,* when there is not one house or tree or any other thing to break the surface of the land, one sees the domes of half-a-dozen scattered churches, rising from the valleys near and far where their villages are hidden). The Church was carrying on, with steadily increasing reinforcement from the school. In 1897, the village population of European Russia, including those officially so classed but found in the cities at the moment of the census, numbered eighty million persons of all ages; of these, 11,431,000 males and 3,923,000 females were literate.[37] Thus the proportion of literates remained less than one-fifth; the channel of written communication was not very wide, but it was widening, and through this channel the flow of ideas moved almost exclusively in one direction — from the city to the village.

That it was the literate peasants who were doing most to develop the contact with the city, is proved (if it requires proof) by the fact that among those villagers who were found in the towns at the time of the census, the percentage of literacy, in the corresponding age- and sex-groups, is very much higher than among the villagers who were registered at their rural homes.[38] Just what may have been the effect upon the village of the peasants' labor-expeditions to the cities, it would be difficult to estimate. Very often the migratory laborer was a petty farmer in his own right at home, with a family who kept the farm-work going in his absence. Experience as a hired laborer, side by side with other peasants from distant villages, and with still other workers who were already completely urbanized, may have developed in him something of the proletarian spirit; but it is not to be forgotten that his earnings served very often to maintain, and no doubt sometimes to strengthen, his own position as a farmer. What was he, then — a farmer or a laborer? And what might one expect his economic and social attitudes to be?

The duality of this situation was less conspicuous in the Central Agricultural *guberniias*, from which the periodic labor-migration moved chiefly toward the grain-fields farther south. In all the *guberniias* below the forest boundary, there was much less contact with the cities than in the forest region, much less opportunity for the infiltration of new customs and new ideas. Specifically, there was less experience of the iron discipline of the machine and of the mass organization of the factory, less opportunity for the inoculation of the revolutionary theories which were finding their way underground along the city streets. If this discipline and this knowledge were the fundamental stuff of revolution, would the *jacquerie* then break out first and burn most hotly in the forest villages which sent their surplus labor to the towns?

But perhaps there would be no more great uprisings. After the outbreaks which followed the announcement of the terms of the Emancipation, there followed a time of comparative quiet in the villages: a police-report of the period tabulates three hundred and thirty-two peasant disturbances which occurred in the Empire during the years 1881–1888, and then remarks that apparently ". . . peasant disorders in Russia have at the present time reached a more or less stable norm, in respect both to their number and to their territorial distribution. There is no reason to fear a strong development of this elemental phenomenon of the people's life — at least not in the immediate future; but on the other hand, there is no ground for the hope that the number of peasant disorders will decrease of itself, unless there is a real change in the existing organization of peasant life. In the present extent of their development, the peasant disorders do not threaten the State with any special danger; but because of certain of their characteristics — their persistence, and their infectiousness — they should be given attention immediately and in good time." [39]

The peasant movement did not remain forever at this stable norm; in the first years of the twentieth century the *jacquerie* again flamed out across a wide horizon. It might be said that the Revolution of 1905 began in 1902, but it will be appropriate to postpone the account of the preliminary terror, and to ask now what had been happening, all this time, in the manor-house where the old *barin* was living out his span of years.

CHAPTER VIII

THE DECLINE OF THE NOBILITY AND THE RISE OF THE THIRD ESTATE

IN VIEW of the large degree of control which the landed nobility exercised over the Emancipation, and the heavy, sometimes ruinous, terms which were imposed, by them or in their behalf, upon the peasants, it might perhaps have been expected that the Great Reform would introduce a period of prosperity for the manor-lords of Russia. However, in the long run at least, such was certainly not the case. If the landlords were most often responsible for the initiation of redemption proceedings, it was partly because they were anxious to realize at an early date the over-charges to be exacted from the peasantry, and partly because they were urgently in need of funds to pay their debts and to set their farming operations going on a more thoroughly capitalistic basis.[1] The extinction of their debts to the treasury alone, took nearly half of the advances made by the government on redemption-account during the first ten years of this huge operation.[2] In the black-soil region, where the forced-labor system had prevailed and the peasants had usually employed their own horses and implements in the cultivation of the manorial fields,[3] the landlord's authority was so diminished during the period of "temporary obligation" that it was sometimes difficult to secure the performance of this work;[4] and once redemption was begun and the peasants were relieved of *corvée*, the southern landlords found themselves not only on a new footing in the matter of labor, but also without the inventory necessary for the cultivation of their lands. In the non-black-soil *guberniias*, where the landlords had drawn their income for the most part not from the direct manorial exploitation of the reluctant soil, or at second hand from its exploitation by dues-paying peasants, but rather from levies on the non-agricultural earnings of these peasants — here, when the government had advanced the sum of the redemption-payments, there was little to tempt the landlords to try to organize the cultivation of their estates in the terms of the new economy.[5]

Again, while the poorest of the peasantry — those who figured chiefly as purchasers, rather than sellers of grain — might perhaps feed themselves more easily, as grain-prices declined, the landlord was almost everywhere a seller of grain and a competitor in the national and international market with the producers of Western Europe, Siberia and the Americas. How far the Old-Russian landlords lagged behind the technical achievements of their West-European competitors, may be judged from the fact that on the private non-allotment-holdings of European Russia, over one-half of which belonged to the nobility, the average annual yield of Spring wheat in the years 1899–1903 was 8.9 bushels per acre, and of Winter wheat 15 bushels, while in 1898–1902 the general average yield on lands of all categories in Germany was 27.5 bushels, in the United Kingdom 35.4.[6]

An imponderable element, but one which nevertheless weighed heavily in the balance, was the fact that the personal traditions and habits of the nobility did not fit them for the new way of life. The Emancipation itself, the subsequent developments in agricultural technique, and the expansion of the market, demanded of them something more than the easy-going methods of the serf-owner; and often enough they lacked the desire or the ability to meet this new demand.

Between the conduct of a thoroughly capitalistic agriculture, on the one hand, and the outright sale of the estate, on the other, various compromises were attempted. Among these, the one that was most sharply reminiscent of the days of serfdom, was the renting of a part of the estate to the neighboring peasants, on condition that they cultivate another part, with their own horses and implements, for the benefit of the landlord. Another system was that of share-renting, where again the landlord furnished nothing but the land, and received in exchange a part of the crop; and finally there was the system of renting all or a part of the estate for a money payment.[7]

But far more significant than all this was the outright sale of land by the nobility. In Russian history there is hardly a more dramatic page than that page of marching tabulations which show the steady retreat of gentry ownership, in every *guberniia* and during every decade, from the Emancipation straight on into the new century. In the forty-seven *guberniias* where these records were kept, the net loss in ownership during the decade 1893–1902 was nearly half again as great as during the preceding decade.[8] In 1877, the personal possessions of the nobles totalled 73,077,000 *desiatinas;* in 1905, only 52,104,000 — a loss by the nobles, in these twenty-eight years alone, of nearly one-third of all their lands.[9] The average size of their holdings also diminished, from 538.2 *desiatinas* in 1887 to 488 in 1905; [10] and their total possession of work-horses from 546,000 in 1888–1891, to 499,000 in 1904–1906 — that is, by 8.5 per cent.[11] Some of the nobles became members of mixed associations formed for the purchasing and holding of lands, but these groups drew their support chiefly from the middle class, rather than the nobility. Economically, the nobles were losing their grip; both as owners and as cultivators of the soil they had gone into a precipitate decline.

It was not in the nature of things that when the social class which had been the chief foundation and support of the government showed such obvious symptoms of disintegration, there should be no official attempt at a shoring-up. The most important of the government's economic measures of relief, was the establishment in 1885 of the Nobles' Land Bank. It was to be the chief business of the Bank to "make more easily accessible to the hereditary nobility the means of preserving for their posterity the estates in their possession"; [12] and to this end, large sums were lent to the nobles with combined interest-and-amortization payments always lower than those charged upon the loans made to the peasantry by the official Peasants' Land Bank.[13] There was a rapid increase in the number of estates mortgaged to the Nobles' Bank,[14] and by 1904 more than one-third of the nobles' land was pledged to this institution alone, to say nothing of commitments to other lenders.[15] By the beginning of this same year, the operations of the Nobles' Bank had expanded until it had on loan about 707,000,000 *rubls,*[16] or nearly twice as large a sum as the Peasants' Bank had outstanding at the same date (380,000,000 *rubls*).[17] Of importance, also, as an indication of the economic condition of the nobility, was the fact that the arrears in their payments to the Nobles' Bank had increased, though they amounted at this time to a total of only 14,714,000 *rubls.*[18]

Although their economic power in the countryside was undoubtedly diminishing, the nobility naturally showed no general disposition to give up their political privileges and functions; in fact, the most important changes made in local government in the latter part of the nineteenth century tended in exactly the opposite direction. Under a law of 1889, provision was made for the appointment by the governors of *zemskii* chiefs, who were required to be chosen as a rule from among the local nobility. These officials were to exercise a general guardianship over the economic and moral condition of the peasantry, to review the acts of the peasant assemblies, and to recommend the repeal by higher authority of any of these acts which they considered to be out of harmony with the law or likely to work an injury to the interests of the commune. Further than this, the *zemskii* chiefs were empowered to judge and to discipline, without appeal, all the officials of the peasant self-government; and without any kind of judicial procedure they might condemn individual peasants to fines up to six *rubls* in amount, and to imprisonment for as much as three days.[19] Four years later (in 1893), the *zemskii* chiefs were given the specific right to interfere in the redistribution of communal lands,[20] and in fact their powers showed more than a little resemblance to those of the serf-owners of other days.

Further to guarantee the predominance of the nobility in local affairs, the representation of the peasants in the *zemstvo* assemblies of the *uezds* was greatly reduced in 1890, and from this time on, the peasants were not permitted to elect their representatives directly, but were to choose a number of candidates from whom the governor would select the persons who were to sit. At the same time the number of places assigned to representatives of the nobles was greatly increased, and the effect of the double change was to leave the local nobility in complete control of the *zemstvo* system, except where the bureaucracy might interfere.[21] The economic foundation of the nobles' power was not as solid as it once had been, but in the provincial towns the façade of their political control rose higher than ever, and on the pediment there appeared, as always, the golden double eagle of the Tsars.[22]

With millions of acres of land slipping away from the nobles into other hands, one naturally inquires to whom these acres fell. During the first years following the Emancipation, the townsmen were the heaviest buyers, and by 1877 their personal holdings amounted to 11,699,000 *desiatinas*, against 5,788,000 *desiatinas* of non-allotment-land held by the peasants personally or in associations.[23] Among these purchasers the lesser townsmen, or *meshchane,* were of no great importance, individually or collectively, as measured by the average size and the total extent of their properties.[24] On the other hand, the 12,621 individual proprietors of the group known officially as "merchants and honorary citizens," held among them nearly ten millions of *desiatinas* — almost one-seventh as much land as was owned by the nobility at the time; [25] and in 1887 the average size of their properties exceeded, by more than one-fifth, the average for the holdings of the nobles.[26] This bourgeois invasion was of such proportions, as even to suggest the possibility of an eventual displacement of the gentry by a new group of magnates of urban origin; but between the late 'eighties and the year 1905, a remarkable change took place. With the passage of time, merchant buying was taking on an increasingly speculative character, sales tended more and more to overtake purchases, and the annual net increase of the merchants' property was reduced, while at the same time that of peasant property was constantly augmented.[27] Between 1877 and 1905, the personal holdings of the merchants and the lesser members of the middle class expanded from 11,699,000 *desiatinas* to 16,241,000. If the calculation be extended to include the holdings of all the non-peasant and mixed collectives (that is, of all the collectives not composed exclusively of peasants), the total for 1877 is 13,416,000 *desiatinas*, and for 1905, 20,591,000. But during this same period, the sum of the personal and collective non-allotment-holdings of the peasants increased at a much more rapid rate, from 6,552,000 *desiatinas* in 1877 to 23,642,000 in 1905.[28] Thus the peasantry were gaining upon the townsmen in the competition to acquire private lands — chiefly the lands which were slipping from the control of the nobility; and among the townsmen themselves, the rate of progress was distinctly slower for the merchants than for the lesser commoners. Not only this, but the number of horses in the possession of both merchants and *meshchane* showed in the period 1888–1906 an absolute decline.[29] If this number may be taken as a rough index of the extent of their cultivation of the land, it would seem that an actual shrinkage had taken place. In sum, it appears that the townsmen were advancing with diminishing rapidity as owners, and were actually falling back as cultivators, of the soil. Between 1877 and 1905, they had acquired much less land than the gentry had lost, and were apparently making little headway in the extension of large-scale capitalistic methods of production to the domain of agriculture.

On the other hand, the ranks of the large holders had received some reinforcement from the peasantry. When conditions vary so widely from place to place, it is of course impossible to fix a definition of large proprietorship; if 200 *desiatinas* (540 acres) be taken somewhat arbitrarily to represent the base-line of "large proprietorship," beyond which the peasant owner and his family, instead of participating in the manual labor of cultivation, were likely to devote themselves to the management of the farm, or simply to the enjoyment of its profits under delegated management, or else to have recourse to renting [30] — then 9,698 peasant holdings of non-allotment-land, with 5,685,000 *desiatinas* among them, might be classified in 1905 as "large proprietorships." If one should arbitrarily lower the line for "large" peasant property to 100 *desiatinas,* then there would be in this class in 1905 21,365 non-allotment-holdings with a total of 7,342,000 *desiatinas* of land.[31] There is no means of determining definitely how this compares with peasant holdings in properties of this size at any earlier date, but simply for the sake of argument one may assume that all these "large" peasant properties were set up after 1877 — an assumption which departs widely from the fact. Nevertheless, proceeding upon this assumption (that these 7,342,000 *desiatinas* constitute a net addition to "large" proprietorship), one may combine this acreage with the net gain in the holdings of the townsmen and of the non-peasant and mixed collectives (7,175,000 *desiatinas* in the period 1877–1905). The total gain, actual and assumed, will then amount to 14,517,000 *desiatinas* — an estimate which certainly runs far beyond the fact. It is all the more striking, then, that this extreme figure of 14,517,000 *desiatinas,* does not by any means outbalance the known loss of 20,973,000 in the individual property of the nobles.[32]

All these data have to do with the non-allotment-lands alone. If it were possible to include the allotments in the computation, the number of peasant holdings above one hundred *desiatinas* in size would be materially increased, but unfortunately there was no country-wide classification of the allotments according to size.[33] Nevertheless, in what has just been said in regard to the non-allotment-properties of the peasants, the townsmen, and the nobles, there is at least an intimation that large holding was not on the increase in European Russia.

In all this, it has been assumed that the noble and bourgeois landowners formed a kind of bloc, while certain of the richer peasants had crossed over to join them. The average size of the holdings of the nobility was, in 1905, 488 *desiatinas;* of the merchant holdings, 559 *desiatinas;* of those of the lesser townsmen or *meshchane,* 42.8; of the Cossack households, 52.7; whereas the average for the non-allotment-holdings of the peasants was 26.0 *desiatinas,* and for their household allotments, 10.2.[34] If one were obliged to adhere to the official class-lines, one might perhaps be justified in grouping all the peasant holders on one side, and all the non-peasant proprietors on the other. However, if an exception is to be taken in behalf of the richer peasants, then exception must be taken also in behalf of certain members of the other classes. Thousands of the properties belonging to nobles and merchants were no more than ten *desiatinas* in extent, and the majority of the holdings of the *meshchane* fell below this line; [35] but here it must be remembered that the statistics deal not with *holders,* but with *holdings* — and at least among the nobles and the merchantry, the probability of the ownership of several non-allotment-properties by a single proprietor was much greater than among the peasants. Still, if there were the possibility of making a purely economic classification of all *holders* in accordance with the total extent of the *holdings* of each, some of the proprietors officially classed as nobles or merchants would certainly fall with the bulk of the peasantry, and some of the peasantry with the bulk of the merchants and of the aristocracy. The effect of all these *if's* and *and's* is somewhat to blur the demarcations of the statistical tables, without setting up anything so definite in their place. If this leaves the reader in a somewhat baffled state of being, it is because there were in the very situation certain elements of confusion and uncertainty. Who could say, at the beginning of the twentieth century, whether the agrarian question would be brought to the test of force ? And if this should really happen, would the socio-official alignments hold — or would they be cut through by economic interests, with some of the richer peasants fighting to preserve their property, and a sprinkling of impoverished nobles joining with the poorer peasantry in the *jacquerie* ?

By no means all the land of European Russia was in private hands; the Church and the State were still to be reckoned as great proprietors. Although the churches and monasteries of Russia had no such vast domain as had been theirs before the secularizations of the eighteenth century, still they held in 1877 some 2,129,000 *desiatinas* of land, and in 1905, a quarter again as much (2,579,000 *desiatinas*). Of these lands nearly three-fourths belonged in 1905 to the churches.[36] A Synodal investigation of 1890 showed that a small fraction of this domain was held by urban churches, and much the greater part by 27,652 Orthodox village churches [37] whose clergy plowed the fields themselves, or employed the gratuitous or paid labor of their parishioners, or rented the church lands to the neighboring peasants.[38] The monastic lands belonged in 1890 chiefly to 640 institutions of the Orthodox communion; 226 of these had modest holdings of 200 *desiatinas* or less apiece, but the six monasteries at the top of the list were proprietors on the grand scale, holding among them 182,000 *desiatinas* of land.[39] Sometimes the monastic lands were cultivated by inmates of the institutions; sometimes they were tilled by hired labor, or rented to the peasants who lived nearby. And thus it came about that some of the peasants stood in the same economic relationship with the village priest or the neighboring abbot, as with the local squire — the relationship of the employee with his employer, or that of the tenant with his landlord.

In 1905, many of the municipalities owned pastures, forests, and farm-lands, and these rural holdings, together with the lands upon which the cities themselves were built, amounted altogether to 2,030,000 *desiatinas*.[40]

The *udel* or appanage land was a scattered domain of 7,843,000 *desiatinas*, the income of which belonged to the Imperial family; this domain was chiefly under forest, but in 1904, 1,737,000 *desiatinas*, consisting largely of hay-fields and plow-lands, were under lease, nearly all to peasant renters.[41] Finally, there was a veritable empire of lands belonging directly to the State. The area of these lands had been somewhat reduced since 1877, by the granting of allotments to various categories of State peasants, and by other grants and sales, but in 1905 the State domain in the forty-nine *guberniias* still included 138,038,000 *desiatinas*, or more than the entire area of the peasant allotment-land. However, the State lands had by no means as great an economic importance as their vast extent would indicate, for the reason that more than eighty-five per cent of their area lay within five sparsely-settled forest *guberniias* of the extreme north and northeast,[42] while as a whole they included a much larger proportion of forest and waste than did the other major categories. Some 4,065,000 *desiatinas* of the State domain were in current use as plow-land, meadow and pasture, and of this area about eighty-seven per cent was rented to peasants, and the remainder to members of other classes.[43] Because the

Emancipation had very often left the peasants with no woodlands of their own, great numbers of them were dependent upon the State forests for their supply of fuel and of structural timber.[44] Thus the peasants had had ample opportunity to deal with both the State and the Church as landed proprietors, and it seemed at least possible that if the day should ever come for an attempt against the private landlords, the domains of Church and State would not escape attack.

It has been one of the objects of this study to show that if the *jacquerie* did flame out again, it would be no novelty in the annals of this peasant empire. The peasant did not always submit; but to put the major stress upon either submission or revolt is to over-emphasize the external relations of the village. In this account, the attempt has been rather to show how the peasants dug their living out of the ground, how they dealt with one another in the household and the commune, even to show what songs they sang and what strange gods they worshipped. If this history has reached out repeatedly beyond these limits, it is because a multitude of influences played upon and radiated from the village; but the intention has been to deal with these matters, not for themselves, but in the terms of village life. By exception there have been occasional excursions to the manor-house, but the major attempt has been to get *inside* the village, — and all this in the high hope of producing a history which would approach as near as may be to factual accuracy, and perhaps would also convey some sense of the reality of life in the log houses of the forests and the post-and-plaster houses of the *step*.

CHAPTER IX

THE REVOLUTION OF 1905: THE RISING TIDE

AT THE beginning of the twentieth century, four decades had passed since the Emancipation was proclaimed, and three times as many since the last great peasant rising, but there was still in Russia a widespread hope — and a widespread fear — that the agrarian history of the country had not yet settled to a quiet and ordered evolution. In the year 1902, these hopes and fears were much enlivened by certain events which took place in the Ukrainian *guberniias* of Kharkov and Poltava. During the five-year period ending with 1904, there were in European Russia some hundreds of instances of agrarian disturbance, including certain cases of the burning of buildings and even a number of fatal assaults upon the landlords or their deputies, but these disturbances were for the most part widely separated in both time and space.[1] By way of exception, the disorders of 1902 in the *guberniias* of Kharkov and Poltava were so highly concentrated that the movement might perhaps be called a miniature revolution. As a rule the bands of villagers here confined themselves to the seizing of grain with which to feed themselves and their animals.[2] Often they claimed to be acting in the name of a ruler who had replaced the Tsar and had authorized the distribution of the landlords' goods and of their estates as well.[3] More than one hundred and sixty villages were involved in this movement, some eighty estates were attacked within the space of a few days, and in the *guberniia* of Poltava alone, seventy-five landlords subsequently brought in claims for losses amounting to a quarter of a million *rubls*.[4] The police and the military were called in, floggings were generously distributed, and the movement was very soon brought to a halt.[5] In justification of the wholesale floggings and of other like measures of "preventative punishment," an official investigator said afterward that in order "to save the other parts of the *guberniia* from just such a critical attack by the peasants . . . the rising had to be put down; there was no one to separate the guilty from the innocent, and no time in which to do it." [6] However, some attempt was later made in this direction, for nearly a thousand persons were turned over to the courts, more than eight hundred were sentenced to confinement for various terms, and the total sum of the damage to the landlords was ordered assessed against the villages which had been involved in the disturbances. To insure against such-like troubles in the future, provision was made for the organization of rural guards to reinforce the police, and by the end of 1904 these guards had been organized in fifteen of the most restless *guberniias*.[7]

Some of the official commentators found the primary cause of this outbreak in the misery of the peasants,[8] while others offered evidence of propaganda, and declared that the whole affair was the work of revolutionary agitators.[9] That there were professional revolutionists in Russia who would have been glad to stir the peasants to revolt, there is of course no question; the matter in doubt is the vitality of the connection between these revolutionists and the peasantry. Four times in the seventeenth and eighteenth centuries the fires of the *jacquerie* had swept through great areas of the country, but no philosopher of revolution had set these fires going. In the eighteenth century, revolutionary ideas had begun to have some currency among educated people in Russia, but evidence is lacking that such people or such ideas had any important influence upon the great revolt of Pugachev. On the other hand, the Decembrist Revolt of 1825, nurtured in the libertarian philosophy of the French Revolution, was born and buried in urban isolation. In the 'sixties, the *narodniks* or "populists" began to celebrate the virtues of the peasantry, and more especially those of the repartitional land-commune; [10] but when some of the young idealists of the 'seventies attempted to "go to the people" (as revolutionary agitators, or for social service as doctors or nurses, or simply as manual workers), the peasants in many instances received these missionaries from the other orders of society with a marked suspicion, and in certain cases even betrayed them to the police.[11] After the arrest of many of the youth who had "gone to the people," the strength of the professional revolutionists was devoted in considerable part to a terrorist attack upon the government which culminated in the assassination of Alexander II and in an extremely rigorous repression by the police.[12]

Toward the end of the century there was a renewal of organized revolutionary activity, and in the period 1899–1901 several radical groups were drawn together to form the Party of Socialist Revolutionaries.[13] This party was the heir of the two strongest traditions of the revolutionary movement of the 'sixties and the 'seventies: peasantism, and terrorism. The leaders of the party did not place all their faith, or even a major part of it, in the propertyless workers who had nothing to lose but their chains; instead, these leaders thought that the proletariat could be united with the idealist intellectuals and the working peasants in a revolutionary "working class." In the belief of the Socialist Revolutionaries, the hope of the "socialization" of landholding (and eventually, of cultivation) rested not upon the landless laborers of the village, but most precisely and explicitly upon the peasants who *did* hold land — in repartitional communal tenure. This socialization would not have to wait upon the development of a capitalistic agriculture, with its accompanying dissolution of the commune and its division of the peasantry into a mass of proletarians on the one hand, and a small number of agricultural capitalists on the other; on the contrary, the commune should be preserved and developed: *preserved*, as an organ for the equalitarian sub-holding of land under the State (with an increased acreage placed at its disposal through a general abolition of private property in land), and *developed*, as an organ of equalitarian, collectivist cultivation. Alongside the agricultural communes should stand communal groups of industrial workers; and all these should be loosely federated in a democratic state. As a matter of tactics, the Socialist Revolutionaries sought to divert the revolutionary energy of the peasants "from its narrow economic channel to the chief center of . . . [the party's] activity at the moment — the struggle for political freedom." In their distrust of the centralized State, in their emphasis upon voluntary co-operation, in their employment of individual terrorist acts to defend and to promote the hoped-for movement of the mass, the Socialist Revolutionaries stood nearer to certain forms of anarchism than to the "scientific socialism" of Karl Marx.[14]

Between the romantic voluntarism of the Socialist Revolutionaries, and the iron-shod determinism of the Social Democrats, there was a difference so profound that not even their common harrying by the government could make these co-revolutionists into friends. In its logical extreme, it was the difference between the man who believes that he is acting freely, in the name of justice, and the man who thinks he is moving with the stars, under the compulsion of immutable law. What does it matter that neither of them was either completely bound, or altogether free; that the Socialist Revolutionaries were sometimes swept headlong by forces as impersonal as the tide; that the Social Democrats acted sometimes as adventurously as Don Quixote? Whoever was right, whoever wrong, the conflict in temper and belief remained — a conflict between two opposing views of the universe and of man's place in it. In thought and feeling there was never even an approximate reconciliation; in practical affairs, the doubtful periods of joint action were forgotten, ultimately, in an open war, with firing-squads to end the argument.

At a congress held in Minsk in 1898, several already-existing groups of Marxians joined their forces to form the Russian Social-Democratic Workers' Party, and in the manifesto adopted by the congress, it is declared that Social Democracy "consciously desires to be and to remain the class-movement of the organized mass of working men." [15] As the party was of course placed under the ban of the government, the sessions of its second congress were held abroad, in Brussels and London, in 1903, and here was adopted a detailed program which opens with a brief restatement of the Marxian theory of the inevitable march of history through a period of capitalism to the victory of the proletariat and the establishment of socialism. And yet, however much the party might emphasize the importance of class-solidarity and class-conflict, and however emphatically it might declare itself identified with the proletariat, most of its own early leaders were drawn from other levels of Russian society — as is clearly indicated by the fact that only a small minority of the fifty-five delegates at the congress of 1903 were themselves members of the working class. In the matter of tactics, the Social Democrats resembled the Socialist Revolutionaries in setting before themselves the immediate task of overthrowing the autocracy.[16]

The agrarian section of the program of 1903 was of course drawn ostensibly in the terms of Marxian theory. It called for the return to the peasants of the lands cut off from their allotments at the time of the Emancipation; for the return also of the redemption-payments already made, and for the abolition of further payments; and finally for the repeal of all laws restricting the peasants in the disposition of their lands (this repeal would involve, of course, the abolition of the laws which gave external support to the repartitional land-commune). It was stated that the agrarian demands were made "with the object of clearing away the remains of the servile order, . . . and in the interest of the free development of the class-struggle in the village." [17] A transfer of some of the lands of the large proprietors to the peasants, as here proposed, would have been a step in the direction of economic equalization: it would have reduced the holdings of the landlords; and at the same time that it increased the holdings of some of the stronger peasants, it would also have expanded the allotments of some of the smallest holders, and would have provided land for some of the peasants who had none. In other words, it would have diminished the numbers of the village proletariat, and would have strengthened the position of some of the smaller farmers who, according to Marxian theory, were about to be "proletarized." It therefore appears that such a redistribution of land would have tended to check and confine the Marxian "class-struggle" — at least for the time being. Indeed, the suggested redistribution might be supposed to contribute to the expansion of the proletariat and the "development of the class-struggle in the village," only if one believed that before the conditions of the Marxian conflict could be fully realized, the estates of the landlords would have to be divided among the peasants and then slowly *reconcentrated* in the hands of a new class of capitalist farmers of peasant origin. To promote the acquisition of land by the mass of the peasants in order to promote their eventual loss of this land and even of that which they had already had — this was the program; but suppose the peasants, having once acquired the land, should fail to divide themselves progressively into capitalists and proletarians, but should simply hold fast to what they had . . . ?

The whole agrarian problem was a surpassingly difficult one for the Social Democrats; small wonder some of them "feared the peasant-agrarian revolution"; small wonder the congress adopted a doubtful half-measure which called for the transfer of only a part of the landlords' acres to the peasants. It is a question how many of the delegates would have voted even for this proposal, if there had not been certain very practical reasons for making friendly advances to a peasantry whose attack upon the landlords might be of invaluable assistance at the time of a proletarian attack upon the government.

It was this same congress that saw the first important development of the factional conflict which was eventually to destroy the unity of the party. The question at issue was chiefly one of organization and discipline: the partisans of extreme centralization, headed by Nikolai Lenin, were able to muster a small majority, and the members of this faction thus came to be called Bolsheviks or "majority-men." The opposing group, led by L. Martov, received the name of Mensheviks or "minority-men," and this name continued to adhere, in spite of the fact that at the general party-congress held in Stockholm in 1906 the Mensheviks very much outnumbered the Bolsheviks. At the only congress held between 1906 and the Revolution of 1917 (the one which met in London in 1907), the Bolsheviks had a somewhat larger delegation than the Mensheviks.[18] From 1903 onward there was a strong antagonism between the factions,[19] and for the time being it was impossible for the party to act as a unit, even in the face of the revolutionary crisis of 1905.

Since the village economy of Russia still rested largely upon the non-capitalistic footing of communal holding and family cultivation, it seemed obvious that if the path of future agrarian history lay *through capitalism* to socialism, the goal must be somewhat more remote than it would be if socialism could be developed *directly* out of the existing land-commune. Again, there could be little point in telling the peasant of the commune to become a proletarian in order that he might become a revolutionist; he would not do this if he could help it, and the number of peasants who had already become landless laborers was distinctly limited. On the other hand, the great mass of communal holders afforded at least a numerous audience for anyone who wished to address them directly in the terms of an increase of the amount of land at their disposal, and a collectivist development of an institution with which they were already thoroughly familiar. No attempt is being made here to show whether socialism could best be established by the one method or by the other — or whether it could (or can) be established at all. The point is simply this: that in the terms of their own basic theory, the Socialist Revolutionaries had someone to talk to in the village, and could at least *believe* in the possibility of some practical result at a time not too far removed; while at the moment, the Social Democrats, equally confident of ultimate success, had (in the terms of *their* theory) a distinctly limited audience in the rural districts, and a somewhat remote prospect of the working out, in landholding and in agriculture, of the capitalistic development which they thought would inevitably increase that audience in the future.

It is not surprising, then, that in the years just preceding the Revolution of 1905, the Socialist Revolutionaries devoted a considerable share of their effort to the villages, and more especially to certain districts of the black-soil region where repartitional holding was the usual form of peasant tenure. The Social Democrats also carried on a certain amount of work in the rural districts, but the activities of both parties were confined very largely to a limited distribution of revolutionary leaflets and to other forms of agitation, and only the most primitive beginnings of party organization were made among the peasants. There was of course some infiltration of liberal and radical ideas by way of the rural *intelligentsiia* (teachers, doctors, and the like), and also by way of the industrial workers who returned to the villages (the police themselves promoted this latter contact by banishing many strikers and other "faithless" people from the cities to their native homes).[20] But even now, at the beginning of the twentieth century, the relations of the peasants with the outside world were still extremely limited; and among the channels through which external influences flowed down to the village, the most capacious were unquestionably the Church, the school, and the conscript army. In the number of peasants whom they affected, and in the systematic persistence of their teaching, these institutions immeasurably exceeded the capacities of the feeble revolutionary organizations of the day. If whole masses of the peasantry held out against the preponderant teaching of conservatism, and presently showed themselves once more to be anything but conservative, the basic reason is most probably to be found in the economic and political conditions of their life, and in their own direct response to these conditions. There is no mathematics for the measurement of such a situation; but in terms of common sense, no other cause seems adequate to so general a result, and there is at least the flavor of plausibility in the testimony on the question of propaganda given by one of the peasants brought before a magistrate after the disturbances of 1902: "No rumors came to me about any little books," he said. "I think that if we lived better, the little books would not be important, no matter what was written in them. What's terrible is not the little books, but this: that there isn't anything to eat." [21]

Somewhere across the fields from almost every hungry village lay the lands of some proprietor, calling to the peasant to come and sink in his plow. The landlord might be a prosperous peasant, or a stranger from some neighboring city, but more often it was the fine gentleman whose father had listened, from the white-columned portico of his mansion, to the petitions of his serfs; or it might be the abbot of some gold-domed monastery whose predecessors had been the lords of scores of villages, and had left him miles-on-end of fertile land; or perhaps it was some broad-bearded official who stood guard over the domains of the State. In any case the poorest peasant (who did not need to be told that he was hungry) hardly needed an agitator to tell him that if he could plow these neighboring lands, and keep the crop, there would be more loaves of black bread in his stove on baking-day, and perhaps leather boots in place of laced-bark slippers between him and the snow.

THAT the government, during the first years of the century, was somewhat doubtful and uneasy in its policy of agrarian conservatism, there can be no question. At its command, numerous local conferences were held, mountains of statistics were assembled, and some of the chief dignitaries of the land were called to take part in the proceedings of three important bodies appointed in the years 1902–03 to inquire into the agrarian situation: the Commission Constituted by Imperial Order, 16 November 1901, for the Investigation of the Question of the Change during the Years 1861–1900 in the Well-being of the Village Population of the Central Agricultural *Guberniias* as Compared with other Parts of European Russia; the Special Conference on the Needs of Rural Industry, Constituted by His Imperial Majesty, under the presidency of Sergei Witte; and the special Editing Commission of the Ministry of the Interior. The facts exhibited by these investigations were disquieting enough, but this did not make it easy to decide what should be done. The nature and effects of repartitional holding were debated at great length, and contradictory attempts were made to prove that the commune did (or did not) benefit the peasant economically, and that it did (or did not) nurture conservatism in the village. It was pointed out that the disorders of 1902 arose in districts where repartitional tenure prevailed; and among those who now discovered in the repartitional commune the threat of every sort of danger, was Witte himself, who said at one of the sessions of the Special Conference over which he presided: "Woe to the country that has not nurtured in its population a sense of law and of property, but on the contrary has established different forms of collective possession which have not been precisely defined in the law, but are regulated by uncertain custom or simply by individual judgment. In such a country, there may take place, sooner or later, such grievous events as have nowhere been known before." [22]

Ten years earlier, Witte had been one of the most active defenders of the land-commune; but it was not he alone who had recently experienced a change of heart. Under the pressure of peasant insolvency and unrest — and no doubt somewhat influenced, too, by the expansion of capitalism in industry — many officials were shifting about uncertainly, or had already settled on new ground. The first important departure from the established policy was made as early as 1899, when joint responsibility for taxes was abolished in communes where the land was held in hereditary tenure; and in 1903 the same change was made in respect to the taxes and the redemption-dues of the repartitional holders in most of the *guberniias*.[23] Thus there began in 1899 a change which was to reverse in less than a decade a policy of at least four centuries' standing — the old policy of recognizing and maintaining group-solidarity and joint-action as the basis of peasant society. But before the Revolution of 1905, the change was only well started. For all its examining of conscience, the government still hesitated uncertainly on the verge of a final repudiation of peasant collectivism; and at the same time, any decisive official action to reduce the obligations of the peasants and to increase their holdings seemed still remote. If changes came quickly during the next few years, it was because the government presently found itself entangled in an unsuccessful war and a temporarily successful revolution.

To take it for granted that at the beginning of the century the landed nobility were everywhere at one with the government, is to lose sight of the fact that the members of a favored class may be divided among themselves by lesser issues, until some crisis comes which threatens the overturn of the whole system whose privileges they enjoy. When, in the 'nineties, the government committed itself to a policy of extreme protectionism for industry, many of the landlords protested that the tariffs and the whole fiscal system were designed to burden the agriculturists inordinately for the benefit of the owners of mines and factories.[24] Upon the question of local self-government, there was also a sharp debate. By and large, the exercise of the functions of government was divided between two different sets of institutions: first, the central government, with its administrative apparatus extending all the way down into the smallest village; and second, the organs of local self-government, from the communal assembly at the bottom to the *zemstvo* assembly of each *guberniia* at the top.[25] Many of the great landlords served, in St. Petersburg or in the provinces, as functionaries of the central government; on the other hand, the lesser landed nobility were more active in the *zemstvos*, where the suffrage arrangements usually gave them complete control. Among the gentry of this second group, there flourished a "liberalism" which expressed itself in the extensive work of the *zemstvos* for the advancement of education and public health among the peasants, as well as in resistance to the intrusions of the bureaucracy within the sphere of *zemstvo* activities, and in attempts to secure the establishment of some form of local representation in the central government of the country. The term "liberal," as applied to the *zemstvo* gentry, included many varieties of opinion, but some notion as to the prevailing limitations of this liberalism may be gathered from the fact that when the *zemstvo* assemblies were asked to consider the question of a change in the franchise for the election of their own membership, these assemblies generally rejected the idea of giving the peasants as a class a voting-weight equal to that of the very much smaller class of private proprietors.[26]

With the professional people, and with the classes which derived their living from industry and trade, this history is not primarily concerned. However, inasmuch as the effect of the Revolution of 1905 upon the landlords and the peasants did not by any means depend upon the temper and activities of these two groups alone, a word must be said of the position of the other classes of Russian society on the eve of the revolution. Like the rural landlords, the well-to-do townsmen received political and economic favors from the government. The arrangements for the election of the municipal *dumas* or councils were weighted in their favor; "the industries of the fatherland" were lavishly supported by subsidies, loans, protective tariffs, State purchases at prices far above those prevailing abroad, and other like measures; [27] and the point-blank advance into Manchuria and Korea of course promised new sources of raw materials and new markets for the industrialists and the traders of Russia. In this situation, it is natural that no important element of opposition had developed among the manufacturers, although the standing of the government with this small but powerful group was undoubtedly threatened by the official experiments made during the first years of the century in the formation of labor unions under police control, and even in the encouragement of strikes — all this in the hope of diverting the labor movement from political to economic aims.

The industrial workers on their part had abundant reason, both economic and political, for a discontent which made itself manifest in a certain responsiveness to the propaganda of both the "police socialists" and the revolutionary parties, and in a scattering of strikes which reached a minor climax in 1903, and involved in that year slightly more than five per cent of the workers in the manufacturing industry.[28]

Among the professional people — doctors, teachers, statisticians, agronomists, and the like, many of whom were in the salaried employ of the *zemstvos* — liberal ideas of various shades had gained an active following, and there was even some support here for socialist doctrines. The *intelligentsiia* had already contributed something to the very limited strength of the Socialist-Revolutionary and Social-Democratic organizations, but as yet no liberal party had taken definite form.[29]

If the Russian Empire had been populated by a single nationality, the foregoing pages might possibly suffice as a sketch of the immediate background of the Revolution of 1905. However, the confusion was worse confounded by the fact that the Empire included not only many nationalities, but increasing numbers of *nationalists* — that is, of people who were conscious of belonging to a particular nationality, and were, to a greater or less extent, guided in their thought and action by this consciousness. In so far as nationalism was developed among the Great Russians, it gave support to the *status quo*. Among the border peoples, on the other hand, it could convert a foreordained conservative (say a Polish landlord) into a revolutionist — of sorts; and it could even make it impossible, for the time being, for the most thoroughly inter-national of revolutionists to merge their forces. Thus the Jewish *Bund* entered the Russian Social-Democratic Workers' Party in 1898 with the reservation of a partial autonomy, and withdrew from the party at the congress of 1903, when the Russians refused to place the union on a federal basis. To this same congress of 1903 came also the delegates of the Polish and Lithuanian Social-Democratic groups, with authority to negotiate a union,

but when the Russians declined to condemn the partition of Poland, the *pourparler* was broken off.[30] In proportion as nationalism had become effective, as it now had to some extent among
many of the subject peoples of the Empire, and more particularly
among the Poles, the Finns, the Esths, the Letts, the Lithuanians,
the Jews, and the Armenians,[31] it of course cut down through the
layers of society from top to bottom, and united the national seg-
ments of the various classes in "vertical combination." The net
political effect of all this is exceedingly difficult to estimate, inasmuch as the growth of nationalism in the borderlands was to some
extent paralleled and counterbalanced by the growth of a Great
Russian nationalism which was easily translated into a devotion to
autocracy as a political system, and a support of an openly imperial-
ist policy toward the border peoples. However, when it is a question, not simply of political change, but of a general economic and
social overturn, it seems probable that nationalism operated against
the success of such a revolution, not so much by dividing the revolutionary forces (for it tended to divide the counter-revolutionary
forces also), as by giving a strictly nationalist employment to energies which might have been devoted to the economic-social cause.
All that has been said here on the subject of nationalism must, of
course, be regarded as only tentative; but even these speculations
are not likely to warp the picture so much as would a complete
omission of the subject.

SUCH was the domestic situation in Russia, when this most Asiatic
of European powers finally blundered and blustered its way into
war with the most European of the Asiatics — the Japanese. The
enormous preponderance of Russia in population, in wealth, and
in the size and apparent strength of her armament, led to a general
belief at home that victory would come soon and easily. But on a
certain night in January 1904, the Japanese, without a formal declaration of war, steamed into the harbor of Port Arthur, and inflicted serious damage upon the Russian fleet, with only negligible
losses to themselves; and from that time onward, the Russian fortunes went lurching down through defeat after defeat to final
ruin. . .

However appalled one may be at the cruelty of war as such, one
may usually find some little exhilaration in a history of military
combat; even the most thorough-going pacifist will perhaps feel
sometimes, in spite of himself, the fascination of this transcendent

game. But this element of exhilaration is almost totally lacking in the history of the Russo-Japanese War — lacking at least for one who approaches it out of the background of the Russian past — and the chronicle of these blunders and defeats settles down upon the mind with the sodden weight of panic and death in a burning theatre or a sinking ship.

In Russia there was no wide popular concern in the series of adventures which brought on the war; but once the troops begin to move, victory-for-its-own-sake becomes a more or less appealing war aim. At any rate, the focus of interest in the *zemstvos* shifted from reform to the war, patriotic resolutions were voted in many of the *zemstvo* assemblies, and within a few weeks after the opening of hostilities, several millions of *zemstvo* money were voluntarily assigned for war purposes.[32] However, the hotter revolutionists would hear nothing of a truce, and at midsummer the most conspicuous of the captains of reaction, V. K. Pleve, the Minister of the Interior, was done to death by a bomb thrown beneath his carriage by a Socialist Revolutionary. If the government had felt moderately sure of its position, at home or abroad, this blow might have been followed by a dragonnade of repression (it had been so, when Alexander II was killed); but just now the temper of the country was doubtful, at best, and the situation in Manchuria was all too definitely adverse. The time appeared to call for a temporizing policy, and for once the government seemed disposed to temporize. A man of more moderate temper was appointed to the Ministry of the Interior, corporal punishment by the *volost* courts was abolished, a large accumulation of peasant arrears in taxes and redemption-dues and a part of the peasant debts for supply-loans were cancelled, and an *ukaz* of 12 December 1904 announced certain "preliminary plans for the improvement of the order of the State."[33]

Turning from the war to the question of reform, the *zemstvo* men had held in November a congress at which they asked for the equalization of the personal rights of the peasants with those of the other classes, for the granting of civil liberty to the whole people, and for the calling of an assembly of "representatives of the people"; yet this congress made no recommendation as to the character of the national franchise. The *zemstvo* moderates would have been unwilling to bring on a serious domestic crisis, even in time of peace; but the more thorough-going liberals and the out right revolutionists were ready for a collision, even in time of war. In the Autumn of this same year, the so-called Union of Liberation allied itself with the Socialist Revolutionaries and with national or national-socialist groups of Poles, Finns, Armenians, and Georgians, for the common object of overthrowing the autocracy and setting up a democratic government with self-determination for the subject nationalities.[34] The Social Democrats did not join in this alliance, but of their revolutionary disposition there could be no doubt. And still the mass of the people did not stir; there was no revolution.

Then within the space of less than three weeks, the government suffered a dire defeat at the hands of the Japanese, and won what may have been regarded as a victory over some of its own people in the streets of St. Petersburg. On the twentieth of December, Port Arthur, "the most nearly impregnable fortress in the world," deserving far better than Vladivostok the title of "Lord of the East," was surrendered to the enemy; [35] but when on the ninth of January, various columns of working men with their women and children marched through the streets and squares of St. Petersburg toward the Winter Palace, to present a petition to the Tsar, there was no surrender. The Emperor having already withdrawn to his Versailles (at Tsarskoe Selo), the soldiery now met the petitioners in his stead, and fired upon them with such effect that some hundreds were left dead in the snow.[36]

If some showman had set out to convince the people that their government was at one and the same time both weak and cruel, he could not have arranged matters more aptly than fate arranged them in that mid-Winter of 1904–05. What was needed to keep the people quiet, was perhaps more force and firmness in Manchuria, and less of it at home. At any rate, the gunning of the working men did not produce the desired result; for during the month of January 1905 more than four hundred thousand factory-workers went out on economic or political strikes — which means that approximately as many strikers were officially recorded in this one month as during the whole course of the ten preceding years. The following months brought wide fluctuations in the number of workers who went on strike, and it was not until Autumn that the record made in January was again attained, and then considerably surpassed.[37] An attempt was made by some of the leaders to direct all this elemental energy into the channels of trade-unionism, but thus far the unions (still outside the law) had gained only a very limited following.[38]

In such troubled times as these, no one who had read the history of the peasants could have counted on them to keep the peace. In the villages the young men had been lined up and herded away to fight the Japanese (whoever they might be); and now back to the village came the news that Ivan would plow no more (he was coming home with only one leg to walk on) — or that Misha would not come home at all, he having been blown up and buried somewhere at the end of the earth. The hardship laid upon the families by the mobilization, and the sacrifice of life and limb in the war itself, can hardly have failed to contribute to the peasants' discontent, and rumors of bungling and defeat may have stirred them, too. But just as soon as one begins to talk of the "causes" of the peasant movement of 1905–07, he falls into a sea of troubles. Of all the major problems connected with this movement, this problem as to its "causes" is the one whose solution is most likely to be obscured by the witnesses' lack of knowledge, and distorted by their personal interests and desires. In 1907, some seven hundred correspondents (many themselves peasants) undertook in reply to a *questionnaire* to discuss the peasant movement of 1905–06 in its agrarian, non-political aspects, as it manifested itself in hundreds of localities scattered throughout European Russia.[39] Among the "causes" of the agrarian movement, as given by these correspondents, there is one that is mentioned far more often than any other: the smallness of the peasant's holding, or his lack of some particular kind of land — meadow, pasture, forest; [40] and frequently it is stated that the peasants believed they had some sort of very special claim upon the lands of the estate to which they or their ancestors were formerly bound as serfs, and particularly upon the acreage cut off from the old serf-allotments at the time of the Emancipation.[41] However, it should be remembered in this connection that the estate of the former master was likely to be the one nearest to any given village of ex-serfs; and this circumstance alone would often be enough to turn the interest of the peasants toward this particular estate. Another "cause" of the movement, often mentioned by the correspondents, is the shortage of the harvest of 1905 or 1906 in the locality concerned; [42] as a matter of fact, the general returns show that the grain-crop for 1904 exceeded the average for the preceding five years, while the figure for 1905 is below this average, and that for 1906 is still worse. In both 1905 and 1906, the *guberniias* which showed the greatest shrinkage in yield, were for the most part in the black-soil region,[43] where the peasant disturbances were most serious, and these disturbances were, no doubt, in part a cause as well as an effect of the crop-shortage. Much less frequently than "little-landedness" or the harvest-failure, the correspondents mention high rents, restrictive leases,[44] and low wages; [45] but the direction taken by the move-ment itself indicates that these matters, and likewise the weight of the tax-burden, were important causes of discontent. All these items are of an economic nature; and both in the resolutions of the village assemblies and in the character of the outbreaks them-selves, there is convincing evidence that the peasants were stirred to active protest much less by their political burdens and disabili-ties than by the economic conditions of village life.[46]

Among these conditions, there is one which is neglected by the correspondents, but can hardly be omitted from consideration on this ground — and that is the *form*, as distinguished from the extent, of peasant land-tenure. The Socialist Revolutionaries re-garded the repartitional holder as already in some part a socialist; and, as will be shown hereafter, this same view of the commune as a school for socialism was adopted during the course of the revolution itself by many conservatives (who accordingly became active proponents of the dissolution of the communes). At any rate, it is probably not a matter of pure coincidence that among the twenty *guberniias* in which the landlords suffered the heaviest losses during the disturbances of the Autumn of 1905, sixteen show a predominance of repartitional tenure over hereditary holding by individual peasant households.[47]

But perhaps it is not in any particular economic or political condition, or in all of these conditions together, that one must seek the most effective stimulus to revolt. A stimulus of a very different order was to be found in the influences which reached the peasants from outside their own class or community. As a rule, the replies to the *questionnaire* just mentioned either omit entirely any reference to the revolutionary parties as such, or assign to them only a very minor role; yet on the other hand, many of the correspondents refer, with varying degrees of emphasis, to the active incitement of the peasants in a given locality by agita-tors from other places — presumably most often from the towns.[48] The soldiers who returned from Manchuria had a certain influ-ence in this direction,[49] while even the leadership and guidance of the agrarian movement in certain localities is credited by the correspondents to peasants who had gone away temporarily to work in the mines or factories and had since returned to their villages.[50] Still, who shall say whether these returned soldiers and workers were acting primarily as peasants, and from peasant motives, or were influenced chiefly by what they had learned in the army or in the cities? When the forty-nine *questionnaire*-replies which were received from one particular region are grouped according to the status of their writers, it turns out that upon the whole, the landlords, the large renters, and the stewards of estates, gave somewhat less importance to economic conditions than to such factors as agitation, class antagonism, rumors, laziness, and drunkenness, as causes of the agrarian disturbances, while the remaining correspondents as a group (peasants, teachers, clergy and the like) tend much more clearly and emphatically to the economic explanation.[51] But suppose for the moment that everyone *except* the peasants had attributed the movement to non-economic causes; after all, the peasants themselves were the voluntary actors in this movement, and who then should know better than they, what it was that had stirred them up?

In an official analysis prepared by the central Department of Police in November 1905 for the inspection of Prime Minister Witte, "revolutionary propaganda" and "the economic conditions of peasant life" are named as equally important causes of the agrarian movement. "Very often," said the Department of Police, "the peasants have too little allotment-land and are not able . . . to feed and clothe themselves, to heat their houses, to maintain their animals and their stock of implements, and to obtain seed for sowing, and [at the same time] to meet all the assessments of the State, the *zemstvo,* and the commune." [52]

At the end of January 1906, the Minister of the Interior, P. N. Durnovo, expressed a somewhat different view. In a report submitted to the Tsar, he said: "In view of the wide distribution of the peasant disorders, and the supposition now arising that their cause lies in the land-shortage of the peasants, I have made inquiry of the heads of those *guberniias* in which the disorders have been widespread, asking their conclusions on this subject [the cause of the disturbances]. . . All the governors assign a pre-eminent significance to revolutionary agitation, as the most immediate cause of the disorders. . . Eight governors . . . believe that the land-shortage of the peasants served as the basis for the development of the disorders, facilitating the penetration among the people of revolutionary socialistic teachings. . . Ten governors fail completely to see the cause of the disorders in a shortage of land." [53] This statement is quoted for what it may be worth — but was it not entirely natural that the officials should minimize the economic difficulties, and magnify the importance of the incitement of the peasants by non-peasant agitators?

It is perhaps unpardonably reckless to undertake an answer to this problem of causation; but even so, one may hardly refuse to raise the question. And in any rash attempt to balance the urge of economic hardship against the stimulus of external influence, there is at least one other fact to be remembered: the practice of going away temporarily to the towns for wage-work was much more widespread, and this particular kind of opportunity for mass-contact with urban ideas was therefore more general, in the villages north of the forest-*step* boundary than in those to the southward, whereas the economic situation of the peasants was in general more difficult in the *guberniias* lying in a broad band along and below this boundary; and — again with exceptions — it was not to the north of this boundary, but to the south of it, that the most serious agrarian disturbances of this revolutionary period took place.[54] Economic hardship created a need for change; peasant tradition, as well as revolutionary propaganda, suggested the remedy; official preoccupation and indecisiveness invited the storm; and soon the greatest agrarian disturbance since the days of Pugachev was under way.

And now, finally and parenthetically: If it be a matter of surprise that this particular problem of cause and effect is so obscured by varying and partly contradictory testimony, let the reader attempt for himself a small experiment in the historical method: let him try to work out, for some crisis of a few years ago in his own personal experience, the true relationship between cause and effect; let him explain just why he acted as he did, and not otherwise, in this personal crisis. The exercise will at least induce a salutary scepticism, and it may even lead the reader to dismiss altogether the attempts of historians to deal with the larger questions of causation.

But to resume the narrative: South of Moscow, in the depths of the black-soil region, lies the *guberniia* of Kursk, and here began the first important agrarian disturbances of the revolutionary period. On the night of 6 February 1905, there was a great stir in the village of Kholzovki, a great tramping and creaking along the road which led to the estate of a certain Popov, much chopping and crashing in his forests, and then a heavier creaking along the homeward road to the village. When the guards appeared, it was too late; the peasants had already cut a large quantity of timber, and now they offered "armed resistance to the police" — though with what result, the chronicle does not say. From Kholzovki the disturbances spread to the surrounding communes, as though according to a plan already agreed upon — or so says the Department of Police. Of an evening, the peasants of several neighboring villages would harness their horses to the wagons, and wait for the order to get under way. Then somewhere on the horizon a signal-fire would be lighted, and with a great outcry and a promiscuous discharge of firearms, the peasants would rattle off along the road to the estate selected for that evening's pillaging, where they would take whatever they could cart away, and then return home again. Detachments of soldiers were marched into the district, but the disorders spread to four other *uezds* or counties before they could be halted.[55]

During the Spring, there were disturbances in many *guberniias,* and in the four months from May to August, the movement manifested itself in one form or another in something like one-sixth of the *uezds* of European Russia, not including the Baltic provinces and the other borderlands.[56] For the eight months ending with August, illicit timber-cutting and pasturing, and rent- and labor-strikes were apparently the most widespread forms of the movement. Instances of the pillaging of estates were rather widely scattered, but seem to have been for the most part isolated and sporadic; and rarer still were the cases of the outright seizure of lands.[57] Because such a seizure aimed directly at a basic change in the relations of landlord and peasant, and because it involved an open defiance of authority, it was a conspicuously revolutionary act, and it is not surprising that the peasants usually hesitated to take so bold a step.

At midsummer a general strike of agricultural workers spread over perhaps a quarter of the area of the Baltic *guberniias,* where most of the landlords were German and most of the laborers Latvian or Esthonian. In part as a result of armed repression, this strike came to an end in a fortnight, but minor disturbances continued in this region.[58] In the Polish *guberniias* there were a number of strikes by agricultural laborers, and a few direct attacks upon the landlords' estates by the peasants; but some of the peasants joined with members of other classes, even with the landlords, in a movement in behalf of a more liberal administration and a free use of the Polish language — from which fact one may conclude that in Poland the nationalist sentiment served in some degree as a check upon the agrarian movement.[59] In Georgia, beyond the Caucasus, there were agricultural strikes, and even numerous seizures of land, but instances of the latter type might possibly have been still more common if the Georgian peasants (no doubt prompted in part by nationalistic feeling) had not attacked the question of local government with a deal more energy than the Russian peasants of the time were expending upon any matter of *politics*.[60]

In the Spring and Summer of 1905, the Social Democrats defined somewhat more clearly their attitude toward the peasant movement. At a conference held in Geneva in April and May, the Mensheviks recognized it as their obligation to support the peasants, even in their seizures of the land; but generally speaking, the faction did not accept this duty whole-heartedly, but still continued to debate among themselves the value and significance of the peasant movement. The establishment of a democratic government was the chief immediate objective of the Mensheviks, and to this end they resolved at Geneva to agitate and organize, especially among the proletariat, for the promotion of an armed uprising. If the *"bourgeois* revolution" were successful, with the help of this uprising, the Mensheviks expected to remain outside the government, with their economic program still waiting upon the future for its accomplishment.[61]

While the Mensheviks were in conference at Geneva, a party-congress under Bolshevik control was held in London. Here the Bolsheviks committed themselves more fully than the Mensheviks were doing to the preparation of an armed uprising, and in furtherance of the revolt against the autocracy they called upon the peasants and the village proletariat for "a collective refusal to pay taxes, or to furnish recruits, or to fulfil the orders and commands of the government and its agents." At the same time the Bolsheviks declared that under certain conditions (not defined), representatives of the Social-Democratic Party might participate in a provisional revolutionary government in order to promote the interests of the working class. Thus, the establishment of a liberal political order is again the chief immediate objective, but evidently this major position was not expected to appeal to the peasants in the mass. At any rate the congress adopted a special resolution in which it characterized the peasant movement as "elementary and lacking in political consciousness," but at the same time it directed all party organizations to make it known that "Social Democracy sets before itself the task of giving the most energetic support to all revolutionary measures of the peasants which are calculated to improve their condition, up to and including the confiscation of the lands of the landlords, the State, the Church, the monasteries, and the Imperial family." Just so: the strength of the peasant movement was now more clearly evident than before, and the Bolsheviks no longer talked simply of the return of the lands cut off at the Emancipation, but of supporting a general confiscation of land by the peasants. Actually the Bolsheviks accepted the peasant movement as an existing fact; they undertook to "support" (they did not claim to lead) the attempt of a part of the peasantry to improve their condition as small farmers, and in doing this the faction undoubtedly had an eye to the destructive, rather than the constructive, possibilities of a movement which would at least help to break the power of the landlords and, indirectly, that of the autocratic government. The peasant-farmer would be a serviceable ally in the early stages of the revolution, but the establishment of socialism would still depend upon the landless proletarian of the village and upon his brother in the town. "As the party of the proletariat," said this same resolution, "Social Democracy should in every case and under all conditions steadfastly aspire to organize the village proletariat independently, and to explain to them the irreconcilable opposition between their interests and those of the peasant *bourgeoisie*." [62]

In view of the declared proletarianism of the Social Democrats — both Menshevik and Bolshevik — and the prominence which they were giving to political issues, it was not to be expected that they would direct their major energies toward the village, or that the peasants in the mass would fall under their leadership. It is true that both the Menshevik and Bolshevik programs were designed in a minor part to appeal to the land-hungry peasants in their own terms, but the rural activities of both the Social-Democratic factions were confined for the most part to the western and southern *guberniias;* and it is not surprising that they attained their greatest success in the Baltic region where agriculture was organized so largely on a capitalistic basis and the mass of landless agricultural laborers furnished just the soil that the Social Democrats liked best to cultivate.[63] The peasant disturbances in

Georgia involved many seizures of land, as well as a deal of revolutionary political activity, and if the Mensheviks were able to play an important role in this movement,[64] it is perhaps due in part to the fact that a nationalist anti-Russian feeling promoted among the Georgian peasants a stronger interest in political affairs than was usually to be found in the villages of Russia.

The Socialist Revolutionaries were naturally very much occupied at this time with the peasant question, and in a manifesto dated March 1905, they said to the peasants: "Drive the landlords and the rich villagers (the *kulaks*) out of their warm, profitable places; beat, cut, choke the lackeys of the Tsarist government — beat them without mercy, just as they have no mercy on you, the defenseless ones." In June 1905, a conference was held for the discussion of the work of the party in the villages, and this conference prepared a proclamation which was subsequently given some distribution among the peasants. The time had come, the proclamation said, to make an end of the old order, economic, social, and political; ". . . the land . . . ought to belong to the whole people, and be employed equally, but only by those who themselves work upon it, and in such a quantity as each himself may cultivate." Eventually, according to the proclamation, there would be a general uprising, but in the meantime the people of each locality should work out the course of action most convenient to themselves: the agricultural workers should strike; the renters should demand better terms, and in case of a refusal by the landlord, the commune acting as a body should immediately carry off hay and grain. In effect, the proclamation said to the peasants: where you are short of pasture-land, act together, use the landlord's pasture for the satisfaction of your urgent needs; when you have not enough timber or firewood, go as a commune and cut what you must have in the landlord's forest; do not pay any more taxes, but collect funds among yourselves for your own needs; fix a tariff for the ministrations of the Church, and drive evil priests out of the village; boycott the courts, and settle your disputes for yourselves; replace any bad officers whom you have elected with good ones; throw out the police — give them their deserts; assemble and discuss how the State may be better organized; if soldiers are sent against you, try to come to an understanding with them and to take away their arms — and don't let the officers get the better of you.[65]

In its detailed recommendations as to immediate action, this program coincides to a certain extent with the course of the peasant movement as it was actually developing, but even this program seems to give more attention to political matters than the peasants themselves were giving, while the most extreme economic measures taken by the peasants — the pillaging and burning of manors, and the outright seizures of the land — are not mentioned in so many words, although the March manifesto does speak of driving out the landlords. The Socialist Revolutionaries said at this time that the peasants ought to do more or less the sort of thing that they were actually doing — but to infer from this that the members of the party were in a large measure responsible for the character and strength of the peasant movement, is to make an assumption which is not required by logic, and to attribute to the Socialist Revolutionaries a degree of influence which the party itself did not claim in its congress at the end of the year. Still, it may at least be said that the party was fundamentally interested in, and hopeful of, the peasant movement. In the Spring of 1905 the Socialist Revolutionaries were at work among the peasants in regions as far separated as the Eastern, the Central, and the Northwestern, and in August the party had already begun the publication of a propagandist journal called the *Peasant Gazette*.[66]

In the Spring of 1905 an official attempt was made to persuade some of the peasant communes of Moscow *guberniia* to make a formal declaration of their support of the war, and of their loyalty to the Emperor. In May, some of the villagers who opposed any such action assembled in Moscow and declared that the peasantry were "in a calamitous condition resulting from land-shortage, from unbearable requisitions and taxes, and from the illiteracy of the population and its lack of rights"; and this situation, they said, "cannot be corrected by the existing bureaucratic administration of the State." Having made this declaration, the conference announced a plan for the organization of an All-Russian Peasants' Union, with elective officers, and local divisions in each *guberniia, uezd* and *volost*.[67]

The Moscow conference was held secretly, but the resolutions with the plan for an all-Russian organization were published shortly thereafter in the *Messenger of Rural Economy* and elsewhere.[68] Local congresses of peasants were now held in various *uezds* and *guberniias*,[69] and on 31 July and 1 August the "Constitutional Assembly of the All-Russian Peasants' Union" met near Moscow. If one may judge by the broad-bearded faces that look out

from an old photograph of the delegation from the Don, the peasants who assembled for these proceedings were men of strength
and dignity. The sessions were held in secret, for fear of arrest;
and according to the somewhat confused testimony of two of the
participants, it seems that on the first day the meeting took place in
a *zemstvo* hospital, and on the second — most appropriately — in
a barn.[70]

If one might only accept this gathering as a microcosm of the
Russian peasant world in revolution, the task of history would be
more than a little simplified. However, there are, unfortunately,
several reasons why this cannot be done. In the first place, the
peasant delegates were drawn from only a part of the fifty *guberniias* of European Russia (the protocol says twenty-eight, and
names twenty-two), and the western regions seem to have been almost entirely unrepresented (only one of the seventeen western
guberniias is named in the published list). Again, the reports given
by the delegates themselves indicate that in most places the work
of organizing the peasants had hardly more than begun as yet; the
apparatus simply did not exist for securing at a national assembly
a true representation of the peasant populace. Finally, in addition
to the more than one hundred peasants who attended the congress,
there were representatives present from the Social-Democratic and
Socialist-Revolutionary party organizations as well as a number of
non-party intellectuals — about twenty-five altogether; and it is
quite possible that their influence modified the actions which
would otherwise have been taken by the assembly.[71] As though to
guard against too strong an influence from the non-peasants, it was
ruled that peasants alone were eligible for membership in the
Chief Committee — the executive body of the Union — while
only the peasant delegates were permitted to vote in the election
of the members of this body. The Bureau of Co-operation, previously organized by the intellectuals, was declared to be subject to
the authority of the Chief Committee, and the question as to
whether intellectuals and other non-peasants might be admitted to
membership in the Union was left for the time being to the dis-
cretion of the local groups, the point being made in debate that
whether or not the intellectuals were formally listed as members,
those who were favorably disposed might give assistance through
"bureaus of co-operation." [72]

For the better part of two days the members of the congress discussed, in such words as these, the problems of land and liberty:

"Land is not the product of human hands. It was created by the Holy Spirit, and therefore should not be bought and sold. No one really bought it [in the beginning] for money; somebody knew how to take it away from the peasants. . . Whether the land was taken away in the time of our ancestors by the Tsars, or by the princes, or by someone else, we do not know, and in any case we are not to blame. Therefore it is not necessary [if the land be reclaimed by the people] to pay compensation to anyone." "It is necessary to take the land and give it to the working peasants. Pay compensation! What for ?" "Comrades! Let us not make the mistake that our fathers made. In 1861 they [the masters] gave us a little, in order that the people should not take everything. The peasants were ignorant and unorganized then, but now things are different. With millions of voices we insistently declare the sacredness of our right to the land. If persuasion does not help, then, friends, plowmen, get up, awake, straighten your backs! For the moment we shall lay our plows aside, and take up the club." Such were some of the most fiery speeches on the land-question; but a more temperate council had also its proponents. For example, one delegate said: "Everywhere among the peasants there is this trend of thought: all private land should be taken with compensation, but the lands of the monasteries, the Imperial family, and so forth, without compensation."

In the matter of government, too, there were wide differences of opinion: "Our peasants say that it is necessary to attain real freedom by revolutionary means. Down with the autocracy! Long live the democratic republic!" — thus the delegate from the *guberniia* of Vladimir, receiving hearty applause. But the delegate from Kharkov *guberniia* said: "Elections by the people are necessary, but the people do not want a republic — they want to keep the Tsar." [73]

There were many who wished to save the monarchy, but not one defender of the private ownership of land, and out of all the confusion there came the resolutions of the congress: "Private property in land should be abolished. . . The land should be considered the common property of the whole people." The lands of the Church, the Sovereign, and the Imperial family should be taken without compensation; in the case of the private proprietors, the alienation should be "in part with compensation, in part without" (a sufficiently ambiguous statement), and the exact conditions of alienation should be defined by a national Constitutional Assembly. The necessity for such an assembly is "unanimously recognized"; in the election of its members, the suffrage should be secret, direct, equal, and universal (but the servants of the present government should not be permitted to vote, nor should the clergy unless their own organization is placed upon an elective basis). One of the institutions of the new constitutional government should be a national assembly or Duma, based upon the suffrage already described, and having large powers over legislation, finance, and administration. All the affairs of local government should be in the hands of officers elected on the basis of a universal suffrage for adults of both sexes, and a large measure of local autonomy should be permitted. In attempting to reach the economic and political objectives of the Union, the members might act openly, or secretly and conspiratively, as local conditions might demand; "in disseminating their views and in securing the satisfaction of their demands, all members of the Union should employ every means available, regardless of the opposition of the *zemskii* chiefs, the police, or the other authorities." [74]

This was not the most extreme program that had yet been launched in Russia, but under an autocratic government supported by a landholding nobility, its aims were certainly revolutionary. As to the means to be employed, the case is not so clear; both conspirative action and the orderly processes of a Constitutional Assembly are mentioned, apparently with the idea that any and all means should be used to bring about the calling of the Assembly, and that this body should then carry through the proposed agrarian and political reforms.

Having framed this program, the congress closed its sessions; and now by road, river, and rail, the one hundred peasant delegates returned to their villages, sometimes as far away as the Viatka forest or the *steps* of the Don, to report the incendiary declaration of the congress that private property in land should be abolished. To the villagers who heard the news and passed it on, this declaration must have meant essentially one thing: that the congress wanted them to have the use of the landlords' fields and of the State domain. How they were to get these lands — that was not so clear. But was it likely that a people with no experience in popular government on a national scale, and with a tradition of direct action against the landlords, would be persuaded by this program to seek for land-reform by way of political reform ? Or was it more likely that they would be stirred to greater activity in the old direct attack ?

For the liberals among the nobility and the *bourgeoisie,* it was easy to think last, or not at all, of any fundamental economic change. As the months passed by, these liberals were engaged in the organization of their forces. Many national unions of professional people were taking form, and in May, fourteen of these groups held a joint convention where they formed a Union of Unions and adopted a democratic political program. The *zemstvo* men held several general conventions of their own, and voted resolutions favoring a liberal, though not a thoroughly democratic, government. At their September congress they criticized the consultative Duma which the government had proposed to set up, but agreed nevertheless to work within it, rather than to boycott it; and with the agrarian disturbances beginning already to threaten the safety of their own estates, they proposed the cancellation of the balance of the peasants' redemption-debt, with the transfer to the peasants of a part of the lands of the State, and "in case of necessity," even of some of the lands of the private holders, with the payment of a "just" compensation.[75] Such was the flavor of the liberalism which had found a following among the middle class and even to a certain extent among the landed nobility. In any general reckoning of the forces of unrest, account must be taken, too, of those national movements along the borderland which have been mentioned previously.

A greater or smaller proportion of the members of every major social class in Russia — the peasants and the nobles, the urban workers and the *bourgeoisie* — were now involved in attempts to change in one way or another the established order of life; but to think of these people as forming one united army, or of "the revolution" itself as a unitary movement upon a single front and toward a single goal, is to misunderstand the situation so completely that certain subsequent developments must seem a miracle. Actually there was and could be no full agreement as to either the direction or the degree of the desired change; and in a concrete and positive sense, there was now in progress not *one* revolution, but a whole series of revolutions in parallel. What the landlords and the peasants did, and what was done to them, is the problem of this history, and it may be well to repeat that the other parallel movements are not here given an accounting in and for themselves, but are mentioned only when this must be done in the interest of the central problem.

The history of the revolution is inseparable, of course, from the history of the war. Before the Summer of 1905, the great game in the East had been played out to a finish, and lost. In seven months, the Russian Baltic fleet had steamed half-way around the world; and then in one ruinous battle most of its ships had fought their way to the bottom of the ocean. The war really came to an end on that mid-May day in the Eastern seas, but the treaty was not signed until August. Defeat might have been endured for a cause; victory might have made good the lack of any cause; but here there was no victory, and no convincing cause, but only dead ships and dead men. The war, while it lasted, had inspired patriotism on the one hand, and discontent on the other; but now that it was finished, the memory of it could nourish only disaffection.

Close upon the treaty, there followed, then, the most spectacular demonstration of the revolutionary period: the general strike of October 1905. Without any sort of pre-arrangement, the strike began early in October among the workers on one of the railway lines running out of Moscow, and spread rapidly among the industrial laborers throughout the country. According to the official registration, about two-sevenths of the workers in the manufacturing industry went on strike during the month of October.[76] But besides all this, most of the railways were brought to a standstill, the telegraphic service was suspended in many places, and even some of the retail shops were closed by the withdrawal of their sales-people. In St. Petersburg a central workers' committee was launched on 13 October, and the working men in all the trades and factories of the city were invited to send representatives.[77] This committee took the name of the Soviet or Council of Workers' Deputies, and similar organizations were soon to appear, or had already been established, in many other cities throughout the country.[78]

That all the hundreds of thousands of striking workers knew explicitly what they wanted, it is hardly possible to believe; and still less possible is it to believe that they all wanted one and the same thing. According to the official analysis, only about one-fifth of the factory workers who went on strike in October left work for economic reasons; for the remainder, the motive is stated to have been not economic but political.[79] This official verdict is confirmed by the actions of the Petersburg Soviet, for this influential body certainly declared political change to be the most important immediate objective of the revolution.[80] In its most obvious aspect, the great strike was a political strike; but in the presence of a movement so spontaneous, so little organized, who could say what degree of political change would satisfy the strikers, or whether any political change, however great, would satisfy them finally ?

At any rate, it was on the basis of its supposed political character and direction that the workers' strike received support from numbers of the *bourgeoisie:* many of the associations of professional men voted their sympathy; the Constitutional-Democratic or "Cadet" Party, then holding its first convention in Moscow, declared its "complete solidarity with the strike movement," and its readiness to support even the conquest of freedom by force, if this should be necessary; the industrialists of Moscow declared that the factory workers ought to be given a restricted suffrage; many civil servants stopped work entirely, and thus clogged the operation of the governmental machine.[81]

Such were the forces of reform and revolution, in town and country, when the urban movement was at its height. Even at this moment of climax, these forces did not, of course, include the entire population of the country; but one cannot fail to be impressed with the fact that the conservatives and the reactionaries, the groups who wanted neither reform nor revolution, were remarkably slow in making themselves heard. The dead weight of the old régime made it difficult to overturn, and the conservatives perhaps trusted too much in sheer inertia; and perhaps also those who were not themselves serving at the time in the bureaucracy, the police, or the army, were too willing to leave the defense of the old order to its official garrison. When the peasants or the workers presented their demands at the manor-house or the factory, the proprietor sometimes complied, sometimes resisted, but only after the strikes and the peasant disturbances had been going on for months and the urban revolutionary movement had already reached and passed its climax — only then did the unofficial forces of conservatism and reaction succeed in making a widespread show of strength.

As one looks back upon the history of the first nine months of 1905, it is clear that not only the government, but the economic system, was in danger. It might have been expected that then, if ever, the privileged members of Russian society would act to-

gether, with unity and decisiveness, in the common cause; and yet
nothing is more obvious than the fact that in the presence of this
crisis, they — even the nobility — were divided among themselves
by the question of political reform.

In this situation, the government hesitated and fumbled. It
tried repression — but there was not force enough to go round.
It made concessions — but until October, these concessions were
so tardy and so limited that they left the opposition stronger and
hungrier than before. In April 1905, the government wrote off a
part of the peasants' supply-debt, and the total of such debts for-
given in August 1904 and April 1905 amounted to about one hundred million *rubls*.[82] In February 1905 a national assembly had
been promised, and in July an appointive conference of dignitaries
was held, with the Tsar himself presiding, to discuss the laws for
the governance of this projected Duma. At the conference, there
was evidence of a paralyzing confusion within the official circle:
one of the Grand Dukes denounced several of the more liberal nobles by name and declared that the class had no sort of solidarity,
while a number of other speakers said that it was not the nobility
but the peasants who were politically dependable. An *ukaz* of 6 August provided for the establishment of the new Duma but gave it
only advisory functions and assigned nearly half of the electoral
votes to the peasants and the Cossacks, at the same time excluding
the urban proletariat and most of the *intelligentsiia* from the franchise.[83] Such was the law; but could the government expect that
this would satisfy even the less radical of the urban malcontents;
and in view of what was going on in the villages, did the government really believe that this political concession would make the
peasants forget that they had wanted land? Or did the Tsar and
his advisers simply not know what to expect, or what to do?

Actually the *ukaz* establishing the consultative Duma was swal-
lowed and soon all but forgotten, and the revolution still moved
on. The war was over now, but the loyalty of the army was in
doubt,[84] and in the face of the peasant barn-burnings and the general strike of October, there was nothing for officialdom to do but
to try once more the policy of retreat. And this time the government offered, in the manifestos of 17 October and 3 November,
the two great concessions of the revolution — the one of general
political import, the other an economic grant to the peasantry
alone.

The famous October Manifesto granted inviolability of person and liberty of conscience, speech, assembly, and association; in the field of "active citizenship," it promised that the franchise would be extended far beyond the limits fixed by the *ukaz* of 6 August; it declared that no law would be made without the consent of the Duma (the Tsar of course reserving an unqualified veto power); and it promised that the Duma would also have a share in supervising the administration of the laws.[85] Then, a fortnight later, came the manifesto of 3 November, announcing that the Peasants' Bank would shortly increase its activities in assisting the villagers to purchase land, and making the much more important declaration that, in the case of all except certain minor groups of peasants, the redemption-assessments for the year 1906 would be reduced by half while all such payments to fall due thereafter would be cancelled outright.[86]

Here, then, were concessions which might be called revolutionary — but would they end the revolution? . . . Actually there was not just one revolution to be heard from, but many different revolutions, and each would give its own answer.

CHAPTER X

THE REVOLUTION OF 1905: *THE EBB*

THROWN out from the palace of Peterhof into the vast confusion of the time, the October Manifesto eventuated in a division of forces and a definition of issues which soon gave a kind of order to this disordered period. Here at last was a constitution — but how would it be regarded by the people? Several different courses of action were conceivable: it was possible to disregard or to denounce the manifesto, and to push forward along the path of "direct action" toward political or economic objectives which were still remote; or an attempt might be made to employ the political means now offered, in order to bring about further reforms; or the manifesto might be accepted as marking the point from which the country should move neither forward nor back — a "conservative" attitude, in the strictest sense of the word; or, finally, the manifesto might be rejected as too extreme, and the attempt made to bring on a reaction — to undo all or some part of what the revolution had already done. In the period now to follow, each of these attitudes was to find its partisan support.

What, first of all, would the working men do? The immediate reply of the St. Petersburg Soviet to the manifesto was a declaration that the revolutionary proletariat would continue the struggle until, as a step toward socialism, a democratic republic had been established. Nevertheless, the Soviet voted on the nineteenth of October to discontinue, at least temporarily, the general political strike.[1] In Moscow the strike had already begun to break up,[2] and now there came a general relaxation of the movement. Early in November, the Petersburg Soviet called for another general political strike in the capital, but this did not lead to such a nationwide demonstration as that of October, and within a few days the attempt was abandoned in Petersburg itself.[3]

This does not mean, however, that the working men had everywhere been pacified by the October Manifesto; there is excellent

statistical evidence that this was not the case. The railroad workers had taken now to more peaceful paths, but according to the
official registration, the number of factory operatives who went on
strike was two-thirds as great in November as it had been during
the preceding month, and in December the number increased
again to about seven-eighths of the total for October. For the
year 1905 as a whole, the number of strikers registered in the manufacturing industry was one and two-thirds times as large as the
total labor-force registered in that industry; in other words, each
worker had gone on strike one and two-thirds times, on the
average.[4]

At the end of November and the beginning of December, the
activities of the Petersburg Soviet were brought to an end by the
arrest of its members.[5] In Moscow there was in December an
armed uprising which was put down only after several days of severe fighting, and might be called the intensive, if not the extensive, climax of the revolution on its urban side. In many other
cities also there were revolutionary outbreaks, but these were
quickly suppressed.[6] During the first six months of 1906, the strike
movement continued to show great vigor; the average number of
strikers registered per month was much lower than in 1905, and
yet the total of nearly 760,000 for the half-year was almost nine
times as great as the total for any entire year before the revolution.[7]
Evidently not all the working men had gotten what they wanted,
nor were they all willing to turn to peaceful political means of getting it. The strikes persisted; the revolution was still going on.

If after the publication of the manifesto the revolutionary movement still continued among the working class, though with diminished strength, the disturbances among the peasants not only continued but increased. The terms of the peasant movement being
what they were, it was not to be expected that any purely political
concession would bring this movement to a halt. Actually the news
of the October Manifesto had an opposite result; nor did the cancellation of the redemption-dues, on 3 November, prove an immediately effective soporific.

The latter concession was only three days old when the second
All-Russian Peasants' Congress, organized by the Peasants' Union,
was convened in Moscow. There was no attempt to keep the sessions secret, and in spite of the floods of fiery oratory at the meetings, there was no interference by the police. The delegates came
from twenty-seven *guberniias*, and the number of those from each

guberniia varied from one to forty-five. This time several of the western *guberniias* were represented, instead of only one as at the preceding congress. About half of the delegates had been chosen by village or *volost* assemblies of the peasants, and the remainder by local committees of the Peasants' Union, or by party-groups of peasants, or by the Bureaus of Co-operation organized by the *intelligentsiia*. Representatives of the official Social-Democratic and Socialist-Revolutionary party-organizations were admitted, but were given only advisory votes, and the president of the Peasants' Union reports that both these party-delegations withdrew before the close of the congress. The number of intellectuals among the delegates was certainly large, but, according to the protocol, they were less numerous than the peasants. It is very evident that the representation was scattering and haphazard in the last degree, and the best that can be said of the congress is, that it brought together from odd corners of the country some two hundred peasants and intellectuals interested in the agrarian problem, and that it did this at the most critical moment in the history of the revolution.[8]

The objectives of the peasant movement had occupied most of the speakers' time at the congress held three months before; the chief question now was one, not of ends, but of means. The delegates from the *guberniia* of Saratov were especially violent in their appeal to force: the Party of Socialist Revolutionaries, they said, invites the people to take the land and to arm themselves against anyone who tries to take it back; what is needed is a general strike and a national armed uprising; lacking this support, the powerful peasant movement in Saratov *guberniia* will be put down by force; "If we endure, they will beat us, and blood will be spilt. Blood is suffocating us now. If we revolt, blood will also be spilt, but out of it will rise the sun of freedom !" From some of the other *guberniias* came such words as these: "To arms, at once ! All means are lawful." "If you yourselves do not take the land by force, the Duma will not give it to you. No peaceful means will give you the land." [9]

Many of the speeches and all of the resolutions adopted were of a far more moderate tone than this, but certainly the congress did not accept the concessions already made as the last accomplishment of the revolution, nor was there any tendency to limit the peasants to the use of the peaceful political means which had now been made available. Rejecting the most important clauses of the October Manifesto, the congress repeated the demand for a Constitutional Assembly, and voted "to consider as enemies of the people

all those who shall take part in the elections of the State Duma."
Pending the reform of local government by the Constituent Assembly, the congress urged the villagers to replace all their own
peasant officials who are favorably disposed toward the higher authorities; and besides this, the peasants should boycott all such
authorities, including the police, and should refuse to give them
any information on any subject whatever, and certainly none in regard to the activities of "the comrades who are struggling for the
land and for the rights and liberties of the people."

To the demand for the nationalization of the land, there was
now added a provision that the use of the land should be granted
only to those who themselves would till it, without the help of
hired labor. In the speeches and resolutions of this congress and of
the preceding one, there is no evidence that the peasant delegates
expected the State to be anything more than an impartial distributor and periodic equalizer of the land. They apparently looked
forward to something like a repartitional commune on a national
scale, and it does not appear that they expected to pay a differential
rent to the State for the use of the nationalized land, any more than
they now paid rent to their own communes. The final settlement
of the agrarian question should be left, the congress said, to the
Constitutional Assembly, but in order to bring about a favorable
decision, the Peasants' Union should immediately come to an understanding with the industrial workers, and the peasants themselves should make no more leases or purchases of land from the
private proprietors. If other means failed to bring about the desired nationalization, it was proposed that the Peasants' Union
organize a general agricultural strike; and finally came the declaration that "failure to satisfy the demands of the people . . .
will inevitably call forth a general popular uprising."

It was perfectly obvious (the reports of the delegates made it so),
that in respect to the means which this program suggested for dealing with the land question, it fell very far behind what was actually happening in many quarters of the country. The peasants who
were already smoking out the landlords — what had the congress
to say to them ? After a stormy and uproarious debate, the assembly
passed a resolution demanding the immediate abandonment of all
military and other exceptional measures for the suppression of the
peasant disturbances, and calling likewise for the release of all
persons held by the authorities as participants. "The congress sends
a brotherly greeting" — so says the resolution, "to those peasants

who are the first to fight in the great cause of the liberation of the people." [10]

Four days after the close of the congress, the members of the central Bureau of Co-operation, and several of the Chief Committee, were placed under arrest.[11] This, however, did not prevent the Committee from joining with the Petersburg Soviet (just before the destruction of the latter by arrests), and with the central committees of the Social-Democratic, Socialist-Revolutionary, and Polish Socialist parties in issuing the famous manifesto of 2 December, calling upon the people to refuse to pay taxes or redemption-dues and to withdraw their funds from savings banks, and declaring at the same time that no repayment would be permitted in the case of loans contracted by the government "while it was openly waging war with the whole people." [12]

Looking backward from this point over the history of the revolution, one sees the Peasants' Union and its congresses always making threats, but never quite ready to unloose the whirlwind. As far as its immediate tactics were concerned, the Union tried for the time being to direct the peasant movement more against the authorities than against the landlords — on the familiar theory that the country must advance toward economic change by way of political change; and if the methods which the Union recommended for immediate use against the government were not particularly drastic, those to be employed against the landlords were tempered with a much greater moderation. Where the peasants out in the villages adopted more cruel measures, the Union sent greetings, and protested against repression. Here it did not lead — it followed.

In a report made to the Tsar in January 1906, the Minister of the Interior stated it as the opinion of many of the governors that the Union and its latest congress had had a "huge influence" in stirring up disorder.[13] On the other hand, when the question came up for discussion at the first session of the Duma, in the Summer of 1906, one speaker after another declared that the local organizations of the Union had acted as a check upon violence and disorder — and no one came forward in the Duma to deny that this was true.[14] In advertising "land and liberty" as ultimate objectives, the Union may indeed have done much to arouse and inflame the peasants; but if it had been able to *direct* as well as to arouse them, would not their forces have been employed chiefly against officialdom as long as the old government was still standing? As a matter of fact, the peasants out in the villages were concerned first and most immediately with the land; when they took up clubs and torches and started down the road, they did not usually march against some local official of the government, but toward some manor-house.

November found the revolution already somewhat past its crest in most of the cities, but just at its climax in the villages, and not since the day of Pugachev had the country seen such a peasant rising. In two-thirds of the fifty *guberniias* of European Russia the harvest was short this year, and the peasants thus had an additional urge to act. The stories of the great strike made stirring news, and at least in certain instances the October Manifesto turned out to be itself a stimulus to new disorders. The "liberty" which was promised in the manifesto was sometimes understood by the peasants as a temporary licence to do what they pleased: "We shall work," said a certain group of peasants who were looting and burning a manor, "while there is freedom. After New Year's, there won't be any freedom any more." So reports one local correspondent, and a number of others write in a similar tone of the effect of the manifesto.[15]

The disturbances of late Autumn were not only more widespread but also more violent than before. During the last four months of the year, estates were robbed (and in some cases the buildings were fired) in about one-quarter of the 478 *uezds* in the forty-seven *guberniias*. Timber-thieving was reported in a still larger number of districts, and rent- or labor-strikes in about half as many, and there were also numerous instances of refusal to pay taxes. During the entire period from September to December, agrarian disturbances of minor or major importance were recorded in about one-half of the 478 *uezds;* that is, in nearly three times as many *uezds* as during the four preceding months.[16]

The fire burned most hotly in the *guberniia* of Saratov on the lower Volga. According to a report made at the national Peasants' Congress in November, the Socialist Revolutionaries had in some places formed groups among the peasants who armed themselves by seizing the equipment of the State foresters, then drove out the authorities, attacked the estates, disarmed the landlords and suggested that they withdraw themselves from the countryside. In some instances the peasants moved about in bands five-hundred strong, with wagon-trains; when a landlord resisted them, he and his steward were beaten, and the manor was burned to the ground

— although, said the report, the Socialist Revolutionaries tried to prevent these burnings.

Another delegate from this *guberniia* reported to the congress that the peasants had decided to establish immediately their right to the use of the land. "They have seized the land of the estates for temporary use," he said, "pending the confirmation [of the seizures] by the Constitutional Assembly. . . The peasants have no arms; hence they have taken to burning the manors in order to 'smoke out the blood-drinkers'. . . The peasants think that the landlords will never come back any more." [17]

These are voices from below; from above, there comes, for example, the report made to the Tsar himself by the adjutant-general who had been sent to restore order in the *guberniias* of Penza and Saratov. The general reached the theatre of operations late in November 1905, and in January he wrote: "In Saratov *guberniia*, more than three hundred estates have suffered losses from the disorders; in Balashov *uezd* there are places where all the manors have been destroyed. A terrible impression is produced by an examination of the ravaged estates. With an astonishing violence the peasants burned and destroyed everything; not one stone is left upon another; everything has been plundered — grain, stores, furniture, household utensils, animals, the sheet-iron from the roof — in a word, everything that could be carried or hauled away; and what remained was given to the flames. Of the things that were stolen, many were thrown into rivers or ponds, or buried in ravines, in order to hide the evidence of the crime. . . There were almost no instances of the killing of the landlords or their stewards, but this is explained in part by the fact that the proprietors of the estates in the majority of cases hastened to quit their homes before the pillage, or saved themselves by running away at the time of the *pogrom* itself." [18]

The time had come for some of the landlords to reap the whirlwind. When the Ministry of the Interior made an estimate of the losses inflicted upon the proprietors by the disturbances of the Autumn of 1905, the *guberniia* of Saratov stood first with over 9,500,000 *rubls*, while the adjoining *guberniia* of Simbirsk was second with nearly four millions. Next came Kursk and Chernigov with about three millions each, and after them a long diminishing series. The estimates for nineteen "true-Russian" *guberniias* (none of them in the borderlands) round out a total of nearly twenty-nine millions of *rubls*.[19] As far as is known, no attempt has since been made to analyse or verify these figures, but whatever the degree of their inaccuracy, they confirm once again the conclusion that in many places the peasants did not stop short of violence and destruction in their attempt to get what they wanted.

At the end of the year, the movement declined considerably,[20] but after a brief and only partial hibernation, the peasants returned once more to the attack. As Spring advanced into Summer, the disorders multiplied, and during the four months from May to August 1906, disturbances were reported in approximately as many *uezds* as during the last four months of 1905. All the old familiar forms of the movement were again represented — timber-cutting, unlawful pasturing, the carting-off of hay and grain from the fields, pillage and arson, renters' strikes, and occasionally the open appropriation and seeding of land; but in the number of *uezds* affected, agricultural labor-strikes now certainly took first place.[21] With due regard to the vastness of the movement and the many shortcomings of the data now available, one may perhaps risk this generalization: that although in the Summer of 1906 the movement still persisted in every quarter of the country, the fires now burned with less fury and destructiveness than before.

In Georgia the peasant movement still continued after the October Manifesto,[22] as it did also with peculiar intensity and bitterness among the Latvian and Esthonian laborers who cultivated the estates of the German landlords in the Baltic *guberniias*,[23] while in Poland the agricultural labor-strikes reached their maximum development in the Summer of 1906.[24] And yet in that Summer one may find the beginning — and more than the beginning — of the end of the peasant revolt.

During the half-year which followed the October Manifesto, the Socialist parties were still trying, according to their lights, to keep the revolution going. At mid-Winter the Socialist Revolutionaries held their first general congress, and here the Commission on Tactics declared that it favored local attempts at the organized seizure of land, but was opposed to the "agrarian terror" — that is, to house-burnings, personal attacks upon the landlords, and other such acts of destruction by the peasants. When the landlords called in the police or the Cossacks — then, said the commission, any terroristic acts by the peasants against these landlords were "political" rather than "agrarian," and under such circumstances these acts were both "necessary and inevitable." In another report by a member of the same commission, it was proposed that in the matter of a general armed uprising of the peasants and of the other revolutionary forces, the party should "preserve its former tactics: it should not invoke it [the uprising], but should prepare for it in case it breaks out of itself." Voting by a large majority to adopt these principles as directive, the congress declared that the party should not incite the peasants to make a general attempt to seize the land during the coming Spring. But recognizing that the peasant movement was not dependent upon the direction of the party, and believing that an agrarian explosion was almost certain to come of itself in the Spring, the congress declared that in the event of such an outbreak, the party should be prepared to assist the peasants by blowing up railroads and bridges, by "removing" local administrative officials (a polite reference to assassination), and by other such terroristic acts. The resolutions of the congress indicate that at least for the time being there was here a willingness to follow, rather than a will to lead, in the most extreme forms of the peasant movement. This seems to be not altogether consistent with the bold actions of the party in the *guberniia* of Saratov, as reported at the national Peasants' Congress in November, but consistency is too much to expect of a scattered organization in such uproarious times as these; and besides, it is to be remembered that in December the government had been notably successful in putting down certain uprisings by force. If the party would not attempt at the moment to bring on a general revolt, it was, nevertheless, quite unwilling to trust to action by political means in the coming Duma, and it declared a boycott of the elections.[25]

The actions of the Social Democrats continued to be hampered by the circumstance that the Mensheviks and the Bolsheviks were neither altogether united nor completely separated. At a conference of their faction held in December 1905, the Bolsheviks once more declared that the party ought to support the revolutionary activities of the peasants to the point of the actual seizure of the land. The Mensheviks were less decisive in their attitude, and it appears that neither faction played a vitally important role in the specific incitement or direction of the peasant disturbances of the Autumn of 1905 or the Spring of 1906 — except perhaps in the Baltic *guberniias* and in the Caucasus. At the end of November 1905, the Moscow committee of the party published a circular in which it summoned the peasants to *prepare* for an uprising, and to select the lands which they wished to take from the landlords and from the State. "Select," said the circular, "but do not take anything now. If you begin now to seize the land, a little at a time, the servants of the Tsar will take it away from you" — and yet this was already the end of the month in which the agrarian movement reached its climax of strength and violence. As far as the Duma elections were concerned, the Bolsheviks maintained an energetic boycott, while the Mensheviks preferred to leave the matter to be decided by the local organizations.[26]

At the general congress of the Social-Democratic Party, convened at Stockholm in April 1906, the agrarian program came in for a thorough overhauling. Lenin believed that the political revolution against the autocracy could not succeed except on the basis of an alliance of the workers with the peasants; the party ought, he said, to come out for the confiscation of all non-peasant land, and for its provisional surrender to local peasant committees. These were the fighting points of his agrarian program. For the rest, the final adjustment of the agrarian question should be left, he said, to the Constitutional Assembly, and in case a democratic government were established, the party should then undertake to bring about the nationalization of all the land. The capitalistic form of agriculture would then be entirely free to develop on nationalized land rented from the State — so Lenin said; indeed, he expected this capitalistic development to proceed even more rapidly after the grand expropriation. At the moment when the Menshevik leaders faced these Bolshevik proposals, they were apparently thinking more of Marxian evolution than of revolution; in particular it seemed to the Mensheviks a reversal of the Marxian order of development to transfer to the peasants, for petty cultivation, any estate which was exploited with the help of wage-labor as a capitalistic enterprise. Accordingly, the Mensheviks proposed that the non-peasant lands should be turned over, not to the peasants, but to the larger organs of local self-government, the notion being that these governing bodies would permit the capitalist farmers to continue their operations upon the payment of a rent, and would lease to the peasants all or nearly all the confiscated land that was not under capitalistic cultivation. It was the Menshevik theory that this would not set back the development of large-scale agriculture, but would enable this development to proceed quite freely until the time should come for the "socialization" of production itself. As the Mensheviks were in a majority at the congress, the program adopted was substantially theirs, but the world would one day have proof that the Bolsheviks had not forgotten their own proposals.

In the matter of tactics, the congress resolved that the party should undertake to "sharpen the clash of the peasants with the government and the landlords"; it urged that the peasants should direct a larger share of their energy against officialdom, and it specifically recommended labor-strikes and the refusal of rent as means of dealing with the landlords. The Bolsheviks advocated "joint and simultaneous armed attacks" by workers and peasants, but the congress resolved to "hold the peasants back from the agrarian terror, the burning of buildings, and the like." Finally, though it was already so late that most of the elections for the Duma had taken place, the congress decided, against the protest of the Bolsheviks, that the party ought to enter the electoral campaign.[27]

It was not to be expected that the revolutionary parties and the Peasants' Union would have a sufficient influence to make their boycott of the elections generally effective among the peasants. There is no evidence of any wide and deliberate abstention of the peasantry from voting,[28] but it must not be concluded on this account that in the Spring of 1906, the peasants had decided to accept the franchise as an end in itself — the rich bequest of a revolution already dead. On the contrary, there is the best of evidence that in the mass they took a quite opposite view: First, it has already been shown that the agrarian disturbances not only continued, but after their Winter decline, actually increased up to mid-Summer; that is, they increased *after* the elections, and while the first Duma was actually in session. In the second place, when the peasants cast their ballots, most of them were apparently in much the same mood as when they cast stones through the landlords' windows — that is, they were expressing their desire for land, rather than their satisfaction with the political reforms. Still, it was not to be expected that they would be left free to work out their agrarian purpose even by political means. The *zemskii* chiefs were instructed by the Minister of the Interior to warn the election assemblies that they would not be permitted to choose candidates who were untrustworthy (*neblagonadezhnye*); and the chiefs were also told, more specifically, to arrange for the removal from the assemblies of any candidates "who deceived the peasants with unrealizable hopes of the gratuitous distribution of private lands." [29] That the great majority of the peasant deputies in the Duma did actually try to realize some such hope is, under the circumstances, all the more clearly indicative of the strength and the constancy of the peasant movement.

Still, in the very act of voting, the peasants expressed in some degree the faith that it was worth while to vote — the faith that they might get the land in this way. How may one fail to believe, then, that the urge toward a direct attack was now less vigorous than it would have been if the ballot had not been offered as a seeming alternative? The peasant movement was powerful enough, this Spring and Summer of 1906, but who knows what it might have been, if this political will-o'-the-wisp had not created so important a diversion? In the weeks immediately following the publication of the October Manifesto, it had not been apparent that the government's policy of *concession* was actually working; but it was working now — it was giving the policy of *repression* a chance to catch up.

SHOULD the revolution still go on; should it stop short with the October Manifesto; should its conquests be reclaimed for the old régime? Time was passing; history was writing down the contradictory answers which must compound into one single answer in the end. The peasants and the working men were giving their several replies; so also the manufacturers, the merchants, the professional men, the nobility. The Constitutional-Democratic or "Cadet" Party, formed during the last days of the October strike, drew for its leadership upon the liberal elements in all the last-named social-economic groups. The program of the party called for civil liberty, equality before the law, an equal and universal suffrage, and a national representative body with the rights of initiative and of veto; in its agrarian program, the party proposed that allotments be made to the peasants from the lands of the Imperial family, the State, and the monasteries, and "when necessary" from the lands of the private proprietors — with the compensation of these proprietors by the State, "not at the market price, but at a fair valuation." [30]

Before the publication of the October Manifesto, the party congress had declared its solidarity with the general political strike, and even its readiness to support, if this should be necessary, the use of force to win political freedom; and immediately after the appearance of the manifesto, the congress made it known that the new reforms fell very far short of realizing the party program.[31] Then came the multiplication of peasant disturbances, and the December outbreak in Moscow; and at its second congress, in January, the party retreated from the position formerly taken in the matter of tactics: the idea of participating in an armed uprising was now repudiated, and although the general political strike was still recognized as "a form of peaceful, organized struggle with the government," it was declared that "the party should and does consider the organized representative assembly to be the chief field of its activities; outside of this assembly, its activities ought to consist of agitation and propaganda." [32] The Constitutional Democrats believed that they still had serious work to do, but for the accomplishment of this work, they were now fully committed to the use of the parliamentary means already made available by the revolution.

To the right of the Constitutional Democrats there arose a party called the Union of the 17th of October — for short, the "Octobrists." This party borrowed both its name and its major principles from the October Manifesto; it called for a union of the monarchy with the people, upon the basis of the manifesto, and for the creation on this footing of a powerful government — for only such a government could "lift the country out of its present social chaos, and guarantee its internal peace and its external security." For the benefit of the peasants, the party proposed a complete equalization of their civil rights with those of other citizens, a new allotment of State and Imperial lands, public assistance in colonization, and other like reformatory measures. A part of the property of the private holders might be alienated, said the Octobrists, in return for a fair compensation, but this was to be done only in instances "of importance to the State," and only if the other measures proposed should turn out to be "insufficient." [33]

In November 1905 another congress of representatives of the zemstvos and of many of the municipal governments was held in Moscow. Sharply conflicting opinions were expressed, and much heat was generated in the debates; the resolutions were liberal in tone, but distinctly more moderate than the program of the Constitutional Democrats.[34] If a similar congress had been held a half-year later, it would certainly have had a less liberal character, for during this period a pronounced "righting of the zemstvos" was in progress. The chief causes of this change of temper were perhaps to be found in the persistence of the peasant disorders and in the agrarian legislation proposed by the First Duma. At any rate, the change itself was made evident by the results of the *zemstvo* elections of the Summer of 1906.[35]

It was the landed nobility whose position was most immediately and directly threatened by the continuance of the revolution, and among the nobles there was an increasing consciousness of this circumstance, and an increasing activity in response. The history of the *zemstvos* is not the only index of this fact. Early in January 1906, there was held in Moscow a national congress of the marshals of nobility. In each *uezd* and each *guberniia*, the marshal stood as the highest official elected by the nobles as a class; and because of the elective character of the office, the marshals may be considered to have represented more or less accurately the temper of the nobility as a whole. The Moscow congress expressed in formal resolutions its approval of the steps already taken to put down the revolutionary movement, and asked that severe but lawful means be employed by the government for the protection of person and of property; the Duma should be summoned at an early date, and it should deal with the agrarian problem upon the basis of the inviolability of private property; the way should be opened for an increase in the holdings of the peasants through the stimulation of colonization, the sale of State and Imperial lands, and an increased activity of the Peasants' Bank in promoting small purchases; measures should be taken looking toward the substitution of consolidated fields for scattered strips, and it should be made much easier for the peasants to divide the repartitional communal holdings into separate proprietorships.[36]

The last point (on the subject of physical consolidations and separations of title) was the most significant of all: it indicated that in the face of the agrarian disorders, many of the nobility — probably most of them — had at last abandoned their old faith in the commune as the great stabilizer of the peasantry. If any doubt remained as to this change of attitude, or as to the reasons for it, that doubt was cleared away by the actions of the "First Congress of Representatives of the Nobles' Societies" which met at St. Petersburg in May, with twenty-nine *guberniias* represented, and left behind it a permanent "Council of the United Nobility" to carry out its policies. At this congress, the speakers again and again attacked the repartitional commune: ". . . the commune is based upon socialistic foundations"; the commune is "the nursery of socialist bacilli"; "if the State wishes to set a limit to socialism, it ought to abolish the commune." In its Most Humble Address to the Tsar, the congress said: ". . . the passing of a land law based upon the compulsory alienation of private property will shake to its depths one of the most important foundations of the life of the State — the inviolability of property-rights — and will also have a disastrous effect upon the prosperity of the people and the proper development of the country. The recognition and confirmation of the full property-right of the peasants in respect to the lands in their possession is a primary need of the national life. The strengthening of property-rights among the peasants . . . will increase their attachment to that which is their own, and their respect for that which belongs to others." This, then, is the gist of the argument: the communal property-right of the peasants must be abolished, in order that the private property-right of the landlords will not have to be; the one is a process in avoidance of the other. The familiar items about colonization and State aid in land-purchasing appear again in this Most Humble Address, but the central plan is to pacify the peasants, not by providing them with the land they want, but by teaching them not to want it.

Furthermore, the address to the Tsar condemns those who have aroused the peasants with the promise of land, but are really trying to get control of the State (a condemnation evidently directed at the majority in the First Duma); ". . . the nobility affirm that the supreme autocratic power . . . must be guarded now more than ever against all encroachments. . . The working landed nobility will not forsake their 'nests' . . . they will sustain to the end the arduous struggle with the revolution." [37]

Just as the revolution in some of its forms or phases had drawn at least a fraction of every class to its support, so the opposition was not confined to any single class. The very names of the classes may hardly be employed here without implying a unity of thought and action which was never entirely in accordance with the fact. Best organized, most open, most easily understood, was the counter-revolutionary movement among the nobles; most obscure, most devious, most baffling, were the reactionary activities of the *pogrom* mobs and of such non-class organizations as the Union of the Russian People. The Union was founded late in the year 1905 upon the old trinity of true-Russian principles: Orthodoxy, Autocracy, Nationality, but it became best known for one particular phase of its doctrine — that is, its anti-Semitism. The organization drew its membership from all classes, including the clergy (though it ought to be said that some of the priesthood — apparently a small minority — were of an entirely different turn of mind and desired a liberal government and an extension of the peasant holdings). In some, if not in all, of its propaganda, the Union announced that every ill of the country was chargeable in the last analysis to the Jews, and that the liberals and the radicals of Russia were the tools or the accomplices of Israel. In a pamphlet called *The Plot against Russia*, the Union declared that the Jewish Social Democrats were not attacking the financial capitalists of their own race, but only the non-Jewish landlords, manufacturers, and merchants: "Inspiring and justifying the pillage by the masses of those propertied classes who are one with the masses in Faith and in nationality, this doctrine [the Social-Democratic] aims, in the first place, to distract the attention of the Christian people from the capital and the riches amassed in their midst, and at their expense, by the Jews themselves; and in the second place, this doctrine aims, through the ruin of the propertied classes in Russia, to reduce these classes to complete material and spiritual subjection to the Israelite ravishers. Then it will not be difficult for the Jews to seize the whole administration of the country, and actually to establish here a Jewish Tsardom. . . The complete bankruptcy of Russia and the enthronement of the Jews would be equally calamitous for all the Christian nationalities of Russia. Hence we call upon you all, Russian Christians, to stand firmly against the Jewish army of anarchists, socialists, and other open revolutionists and deceitful liberals, directed and supported as they are by the Jews and their sympathizers, the Russian and foreign Masons. Stand firm, Russian people, for the Orthodox Faith, for the Autocratic Tsar, for Russia, the One, the Great, the Indivisible, the Holy . . . ! Let the Lord arise, and let His enemies be scattered !" [38]

These hot words were published in 1906, but the activities of the Union date back to the later months of 1905; and even before this there had been some organized propaganda of the same general character from other sources.[39] Toward the end of the great October strike, and during the weeks which followed, riots broke out in scores of Russian cities; nor was the year 1906 by any means free from such occurrences. The rioters directed their attacks sometimes against the Russian *intelligentsiia*, but most often against Jews of every class, and upon the basis of the newspaper reports of the time one writer has estimated that the number of the killed and the wounded ran into thousands.[40] No assumption whatever is made here as to the accuracy of this estimate; it is mentioned simply as a vague indication of the strength of the outbreaks.

But what was in the minds of the rioters? No doubt some of them struck out against the Jews in the belief that this would somehow alter the conditions of life under the old régime. That is, they acted not out of contentment and in opposition to all change, but out of discontent and in behalf of change; they were revolutionists, of a sort, whom every other revolutionist called blind, befuddled, black-ignorant. At the least, then, anti-Semitism diverted certain forces which might conceivably have strengthened the major revolution; and yet one may hardly escape the belief that a genuine devotion to some aspect of the past, a genuine opposition to change, also played a part in the *pogroms* against the liberal and radical *intelligentsiia* and the Jews. It is unnecessary to discuss here the much-debated question as to how far the officials of the government were responsible for the *pogroms*. The one point to be made is this: in the critical late-Autumn weeks of 1905, the chiefs and guardians of the old régime might look down into the streets and see there not only processions of revolutionists, but processions of another kind carrying holy icons and pictures of the Tsar — processions of men ripe and ready for violence against the revolutionists as such, or against a race who might be sacrificed, so some thought, without serious danger to the established order of politics and of property. . . Under such circumstances, one might draw the curtain and sit down more comfortably to consider the cancellation of some reform which had recently been granted under pressure, and perhaps in too great haste.

Even among the peasants, some encouragement might be found for such a policy of reaction. There was an abundance of political indifferentism in the villages, sometimes a positive monarchism; even occasionally an open collision in the matter of the land, between the well-to-do peasants who had something to lose, and the mass of their neighbors who had so much to gain. But of this, there is more to be said hereafter.

In compounding any decision as to what concessions must be made, or what and how much might be withdrawn, there was still one other matter to be considered: the strength and temper of the army. There were a number of instances of insubordination and outright mutiny in the military and naval forces, more particularly during the last three months of 1905, and at the end of the year the field-army, beginning at about this time to return from the Far East, was more than suspect of a revolutionary taint.[41] The officers were drawn for the most part from the nobility or the middle class, and only rarely was there any question of their loyalty. The peasantry formed the bulk of the rank-and-file, but in uniform and under discipline they showed a much less rebellious spirit than did their fellows at home in the villages. Not only did the soldiers fail to make any great disturbance on their own account, but in general they showed themselves willing to act without protest against the civilian disturbers of the peace. The doubt as to their morale was gradually resolved by experience; in the crisis of this Winter and Spring, the army was not found wanting.

Thus the balance of power was shifting slowly toward the side of counter-revolution; the central figure was called upon to act:

In the park of Tsarskoe Selo (Tsar's Village), about fifteen miles from old St. Petersburg, there are two Imperial residences. The Catherine Palace, extending its elaborate façade of white, green, and bronze for nearly a thousand feet across the face of a great paved square, is the Versailles of the North, unbelievably fantastic in the snow. The other, the Alexander Palace, is much smaller, much more severe in the style of its exterior, with the rooms of its eastern wing done over to please the pitifully mean and paltering taste of the last Nicholas and his consort. Here in the Alexander Palace, on the first day of December 1905, several deputations presented themselves for a simultaneous audience with the monarch. One would like to think that these deputies were received, not in the gew-gawed modern chambers, but in the columned portrait-hall which still preserved the dignity of an earlier time. The chronicle leaves this question to conjecture, but not so the name and station of the deputies: they ran the scale from prince to peasant, and "as the Lord Emperor entered the hall, all . . . bowed to the floor in salutation." Having received and kissed the holy picture offered by the Society of the Bearers of Icon-Standards, the Lord Emperor said to the deputies: "Repeat it to all who love our dear fatherland that the manifesto which I gave forth on the seventeenth of October is the full and sincere expression of my inflexible and unchangeable will — an act that is subject to no alteration." [42]

These words are excellent drama, but bad history. They assume, not "divine right" only, but two separate attributes of divinity itself: immutability, and a will that "moves not by the external impulse or inclination of objects, but determines itself by an absolute autocracy." Yet in the very appearance here of the deputies to whom the Tsar addressed himself, one finds the suggestion of pressure from one direction; while, on the other hand, in the necessary maintenance within and all around the palace of a heavily armed "protection," there is more than a hint of the existence of an opposing pressure from the revolutionists. In the vacillations of the Tsar and of the changing company of his advisers, there was, of course, some self-generated motion, but unquestionably one must also see here the variable resultant of contending external forces.

An attempt has been made to show what these forces were — to show that in the period following the October Days, the revolutionary drive continued, but with somewhat diminished strength, while the unofficial opposition to this movement increased in vigor and in aggressiveness. It now becomes appropriate to sketch out the history of the official policy as such, in this most critical situation.

The publication of the October Manifesto certainly did not mean that the government had gone over completely to a policy of pacification-by-concession. The new election-law of 11 December extended the franchise considerably beyond the terms of the law of 6 August, but still fell somewhat short of providing a universal manhood suffrage, while the grouping of the electors in separate classes and the system of indirect elections produced a marked inequality among the voters and gave to the working men and the peasants an influence much less than proportionate to their number. The October Manifesto was only ten days old when Poland was placed under martial law; soon after, as has been said, there came the arrest of a number of officers of the Peasants' Union, and of the members of the Petersburg Soviet of Workers' Deputies; in many of the rural districts, and in Moscow at the time of the December uprising, revolutionary force was met and overborne with force. Instances of the employment of repressive measures are frequent enough during these last months of 1905, yet Premier Witte and the Minister of the Interior, Durnovo, complained of "do-nothingness" and a lack of boldness on the part of the local authorities, while some of the governors said in their turn that the policy of the central government itself was vague and undefined.[43] For both these complaints, there was a certain justification, from the point of view of those who made the criticisms. The government was feeling its way, testing the temper of the army, watching the effect of the October Manifesto and the progress of the *pogroms,* listening for reassuring voices from the nobility, from the mob, from anywhere. At mid-Winter, neither the staff nor the ranks of officialdom were yet altogether sure what should or could be done.

The uncertainty of the time is perfectly reflected in the official handling of the land-question. "Many of the nobility," says Witte, "had completely lost their heads." One of the most influential men of the day was the Governor General of St. Petersburg, D. F. Trepov, and shortly after the publication of the October Manifesto, he said to Witte: "I myself am a landed proprietor, and I shall be very glad indeed to surrender without compensation one-half of my land, since I am persuaded that only under this condition shall I succeed in keeping the other half for myself." The Council of Ministers actually considered a proposal for the compulsory alienation of a part of the private lands, but instead there was published the manifesto of 3 November cancelling the redemption-dues and promising an expansion of the activities of the Peasants' Bank. However, the question would not down, and before the middle of January the Council had examined two other alienation-projects of the same general character, one of them supported by the Minister of Agriculture.[44]

In a report to the Tsar, under date of 10 January 1906, Witte says that except in the Caucasus, the Baltic provinces, and Poland, there will be "no further serious mass-movements of a revolutionary character" — at least not during the next few months. "As to the agrarian disorders — there the situation is quite different. Not only have these disorders not come to an end, but probably it must be considered that they are only entering upon their initial period. New and stronger manifestations may be expected in the Spring, if only they are not forestalled by appropriate measures." [45] The measures recommended by Witte were: first, a more strenuous repression, with an increased employment of the army, and second, the adoption of that new attitude toward the land-commune which was to become the basis of the government's agrarian policy from the end of this revolution down to the beginning of the next. The Council of Ministers had not previously agreed upon the compulsory alienation of any of the private lands, and the Tsar now rejected the idea; upon the margin of Witte's report he wrote, "Private property should remain sacred." The Council had, how-

ever, expressed the belief that the final break-up of the repartitional lands into private holdings would inspire in the peasants "a
sounder view of the property-right of others"; and here the Tsar
wrote, "I approve." [46]

This last was to be the dominant idea of the decade to come: not
to give the peasants land, but to teach them not to try to take it.
Still, whatever might be hoped for from the development of a
property-sense in the peasantry, this remedy could not be expected
to work quickly enough to meet the current crisis. Repression was
still to receive a further trial; the landed proprietors were to have
many months in which to organize and to make themselves more
clearly heard; and only then would the government be ready to
offer and to impose its new system of property-right — its moral
equivalent for land.

The revolution had made the appeal to force, and by force it
would finally be destroyed. When the revolutionists seemed to be
the stronger party, the government made concessions, but many
of these concessions were withdrawn as the balance of force
swung slowly back again. Of the campaign of repression in town
and country, there is no existing account which approximates to
completeness — and because of the endless variety of legal, half-
legal, and illegal measures, and the wide distribution of the areas
affected, it is probable that no complete record of the dragonnade
can ever be assembled and no full history ever written. Against
the peasants, military detachments were frequently employed in
place of, or in addition to, the police. Upon the arrival of the force,
the peasants usually made immediate submission; but sometimes
there was a show of resistance, and then the troops would fire into
the crowd, and there would be a toll of killed and wounded. When
the peasants had submitted, there often followed a series of floggings, sometimes even the burning of houses and summary executions; then came the more regular administrative or judicial trials
and punishments. In a telegram to one of the governors, the Minister of the Interior, Durnovo, said: "Take the sternest measures
to bring the disorders to an end: it is a useful thing to wipe the
rebellious village off the face of the earth, and to exterminate the
rebels themselves without mercy, by force of arms." As far as may
be judged from the reports available of actual operations in the
villages, the commanders of the punitive detachments were not
usually so ferocious as this, but the telegram may be worth quot-
ing to show the lengths to which officialdom could go.

To facilitate the repression, one region after another was placed under exceptional law — that is, the usual laws were to a greater or less extent suspended, and one of the several emergency codes, varying in the degree of their severity, was applied. Thus, out of the eighty-seven *guberniias* of the Empire exclusive of Finland, thirty in their entirety and thirty more in part were on 1 March 1906 under the rules of "strengthened protection," or of "extraordinary protection," or of "a condition of war." In certain of the illustrated journals dating from 1906, one may see photographs of Cossack posts on the estates, Cossacks patrolling the fields, armed guards standing by at the threshing. In the Baltic provinces and in the Caucasus, the punitive expeditions showed their maximal severity, and from the Baltic comes one not-to-be-forgotten photograph of bodies lying beside a fence, in the snow.[47]

In sum, if the first three months of 1906 be compared with the last quarter of the preceding year, it will be seen that the industrial labor movement (as reflected in the strike statistics) now showed a diminished strength; that the peasant disturbances were much less frequent; that the liberals were much more favorable than before to peaceful political action; that the conservative and reactionary elements were better organized; that the army was being reinforced by troops from the East; that the temper of the soldiers was now less doubtful, while the list of their domestic victories was growing day by day. A short time before the Duma opened, the government succeeded, too, in concluding an agreement with an international syndicate of bankers for a huge loan — according to Count Witte the largest foreign loan ever yet made in the history of mankind. The Tsar called it "a guarantee of the future tranquillity and peaceful development of Russia," while Witte says somewhat more specifically that the return of the army and the flotation of the loan "re-established order and self-confidence in the actions of the government." [48] It was not soon to be forgotten that this financial bargain helped the government to put down the revolution. The Socialist parties had already declared, in December 1905, that they would never permit the repayment of any such loan as this.

As the balance of power shifted, the repressions were gradually extended from the region of fact, where they might possibly have been thought temporary, to the region of law, where they were obviously intended to be permanent. It was the working men and the liberals whose fighting strength had apparently been most reduced (respectively by repression and by deflection into parliamentary channels), and the first major laws of the reaction were within the field where these groups had expended most of their strength — that is, the field of political reform. The laws of 20 February 1906 provided that the old Council of State, formerly appointed by the Emperor, should hereafter have half its members elected by certain highly restricted groups, and should possess a legislative authority equal to that of the popularly elected Duma. Also it was provided that when the legislature was not in session, the government might issue temporary laws, which would lapse, however, if they were not approved by both houses at their next convention. Far more important, however, were two other rules laid down by the new legislation: first, no project for the revision of the Fundamental State Laws (which were concerned primarily with the "sacred rights and prerogatives of the Supreme Autocratic Power") might be so much as discussed by the Council of State or by the Duma except upon the initiative of the Tsar himself; and in the second place, the right of the Duma to inquire into the legality of administrative actions, as provided in the October Manifesto, was so hedged in as to make it of questionable value in practice.[49]

The manifesto accompanying the laws of 20 February was published in the full panoply of the old régime: "By the Grace of God, We, Nicholas the Second, Emperor and Autocrat of All the Russias, Tsar of Poland, Grand Duke of Finland, etc., etc., etc. . ." In the face of all this, one of the journals of the time still had the courage to say that the country had "an autocracy without content, and a constitution without the name." However, it would soon be possible to see somewhat more clearly which was the reality — the autocracy or the constitution — and which the shadow.

On 23 April, four days before the opening of the Duma, a whole series of laws defining and limiting the powers of that body and of the Council of State were confirmed by the Tsar: "On the original document there is indited by the Own hand of His Imperial Majesty, 'So let it be' " — thus reads the autocratic formula. But even more significant than the content of the statutes was the fact that they were denominated Fundamental State Laws; hence, under the terms of the law of 20 February, they might not be tampered with by the legislature except on the initiative of the Emperor himself. Among the untouchable principles now set out, was this: "To the Emperor of All the Russias belongs supreme autocratic power. Submission to His power, not only from fear, but as a matter of conscience, is commanded by God Himself." And yet it was stated once more, a little farther along, that except for the temporary legislation promulgated under the conditions described above, no new law might be enacted without the approval of the Duma and of the State Council as well as that of the Emperor. To the Tsar, a number of powers were specifically reserved: the control of foreign affairs, the right to declare war and to conclude peace, the direction of the military and naval forces, and the appointment and dismissal of the Ministers of State. If in any instance the chambers should refuse to approve a new budget, the old budget (as modified by the requirements of subsequent laws) might still be kept in force by the government; and should the flotation of loans be necessary for the maintenance of the old schedule of expenditures, the legislature might not block the making of such loans, or their subsequent service and repayment.[50] Evidently, then, the Duma would have little opportunity to apply the formula of grievance before supply. The publication of these Fundamental Laws on the eve of the opening of the Duma was a direct challenge to that body; it was called by one of the public men of the time a *coup d'état,* but had this gentleman been able to foresee what was soon to happen, he would have held this term in reserve for use a few weeks later.

When the Duma opened on 27 April, the Constitutional Democrats were easily its leading faction. They were the only party who had conducted a general and well-organized campaign, and the complex electoral process gave them more than one hundred and fifty seats out of a total of some five hundred. Many of the other deputies came up to Petersburg uncommitted to any affiliation; and the wide discrepancies which exist among the various accounts of the party-composition of the First Duma, while perhaps due in part to the carelessness of the compilers, are doubtless in part also a result of a certain vagueness and inconstancy in the party-allegiance of some of the deputies. Second to the Cadets in strength was the Labor Group, with about one hundred members. The history of this group did not run back of the election period itself, and a considerable part of its membership was recruited from among those peasant deputies who arrived at the capital as non-partisans, and were attracted to this group by its special preoccupation with the land problem and its demand for compulsory alienations for the benefit of the peasantry. Most of the Socialist Revolutionaries and Social Democrats had boycotted the election, and yet seventeen or eighteen Social Democrats were returned to the chamber. Of the remaining deputies — less than half of the total membership — a few were adherents of the small Russian parties standing to the right of the Constitutional Democrats, while a much greater number either had no affiliation or belonged to some one of the non-Russian national groups which were federated in the Union of Autonomists.[51]

It was obvious from the beginning that the Duma and the government could not possibly work together, unless one or both made radical concessions. Most of the deputies expected the major concessions to come from the side of the government; at this late day, when the revolution was no longer making headway by direct action, they still hoped to carry it forward by political action. In making reply to the address from the throne, the Duma proposed many reforms — such, for example, as the establishment of the equality of all citizens before the law, the institution of universal suffrage and of ministerial responsibility to the Duma, and the employment of the compulsory alienation of private lands as one means of satisfying the needs of the peasantry.[52] In the government's answer, read by the new Prime Minister, I. L. Goremykin, who had recently succeeded Count Witte, the deputies were reminded that many of the political measures which they proposed lay within the scope of the Fundamental Laws and were therefore not subject to the Duma's initiative; also, the Premier declared that the solution of the land question upon the basis proposed by the Duma was "absolutely inadmissible." [53] In the course of his address, Goremykin mentioned certain measures which might be admitted to consideration, but the differences between the program of the government and that of the Duma were so wide that it is hard to see how anyone could still have hoped for a compromise.

This is not a general history of the revolution, and there is no point in discussing here the cause and course of the thousand and one collisions between the Duma and the government. The agrarian problem occupied far more of the Duma's time than all other matters put together, and upon this question the final conflict centered. Three agrarian projects were presented in the Duma, all of them involving to a greater or less extent the expropriation of private holdings, with or without compensation.[54] The government had already declared that it would not tolerate any such measure, and toward the end of May the Nobles' Congress published its declaration of loyalty to the Tsar and its protest against any trespass upon the right of private property. With this show of outside support, the ministry now announced to the country a land program of its own: to the better-off peasants, it was suggested that any expropriation of the lands of the large proprietors would lead naturally to a general redivision of the peasant holdings also, with a consequent loss to many peasants; for the benefit of the land-short villagers, there were proposals to sell the lands of the State on favorable terms; to buy private lands for the same purpose with State funds, and to re-sell such lands to the peasants, at a reduced price if necessary; and finally to give increased State aid in colonization. As to the physical arrangement of the allotment-lands, the government proposed that each holder should receive a consolidated plot in exchange for his scattered strips; and as to the legal form of allotment tenure, the official plan was that those land-communes in which there had been no redistribution for twenty-four years should be recognized as already in fact dissolved and should not be permitted to revive the practice of reallotment, while in the case of the other repartitional communes the establishment of separate hereditary titles for individual holders should be facilitated.[55] When this program is compared with the proposals made by the major groups in the Duma, on the one hand, and on the other with the program so recently adopted by the Nobles' Congress, the result is so striking that any comment is a waste of words.

"The commune — there is the enemy!" The Nobles' Congress had said it, with ample explanation as to why and wherefore; and now at last the government had said it, by implication, in announcing openly its agrarian proposals. By the sale of lands, and especially by the dissolution of the communes, a prosperous and trustworthy class of petty individual proprietors was to be built up; and in fixing this goal for itself, the government had adopted the policy with the fulfilment of which the name of P. A. Stolypin, then Minister of the Interior, was to be so intimately associated — the policy of which Stolypin was speaking when, as Prime Minister, he addressed these words to the Third Duma more than two years later: "The government has placed its wager, not on the needy and the drunken, but on the sturdy and the strong — on the sturdy individual proprietor who is called upon to play a part in the reconstruction of our Tsardom on strong monarchical foundations." [56]

The announcement of the official agrarian program only sharpened the war of words in and around the First Duma, and in an attempt to counteract the action of the government this body issued an appeal to the country. In this appeal, the Duma stated that it was preparing a land law calling for certain expropriations of private property, and it urged the people to await quietly the completion and publication of this law.[57]

But would the *government* wait? The vigorous Stolypin was appointed Prime Minister, and on 8 July 1906, the second day after the Duma's appeal to the people, the assembly was dissolved and the city and *guberniia* of St. Petersburg were placed under "extraordinary protection." The next morning, a Sunday, St. Petersburg was plastered with a manifesto on the dissolution, beginning as always, "By the Grace of God, We, Nicholas the Second, Emperor and Autocrat of All the Russias . . ." [58] And that day any of the idle and curious of the town who wandered eastward along the Neva toward the Taurida Palace, where the Duma had been sitting, might see troops on guard to block the entrance beneath the eighteenth-century portico — no place now in these classic halls for the deputies who had so thoroughly worn out their welcome.

IN THE imperial manifesto on the dismissal of the Duma, there is no open declaration of an intent to bring back the good old times: the Duma still exists, as an institution, and when fresh elections have been held, the new deputies are to be convened, in February of the coming year. The land problem is the center of attention: the Tsar declares that the improvement of the condition of the peasants is his chief task, and that "where a shortage of land exists, the Russian plowman shall be given a lawful and honest means of extending his holding without inflicting loss upon the possessions of others." The peasant outbreaks are mentioned, too, and in general terms the manifesto says: ". . . We will permit no lawlessness or insubordination, and with the full power of the State We will subject the law-breakers to Our Imperial will." [59]

On the day of the dissolution, about two hundred members of the Duma, including the leaders of the Cadets and of the Labor Group, assembled at Viborg, in Finland, and prepared the famous manifesto in which they called upon the people to boycott the government by refusing to pay taxes or to furnish recruits. Peaceful political action having failed of its objective, most of the Cadet and Labor members were now ready for a try at passive resistance; but there were others who wished to go much farther. The Executive Committee of the Social Democrats, dominated by the Menshevik faction, announced a general political strike, and the Socialist Revolutionaries called for an uprising of the peasants, but the trend of the times was, or soon would be, in quite the opposite direction. There were two cases of mutiny among the soldiers and sailors, but these disturbances were quickly suppressed.[60] The number of factory workers who went on strike for political reasons was very much greater in July than it had been in June, but only about equal to the number for May, and very far below the figure for any of the last three months of the preceding year. The number of men who struck for economic reasons was less in July than in June; and as the end of the year 1906 approached, the industrial strike-movement in both its economic and political phases diminished very rapidly in strength. The total number of strikers in 1905 was 2,863,000, while in 1906 it was 1,108,000, and more than two-thirds of the total for 1906 belong to the first half of that year.[61] The revolutionary movement among the factory workers was most certainly in decline.

Of the movement among the peasantry, the same thing must be said. Here the decline begins approximately with the middle of the year, and during the last four months of 1906 disturbances were reported in only about as many *uezds* as during a similar length of time at the beginning of 1905.[62] The revolution had been young and growing then, but now it was already old.

This change is reflected also in the attitude of the revolutionary organizations and parties. Apparently losing hope of energetic direct action by the masses in the near future, the Peasants' Union, the Socialist Revolutionaries, and the Social Democrats made no attempt to boycott the polling for the Second Duma, but joined in the electoral campaigns instead. The change of attitude is nowhere more clearly shown than in a resolution which the Bolsheviks offered at the congress of the Social-Democratic Party in the Spring of 1907: ". . . at the present moment, in the absence of the conditions for a revolutionary explosion of the masses, partisan attacks are not desirable, and the Congress recommends an ideational struggle against them." [63]

If the revolutionary parties were now less hopeful and less resolute than they had been after the October Manifesto and before the dissolution of the First Duma, the conservative-reactionary forces were more aggressive than ever. In December 1906, the

Most Holy Synod called upon the Orthodox clergy to take an active part in the election of the Second Duma and at special services to explain to the voters that "just as a Duma of wise and faithful men will bring good to the people, so evil will come from a Duma into which the enemies of the holy faith and of the throne have managed to penetrate." In November 1906, and again shortly after the Second Duma opened in February 1907, national congresses of representatives of the nobles' societies were held, and at these meetings a lusty cry was raised for the suppression of the revolution, the protection of property, and the break-up of the land-commune, and also for the dissolution of the Second Duma and for such a revision of the electoral law as would place the control of future Dumas in the hands of men of property.[64] A few days after the new parliament opened in February, a famous reactionary paper, the *Moscow Vedomosti*, published an editorial under the heading: "Why the State Duma Should Be Dissolved," and in this article it declared that the Duma was "fit for nothing but to kindle revolution and to destroy everything in the country." A few more weeks passed, and this paper began to carry every day at the top of its first page this seven-column headline: "First of all, the Duma should be dissolved." The Union of the Russian People continued its reactionary work, and the "Fourth All-Russian Congress of the United Russian People," meeting in April and May, demanded the suppression of revolutionary activities and declared it indispensable that the Duma be dissolved immediately and the electoral laws revised.[65]

Thus the government certainly did not act entirely without support as it pushed ahead with the policy of repression. Before the end of the Summer of 1906, the application of the exceptional laws had been so extended that almost all the *guberniias* of the Empire were now in part or as a whole under the rules of "strengthened protection," or of "extraordinary protection," or of "a state of war." [66] The newspapers literally swarmed with reports of repressive activities of every familiar kind, and under special regulations published late in August, a new instrument of control was added — the military field-court. According to these new regulations, the governor-general of any region which was under "extraordinary protection" or in "a condition of war" might turn over an accused person to a court composed exclusively of military or naval officers selected for the occasion; the investigation was to be completed if possible in a single day; the trial was to be conducted in secret and finished in not more than two days; and then immediately, and not on any account with a delay of more than twenty-four hours, the sentence was to be carried out.[67] The number of civilians executed during the next eight months by the new field-courts has been officially reported as 683, while the ordinary courts-martial are officially credited with the execution of 10 civilians in 1905, 144 in 1906, 456 in 1907, and 825 in 1908. These figures do not include the numbers of persons executed upon administrative order, without the formality of a trial, and an unofficial tabulation places the number of such executions at 376 in 1905, 864 in 1906, 59 in 1907, and 32 for the first ten months of 1908. The total number of executions here listed is therefore more than three thousand four hundred.[68] The word "execution" is to be understood literally, since no account is taken here of the unknown number of persons who were shot down during the actual disturbances without first being captured by the authorities.

In addition to all this, the Department of Police reported that during the year ending 1 November 1906, the following results had been accomplished by "administrative process": seven thousand persons fined, two thousand prohibited from living in regions which had been placed under extraordinary law, and twenty-one thousand banished — most of them to the northern *guberniias* or to Siberia.[69]

A history of these repressions is not, however, a complete history of the policy of the government during this period and especially of its policy respecting the peasant question. The government no longer thought it possible to deal with the villagers by repressive measures alone. Private property was of course to be protected, but the peasants — some of them — were to have more land, and the reversal of the old policy of maintaining the solidarity of the household and of the commune was to be given a practical effect. The manifesto of 3 November 1905 had promised that the Peasants' Bank would increase its activities in the promotion of land purchasing by the villagers, and the story of some of the steps taken in fulfilment of this program is most illuminating. In the single year 1906, the Bank purchased from private proprietors, for resale to the peasants, more land than it had bought during the whole thirteen-year period from 1893 to 1905, and for this land purchased in 1906 it paid an average price of 108 *rubls* per *desiatina*, as compared with ninety-four *rubls* in 1905. On the other hand, the Bank's sales of its own lands fell off very materially

in 1906 — and this in spite of the fact that the average sale-price
of seventy-one *rubls* per *desiatina* was very much below the price
level for the years just preceding, and far below the price at which
the Bank was making its own contemporary purchases.[70] The re-
luctance of the peasants to buy land from the Bank, even at a reduced price, reflects their continuing hope that there would be a
thoroughly revolutionary land settlement, or that they would at
least be able to make purchases directly from the landlords at a
still lower figure. On the other hand, the eagerness of the Bank
to buy lands from the landlords at an increased price, gives evidence of the desire of the government to use its resources to assist
the proprietors at a time when their fear of the peasant disturbances and of possible confiscation would otherwise have driven
prices sharply downward. "In the current situation, there remained
no doubt of the immediate necessity . . . of giving attention to
the maintenance of the balance . . . in the land market" — so
said an official report of the Bank.[71] To restore and maintain this
balance of supply and demand between landlord-sellers and
peasant-buyers was to oppose the natural out-working of the revolution, and this is exactly what the Bank had set itself to do at
the moment.

However, the private lands purchased by the Bank were not the
only ones intended to be sold to the peasants; the revolutionists
had talked freely of the gratuitous distribution of the holdings of
the State and of the Imperial family, and now, under two *ukazes*
of August 1906, considerable areas of these lands were designated
for transfer to the peasants, not as a gift, but at prices to be determined with the help of the Peasants' Land Bank or in accordance with its methods. By other *ukazes* published in October and
November 1906 the interest rates of the Bank were reduced and
provision was made for the expansion of its loan operations.[72]

All these measures dealt with what might be called the quantitative side of the land question; but more novel and far wider in
their influence were the celebrated *ukazes* of 5 October and 9 November 1906 which so materially affected the qualitative aspect
of peasant holding and the general organization of peasant society.
In furtherance of the program which had been put forward in
May by the Nobles' Congress, and announced by the government
as its own shortly before the dissolution of the First Duma, the
new laws introduced a novel degree of freedom and individualism
into the personal and property relations of the village. The *ukaz* of

9 November stated in its introductory paragraphs that the new measures to promote the individualization of peasant holdings followed quite naturally from the cancellation of the redemption-debt, but as a matter of fact this is a wholly inadequate explanation of the new policy. If the repartitional commune had been kept alive by the government only because it served as a guarantor and collector of the redemption-dues, then the measures to promote the dissolution of the communal land-relations might quite properly have been introduced in 1903 when the joint financial responsibility of the repartitional communes was abolished in most of the *guberniias*. As a matter of fact, these measures were not undertaken then, but only after the agrarian disturbances had taught the nobles and the government that the commune did not guarantee a stable and conservative peasantry. Then, and only then, did the government commit itself to the idea that the régime of autocratic power and economic privilege could best be maintained by individualizing the peasant holdings and by helping the stouter and abler peasants to build up a proprietary interest in the established order.

There is no convincing proof that the existence of the old laws supporting the system of common property was one of the grievances which led to the peasant disorders, nor is there any reason to believe that the new laws on property and person, as published in the Autumn of 1906, helped materially to bring the revolution to a close. The provisions of these laws, and of others of the same type enacted subsequently, will therefore be examined later, in connection with an account of the changes which actually took place, during the post-revolutionary decade, in the peasant household and in the commune. But first there remains the duty of watching to the end the final throes of the revolution itself.

In the Spring of 1907, the government was stronger, more self-assured, than it had been when it dissolved the First Duma, while the forces of revolutionary direct action were conspicuously weaker; and yet (partly because there had been no boycott of the new elections) the Second Duma contained a much stronger radical group than had the First. In this situation, there was little hope that the assembly would be permitted to live out its time. According to an official tabulation of the membership, the Constitutional Democrats or Cadets (now calling themselves officially the Party of the People's Freedom) had only ninety-one deputies in the Second Duma, as against more than one hundred and fifty in the First;

the Labor Group, with 101 members, had approximately held its own; the Socialist Revolutionaries had returned thirty-six deputies; and the Social Democrats had made a conspicuous advance, from seventeen or eighteen members to sixty-five.[73] The Cadets wanted the Duma really to function as a parliamentary institution, and to this end they tried to hold it within the limits of the law, but the left-extremists were too much for them. One of the leaders of the Cadets said that the parties of the extreme left "desired that the Duma, powerless in its own affairs, should transform itself into an all-powerful government and assume the leadership of a non-existent movement of the people." [74] The extremists in their turn accused the Cadets of weakness — and worse; and at the congress of the Social-Democratic Party held just at this time, the Bolsheviks argued that the immediate task of the party's deputies in the Duma should be to make it clear to the people at large that the demands of the workers and the peasants could not possibly be realized through the work of the Duma — that success could come only through "the open struggle of the mass of the people with the armed autocracy." At the moment the conditions for such a mass revolution were lacking, the Bolsheviks said; [75] but apparently they thought that the very failure and expulsion of the Duma might help to bring these conditions into being.

Since the government and its supporters had been able to check the revolutionary movement in its most substantial actuality, it was not likely that they would fail to stop the revolutionary talk in the chamber. When the Duma had lived through something more than three months of hot debate, the Prime Minister suddenly brought a charge of conspiracy against the Social-Democratic deputies, and demanded the expulsion of the whole group, with the arrest of their leaders; and then while a parliamentary commission was still considering these demands, the Duma was arbitrarily dissolved.[76]

In the manifesto of dissolution, the Emperor said: "The Tsarist Power over Our people was committed to Us by the Lord God. Before His Throne We shall answer for the fate of the Russian Empire." [77] Under this broad authority (and in direct violation of the Fundamental Laws), there was issued on the day of dissolution (3 June 1907) a new law governing the future elections to the chamber. The members of the first two Dumas had not been "true representatives of the needs and desires of the people" (so said the manifesto), and the new election law had its own particular way of making good this defect. The people of Central Asia were deprived of all representation, and the number of deputies from Poland and the Caucasus was greatly reduced. Of the twenty-five cities, each of which had formerly been separately represented, only seven preserved this privilege. Within the cities, as between the non-propertied voters and the owners of real estate and of commercial and industrial establishments, the balance was altered by the assignment of a greatly increased voting-weight to the propertied group. In the rural districts there was a drastic readjustment in favor of the larger landed proprietors, and the net result of the changes in city and country was this: in the electoral colleges of twenty-eight *guberniias* out of the fifty-three in which comparisons may be made, the number of electoral seats to be filled by the larger rural proprietors, acting separately, was greater than the number assigned to all the other classes of the population put together; in four other colleges the electors of this class exactly equalled in number all the other electors combined, and in every other one of the fifty-three colleges, the rural proprietorial electors, with the help of those of the urban propertied group, could out-vote all the rest. Disregarding entirely the second and third groups of colleges (those in which the rural proprietors acting separately could control only half or less than half of the electoral votes), and considering only the twenty-eight colleges in which this class held an absolute majority, one finds that these twenty-eight colleges *alone* were to elect a substantial majority of the Duma — 255 deputies out of 442.[78] In 1905, when the first election law was taking form, some of the bureaucrats had been doubtful about the dependability of the nobles as a class, and some of the nobles had certainly been tainted with the spirit of reform; but under pressure of the revolutionary attack upon prerogative, privilege, and property, certain old lessons had been re-learned. Inasmuch as the larger landed proprietors were for the most part nobles, the new election law was essentially a confirmation of the old alliance between monarchy and nobility — an alliance which might be expected to act in the name of Autocracy, Orthodoxy, Nationality — and now as before in the name also of one other cause: Landed Property.

During the months which preceded the dissolution of the Second Duma and the publication of the new election law, the strike movement among the factory workers had gained considerably in strength; but instead of a more general resort to direct action after the expulsion of the chamber, there came then a gradual decline in economic strikes, and an almost complete collapse of the political strike movement, with a brief revival in November 1907. The number of strikers recorded in 1906 was two-thirds of the total number of factory workers; in 1907 the proportion was two-fifths; in 1908, one-tenth.[79] The labor movement had lost, at least for the time being, its revolutionary vigor; the workers were too tired to fight.

For the peasants, the story was somewhat the same. The Summer of 1907 brought some revival of the agrarian disturbances, but the number of *uezds* affected was far below that for the preceding Summer, and by Autumn the movement had almost completely vanished.[80]

The political concessions of 1905 had satisfied some men as an end in themselves, and by many others they had been accepted as offering a means of working forward peacefully toward further political and economic changes. Thus these concessions had weakened the forces of revolutionary direct action; the government and the counter-revolutionary elements of the population, the latter at last thoroughly aroused, had then defeated the revolutionary extremists on their own ground, by direct action; and finally the political concessions themselves had been in considerable part withdrawn. Concession, repression, exhaustion, had combined to do their perfect work. The new elections returned to the Third Duma a mere handful of Socialists and Laborites, and only some fifty Cadets; [81] the government had at last achieved a legislative majority with which it could carry on.

The whole history of the rise and fall of the Duma is hardly more than a pale reflection of a thousand much more brutal histories which worked out their own climax in the streets, the factories, the manor-yards, and the far villages of the Empire. On this wider stage and in this more vital drama, the peasants had played a leading role.

From the government itself the peasant trouble-makers had certainly received more attention than any other opposition group, and now the peasantry emerged from the revolution with their civil and political status somewhat improved, and with a whole mass of agrarian legislation designed in part to deflect or defeat their demands, but in a small part actually to satisfy them. Certainly the peasants had not gotten all that they wanted — far from it; but here and there, when the landlord took to flight and the red cock crowed on the manorial roof, they had tasted power; some of them had felt for a moment that they held the world in their hands. and they as a class had gained something out of the revolution.

To say exactly *what* the peasants wanted is not easy — not even possible. In the resolutions of the village assemblies and the national Peasant Congresses, in the peasant balloting for the Dumas,[82] and in the attitude of the peasant deputies in that body, there seems to be evidence that in so far as the peasants were concerned with *political* issues as such, the major weight of their opinion was probably on the side of at least a limited democratization of central and local government. But even if one suppose that political liberalism or radicalism was widespread in the villages, this sentiment still need not have been particularly vital. In rare instances, indeed, the peasants removed their own elective officers in the village and the *volost,* and replaced them with others.[83] Again, there were frequent refusals to pay taxes, but in taking this action the peasants were undoubtedly more influenced by the desire to keep their *rubls* than by any hope of weakening the government.[84] There were collisions, too, with the local representatives of governmental authority — the *zemskii* chiefs, the police, and the soldiers, but these difficulties usually arose, not out of initial attacks by the peasants upon the officials as such, but out of peasant demonstrations against the landlords whom the officials were trying to protect. The revolutionary parties did their best to persuade the peasants that a thorough land reform could come only by way of a political revolution, but they failed to make the mass of the peasants act upon any such belief. In the end, one may hardly escape the conclusion that as compared with the peasant's interest in the land and even in the question of agricultural wages, his interest in political change — whether for itself or as a step toward economic change — was lacking in vigor and driving force.

To say that the widest and deepest interest of the peasants was in the land, is not to say, of course, that the peasants were everywhere agreed upon a single agrarian program. Instead, one finds such programs in bewildering variety; but apparently the bulk of the peasant demands could be bracketed somewhere between a simple reduction of rents, at the one extreme, and at the other, a nationalization of all the land (including that already in peasant hands) without compensation to the owners, with a subsequent allotment and periodic readjustment of holdings in accordance with the labor norm — that is, in proportion to the ability of the households to till the soil with their own hands, and without the help of hired labor. The second Peasants' Congress had voted for a general nationalization, with the use of the land to be allotted according to the labor norm, but had not definitely decided the question of compensation to the former owners and had made no mention of any charges to be levied upon the allottees for the use of the soil. The Labor Group in the First Duma had proposed an immediate nationalization such as would reduce to the labor norm all private holdings which exceeded that measure, and had spoken also of the compensation of the expropriated owners at State expense. For all holdings within the norm, the Group had proposed a "gradual" nationalization. According to this same plan, the use of the nationalized land, including the old State lands and those of the Church and of the Imperial family, was to be allotted in accordance with the labor norm, and the allotments were to be subject thereafter to readjustments in accordance with this same standard, always providing that in any given district the needs of the local agricultural population were to be satisfied before those of non-agriculturists and persons from other localities. For those allottees who did not have enough capital to cultivate the land assigned to them, State loans and subsidies were proposed. In return for the use of the allotment, the holder was to pay a tax proportioned to the size, the quality, and the location of the holding.[85] If this Labor program had been realized, it is hard to see how the capitalistic evolution expected by the Social Democrats could have made much progress in the villages.

Considering the character of the Peasants' Congress and the special conditions surrounding the elections to the Duma, and considering also the fact that not nearly all the peasant deputies aligned themselves with the Labor Group, one is by no means certain that either the resolutions of the Congress or the proposals of the Laborites in the Duma were representative of the bulk of peasant opinion. The numberless petitions and resolutions of the village assemblies must have reflected more directly and more authoritatively the ideas of the peasants, but it does not appear that this mass of material has been collected and analysed with sufficient care to produce a definitive result.[86] The form taken by the direct action of the peasants against the landlords gives also some notion as to the objectives of the movement, but here the easy inference is not always the accurate one: for example, it appears that in some of their strikes the peasants demanded an excessive wage, not with any expectation of obtaining it, but in the hope that the landlord would find it impossible to employ labor at such a price and would therefore abandon his estate.[87] Such a strike was not what it appeared to be: it was not a wage-strike, but an attempt to get control of the land.

In sum, it is impossible to say just where, between the minimum of lower rentals and the maximum of general nationalization, the bulk of peasant opinion centered. Indeed, it would be going very much too far even to assume that the peasants had everywhere a definite program — and yet it is probably safe to say at least this: that those peasants down in the villages who talked of the nationalization of landholding rarely had any thought of a general "socialization" of their equipment and other capital and of the productive process itself. Such revolutionary leanings as existed in rural Russia had come chiefly out of the relations of small, land-short farmers with large landholders, rather than the relations of proletarian and "half-proletarian" laborers with capitalistic cultivators; and such limited capacity as the villagers possessed for collective thought and action was connected primarily with the old communal land-system, and only in a much less degree with proletarian experience under a capitalistic discipline. A substantial minority of the peasant deputies in the Second Duma were members of the Socialist parties and must therefore have hoped for an ultimate "socialization of production"; yet a reading of the debates at the Peasant Congresses and of a scattering selection of the resolutions adopted by local peasant meetings will still give the impression that out in the villages, "nationalization" usually meant (when it meant anything at all) a vague collective ownership, but not a conscious step toward collective cultivation — that it meant essentially an opportunity to extend the old system of peasant agriculture to a wider acreage.

Even if it were possible — as it certainly is not — to define with accuracy the opinions which controlled the bulk of peasant thought, there would still remain a minority opinion, or many different minority opinions, to be accounted for. Of the persistence in some quarters of a devout and whole-hearted Tsarism, there can be no doubt; nor can there be any question that some of the villagers were in outright opposition to the movement against the landlords. Sometimes the better-off peasants joined with the rest in depredations upon the estates, and particularly in the cutting and carting-off of timber and in the illicit pasturing of cattle.[88] However, there were at least a few cases in which the attacks of the peasants were directed against the richer members of their own class, rather than against the landlords; and no doubt because of a fear of loss to themselves, the richer peasants, and especially those who had purchased plots of non-allotment-land, were often indifferent or openly hostile to the agrarian movement.[89] On the other hand, the agricultural wage-workers who had no land, or at least none in the immediate neighborhood of their place of employment, were not usually the leaders of the agrarian movement in general, or even of the labor strikes on the estates (except in the Baltic provinces). Instead, the leading part in these strikes was usually taken by laborers who had some land of their own near by; and indeed there developed in certain instances a definite hostility between the agricultural proletariat and those peasants who divided their time between the landlords' fields and their own.[90]

Thus it was clear that the plowmen of Russia did not form one wholly undivided and ever indivisible peasantry; but this was soon to be clearer still, now that the government had decided to lay its "wager on the strong."

CHAPTER XI

THE WAGER ON THE STRONG

THE REVOLUTIONS of 1905 and 1917 were linked and bound together, rather than divided, by the decade which intervened; and
for many of the peasants this intervening decade was a period of
change so rapid and so profound as in itself to constitute a kind
of revolution. In many thousands of communes, the relations of
peasant with peasant were altered fundamentally, and the mark of
this change was written upon the very face of nature: the old land-
relations were dissolving, the old scattered strips of plow-land were
being assembled into individual farms, and the countryside was
beginning to lose that minutely patched and quilted aspect so un-
familiar to the American eye.

Measured by the breadth and depth of their effect, the laws
which permitted or directed these changes were certainly the most
important agrarian measures that had been enacted in Russia since
the period of the Great Reform. Before the Revolution of 1905
the peasants had been bound more or less effectively to their households and their communes by restrictions upon their personal freedom and by the common holding and the common use of property.
Not all the many forms of linkage were present everywhere, and
the catalogue of details and exceptions has filled many pages of
this book — but by and large, the picture is a true one. Now, however, as a result of the actions of the government and of many millions of the peasantry themselves, these ties were to be greatly
weakened, sometimes dissolved entirely, in favor of a far more
individualistic order.

From the Revolutionary Autumn of 1905 down to the Revolutionary Spring of 1917, the most important legislative measures
dealing primarily with the economic, social, and political status
and inter-relations of the peasantry were those of 3 November
1905, on the cancellation of the redemption-debt; [1] of 4 March
1906, establishing the Land-Organization Commissions; [2] of 5 October 1906, on the abolition of certain restrictions upon the per-

sonal rights of the peasants; [3] of 9 November 1906, on the tenure
and reallocation of the peasant allotment-lands; [4] of 14 June 1910,
extending the *ukaz* of 9 November 1906; [5] and of 29 May 1911,
consolidating and amplifying the regulations governing the allo-
cation of lands.[6] The first four of these measures were issued as
temporary enactments, by authority of the Tsar alone; the last
two were the result of the submission of the temporary land-decrees
for reconsideration by the Council of State and the mild-mannered
Third Duma. These acts will not be dealt with separately here;
instead, an attempt will be made at a systematic grouping of their
terms around the institutions which they affected so profoundly:
the commune and the peasant household.

But first of all, there is some improvement to be recorded in the
relations of the villagers with the administrative hierarchy. The
peasant representatives in the *zemstvo* assemblies were now no
longer to be appointed by the governors from among the candidates elected by the peasants, but were to be chosen by these elected
candidates themselves from their own number. The scope of the
administrative review of the acts of the peasant assemblies was
materially reduced, and the general power of the appointive *zemskii* chief to sentence the peasants, without any sort of formal procedure, to a small fine or a brief imprisonment, was now abolished,
although he might still use these same weapons against the petty
officials elected by the peasantry. Not quite so powerful as he had
been, the *zemskii* chief was still something of a little tsar in the
village, and among the saddest of the peasant folk-songs is a certain
lament devoted to his name.

The reforms just mentioned were made by the *ukaz* of 5 October 1906, and in 1912 there came another important administrative change: the jurisdiction of the *volost* courts was materially
reduced, but in respect to the functions left to them these courts
were given a much greater independence of external authority.[7]

Under the *ukaz* of 5 October 1906, the old joint responsibility
for public obligations was abrogated in the few districts where this
had not already been accomplished by the law of 1903. The corporal punishment of the peasants by the *volost* courts had been
abolished in 1904, and the *ukaz* of October 1906 deprived the communal assemblies of their power to put out at forced labor any
peasant who had fallen behind in his public obligations. Under
the same law, the elective peasant officials and the heads of households lost their rights in respect to the control of passports; that

is, they might no longer prevent a member from going away from the commune or compel him to return. The member was therefore comparatively free in the selection of a place of residence, and when he took advantage of this privilege to settle in a city, he fell under the jurisdiction of the general non-class laws and institutions of the State; but wherever he might reside, he was still subject to the taxing power of his old commune so long as he remained registered there as a member.[8]

If he wished not simply to live elsewhere on a passport, but to withdraw from membership in the commune, he was now in general required, if he had not previously been accepted by some other commune, to register as a kind of member-at-large in his own *volost*, and the authorities of the *volost* were on their part obligated to grant him this registration. Thus, under the *ukaz* of October 1906, a separation from one commune was no longer conditioned upon the voluntary acceptance of the separator by another commune; and yet the separator was still required, as a peasant, to be a registered member of some commune or *volost* — that is, of some purely peasant group.

Under this decree of 1906, the only other requirement for withdrawal from the commune was one that had to do with the land-relation and applied only to certain classes of householders-with-allotments. Heretofore the most serious obstacle to the personal withdrawal of an allotment-holder had been the requirement (often difficult if not impossible to fulfil) that the separator should divest himself of any land still held in repartitional tenure, and of any land under hereditary tenure and still in process of redemption. In the interpretation of the October decree, the Minister of the Interior preserved the old rule respecting the lands which continued to be held in repartitional tenure, and required now the alienation by the separator of any allotment in hereditary tenure which had not been physically consolidated. These restrictions were severe enough; but on the other hand the cancellation of the redemption-debt removed a major obstacle to the transfer of the land, while the new agrarian laws (presently to be described) were designed to facilitate the conversion of repartitional allotments into hereditary holdings, and to make all hereditary holdings more easily salable, as well as to promote the formation of consolidated farms, which might be either sold or retained in the event of a personal separation.[9] Thus, under certain conditions, a personal withdrawal might still be hampered by the holder's connection with the land, but in general this impediment was less serious than it had been before the revolution.

By and large, it comes to this: the peasants had not lost their identity as a class (a major section of Russian law was still devoted to their distinctive rights, duties, usages, and institutions), but the gap between the peasantry and the other classes was not so wide as it had been hitherto; the interference of external authority in the affairs of the commune was now somewhat restricted; the tie of joint responsibility had been broken; the power of the commune over those members who lived in the village was materially reduced; and a temporary removal or a permanent separation might be effected far more easily than before.[10]

Next to be considered is the fate of those communal relationships which linked the peasants together on the basis of their interest in the allotment-lands; and it is precisely here, in the field of these land-relationships, that the history of the inter-revolutionary decade finds its center.

In 1905 the communes of Russia were of two major types: those in which the tenure was essentially collective, with the right of quantitative repartition among the households as the clearest embodiment of this collectivism; and those where the households were joined by certain secondary land-relationships, but where the greater part of the land (sometimes all of it) was divided into hereditary holdings which could not be subjected to reallotment. In addition to these two major groups of communes, there were a few in which some of the allotments originally granted in repartional tenure had since been converted into hereditary holdings. More than three-quarters of the peasant households with allotments belonged in 1905 to repartitional communes, and would be directly affected by any change in this communal land-relationship; that is to say, more than nine million households were afloat in this particular stream of history.

In the repartitional communes, the house-and-garden plots had been held in heredity, but the holders had not hitherto been permitted to sell such plots to anyone outside the commune without the consent of the peasant assembly. Now, however, the law of 9 November 1906 cleared these plots of this restriction. But much more important was the question as to what was to happen to the other lands — those which were divided for household use, but remained subject to quantitative adjustment through repartition (these were chiefly the plow-lands and the meadows), and those which remained undivided and in common use (chiefly the natural pastures). In the case of lands in repartitional tenure and still under redemption, it had been impossible, since 1893, for any peasant to convert his allotment into an hereditary holding without the consent of the assembly, but this and all other special restrictions applicable exclusively to lands in process of redemption were voided automatically by the cancellation of further payments. And besides this, the old provision for individual conversions of tenure in the case of lands free from redemption-dues (a provision which had been hitherto of little practical importance, inasmuch as almost all the allotment-land was still undergoing redemption down to 1906), was now modified in such a way as greatly to facilitate these individual conversions: that is, a practical if not an equitable method was provided for determining the size of the allotment to be assigned, definite rules were laid down respecting the separating holder's rights in the undivided lands (such as the common pastures), and the commune was deprived of its old privilege of offering a money indemnity instead of granting an hereditary title.

The practical effect of this new legislation was so wide and so deep that its provisions deserve a more detailed statement. Under the *ukaz* of 9 November, the householder might demand and receive, with or without the consent of the communal assembly, a separate and permanent title to all or a certain part of the strips of plow-land held by his household. If there had been no general partition within the twenty-four years preceding the demand for separation (or, according to the law of 1910, no general partition since 1893), then the holder was to receive all the strips which were in his hands at the moment of his demand, even though his household might have so changed in composition that any new partition might be expected to deprive the family of some of these strips. If a general repartition had been carried out within the period named, then any surplus of land in the hands of the family was to be deeded to the householder only if he paid the commune for this surplus at the original redemption-rate. When the concrete and specific strips of plow-land were deeded over in the manner described, the holder was also to be guaranteed in the perpetual use of the same quantity of meadow land as was in the hands of the household at the time of his demand for separation, and was to share perpetually in the use of any undivided lands (such as the natural pastures). Thus the share in the meadows was to be fixed only as to quantity — not as to place; and in the law of 1910 it was provided that wherever possible the share in the use of lands previously undivided was also to be given a quantitative determination.[11] And like the house-and-garden plots, the separated strips and the accompanying use-rights might be sold without the consent of the communal assembly.[12]

Under the stimulus of these provisions of 1906 and 1910, more than two and one-half million householders applied specifically, before the end of the year 1915, for separation of title. Certain of these applications were withdrawn, or were for some reason denied or delayed in their execution, but by 1 January 1916, confirmation had been granted in approximately two million cases.[13]

All this has to do with the opportunities and inducements offered to the individual householder hitherto under repartitional tenure to secure a separate and negotiable title to his share of the communal land. But besides this, the commune as a body still had its old right to do away with repartition, and by a two-thirds' vote to divide its lands in perpetuity among its member-households. Incomplete returns show that during the period 1906–1916, more than one hundred and thirty thousand households were affected by general dissolutions carried out under this old provision.[14]

However, it was scarcely to be expected that any question of such importance to the peasantry would be left to find its answer in the voluntary actions of the peasants themselves. The old land-relationships had been maintained in part by force, and force was also to be used in their destruction. In eight brief paragraphs, the law of 1910 proclaimed the dissolution of repartitional tenure and the establishment of hereditary holding in every commune where there had been no *general* redistribution since the land was originally allotted in the course of the Great Reform. This arbitrary dissolution-law included within its scope many communes where partial rather than general redistribution had taken place, as well as all those where there had been no redistribution of any kind; in other words, it included many communes where the repartitional function was more or less alive. In the communes covered by the law, the head of the household was recognized as the owner of those plow-lands which were in the factual possession of the household at the time of the publication of the law, and also as the hereditary holder of a share in the other lands of the commune, to be apportioned in the manner already prescribed for cases of individual conversion of tenure. In these communes — the ones which had possessed, but had not exercised, the right of repartition

— the hereditary tenure did not have to be established by any action on the part of the peasants; it was declared by the law to be *actually in existence,* and provision was made for the issuance, upon application, of documents which would attest this fact in each particular case.[15]

Inasmuch as no general and systematic record had been kept of the practice of reallotment, it was impossible to say, without a thorough local investigation, just how many communes and how many households should fall within the scope of this arbitrary dissolution-law. A Ministerial estimate (of doubtful accuracy, and officially declared to be incomplete) announced the number of such households as more than three and one-half millions; [16] but down to the end of 1915, documentary confirmations of title had been issued under this decree for the holdings of only about 470,-000 households.[17] It appears that as a rule this dissolution-law had little or no practical effect in the communes where no one applied for a confirmation of title, and it is probable that most of these groups continued to repartition the meadows every year, and in general to carry on their communal life as before. On the other hand, it seems that the law was arbitrarily applied in practice to all the households in each commune where even a single household requested a confirmation of title under this statute. It has been estimated that perhaps 1,700,000 households were dragged into hereditary tenure in this fashion, with no application on their own part, but this figure must be regarded as only a very rough approximation, and it is probable that it includes a second counting of some of the households which had previously effected a separation of title under the law of 1906.[18] To the 470,000 documentary confirmations one may add, provisionally, this very doubtful figure of 1,700,000, thus producing a total number of effective conversions of tenure under the arbitrary dissolution-law which runs to some 2,100,000 or 2,200,000. The remaining households covered by this law (1,300,000, more or less) were in a thoroughly unstable and transitory situation, and indeed the status of all excepting the 470,000 is so uncertain that one ought perhaps to give up any attempt at differentiation.

In sum, the conversions thus far accounted for are: 2,000,000 under the optional clauses of 1906 and 1910; about 130,000 under the old provision for general dissolution by a two-thirds' vote; and under the arbitrary dissolution-law of 1910, about 470,000 documented cases, and perhaps 1,700,000 others not yet certified — a grand total of some 2,600,000 with all the necessary seals and records, and 1,700,000 or so without. But even this is not the whole story, for there were cases of individual conversion and of general dissolution which are not included in any of the groups already mentioned — the cases which occurred when, under the conditions presently to be described, certain lands, *up to the moment repartitional in tenure,* were subjected to a physical consolidation of the scattered strips into unitary holdings — a change which always (or nearly always) here involved in itself a separation of title.[19] For the period 1907–1915, there are records of the formation of 1,200,000 consolidated holdings on allotment-lands,[20] but the writer can find no means of determining how many of these consolidations involved in themselves new *juridical* conversions, and how many, on the other hand, affected only such lands as had been allotted in heredity during the Great Reform or allotted at that time in repartitional tenure but judicially separated *before* the date of their physical consolidation. The total number of consolidations of the former class (those which in themselves involved conversions of title), ought to be added to the grand total of some 4,300,000 conversions already given above, but inasmuch as the number proposed to be added remains an unknown quantity, all that one may say is that the true total of conversions evidently exceeded 4,300,000.

Now among the twelve million peasant households with allotments in the fifty *guberniias* in 1905, about 2,800,000 held their land at that time in hereditary tenure, and 9,200,000 in repartitional tenure. There are no inclusive data on the number of households with allotments ten years later, but if their number continued throughout the decade to increase at its former rate through subdivisions, there must have been between thirteen and fourteen million of such households in 1915. By this time, the 2,800,000 hereditary holdings of 1905 had probably been increased, from within, by subdivision, to more than three million, and to these there had been added by the conversions of title already described about 4,300,000 holdings which had formerly been under repartitional tenure. It would therefore appear that toward the end of 1915, the total number of households with hereditary allotments was something like 7,300,000 (3,000,000 under the old tenures, more than 2,600,000 under new documents, and 1,700,000 under heaven-knows-what arbitrary rulings of the administration) — altogether more than half, then, of all the allotment-holding households, and indeed far more than half if one should add also the remainder of those covered by the arbitrary dissolution-law.[21]

This question of the balance of forces between the two kinds of peasant tenure is one of such importance that it simply must be faced — and this necessity is the only excuse for presenting here an estimate which is so riddled with *if's* and *and's*. Within the limits of the published materials, the obstacles to accuracy are apparently insurmountable, but no harm can be done by the offering of this estimate, unless the reader attribute to it a quality to which it has no claim; and in any case the figures will serve to emphasize the fact that in many thousands of communes, the old land-relations were being strained and broken from within, or demolished by official pressure from without.

Of the vast importance of this change, there can be no doubt whatever; and yet the American reader, accustomed to a country-side divided into isolated farms, is more likely to exaggerate than to minimize the significance of these developments and the degree of individualization which resulted. The point is, that separation of title did not in itself result in the establishment of an isolated and independent farm — far from it. It has already been said that before the Revolution of 1905 almost all the household allotments of plow-land (whether under repartitional or hereditary tenure) were made up of small strips scattered among the several great fields which lay about the village; and most of the separations of title recorded during the inter-revolutionary decade did not result from, or lead to, the physical consolidation of the scattered holdings. It is probable that on the eve of the Revolution of 1917, among more than five and one-half million allotments with old or newly-documented hereditary titles, at least three-fourths were still made up of scattered strips; and among such unconsolidated hereditary holdings, whether their titles dated from the Emancipation or from some current act of separation, the familiar land-linkage still persisted in many forms. Equalizing repartition was, of course, prohibited here — that was the central fact. Then, too, the newly separated holdings might be sold without the consent of the peasant assembly, while the sale of the old hereditary allotments was greatly facilitated by new rules governing the documentary procedure in such transactions.[22] And yet wherever the holdings remained in scattered strips, the plow-lands might not be enclosed or built upon without the consent of the assembly, the compulsory crop-cycle and the right of common pasturage after

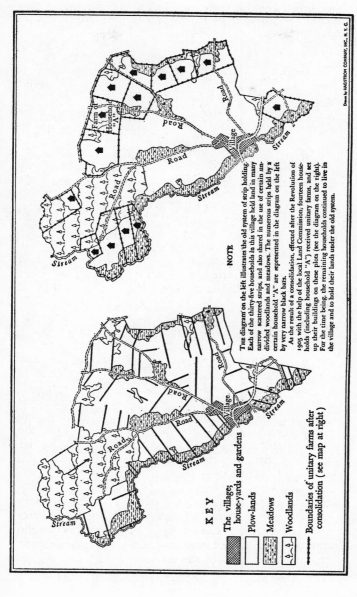

KEY

The village; house-yards and gardens

Plow-lands

Meadows

Woodlands

Boundaries of unitary farms after consolidation (see map at right)

NOTE

THE diagram on the left illustrates the old system of strip holding. Each of the thirty-five households in this village held land in many narrow scattered strips, and also shared in the use of certain undivided woodlands and meadows. The numerous strips held by a certain household "A" are represented in the diagram on the left by very narrow black bars.

As the result of a consolidation, effected after the Revolution of 1905 with the help of the local Land Commission, fourteen households (including household "A") received unitary farms, and set up their buildings on these plots (see the diagram on the right). For the time being, the remaining households continued to live in the village and to hold their lands under the old system.

PEASANT HOLDINGS — OLD STYLE AND NEW

The diagrams are based on: Direction Générale de l'Organisation agraire et de l'Agriculture, *Les Travaux des Commissions Agraires (1907–1911)*, St. P., 1912, pp. 107–108 and plates 27 and 28.

harvest and in fallow years were still in force under the control of this same assembly, and almost always a *part* of the land remained even yet in *common tenure* — sometimes with the individual use-right fixed as to quantity (though not as to place), sometimes with the whole matter of use left to the regulation of the peasant meeting.[23] Thus, where there was no physical consolidation, the divorce of holding from holding was by no means complete: under hereditary tenure, the interrelationships had always been comparatively weak, and now the new separations of title had weakened these relationships in many a village where they had once been strong; but wherever the land-interests of the peasants were still interlocked in one or more of the ways described, there the commune still had something more than a political significance.

All this with respect to the surviving land-relationships applies, as has been said, to the allotments with old or newly-established hereditary title, and only to those allotments of this type where the plow-land remained in scattered strips. But it has been said, too, that (as far as the records of the Land Commissions reveal the matter) there were among these juridically separate holdings at the end of the year 1915 about 1,200,000 which had recently undergone at least a partial physical consolidation. And it was precisely the achievement of this fuller individualization that was the dear and special objective of officialdom in the inter-revolutionary period.

In any attempt to deal with the laws on this subject of physical consolidation, a line may be drawn between commune and commune upon the basis of the original character of the land-tenure established in each at the time of the Great Reform. Where the allotments had first been granted in hereditary tenure, the provisions of the new laws were comparatively simple. Now as before, the individual householder might effect a consolidation only with the consent of every other hereditary holder whose lands would be displaced in the process;[24] but where it was a question of a general consolidation throughout the commune, the law underwent a fundamental change. The *ukaz* of 9 November 1906 provided that upon the demand of a two-thirds' majority in the communal assembly, the scattered lands of each household should be consolidated, in so far as possible, into a single plot;[25] the law of 14 June 1910 reduced the required vote to a simple majority;[26] and the law of 29 May 1911 specifically provided a means of dividing permanently, by a similar vote, the lands which had not before been subjected to even a temporary division for separate use.[27] It will be remembered that under hereditary tenure the displacements involved in a physical consolidation had as a rule been permitted, before the Revolution of 1905, only with the consent of all the peasants whose holdings were affected; but now the government and the Duma had assigned to a simple majority in the commune the power to shift the holdings of all the members in the process of establishing unitary farms. Thus, in the cause of economic independence and individual property-right, this legislation increased for the moment the power of the commune over the hereditary holding, and violated the already existing property-right of the hereditary holder.

So much, then, for the communes where the original tenure had been hereditary. Turning now to the case of the communes where the land had originally been granted in repartitional tenure, one finds the new legislation more complex and the possibilities more varied — for here under the new laws the individual householder was not usually obliged to wait for the consent of his neighbors, but might under certain conditions obtain a permanent and more or less unified holding even against the unanimous opposition of the communal assembly.[28] Under the law of 1906, the commune was obliged to grant to any householder who demanded it at the time of a general repartition, his household share of the plowland in the form of a holding consolidated "in so far as possible" in one place. If the householder had previously secured a separation *of title* under this law, he might make his demand for a consolidated plot *at any time,* and the commune was obliged either to comply, or to offer instead a certain money payment.[29] In the laws of 1910 and 1911, the provisions were pushed much farther, and the commune was required to comply at any time with the demand of any householder for consolidation (whether or not he had previously secured a separate *title*), provided only that in the judgment of the local Land-Organization Commission, the consolidation would involve no "special difficulties." Thus it was the commission, not the commune, that was to decide whether the demand should be met; and in case the former body found the consolidation especially difficult, or impossible, the commune was obliged to offer in place of the land a money indemnity, the amount of which would also be determined, in case of dispute, by the commission.[30] Further than this, the law of 1911 provided that wherever the plow-land was consolidated in the manner described, the householder might also enforce the physical separation, for his benefit, of his due share of the meadow, and of any other communal holdings (such as pastures, wood-lots, and the like) if the basis for a permanent partition could be determined; and finally, if he wished to remove his buildings from the village to his consolidated acres, he might claim the annexation thereto of an additional bit of plow-land in exchange for the old site of his house and garden.[31] Even the most casual comparison of these measures with the laws in force at the beginning of the century will show how far the government had gone since 1893, when it had withdrawn the only means then available for the separation and consolidation, without the consent of the commune, of a repartitional allotment in process of redemption. Now under the new laws, the situation was exactly reversed — and however reluctant the commune might be to carve out a single unitary farm from the complex pattern of its holdings, it could not escape this Shylock's forfeit, even by the payment of an indemnity, unless it had the support of the Land Commission in its refusal. And as to whether the commissions were more likely to lean toward the individual separatist, or toward the commune — this important question will be examined presently.

In respect to the wholesale consolidation of all the allotments in communes which remained up to the time of consolidation wholly under repartitional tenure, the laws of 1906, 1910,[32] and 1911 preserved the old rule which required a two-thirds' vote of the assembly, and this same majority was required by the law of 1911 in communes where a part of the holders had effected a separation of title before the consolidation. In behalf of the old system of tenure and of physical arrangement, an important reservation was made in the law of 1911 when it provided that at the time of a general consolidation, any minority in the commune who held scattered strips in repartitional tenure might preserve both features of this system for themselves if they so desired. Where, on the other hand, all the holdings had been transferred to hereditary tenure before the question of consolidation was raised, the vote required for a general consolidation was fixed by the law of 1911 at a simple majority.[33] It is evident, then, that a mere conversion of title did not give the holder secure possession of such-and-such particular strips of land; a full security of tenure was established only after a physical consolidation.

The wholesale readjustment of the communal holdings was not necessarily confined to the plow-lands: the law of 1911 provided for the final partition, under the voting-rules above described, of lands (such as natural pastures) which had hitherto been used in common without even a temporary physical division.[34] And finally, it was provided that when a general consolidation took place, each householder who wished to move out to his new farm might, by agreement with the commune, exchange his old house-and-garden plot in the village street for an additional area adjoining his culti- vated fields.[35]

Now it is clear that quite irrespective of the juridical form of tenure — whether hereditary or repartitional — which had ex- isted up to the moment of consolidation in any particular case, this legislation aimed at physical readjustments of two kinds; first, the final assortment into unitary plots of the lands which had pre- viously been held in scattered strips; and second, the final parti- tion (and if possible the physical annexation to these unitary hold- ings) of the lands which had previously been used undivided. The change, however, was more than physical; it produced a form of holding which was economically and juridically much more thor- oughly individualized than any holding could be, even under he- reditary title, so long as it remained in scattered strips.[36] Where the plow-land was now consolidated, a part of the other lands very often remained in common use, but the proportion of such land was unquestionably much smaller here than elsewhere. The fun- damental difference was, however, that consolidation gave the right to enclose the unified plot, and automatically abolished in respect to it the compulsory common crop-cycle and the right of common pasture after harvest and during fallow years.[37] Here, then, upon the unitary holding, as nowhere else upon the allotment-land, the holder might sow and reap as he pleased, within the limits of the means and the knowledge which he pos- sessed. Even here, however, the holding did not have all the char- acteristics of private landed property; that is, in all but the most exceptional circumstances,[38] it still retained the special character of "allotment-land," [39] and as such it might not be mortgaged to any individual or to any private institution, nor might it be sold to anyone other than a peasant,[40] and even as among the members of the peasant class, the purchase and sale of allotment-lands was not unrestricted, since the law of 1910 placed a limit upon the amount of such land that any one peasant might purchase within the boundaries of a single *uezd* — a limit fixed in most of the *guberniias* at six maximum "soul-allotments" as defined in the old Statutes of Emancipation. And besides all this, the inheritance of every form of allotment-land was still governed, not by the general laws on real property, but by local peasant custom.[41]

In all that has been said thus far about the right to set up unitary holdings upon the allotment-lands, little direct attention has been given to the practical difficulties which stood in the way of the exercise of this right. Still, if the reader has before him a picture of the houses, barns, and sheds all clustered along the village street, of the open fields with their quilting of intermingled strips, of the meadow staked off in patchwork for this year's mowing, of the natural pasture with its browsing fellowship of all the animals of the village — if the reader visualizes some such panorama, he will have no trouble in seeing that to convert this conglomerate of plots and rights into individual farms was a task of almost incomparable difficulty. Once man and nature had been accommodated to each other under the old system, nature herself seemed to resist the change: for under what terms could the good land in this field be exchanged for the poor land in that; how could every new farm be so located that a proper share, or any share, of the natural meadow and the pasture-land would fall within its borders; how was a supply of water to be provided for every isolated farm, especially in the treeless *step*, where the traveller might drive for a whole day along a water-course, through an almost continuous double line of peasant houses, and then turn away from the stream and drive all the following day through waterless grainfields without seeing a single dwelling ?

To advance the enormous task of disentanglement, the government established Land-Organization Commissions in most of the *guberniias* and *uezds* of European Russia. According to the instructions of 1906, these bodies were simply to co-operate in the reallocation of the land when requested to do so by the peasants,[42] but in 1911 it was provided that the execution of all such physical readjustments as have here been described was to be in charge of the commissions — except in the few districts where they had not been established — and was to be carried out chiefly at public expense.[43]

It has been shown that a physical reallocation did not require the consent of all the parties concerned; on the contrary, the new laws made it possible for one or more peasants to enforce such a consolidation of their own holdings as could not possibly be effected without the rearrangement of all or a part of the other holdings in the commune and might therefore arouse the strongest opposition on the part of the other holders. Who, then, would have the Land Commissions' favor — the peasant individualists, or the communal opposition? The answer may perhaps be found in a study of the composition of the commissions, and of the instructions under which they were called upon to act.

The question as to personnel is soon answered. Of the twelve (or thirteen) members of each *uezd* commission, three (later four) were elected by the peasants, while the others were either officially appointed, or became members by virtue of their holding of other official posts, or were elected by the *zemstvo* assembly (which was controlled in its turn by the larger landed proprietors). Among the fifteen (or sixteen) members (later reduced to ten) who made up each *guberniia* commission, six (later two) were elected by the *zemstvo* assembly of the *guberniia,* and it was required that three (later one) of this number should be from the peasant class. However the peasants, as such, did not at any time have the right to act separately in the election of representatives to the *guberniia* commissions.[44] It is therefore clear enough that in both the *uezds* and the *guberniias* the commissions were in the complete control of the bureaucracy and the non-peasant proprietors.

In the official instructions of 1908, 1909, and 1911, the commissions were advised that the preferred form for the reorganized holdings was the completely consolidated farm within which were included all the lands of the holder, and upon which the house and other buildings were established.[45] If the organization of such holdings proved too difficult, then at least all the plow-land of the holder must be assembled in one plot, and the commissions must use all their influence to bring about the final partition of the meadows, the pastures, and other such holdings, with the establishment for each holder of a single plot of each of these types of land.[46] In order to facilitate the consolidation of all the lands of each claimant, irrespective of any differences in the legal form of their tenure, the law of 1911 provided that not only allotment-holdings but non-allotment-lands owned by individual peasants, by peasant associations, and by entire communes might be included in the local readjustment.[47] Under certain conditions, the commission might enforce the acceptance of one type of land in lieu of another, say of meadow land in place of plow-land; but in all exchanges compulsory upon one party the commissions were directed to give attention not only to acreage but to quality — that is, they were to exchange value for value, and they were also directed to use every effort to bring the parties into an agreement.[48] "The fundamental purpose" of the land-settlement was officially declared to be "the formation of independent farms through the concentration in one place of all the lands of different types and of various tenures which pertain to a given holder." [49] The attitude of the government toward the commune was clear enough; and as far as the Land-Organization Commissions were concerned, the character of their membership and the tone of their instructions made it certain that they would favor and support the cause of individualism against collectivism in the contest now under way.

To assist in the establishment of new individual farms, the government took measures still other than those that have been mentioned. In certain cases, for example, it granted fifteen-year loans without interest, or paid out non-returnable subsidies to the farmers. The reports of these financial operations do not differentiate between the farms established through the consolidation of allotment-holdings and those set up upon non-allotment-lands newly purchased by the peasants, but down to the end of 1915, three hundred thousand loans averaging about one hundred *rubls* each, and fifty-eight thousand grants averaging about twenty-two *rubls*, had been approved and paid. Further than this, the government employed "farm-advisers" and model farms in increasing numbers to stimulate the development of peasant agriculture in general, but more particularly in its individualized form.[50]

Besides providing for the establishment of consolidated farms, the statute of 1911 was also concerned with other less radical measures, both physical and juridical, for the readjustment of the land-system. For example, it provided that where the land was held in repartitional tenure, some of the members might withdraw and set up a smaller commune of their own upon the consolidated lands which the parent commune would be obliged to assign to them.[51] Within the new group, the system of strip-holding might or might not be preserved, but the establishment of a village upon the newly separated tract would at least bring the re-settled households nearer to the lands which they would cultivate. Again, where a commune owned certain lands in common with another commune, or with a private proprietor, either party might secure the consolidation and separation of its share,[52] and where the lands owned by one commune were physically intermixed with those of another commune, or of a private proprietor, or of the Church or the State, the holdings were to be sorted out upon the demand of either party if the existing intermixture were recognized by the local Land Commission as "prejudicial to the exploitation" of the land.[53]

These last-named provisions were important enough, yet they did not stand at the central pressure-point of agrarian change, and history must place the emphasis where the government placed it, upon outright individualization. The Land Commissions were flooded with requests for physical readjustments, though only a part of the petitioners aimed at the establishment of individual consolidated farms. According to the official returns, nearly six and one-half million households were covered by applications of various kinds received before the end of 1916, and even if this number be reduced by two millions (as one critic says it should be) through the elimination of requests not made in proper form or afterwards withdrawn,[54] the remaining number was still enormously in excess of the technical capacity of the commissions for fulfilment.[55]

The only application figures of which a detailed analysis has been published are the official ones, unreduced. According to these data, for the period down to the end of 1914, almost half of the total number of households involved were covered by petitions which called for the establishment of individual farms, rather than for the other forms of physical readjustment which have been described.[56] By the end of 1915, the commissions had made changes affecting the allotments of nearly 2,400,000 peasant households. Of this number more than 1,200,000 had been provided with consolidated farms in place of their old scattered allotments,[57] and during the year 1916 approximately another hundred thousand consolidated holdings were established.[58] Thus, among all the allotments in existence in the fifty *guberniias* on the eve of the Revolution of 1917, something like one-tenth had been consolidated by the Land Commissions during the inter-revolutionary period.

However, it is not to be inferred from this statement that the remaining nine-tenths of the allotments still retained in every case the form of scattered strips. A small minority of these holdings had originally been allotted in unitary form or had already been consolidated before the Revolution of 1905 — though no one knows their number; and besides this, it was possible under certain conditions to arrange for consolidations after 1905 without the help of a Land Commission, though there is every reason to believe that the number of adjustments so effected was comparatively small. Still, the fact remains that the commissions recorded only those changes in which they actually took part; the unitary holdings previously in existence or independently established upon the allotment-lands, are therefore not included in the grand total of 1,300,000, and their number constitutes the x-quantity so familiar in Russian statistics.[59]

On the other hand, it is not to be assumed that in the case of the farms set up by the commissions (the 1,300,000), every one of the old land-ties had been cut. On the contrary, 6.7 per cent of the land assignable to the farms so established before the end of 1916 was left physically undivided but subject to fixed use-rights assigned to the peasants concerned.[60] Of much greater significance is the fact, revealed by a limited investigation made in 1913, that the proportion of the individualized farms which still shared in these undivided lands was very considerable — perhaps more than one-half of the total number. Even in the case of the so-called *khutors*, where the farm-buildings stood upon the plow-land rather than in the village, the proportion of farms with shares in lands still undivided was almost one-fourth.[61] Also, these *khutors* apparently formed only a minority of the consolidated farms, and in most cases the houses and barns of the owners of such farms still stood beside that great avenue of concourse for geese, pigs, sheep, cows, dogs, horses, chickens, and human beings — the village street.[62]

So much, then, for this decade of change in the tenure and the physical arrangement of the allotments. A great deal of fundamental history had been written during these years and now in the last days of the old Empire the thirteen or fourteen millions of peasant allotments might be classified, with respect to the degree of their individualization, somewhat as follows: first, some five millions of holdings in unchanged repartitional tenure; second, 1,300,000 holdings covered by the arbitrary dissolution-law of 1910 but thus far apparently not brought under its actual operation; third, 1,700,000 holdings already practically affected in some degree by this law but not yet fully documented; fourth, about 4,300,000 holdings with fully-established hereditary title but still in scattered strips; and finally, at least 1,300,000 with similar titles and with a partly or wholly consolidated form. The figures are no more than rough approximations, but they will have to serve.

In the face of so much that is new, it is easy to forget that after a separation of title alone, the old land-linkage was still preserved in many of its aspects, and that even a physical consolidation failed in many cases to cut the last tie of common property. Under the combined stimulus of peasant ambition and official policy, the structure of rural society had been changing at a headlong rate — of that there can be no question; yet it is also clear that a great deal still survived of the old collective interests and the old apparatus for collective action. . . The writing of history is a task of many difficulties, and one of the most serious of these (the one that is most obvious just here) is the difficulty of maintaining a proper balance of emphasis between the novel elements in any given time and situation, and those survivals which continue to have a profound importance in the life of the time, but are so easily taken for granted by contemporaries and so often forgotten by the chroniclers of a later day.

If the commune in its economic and political aspects was profoundly affected by the changes of this decade, so too was that miniature collective, the peasant household. Wherever the allotment was held in hereditary tenure upon the basis of the original grant, or came to be so held as the result of a subsequent conversion, the new laws arbitrarily declared the entire holding to be the property, not of the household, as hitherto, but of the head of the household as an individual.[63] It will be remembered that even in the communes with repartitional tenure, the house-and-garden plots had never been subject to reallotment, but had been held in heredity by the households; and now by the law of 1906, these plots, too, became the individual possession of the head of the household.[64] In these laws on the individualization of the family property, certain exceptions were made in favor of members of the household who were not descendants of its acting head, and some of these members were recognized as joint holders with the head,[65] but under the major provisions of this legislation, millions of peasants were deprived, at one grand sweep, of their most important property-right — the right to share in the use of the household allotment, and under certain conditions to secure, even against the will of the head of the house, a partition of this land for their own benefit. Thus the old system of collective household tenure no longer applied to the hereditary allotments, or to the house-and-garden plots in the repartitional communes, but only to other lands still held in repartitional tenure. In respect to these lands, the law requiring the consent of a majority of the peasant assembly for a partition of the allotment was still in force, but the additional restrictions which had been imposed upon such partitions by the law of 1886 were now abolished.[66] In respect to the non-allotment-holdings of the peasants, no change was made, since these holdings had never been regarded as household property, but as the property of the individual under the general terms of the Civil Code.

So much for the household and its land — but what of the implements and the animals necessary to the cultivation of the allotment? When all or a part of the holding was converted from household property into individual property, were these movables individualized too? The question would seem to be important enough, but the law made no mention of it.[67] And what of the earnings of the junior members of the household, present or absent — earnings which had also been regarded as collective property, subject to the control of the head of the house? It cannot be discovered that there was any direct attack upon this question, but as will presently be shown, the personal freedom of the junior members was greatly increased, and this must have made it difficult and often impossible for the householder to maintain his old economic control.

It might have been expected that the partial abolition of the joint-property system within the household would have been accompanied by the abolition of the members' joint responsibility for taxes, but as a matter of fact the solidarity of the household in this respect was still preserved.[68] On the other hand, the head of the house was deprived of his power over the passports of the members,[69] and the consent of the parents was no longer prerequisite to the personal separation of junior members from the commune.[70] Thus the peasant household, like the peasant commune, was weakened by the removal of old legal supports, and by the positive legal measures taken to cut away some of the old ties. It was clearly the intention of the law-makers that both the minor and the major collectives should be stretched or broken to make way for a prosperous (and conservative) individualism, but the change was far from complete and there was much that still survived of the older order.

In describing the changes of the decade in the land-relationships of the peasants, attention has thus far been given almost exclusively to their allotment-holdings, and yet it will be remembered that before the Revolution of 1905 the villagers had purchased a considerable body of non-allotment-lands. These purchases were made by the old communes, or by new associations formed especially for the purpose, or by individual peasants; and it has been shown that before 1905, collective purchasing was responsible for a constantly increasing share of the acquisitions. During the inter-revolutionary decade, this situation was exactly reversed, and individual purchases increased rapidly in relative importance. A very large part of the land acquired by the peasants during this decade was bought with the help of loans advanced by the Peasants' Land Bank, with that institution either acting simply as intermediary in the sale, or first acquiring the land outright on its own part and then reselling it to the peasant purchasers. With the help of subsidies from the State, the Bank made loans at terms with which no private lender could possibly compete, and in all this it extended exceptional advantages to individual buyers, as against the collectives.[71] In part at least as a result of this favoritism, an impressive change took place in the relative importance of the three types of purchasers who bought land from (or through) the Bank: speaking in terms of proportion only, there was a moderate decline in the part played by the associations, a precipitate decline in the case of the communes, and a sharp rise in the case of individuals. During the period 1906–1916, the associations and the communes together purchased nearly one-third again as much land as the solitary buyers; and yet when the returns of the Bank are examined year by year, there is no mistaking the *trend* toward individual purchasing [72] — a trend toward individualization such as has already been discovered on the other data on the commune and the household.

Leaving now the question as to whether the buying was individual or collective, and considering only the quantitative net result of purchases and sales for the years 1906–1914, one finds that during this period more than nine and one-half millions of *desiatinas* were added to the non-allotment-holdings of the peasants and the Cossacks in forty-seven *guberniias*. The returns, in part unpublished, indicate that there was a rapid increase in the annual net gains of the villagers during the years immediately following the Revolution of 1905, and that the average net gain per year for the entire period (1906–1914) was far above that for any preceding decade. Also the returns for the period as a whole indicate that the increase was not localized, but extended to every one of the forty-seven *guberniias* covered by the reports; and yet in spite of all this, the growth of the peasant population was far more than proportionate to the expansion of the peasant holdings.[73]

Among the other landholders for whom data are available for the period 1906–1914, the Peasants' Land Bank is the only one which shows a gain — and the Bank was, of course, only a kind of broker, a transitional holder of lands destined for resale to small cultivators. In 1914, the Bank had in its possession two million more *desiatinas* than in 1906. The losers, in so far as the writer is able to identify them, were the State, the Imperial family, and — above all — the nobles. The State completed the sale of 239,000 *desiatinas* directly to the peasants, while 1,258,000 *desiatinas* of the lands of the Imperial family were sold to the Peasants' Bank, for resale. In spite of all the earlier talk of devoting the State and Imperial lands to the needs of the peasantry, the total amount of these lands actually sold to the Bank or directly to the peasants is not particularly impressive. The nobles, on the other hand, suffered a huge net loss, amounting to more than 10,200,000 *desiatinas* in the forty-seven *guberniias*.

With the help of such data, published and unpublished, as are available, the changes of the inter-revolutionary period, and the situation at the end of 1914, are summarized in the second table appended to this volume. It appears that on the latter date, with the Great War already under way, and the new revolution not far beyond the horizon, the peasants and the Cossacks of the forty-seven *guberniias* owned about one hundred and seventy million *desiatinas* of land out of a total of three hundred and eighty-eight million *desiatinas*. The Cossacks were on the average so much better provided with land than were their peasant neighbors that the former ought properly to be excluded from the calculation, if the data available for the later years would permit this to be done. As a step in this direction, one may at least subtract from the combined peasant-Cossack holdings the fourteen and one-half million *desiatinas* of Cossack allotment-land reported in 1905. It is apparently safe to say, then, that at the end of the year 1914 the peasants held not more than one hundred and fifty-six million *desiatinas* in the forty-seven *guberniias* — or about forty per cent of the whole. However, the remaining sixty per cent of the acreage included a large amount of forest and of waste, and certainly represented very much less than sixty per cent of the land-value of these *guberniias.*

The peasants were still trying to get control of the non-peasant land, but during the period between the two revolutions the visions and the violence of 1905 were replaced (partially and for the time being) by a campaign of working, saving, and buying. It is not to be supposed, however, that this campaign was without its casualties. The purchases from (and through) the Peasants' Bank were made at prices materially higher than those paid before 1905,[74] and at the end of 1914 about three-sevenths of all the non-allotment-land of the villagers in the forty-seven *guberniias* was under mortgage to the Peasants' Bank for loans totalling nearly one billion, two hundred and fifty million *rubls,* or more than three-quarters of the official valuation of the mortgaged land. The returns of the Bank for the Empire as a whole show that arrears were accumulating after 1910, and amounted at the end of the last pre-war year to some eighteen and one-half million *rubls,* or nearly one-third as much as the new sum which currently fell due to the Bank during the year.[75]

IT IS impossible to discuss the buying of non-allotment-land by the peasants, or the conversions to hereditary tenure, or the physical consolidations, without raising again the old problem of economic differentiation in the village. Before the Revolution of 1905, the peasants lived on various levels of well-being and ill-being, and one may hardly take it for granted that the best-off and the worst-off were all affected in the same manner and degree by the changes of the following decade. It is therefore perfectly natural to ask: *Who* separated ? *Who* consolidated ? *Who* bought land ? *Why* did these particular peasants act as they did ? And *just what* — if anything — did all this have to do with economic differentiation and with conflicts of interest within the village ?

In the method by which individual conversions to hereditary tenure were in practice effected, there is more than a hint of friction between peasant and peasant. The laws of 1906 and 1910 provided that each petition should be presented first of all to the communal assembly; if the assembly refused to consent to the separation, or simply failed to act, the case was to be turned over to the *zemskii* chief — an appointive official who represented the higher administration, rather than the peasants.[76] Now among the two million individual separations of title which were effected

under these provisions, only about one-third had the approval of
the assemblies,[77] and one may therefore infer that in many thousands of villages, the communists and the separatists were at outs,
and that many of the individual conversions of tenure were carried through in the face of a strong opposition to any break in the
old communal system. This conclusion is confirmed by the record
of what happened under the arbitrary dissolution-law of 1910. In
the communes to which this law extended, requests for confirmation of hereditary title might be made by individual householders,
or by the commune in behalf of each and all of its members,[78]
and the records show that of the 470,000 confirmations actually
issued, more than two-thirds were based upon individual petitions.[79]

When it was a question, not simply of separation of title, but
of consolidation into unitary farms, the establishment of even a
single consolidated holding usually required the partial readjustment of many others; and yet in most cases, as has been shown, the
law did not wait upon the consent of all those whose holdings were
affected. Among the farms consolidated by the Land-Organization
Commissions, about two-thirds were formed as a result of the general reorganization of the lands of the communes affected.[80] In
every such instance, the commissions must have acted upon the
demand of at least a simple majority of the householders, and
under certain conditions a vote of at least two-thirds in the peasant
assembly had been necessary to initiate the action (the requirement varied, as has been shown, in accordance with the character
of the tenure already in existence in the commune). In some cases,
the vote for consolidation was no doubt unanimous, but the published records of the commissions do not cover this interesting
question, and inasmuch as there is other evidence of a sharp and
widespread difference of opinion among the peasantry in general
as to the value of consolidation, one may not doubt that an active
minority-opposition existed in many villages where a general readjustment was actually effected. And finally, in the cases where
consolidations were made upon individual demand, there is official evidence that the work was often carried out against the will
of a majority in the commune.[81]

In the laws of the period and in the activities of the *zemskii*
chiefs, the Land-Organization Commissions, and the Peasants'
Bank, the official partisanship is clear enough; but this alone can
not explain the great changes that were taking place. In spite of

natural inertia, and often in the face of active opposition in the village, there was a demand on the part of many of the peasants for separation of tenure and for consolidation, and this demand must have been stimulated by motives of some urgency. Who were they, then, who felt this urge to break the old ties?

In 1910 and 1911 a *questionnaire* on the land-settlement was circulated in the Central Agricultural and Central Industrial regions, and the answers, chiefly from peasant correspondents, describe more or less systematically the conditions existing in about four hundred communes.[82] In one of the questions, the correspondents were asked to state whether it was the "middle peasants," the "poor peasants," or an indiscriminate mixture, who had separated their lands from those of the commune (with or without effecting a physical consolidation). The answer most often given was the last, "a mixture"; the middle peasants were separately mentioned about as frequently as the poor, but the "rich" peasants much less often.[83] All this is vague and hazy in the last degree — yet one must at least conclude that the individualist movement was not confined to any one economic level of the peasantry.

It has been pointed out repeatedly in other writings on this subject that the allotments for which separate title was established or confirmed under the laws of 1906 and 1910, were smaller, region for region, than the allotments which remained under repartitional tenure.[84] However, the recorded area of the separated allotments takes no account of the use-right of their holders in lands still undivided, and for this reason there is no sound basis for a comparison with the repartitional holdings, whose area is determined by dividing the whole acreage of the communal land by the number of allotment-holding households in the commune.[85] Even if this difficulty could be eliminated, the size of the households would have to be considered, too, in any valid comparison of household allotments. There is some evidence, of doubtful quality, that the households of the separators were of less than average size; [86] hence they could hardly be classified as poor, on the basis of the size of their holdings, unless these holdings were disproportionately small. The difference in the size of the holdings of the separators and the non-separators was in many regions so substantial as perhaps to indicate that the former were, on the average, in an inferior economic position; and yet it seems impossible to say with certainty that this was so.

Whatever may have been the connection between the movement

234 RURAL RUSSIA UNDER THE OLD RÉGIME

for the separation of title, and the economic differences which already existed in the village, it is at least certain that wherever the repartitional tenure was dissolved, this meant the end of a practice which had made for economic equalization — the practice of making a periodic redistribution of the land. Further than this, the new form of title gave an unprecedented freedom in the buying and selling of lands which had formerly been held in repartitional tenure; and it will be remembered that measures were also taken to facilitate the trade in those lands which were already held in heredity before 1905. Thus at one and the same time, communal redistribution was restricted to a narrower area, while redistribution by purchase and sale was made easy; and quite naturally there arose the question whether the transactions of the latter variety would make for a concentration, or for a diffusion, of landownership. Only the peasants were concerned in these dealings, for they alone might buy allotment-lands. The question therefore was: would the land-shortage of the poorer peasants be relieved by purchases on their part, or would they sell what few acres they had to their more comfortably situated neighbors?

Under the new laws there was a rapid expansion of trading in allotment-land,[87] and the records show that for European Russia as a whole, and for each region separately, the average size of the plots transferred by sale was very much less than the average for the allotments in general — in fact, nearly everywhere less than half.[88] If the plot transferred had constituted in each case the entire allotment of the seller, then one would be justified in concluding that most of the sellers were small holders; but as a matter of fact, the tables make no distinction between the sales of entire allotments, and those of a part only. Certain detailed local records of the sales made by nearly thirty-five thousand allotment-holders (a very small fraction of the total number of allotment-sales negotiated in European Russia during the period) have, however, been assembled from seven scattered districts; and in four of these districts, as well as in the general total for the seven, more than half the sellers did actually dispose of their entire allotments.[89] All this suggests, though it certainly does not prove, that the smallest holders as a class furnished a considerable proportion of the sellers of allotment-land. If it does not seem possible to demonstrate with finality that purchase and sale tended to produce a concentration in the ownership of allotment-holdings, still the fragmentary evidence appears to lean rather more toward this in-

terpretation than toward the opposite theory that large numbers
of the poorer peasants were buying portions of the allotments of
their richer neighbors and were in this fashion solving the land
problem for themselves.[90]

If the net result of the trading in allotment-land remains obscure, the effect produced by peasant purchases of non-allotment-
land is somewhat less so. A considerable share of these purchases
were made from, or with the help of, the Peasants' Land Bank,
and the returns of the Bank show that among its total of nine
hundred thousand buyers for the years 1909–1915 — a total including both individual purchasers and the members of purchasing associations and communes — sixteen per cent had no land at
the time of the purchase, while an additional fifty-three per cent
were small holders with not more than six *desiatinas* each, counting both their allotment-land and any non-allotment-land which
they already owned. Undoubtedly the group here recorded as
"landless" included many prosperous peasants who had recently
sold their old allotments in order to buy new farms; and yet the
majority of all those who purchased from the Bank may safely
be classified as land-short peasants. On the other hand, the average
size of the purchases made by individual buyers (those who did
not act as members of associations or communes) was well above
the general average for the allotment-holdings in 1905; [91] hence
an average individual purchase from the Bank would have raised
even a landless purchaser above the general norm of land-holding.
It goes without saying that with the average size of the individual
acquisitions as large as this, and with many of the buyers already
provided with land, the operations of the Bank not infrequently
resulted in the creation of holdings that conspicuously exceeded
the peasant norms for the regions in which they were located.[92]

When one turns from the reports of the Bank to other data
which cover *all* peasant purchases of non-allotment-land — those
made from both peasants and non-peasants, and with or without
the intervention of the Bank — one discovers that during the years
1909 and 1910 the total amount of land bought by the peasants as
individuals was somewhat less than the total acreage purchased by
their associations and communes, while the average size of the purchases made by individuals was 14.8 *desiatinas* in 1909 and 16.1
desiatinas in 1910, against a general average of 10.2 *desiatinas* for
the peasant allotment-holdings in 1905. That this difference in
average size represents in some degree a differentiation, not be-

tween region and region, but within each separate region, is indicated by a comparison of the size of the allotments with the size of the purchases of 1910 in eight *guberniias* scattered in every quarter of the country. In every case the average individual purchase of non-allotment-land was much larger than the average allotment — in several *guberniias* more than twice as large.[93] Also one finds that in 1909 and again in 1910, more than one-half of the total net gain in the individual peasant holdings of non-allotment-land was acquired in the form of purchases of fifteen *desiatinas* or more — purchases at least half again as large as the average allotment of 1905.[94]

All this is but a poor substitute for the comparative tables one would like to have for peasant landholding on the eve of the Revolution of 1917 and at earlier dates — tables that would unite the allotments with the non-allotment-lands and arrange the peasant holders in a single series in accordance with the extent of each man's acreage. But there are no such tables for the country as a whole, and in their absence one may hardly say more than this: that the trading in allotment-land perhaps showed some tendency to promote a concentration of ownership; that the purchase of non-allotment-land by associations and communes apparently left most of their members still at a very modest level of land-holding; and that, on the other hand, a considerable share (probably much more than one-half) of the non-allotment acreage purchased by *individual* peasants apparently went into the establishment (or the enlargement) of substantial, and sometimes even conspicuous, holdings.

In many instances the individual purchaser moved from the village to the newly acquired land, and set himself up there as an independent farmer. What proportion of all the individual purchases were utilized in this fashion, it is impossible to say, but the reports of the Peasants' Bank indicate that an increasing share of the sales made by or through this institution were conditioned upon the actual settlement of the individual buyer upon the land. A consolidated farm upon which the peasant actually lived was called, as has been said, a *khutor,* while a similar holding cultivated by a family who still lived elsewhere (usually in the old house beside the village street) was called an *otrub.* As a result of the activities of the Peasants' Bank, about seventy-five thousand *khutors* were established during the years 1910–1915, and it has been estimated that the total number of *khutors* and *otrubs* sold by the Bank during the period 1906–1916 was about two hundred and eighty thousand.[95] Thus the establishment of unitary peasant farms was promoted by the purchasing of non-allotment-land, as well as by the consolidation of the old allotments.

In the further search for light on the question of differentiation, one may examine the status of the *otrubs* established through the consolidation of the allotment-lands. In the scattering data on the size of these holdings and on the technique of cultivation practiced by their holders, there is little to distinguish the *otrubs* from the allotments which still remained in scattered strips. There can be no question that the disentanglement of the land from repartition and from the common crop-cycle gave the household a greater economic independence — for better or for worse; but there is little evidence that the peasants who embarked upon this way of life were either better off or worse off than the average in the beginning; and at the end of a brief decade of experiment, there were only uncertain indications that the *otrubs* had been raised above the general economic level of the unconsolidated holdings.

In the case of the *khutors* established through the consolidation of allotments, the break in the old land-ties was more complete (though it was not always absolute, as has been shown), and the superiority in economic status was hardly to be doubted; and what was true of the *khutors* on the allotment-lands, was all the more true of those established on non-allotment-holdings newly purchased by the peasants. The outright removal of the old buildings from the village, or the construction of new ones from mud-sill to roof-tree, was in itself an undertaking which required not only a pioneering energy but certain material resources, and the advances of money offered by the government were by no means adequate to this need. There is substantial evidence to indicate that although many of the best-off peasants still held fast to the old system of scattered strips and periodic repartition, the average *khutor* was, region by region, considerably larger than the other peasant holdings. On the other hand, the history of the *khutors* after their establishment is far from clear, and it is extremely doubtful whether they prospered in such a way as to produce a further widening of the economic gap between their holders and the bulk of the peasantry. The establishment of the *khutor* was costly, the situation novel, the testing-period short; the pioneers had much to learn and a great deal to forget. It had been rather generally assumed that these pioneers would take advantage of their exceptional isolation to increase the economic differential in their favor, and yet, when the new revolution came in 1917, the truth of this assumption had hardly been clearly demonstrated, as yet in the history of the Russian countryside.[96]

In the depths of this countryside, on a certain morning in the late Summer of 1926, the writer had himself jostled over several miles of country road from a river-town on the upper Volga (green bluffs, white walls, gold domes) to a village which was to serve as the first halting-place on a wagon-journey northward; and he had not spent an hour here, beside the samovar (drinking tea, eating carrot-cakes, and watching respectfully a large cockroach which scuttled several times across the table) when he learned that there was in the neighborhood of this village a curiosity which every traveller must see. Accordingly there was more joggling along the street with its double row of houses, then on through a motley of scattered strips of plow-land, and around the easy slope of a hill to a fence where the patchwork came abruptly to an end. Beyond the fence was a substantial and prosperous house of logs set down alone in the midst of unbroken fields — the special marvel of the neighborhood, an isolated peasant farm. If this *khutor* had been established here in accordance with some pre-plan to dramatize the double contrast between the individual and the collective, the well-off and the not-so-well, the thing could hardly have been better done.

The *khutors* were not everywhere such a rarity as in this district; and yet the attention which they attracted, whether among the peasants or at St. Petersburg, was out of all proportion to their immediate economic weight — an interest measured not so much by what they had done, as what they might do. The *khutor* was still a Promise or a Menace — the Russians could hardly talk of it in other terms.

It has been shown that there was during the years between the two revolutions a widespread change among the peasants in the direction of a more individualistic way of life (though it is easy to exaggerate the breadth and depth of this change, and at the same time to lose sight of the growth of the co-operative movement, to be discussed hereafter). It is not simply to be taken for granted, of course, that the increase in individualism involved of necessity an increasing economic differentiation among the villagers, but many of the new developments seemed to point that way: the disendowment, under certain conditions, of the junior members of peasant households was a move in this direction; the old procedure of equalization by reallotment had been ruled out, wherever repartitional tenure was converted to hereditary; the increased salability of the allotments may have resulted in some concentration of these lands in the possession of the stronger peasants; the consolidation of scattered strips in *otrubs* and *khutors* created an opportunity, at least, for a differentiation upon the basis of technical skill and individual initiative; and finally, the purchasing of non-allotment-land contributed increasingly, it seems, to the strengthening of those peasants who were already strong beyond the average. To review all this evidence and half-evidence, doubtful as much of it is, is to convince oneself that this decade of individualization was probably also a decade of differentiation within the peasant class.

By way of farewell to this troubled question, one may point out that the contrast between well-being and ill-being was most conspicuous when a peasant household with more land than its members could cultivate turned to leasing-out, or to the hiring of labor, as a means of exploiting the surplus acreage. In many *guberniias,* a substantial proportion of the peasants were listed as lessors of land, but in most of the tables it is impossible to distinguish between the lessors who actually lived in the villages and those who had settled elsewhere. In the *guberniia* of Tula, where this distinction may be drawn, records dating from the period 1910–1912 show that among the 220,375 peasant households actually present in the rural districts, 27,406 were lessors of allotments or of non-allotment-lands, while in addition 33,406 absent households figured as lessors of allotments. The relation between the lessee and the absent lessor was vital and significant enough, but inasmuch as the latter was usually a small holder who had gone elsewhere to work for wages, the data on renting-out by peasant absentees certainly cannot be employed to build up a picture of prosperous peasant landlords and a humble peasant tenantry. Again there are data for certain limited districts which make it appear that some of the lessors actually present in the villages did not rent out land because of their own abundance, but because of their poverty; for the lack of animals and of implements, they leased their petty holdings and hired themselves out for wage-work in the neighborhood. There can be no doubt that the relationship of well-to-do landlord and poor tenant sometimes existed as between peasant and peasant, but to show just where and when — this seems to be impossible.

Not quite so much befogged is the question of the employment of paid labor by the peasants. Under certain conditions, a small holder might perhaps hire a farm-hand, but the great majority of the peasant employers were probably well supplied with land and in general somewhat better off than their neighbors. Unfortunately the available data on this subject extend only to the employment of agricultural "term-workers" by the peasants, as distinguished from the hiring of day-workers for short periods of special stress. The latter form of employment was undoubtedly more widespread, but the former suggests a closer approach to a capitalistic system of agriculture. Some of the peasants of course employed the help of term-workers in connection with industrial and trading operations, but such non-agricultural workers are not included in the table presented on the opposite page. The purpose of this table is to show something as to the variation in the size of the peasant holdings and as to the employment of agricultural term-workers by the peasant holders. In determining the size of the holdings, the allotment-lands and the non-allotment-lands were merged.

Abundant materials might be brought forward to support the statement that a considerable variation in the size of the peasant holdings in any given locality was quite normal; and yet, among more than a hundred thousand households covered by this table, only a very few had moved so far toward a capitalistic agriculture as to employ a term-worker, and few indeed had more than one such helper. Whatever supplementary use may have been made of day-labor at seeding and at the harvest, one hired worker could hardly do all that was necessary on a peasant farm even in the slacker times, and it seems fair to assume that among the employing households there were almost none that did not send their own members into the fields. The *uezds* listed in the table are located, respectively, in the north-central, south-central, southern, and southwestern regions of European Russia, but reports for four *volosts* in the east-central *guberniia* of Penza, and for Stavropol *uezd* in the *guberniia* of Samara on the Volga, indicate that in these districts also there was only a very limited development of the hiring of term-labor by the peasants. There may have been more of such hiring in the Southeast and the extreme South, but it seems probable that in most of the *guberniias* there was rarely to be found a family of peasants who conducted the operation of a farm and yet did not share in its roughest labor. Some of the peasants were "capitalists," to be sure, in that they were employ-

LANDHOLDING AND THE HIRING OF AGRICULTURAL TERM-WORKERS, BY PEASANT HOUSEHOLDS

Guberniia.	Uezd.	Date of investigation.	Total number of peasant households present in the villages.	Landholding of households present in the villages. (Households with middle-sized holdings are omitted; only the smallest and the largest holders are shown.)				Hiring of agricultural "term-workers."	
				Number of landless households present.	Number of households with smallest holdings.		Number of households with largest holdings.	Number of households hiring such workers.	Number of workers so hired.
Vologda	Veliko-Ustiug	1911	27,769	707	(Up to 3 d.) 737		(With more than 20 d.) 9,745	803	883
Tula	Aleksin	1912	12,691	161	(Up to 3 d.) 1,657	(With 12-20 d.) 1,164	(With more than 20 d.) 285	668	750
Poltava	Gadiach	1910	23,110	929	(Up to 1 d.) 3,502	(With 15-25 d.) 1,523	(With more than 25 d.) 629	1,098	1,631
Volyn	Vladimir-Volynskii	1910	42,024	2,917	(Up to 1 d.) 1,575	(With 15-25 d.) 1,297	(With more than 25 d.) 254	666	793

ers of labor (and if day-labor be included, no one may say how many such there were), but even among these "capitalists" nearly all were laborers too, in that they still knew the jerk of an unruly plow-handle and the drag of a sackful of grain between the shoulders.[97]

CHAPTER XII

ON THE EVE

HEIRS to a history of landed serfdom, not of landless slavery, the peasants were by taste and tradition petty cultivators, ready and eager to buy land, to rent it, sometimes even to rise up and seize it, but reluctant to turn instead to wage-work for a supplementary income. Only this essential *peasantism,* this *non-proletarian* habit of thought and action, can explain the fact that the villagers crowded one another for the opportunity to rent lands at a figure which did not leave them, in return for their labor, as much as they might have earned by working for wages on a neighboring estate. The renting of non-allotment-lands by the peasants is a subject which was never brought under thorough statistical control, but there is good reason to believe that in respect to the vastness of the rented area and the burdensomeness of the rental charges, the conditions which existed during the later pre-war years were not notably different from those which helped to bring on the Revolution of 1905.[1]

The later decades of the nineteenth century had witnessed some improvement in the methods and the productivity of peasant agriculture, and during the short period between the Revolution of 1905 and the Great War the improvement continued, in part as a result of the influence of the model farms and the "farm advisers" maintained by the *zemstvos* and the Ministry of Agriculture. There was a rapid increase in the importation and the domestic manufacture of agricultural implements and machines, and in their employment by the peasants; and this, too, helps to explain the fact that the average yield in the fifty *guberniias* for each acre of allotment-land planted with grain, potatoes, or flax, was materially improved. Also, between 1901 and 1916 the acreage which the peasantry devoted to artificially-seeded hay-crops was increased several times over, and among these cultures were clovers of various kinds which did the double service of improving the soil and supplementing the stores of forage produced upon the natural meadows.

These were some of the signs of technical progress; but a pre-war traveller from the United States would still have been strongly impressed by what might be called the mature and complex primitiveness of Russian peasant agriculture. It was not the primitiveness of pioneering; not new and raw, but stained and weathered, and worn round by time; not the beginning of a new history so much as some late chapter of an old one. All about, in the compact village, in the intricate pattern of the fields, in the routine of the seeding and the harvest, there were the evidences of a venerable tradition.

For the most part, the villagers still followed the three-year cycle of Winter grain, Spring grain, and fallow, or the even more primitive routine of sowing a field for several successive years with the same cereal and then abandoning it for a long period of recuperation. Of all the land which the peasants put under crops, by far the greater part was still seeded to grain, and only a small fraction (in forty-eight *guberniias* in 1916, about one-ninth) was used for other cultures, such as clover and other forage-plants (1.9 per cent of the crop-area in 1916), flax (2.0 per cent), and potatoes (3.4 per cent).

Among the implements used by the peasants to cultivate the soil, those classified as "unimproved" still predominated in nearly three-quarters of the *uezds* of European Russia in 1910. In 1917 the number of iron plows found on farms "of peasant type" was less than half the number of such farms in twenty-one scattered *guberniias* out of the twenty-six for which the returns may be compared — and in most of the twenty-one *guberniias* the proportion of plows to farms was very much less than one-half to one. The investigation of 1917 was incomplete and defective in many respects; yet it is probably quite safe to say that more than one-half of the peasants still broke and stirred the surface of the soil with the *sokha* (a primitive horse-drawn implement which somewhat resembled a single- or double-bladed cultivator), instead of turning the soil upside-down to a reasonable depth with the curving blade of a modern plowshare. The sickle was still a common instrument of reaping, and in many villages the grain was threshed with the flail.[2] On the allotment-lands of European Russia, the yields were still markedly lower than those on the estates, and far below the average yields in Western Europe and in the United

States, and in 1911 a crop-failure brought another widespread famine on the Volga. The peasant cattle were usually light in weight, the peasant horse a "small, weak-limbed, and weak-boned creature" inadequate to heavy work. In the black-soil region — say in the *guberniia* of Tambov, an American traveller who rode through the grain-fields in 1913 might have expected to find a scattering of farm-houses supported by this casual culture; but instead he would have found, perhaps, a village of a hundred households, and then, a few miles farther on, a village of four hundred more. A constricted acreage, a non-intensive agriculture, a comparatively dense population — the landscape told no lies; there was really a malignant discord here.

In the relations of the peasants with the market during the period 1906–1913, there were developments both favorable and unfavorable. The sharp rise in the price of animal products was to the advantage of the villagers, as was also the prevailingly high price of wheat — a grain which the peasants produced very largely for the towns or for the export-market. In the case of rye, the situation was far more complex. This grain was at one and the same time the chief product of the peasantry, and their chief article of consumption; there were many villagers who produced a surplus for the market, and many others (especially north of the line between the *step* and the forest) who regularly purchased rye for their own subsistence; and these two groups, the sellers and the buyers, were of course oppositely affected by the circumstance that during most of this period the price of rye held well above the levels of the decade before the Revolution of 1905 although it stood at a somewhat lower point in 1913 than in 1906.

As a result of the economic backwardness of the country and the attempt to stimulate industrial development by a protectionist policy, high and increasing prices were maintained for most non-agricultural products — and without entering upon the argument as to the ultimate advantages or disadvantages of an artificially-stimulated industrialization, one may perhaps say that at least for the time being the bulk of the peasantry were most unfavorably affected. When a general comparison is made of prices in the last pre-war year in Russia, England, Germany, France, and the United States, the one most conspicuous fact is that most food-stuffs, whether animal or vegetable, were about one-third cheaper in Russia than in any of the other countries mentioned, while most manufactures (cotton yarn, cotton cloth, metals) were very much higher.[3] If the price-structure had been deliberately contrived as a yoke to fit the necks of the men who sold the products of agriculture and bought those of industry, the design could hardly have been more perfect.

It was thoroughly characteristic of the conditions of Russian village life that the peasants should be in part dependent upon "side-earnings" drawn from the production of craft-wares for the market and from wage-work. To appraise these activities in any sort of quantitative terms is difficult in the last degree, and for information on this question one catches perhaps too eagerly at the returns of certain local budget researches made at various times between 1905 and 1915. Of 228 peasant households investigated in two different localities in the forest region, all but two were engaged to some extent in side-work, and on the average about forty-four per cent of their net income was derived from this source; in one locality in the upper black-soil belt, the number of households with side-earnings was eighty-one out of eighty-five, and the average contribution to their income was twenty-six per cent; in a district farther south in the *step*, the returns showed seventy-two households with side-work out of a total of ninety-one, and a contribution of about twelve per cent. Whether or not these figures have the more or less representative character which has been claimed for them, they at least support the prevailing view that side-earnings were of very great importance to the peasants who lived north of the forest boundary, and had a place of consequence even in the South.[4]

Speaking still with the greatest diffidence, one may say that there is some ground for believing that between the Revolution of 1905 and the Great War there was a change in both the absolute and the relative importance of certain sources of side-earnings: the question as to whether the handicraft-industries developed or declined is apparently insoluble, but the employment of peasant wage-labor in agriculture probably showed a relative and possibly even an absolute contraction,[5] while on the other hand the expanding machine-industry [6] enlisted an increasing army of peasant workers.

It might have been expected that as mechanized industry advanced, the handicraft-industries would be forced to retreat, and indeed this hypothesis seemed to be confirmed by the results of a *questionnaire*-investigation conducted by the *Gazette of Trade and Industry,* an organ of the Ministry of Finance. The returns of this country-wide inquiry were published in 1913, and the tables show that 950 correspondents reported that the handicraft-industries were in a decline, while only 170 reported an improvement — eighty-five per cent against fifteen. Of 480 correspondents who commented, for example, upon the state of the furniture-industry, 440 reported an unfavorable trend.[7] Such evidence is certainly not of the first quality, but for the lack of anything better, one might accept it provisionally, were it not for the fact that at about the same time the Chief Administration of Land-Organization and Agriculture also circulated a country-wide *questionnaire* and learned from "a vast majority" of *its* correspondents that the cottage-industry of furniture-making was expanding, and was therefore engaging the labor of an increasing number of craftsmen. In fact, only five per cent of the correspondents of the Chief Administration reported any recent diminution of the working force in this particular industry.[8] Make what allowance one will for the agrarianism of the one Ministry and its correspondents, and the industrialism of the other — the outcome is still a stalemate, and the whole matter is reported here only by way of showing how deep was the fog which surrounded the cottage-industries. In respect to the value of the annual output and the total number of persons engaged, the estimates vary in a fantastic degree,[9] and all that may be said with any certainty is that in thousands of villages, and in a multitude of peasant homes, one might still hear the noises of cottage craft-work — hear them as the writer did one day in the Autumn of 1925, when he drove through the fields toward a village that rang with the sound of metals, and found the peasants in their homes and shops all black with iron and soot, all forging, tapping, filing away at locks or pulleys, or doors for the tile stoves of Moscow.

Turning to another major field of side-work, one discovers two changes which tended to limit the demand for wage-labor in agriculture: the sale of millions of acres of the proprietorial lands to the peasants, and the increase in the use of farm-machinery on the lands which remained in the hands of the large proprietors. At some of the customary gathering-points where the itinerant laborers still assembled to meet with possible employers, the local *zemstvos* provided shelter, meals, and medical care, but at other centers of this kind the workers "were soaked by the rain, shivered, starved, sickened, and died," just as others had before them through the run of years.[10] In the matter of wages, the trend of the time was apparently favorable to the laborers: in eleven of the thirteen regions of European Russia, the money-wage of agricultural day-workers was higher in 1912 than in 1906 (in most cases markedly higher), and in terms of rye at the local price the wage also showed an increase in each of these eleven regions.[11] For the years 1901–1905, the average wage for a male day-laborer during the harvest was fifty-eight *kopeikas* a day with subsistence, or seventy *kopeikas* without; in 1912 it was seventy-seven *kopeikas* — or ninety-seven; in 1913, eighty-seven — or one *rubl* eight.[12] Rye is of course anything but an adequate general measure of the "real wage," but a comparison of the money-payments with the prices of certain other commodities (such as meat, sugar, calico, wool, and kerosene) [13] gives some further ground for the inference, diffident and uncertain as it must be, that the real wage increased, though only very moderately. Still, one *rubl* and eight *kopeikas* (something like fifty-four cents), without rations, was hardly a munificent wage for a day's work at the crest of the agricultural season, and the rate of payment to year-round workers was far lower than this. Black bread was cheap enough, but in 1913 sugar cost about sixteen *kopeikas* a pound — perhaps one-seventh of a day's harvest-wage, while a pair of workman's boots was priced at five or six *rubls* [14] or something like five days' wages. It is not surprising, then, that many of the agricultural laborers walked their long road in shoes of plaited bark; nor is it difficult to understand the Russian folk-custom of holding a small lump of sugar in the teeth and drawing the tea in past it (with a delightful, swishing sound) — an invention of necessity, no doubt — a means of drawing out to the full this bit of lingering sweetness.

If by any chance the agricultural workers thought of trying to improve their condition by a strike, they found themselves faced with numerous perils. An individual laborer who quit work before the expiration of his contract was liable to a month's imprisonment. If a group of laborers stopped work in this way, and by means of force, threats, or "exclusion from intercourse" (personal boycott) compelled other workers to do the same, the offenders were liable to imprisonment for from six to twelve months. Still more severe was the punishment provided for the members of any organization which incited agricultural laborers to stop work in violation of contract; the penalty here was imprisonment in a fortress for from one year and four months to four years, with a permanent loss of the right to vote or to hold office.[15] The government was apparently determined not to tolerate any foolishness among the agricultural laborers, and in particular it aimed to check the activities of individual agitators and of radical organizations. In part, no doubt, as a result of this policy of repression, the farm-workers remained almost entirely unorganized (except for the many small and primitive *artels*) and the number of strikes between 1907 and 1913 was inconsequential.[16]

The expansion of large-scale industry and the increase in its demand for labor from the villages was especially rapid during the last five years before the Great War,[17] and the general trend was reflected in the growth of the cities. In 1897, the urban population of the fifty *guberniias* was about twelve millions, or 12.8 per cent of the whole; by 1914, the population of the cities was more than half-again as large (about nineteen and one-half millions), but it still formed only 14.8 per cent of the total.[18] Now, as before, the cities were swallowing a part, but a part only, of the natural increase of the villages.

It has been shown that the new laws of the inter-revolutionary period made it much easier than it had formerly been for the peasant who went to the city to dissolve the personal and property ties which bound him to the household and to the commune; but to assume on this account that all or nearly all of the peasants who found work in the towns actually did break their connections with the village would be to misunderstand completely the relations of town and country. Some of the latest pre-war investigations show that there was still a vital connection between the factory and the farm; for example, it was found that among the workers in the printing-trades in Moscow, forty-six per cent were still conducting farming operations, while an additional 16.7 per cent were no longer personally engaged in farming but still had households in the village.[19] If nearly two-thirds of the workers in this skilled trade continued to maintain such important rural connections, who then was to say where the peasantry left off and the proletariat began? The question was a vital one at any time — and it would be all the more so during the coming years of war and revolution.

Inasmuch as a great number of peasant households were in part dependent upon the earnings of some of their members in industry, it is obvious that the movement and the level of real wages in mining and manufacturing were matters of immediate consequence in the economy of the village. It may therefore be recorded here that between 1908 and 1913 there was apparently an increase in the real wage of Russian miners and factory-workers; and it may also be noted that between 1904 and 1913 there was a reduction in the average length of the working day in industry.[20] The comparison of real wages at different periods, and in different countries, is at best a difficult and doubtful business, but it is hardly to be questioned that before the war the wage-level in Russian industry was far below that in the countries to the westward. In the mines and factories of Russia, the general average wage in 1913 was apparently about twenty-five *rubls* per month; in the metal industries, the average was thirty-five *rubls* — in the textile mills, at the opposite end of the scale, it was only about seventeen *rubls*. Translated into the terms of American currency, this means that the Russian textile worker received only about two dollars per week; but in 1913 in Germany, collective agreements in this industry provided for payments ranging from about three dollars and a half per week for unskilled female labor, to about six dollars and a half for male spinners and weavers; and in the United Kingdom just before the war, operatives in the worsted mills earned about four dollars per week, and in the cotton mills nearly five dollars.[21] Such international comparisons are of course meaningless unless account be taken of the price-levels in the countries concerned, but a comparison of prices in 1913 indicates that while most of the important food-stuffs were about one-third cheaper in Russia than in Germany, in England, or in the United States, manufactured goods were in general somewhat higher in Russia than in the other countries mentioned.[22] When allowance is made, very roughly, for these differences in price, it still appears that the Russian industrial worker was having a much worse time of it than the workers in Germany, in England, or in America, and indeed might very properly regard the foreign proletariat as favored sons of the industrial revolution.

Besides the flow of population from the villages to the towns, there was also a considerable movement to Asiatic Russia and to foreign countries. Between 1907 and 1913, the emigration beyond the frontiers of the Empire varied between a minimum of forty-six thousand and a maximum of more than two hundred thousand per year, but as this emigration was made up chiefly of Jewish townsmen rather than of Russian peasants, it had no important direct effect upon the agrarian situation. The movement to Asiatic Russia reached its climax just after the Revolution of 1905–06, and in 1907 more than six hundred and fifty thousand colonists made the long journey to the Russian New World. Thereafter, the annual movement declined to something less than two hundred thousand in 1911 and then increased once more during the years 1912 and 1913; but the sum of all the removals to the cities, to Asiatic Russia, and to foreign countries, exhausted only a fraction of the natural increase of the peasant population.

Among the peasants west of the Ural, Siberia was regarded as a kind of Utopia; but many of the colonists did not actually find it so, as is indicated by the strength of the counter-movement back to European Russia. Between 1907 and 1913, the number of these returning colonists was never less than twenty thousand a year, and in 1910 it mounted to seventy-six thousand.[23] The best of the Siberian lands had already been claimed by the earlier settlers; the return of a colonist was usually a confession of his defeat, and the statistical tables which record the counter-march are themselves a kind of figurative burying-ground of peasant hopes.

As to the general state of well-being, or its opposite, in the villages of European Russia, one may gather something from the local investigations of peasant budgets. Of the budget-data in general, it must be said at the outset that they are subject to all sorts of doubts and reservations; the peasants must often have told the recorders to "write down what they pleased and go with God"; and furthermore, the families from which the data were obtained were no doubt above the average in economic status and in education, for the simple reason that the poorest and worst-managed households could hardly supply the information required by the complex schedules. And yet, for all their faults, the budget tables are no doubt worth more than the usual run of observations, impressions, and intuitions on the subject of peasant life. It is worth noting, at any rate, that five local group-investigations made in various quarters of the country between 1900 and 1915 showed that for the year of record the total outlay for personal needs (including the computed value of the goods consumed by the family out of its own production) averaged 202 *rubls* per household in the local group which made the poorest showing, and 539 *rubls* in the group at the opposite extreme — that is, from $101 to some $270 per year per household, in a country where most of the principal food-stuffs were perhaps one-third cheaper than in Germany, in England, or in the United States, while manufactures were apparently somewhat higher priced than in these other countries.[24] The budget-data may be neither accurate in themselves nor properly representative of the general condition of the peasantry (indeed there are other budget reports which indicate that the figures here quoted give perhaps too dark a picture), and the international price-tables may also suffer from a variety of defects; but by how much would one have to raise these budgets and depress these prices in order to make possible a decent level of consumption?

In a certain community in the western part of the United States, there is — or used to be — a saying that "nothing is sure but death and taxes"; and for this saying the Russian peasant must certainly have had a counterpart. It will be remembered that during the height of the Revolution of 1905, the redemption-debt of all excepting a few minor groups of peasants was cancelled; but even after this, the villagers still had a heavy fiscal load to carry. In the year 1912, the direct taxes collected by the State, the *zemstvos*, the *volosts*, and the communes from the peasants of the fifty *guberniias* amounted to something like ten *rubls* for each household, while the indirect levies falling upon the peasants probably came to a good deal more than this. The budgetary demands of the central government were increasing rapidly, and in the satisfaction of these demands, indirect taxes and customs duties played a larger part than in any other important country in Europe.

When the peasant could afford a luxurious evening, he filled his lamp with taxed kerosene (if he had a lamp), lighted it with a taxed match (or with a splinter from the stove), poured a little taxed tobacco into a cigarette-paper, also taxed (or into a cone of newspaper), and puffed himself into a cloud of smoke. If this operation made him thirsty, he drank a glass of taxed tea, with a lump of taxed sugar gripped between his teeth. Or perhaps he went out to buy a bottle of *vodka* (colorless as alcohol, and strong as whisky), smacked the bottom of the bottle to loosen the cork, drew it with his teeth, and drank off the liquor in large gulps from the bottle-mouth or from a tea-glass; and as a result of this act of consumption, the State received a handsome revenue, in its double capacity of tax-collector and of merchant under the Spirit Monopoly. On the basis of reports as to the total revenue derived by the State from the commodities just mentioned, and with the help of doubtful estimates of the share of these commodities consumed by the peasants, a Russian statistician has attempted to show that the indirect payments of the peasantry under this head exceeded the total of all the direct taxes which rested upon them; and over and above this, there were a number of stamp-fees, cus-

toms duties and the like which were also borne in part by the
village population.

In considering the position of the peasantry under the Russian
fiscal system, it is worth noting that although the goods that have
just been mentioned were very widely consumed, most of them
would hardly have been classified by the peasants themselves as
prime necessities. That is, the poorest peasants might escape the
tax on most of these commodities by refraining from consuming
them. In the case of many of the duties on imports, however, the
situation was altogether different, since these duties in many instances rested upon articles, or upon the materials for the manufacture of articles, which most of the peasants, even the poorest,
were obliged to have at any price. Such, for example, were the
duties of thirty-nine per cent on raw cotton, fifty-eight per cent on
pig iron, and seventy-nine per cent on steel, (in 1913). In order
to determine the cost to the Russian peasantry of this tariff-system
— the most thoroughly protectionist in Europe at the time,[25] one
would be obliged not only to apportion a proper share of the
customs-duties actually collected, but to consider other items
which could have no place in the budget of the State — such, for
example, as the effect of the artificial stimulation of industry upon
the demand for, and the wages of, peasant labor, and the extent
to which this factor balanced the excess-price paid by the peasants
to the Russian producers of protected goods. An attempt to get
to the bottom of this question would involve all sorts of astronom-
ical calculations, with only the most doubtful results in prospect,
but at any rate it is not difficult to see that under the existing
fiscal system the peasants were carrying, in addition to their visible
load of assessments, an invisible burden of heavy weight.

From tax-rates to the death-rates is not so long a leap as may at
first appear. The death-rate is in some sense an index of the general material condition of the people, and the records show that
the number of deaths per year for each thousand of the entire population declined markedly during the new century. For the years
1901–1905 the average rate for the fifty *guberniias* was 31.0, while
for the years 1911–1913 it was 27.2; but for France the average for
the years 1901–1910 was 19.4, and for England and Wales it was
only 15.4. The figures for the annual birth-rate in the fifty *guberniias* in 1901–1905 and in 1911–1913 are 47.7 and 44.1, and a simple subtraction shows that the rate of natural net increase was even
higher in the second period than in the first (16.7 in 1901–1905, as

against 16.9 in 1911–1913). The *zemstvos* had done a great deal to make good the shortage of doctors and hospitals in the rural districts, but by comparison with the populations of a dozen other European countries and with the townspeople of Russia itself, the Russian peasants still carried an overload of birth and death.[26]

A CONSIDERABLE part of the preceding chapter was taken up with an account of the loosening of old ties in the commune and the household — but this did not cover all, by any means, of the group-forms and group-activities that figure in the history of the peasants. As distinguished from the collective holding of the land, its collective cultivation with a subsequent division of the crop was comparatively rare, though certainly not unheard of; but perhaps somewhat more common was the employment on several holdings in succession of all the animals and implements owned by the several holders, or of agricultural machines which had been purchased by the holders as a body. Records touching this subject were made during the last pre-war years in sixteen *volosts* scattered among the four *guberniias* of Tver, Tula, Penza, and Poltava, and these records show that in some of the *volosts* only a very few of the peasant households owned or shared in the ownership of such machines as seed-drills, harvesters, threshers, winnowers, and the like, while in several other *volosts* the proportion of such households was about one-quarter. However, the point at issue just here is not the general distribution of such equipment, but the question as to whether the comparatively few machines actually in use were owned individually or collectively; and here one finds that in several *volosts* the ownership was wholly individual, while in four other *volosts* more than a third of the families listed as machine-owners did not possess the machines independently but were shareholders with one or more of their neighbors. The total number of the registered households was 15,480, and among this number 1,478 were independent owners of machines, while 321 owned shares in such equipment.[27] These figures will hardly justify any sort of generalization, except perhaps this: that even before the Great Revolution, the collective holding and use of complex agricultural equipment was not altogether unknown and unheard of in the Russian village.

By 1914, the number of registered societies and associations for the promotion of agriculture had grown to several thousand, and the peasants among their members were profiting considerably by the activity of some of these organizations in supplying agricultural machines on a rental basis, and in the marketing of the crops. Much more important to the peasants, however, was the work of the co-operative savings and credit associations which multiplied nine times over between 1905 and 1914, and numbered at the beginning of the latter year about thirteen thousand, with a membership of more than eight millions, drawn very largely from the peasantry of the fifty *guberniias*. The principal function of these associations was the acceptance of deposits and the granting of loans, and at the beginning of 1914 they had loans outstanding to the amount of more than half a billion *rubls,* chiefly in the form of advances made for the purchase of land, live-stock, fertilizer, and implements, and for other such productive purposes. Besides this, an increasing number of these associations purchased, for the account of their members, such things as agricultural machinery, fertilizer, and seed, and a few of the associations also undertook the marketing of their members' agricultural products. In 1913 about thirty-seven hundred savings and credit societies were engaged in purchasing operations, and the amount of that year's purchases was some twenty-three million *rubls,* but less than 250 societies had undertaken the marketing of goods, and their total sales had not exceeded four million *rubls* in any one year.[28]

In European Russia there were some hundreds of co-operative groups which maintained creameries for the manufacture of butter and cheese from the milk delivered by their members.[29] In the northern *guberniias* the collective conduct of hunting and fishing operations appears to have been quite common, but in the craft-industries co-operative production in the full sense of the term was rarely met with. The workers did sometimes combine, however, to provide a furnace, a smithy, a tar-still, or some other equipment which the members then had the right to use in turn; and less frequently they united for the common preparation or purchase of raw materials and for the marketing of the finished wares which they had separately produced. In some instances the co-operative credit societies and the *zemstvos* granted loans to the hand-workers for the purchase of tools and materials, and less frequently they mediated in these purchases or undertook the marketing of the products.[30] Again, among the peasants who left their villages temporarily to work as hired laborers in agriculture, in lumbering, in freight-handling at the river-landings, in carpentry, in bricklaying, and in certain other fields, it was not uncommon to find small groups or *artels* which housed and fed their members and received and distributed their earnings.[31] In the field of consumers' co-operation, as conventionally defined, the number of rural societies increased about twenty-three times over between 1905 and 1914, and on the eve of the war there were in the Empire (exclusive of Finland) about 8,600 of these rural societies, with perhaps eight hundred thousand members, chiefly peasants of the fifty *guberniias*.[32]

By way of summarizing this discussion of collective activities other than those of the households and the communes as such, it may be said, first, that groups of peasants sometimes co-operated in the actual work of production — but how often, it is impossible even to guess, for the reason that these activities were not covered by any inclusive statistical record. In the providing of credit for productive purposes, co-operative action had taken a place of great importance, but the co-operatives had apparently made only a very limited headway as intermediaries in the supplying of raw materials and equipment, and still less in the marketing of their members' products. In the matter of providing consumption goods, co-operative action was developing with great rapidity; but even so, it had been extended, on the eve of the war, to only a small fraction of the peasant families of the country. It is clear, then, that in their relations with the market, whether as sellers or as buyers, the peasants still acted for the most part through private grain-traders, private store-keepers, and other such professional middlemen.

Turning from the trade in material goods to the trade in ideas, one finds a wholesale expansion in the apparatus of exchange. In 1908 the Third Duma launched a program designed to provide ultimately a free, primary education for all the children of Russia, and between 1908 and 1914 the total number of primary schools in the country was increased by about fifty per cent (from one hundred thousand to one hundred and fifty thousand, approximately); and yet the *zemstvos*, the municipalities, the Church and the State had thus far provided only about half the facilities that were necessary to carry out the Duma's program, and only about one-half of the children of primary-school age were actually enrolled.[33] But that there had been a marked increase in literacy, there can be no doubt; the percentage of literates among the recruits called for military service is reported as forty-nine in 1900, and seventy-three in 1913. It may very well be that much of this literacy was purely nominal, and yet the figures serve at least to give some general notion of the rate of change.[34] If the proportion of literates for the entire male population of the villages of the fifty *guberniias* had increased between 1897 and ·913 at the same rate as that for the recruits, then something like forty-five per cent of the male villagers of all ages would have been literate in 1913; but the assumption as to a parallel rate of increase is, of course, not much better than a guess.

One tends to take it for granted that the schools not only introduced certain common ideas directly into their pupils' heads, but at the same time provided them with the means of thereafter acquiring other ideas through the medium of the printed word. Certain investigations have shown, however, that the second assumption is not to be taken too seriously. For example, there is the examination made in 1909 of the budgets of 107 peasant households which were selected as more or less representative of conditions existing in the southwestern section of the *guberniia* of Kostroma, some two hundred miles northeast of Moscow. It is reported that in ninety-nine of these 107 households, there was at least one member who was literate;[35] and in this connection it is worth remembering, too, that an unusually large percentage of the peasants of this region were engaged in factory wage-work, with the result that these villages received a more-than-average stimulation through urban contacts. What, then, of the *quality* of the literacy in the investigated households ? The tables show that during the year of record, only six among the 107 households spent more than one *rubl* (fifty cents) on "books" (an item which probably includes all printed matter); forty-four households spent something less than that (usually ten or fifteen cents); fifty-seven reported nothing at all; and only four laid out anything for schooling (that is, anything in addition to the assessment for this purpose which was included in their tax-payments).[36] Five similar group-investigations made in various quarters of the country between 1900 and 1915 showed for the given budget-year an average expenditure per household for books and education (aside from tax-payments) which varied from ten *kopeikas* in the local group which made the worst showing, to two and one-half *rubls* in the best group.[37] Thus the budget records, whatever their faults, would seem at least to suggest that the villages had hardly as yet been flooded with new ideas through the channel of the printed page.

Somewhere beyond the village horizon, drawing recruits and

sending them back again, the system of universal military training still carried on its standardizing function; and behind the school and the army there was still the ancient Church. From every one of the 107 households investigated in this particular corner of Kostroma *guberniia,* the priest received some contribution, and here, as well as in all of the five other budget-groups which have been mentioned, the payments to the priest and the Church were very much larger than the voluntary outlay for books and schooling.[38] As to the character of the peasants' religion, one may gather something from the fact that for such ritual goods as incense, and oil to burn before the holy pictures (which probably hung in every house), the 107 families spent more than five times as much as they gave to the poor.[39] Turning now to the five other budget-groups, one finds that the average expenditure per household for "spiritual needs" (that is, for education aside from that provided for out of taxes; for books; for payments to the priests and the Church; and for weddings and christenings) amounted in one group to less than one and one-half per cent of the total outlay for personal needs, and in the group at the other extreme to only a little more than five per cent. The balance was devoted almost exclusively to the provision of food and drink, clothing and shelter.[40]

The Church, the conscript army, the school, and the press, all helped to wear down the cultural isolation of the village and to give general currency to ideas of one kind and another. As to the quality of these ideas, one may say at least that wherever they touched directly upon the economic, social, and political life of the country, they were usually conservative, sometimes reactionary, seldom progressive. That this should be so was guaranteed by the character of the government and by its direct control of the Church, its minute inspection of the schools, its omnivorous censorship of the printed word.[41] A venturesome school-teacher, a stray newspaper or pamphlet, a peasant worker returning from the city, might impart a dash of liberal or revolutionary thought, but the sheer weight and size of the official forces gave them control of most of the avenues of communication with the village.

This *qualitative* control was severe enough, but the intercourse of the peasants with the outside world was so limited in *quantity* — if one may employ the term — that much of the ideology of the village was still derived, not from any outside source, whether officially approved or unapproved, but from the past of the village itself. The peasant was ignorant — so men said; that is, he was ignorant of most of what the learned recognize as learning. He knew little of the systematic theology of the Church, and still less of the secular discipline of the schools, but other lore he knew in plenty: how to read signs and portents; how to circumvent spells; how to tell stories and sing songs that had never been set down in any book; how to bend a horse-yoke, or thatch a house; how to act in concert with his neighbors in some vital matter — say the annual redivision of the meadow; how (after mass) to dance, sing, and drink down sorrow on numberless holidays of Christian name and somewhat Bacchic character.[42]

In the life of the peasantry there was good deal that they could well afford to forget, and in order to accomplish this end and to achieve for the moment a state of bliss, many of the villagers had recourse to the bottle. A certain amount of *kvas* and of other mild brews was drunk, but hard white liquor, hot and straight, was much used in periodic carouses. The budget-investigation of the 107 households in Kostroma *guberniia* showed that during the given year all but two of these households expended something for *vodka*, while the total outlay for this item did not fall far short of the sum of all that these families spent for education (aside from taxes), for books, for oil and incense, for gifts to the priests and to the poor, and for weddings and funerals.[43] It is true that the general per capita consumption of spirits in this *guberniia* was somewhat above the average for the country as a whole, but other budget-investigations in two *guberniias* with a general below-average consumption showed that in the small groups of peasant households examined, the percentage of families which made use of *vodka* varied from 94.1 to one hundred.[44] "According to an established custom, sanctified by time and by tradition, not one event in the social life of the community (such, for example, as the cutting of the hay, or the celebration of the local saint's day), can be gotten through without the drinking of *vodka;* and in just the same way *vodka* is indispensable on every important occasion in the life of the family: at births, marriages, funeral-feasts, the leave-taking of recruits, and the like" — so said a government report in 1903, and there is no reason to believe that the drinking-customs had since declined.[45]

WITH many of the landed nobles, things had gone badly indeed during the Revolution of 1905; with many they had gone badly since. It has been explained that an important part of the area owned by the nobles and the larger proprietors of other classes was let to the peasants under various rental arrangements, while the remainder was cultivated under the management of the estate, either with the help of the peasants' equipment or with inventory belonging to the estate itself. After the Revolution of 1905, there was a considerable increase in the employment by the estates of agricultural machinery of many kinds, though it seems that in 1912 there were, for example, only 166 tractors in the country. During the period between the Revolution of 1905 and the Great War, the yield of grain per acre was also materially improved, and continued to exceed by a substantial margin the improving yield on the allotment-land of the peasants. In the data on yields collected by the Ministry of Agriculture, the line was drawn between the peasant allotments and all other lands; that is, the lands which the peasants rented from non-peasant proprietors, and even the non-allotment-lands which the peasants had purchased, were grouped with those cultivated under the management of the estates. If there were any inclusive data on productivity which distinguished between the lands actually *cultivated* by the estates on the one hand, and those *cultivated* by the peasants on the other, the superiority of the former would undoubtedly be revealed as greater than was that of the non-allotment-lands in general as compared with the allotments.

With an extensive acreage, a trained management, a superior equipment, and an improved technique, some of the proprietors were demonstrating what might be accomplished by a large-scale, capitalistic agriculture; they had already set up what some of the Marxian writers of Soviet Russia have called "agricultural factories." In the northern and central *guberniias*, one rarely met with estates which were organized on this footing, but in the West, and especially in the Southwest, they were much more common. In some cases, indeed, several latifundia belonging to a single grandee, with a total area of thousands or even tens of thousands of acres, were operated under a central management, just as are the separate factories of some great industrial corporation. It is impossible to estimate, even approximately, the area of large-scale, capitalistic *cultivation* before the war, but certainly this area was far smaller than that of large-scale *ownership*, and small indeed as compared with the area of petty cultivation. The peasant cultivators produced a very much larger quantity than did the non-peasants of both wheat and rye, and sent into the general market a much larger gross tonnage, but it was in the nature of things that the marketable surplus of the non-peasant producers should be larger in *proportion* to their gross production — and this of course gave to non-peasant farming a place of very special significance in the domestic and foreign grain-trade.[46]

In the old system of large holding by the nobility, there had existed the physical basis for agriculture on the grand scale, but by and large, the nobles had failed to build upon this foundation. Whether from indifference, or ineptitude, or necessity, many had rented their land to the peasants, and many others had eliminated themselves from the rural scene by the outright sale of their estates. The story has already been told of how the nobles lost, between 1877 and 1905, nearly twenty-one million *desiatinas* of land, and during the following decade ten millions more — a total net loss of about three-sevenths of all the land that they had held in 1877. Further than this, more than one-third of the land remaining to the nobility was under mortgage, on 1 January 1915, to the Nobles' Bank for loans totalling 831,000,000 *rubls*, or considerably more than half of the value of the mortgaged land (this of course takes no account of mortgages to private lenders); and in 1913 the arrears in the account of the nobles with the Bank amounted to more than two-fifths as much as the current payments which fell due that year.[47]

Inasmuch as the land sold by the nobles passed for the most part not to large proprietors of other classes but to petty holders or to groups of such holders, the change of ownership meant not only the economic decline of the nobility but the partial breaking up of the foundation for a capitalistic agriculture. It has often been argued that the loss of land by the nobles cleared the ground for a capitalistic re-integration that was to follow, and it has been argued, too, that the sale of land to the peasants had already helped to produce a differentiation within the peasant class; but however this may be, and whatever may have been the promise of the future, the readjustment which had actually taken place in the transfer of land from the nobles to the peasants was primarily an agrarian levelling-down. Already, before the Great War and the Great Revolution, many of the nobles were (for a price) surrendering their land.

Yet at the end of every road, one might still find a "nobleman's nest" — in a house of wood or of plastered brick which would

almost certainly present (if it were a building of any size) at least
four of those classical columns which had been since the eighteenth
century so necessary a part of the stage-setting of manorial life.
The house might of course be a small and tumble-down affair, not
much better than a peasant's. Or it might be a modest place of a
single storey with several thousand volumes in its library, and the
walls of its drawing-room over-crowded with eighteenth-century
portraits in wig and powder, and nineteenth-century photographs
in sideburns and epaulets, or expansively *décolletée* (such was the
home on the small estate of the Marshal of Nobility of a certain
northern *guberniia*).[48] Or again it might be a more elaborate residence, like that on the two-thousand-acre domain of the Marshal
of Nobility of one of the *guberniias* of the *step,* where the drawing-
room contained the following properties (all of which were seized
by the peasants in 1917, and duly catalogued by the Marshal,
Prince Ch——, in a subsequent complaint to the authorities): [49]

1 icon	2 small round tables
1 silver icon	1 small three-cornered table of
1 grand piano	apple-wood
1 harmonium	1 large round table
1 large upholstered divan	1 rocking chair, Viennese style
4 large upholstered armchairs	2 tall circular stands
4 small upholstered armchairs	3 bookcases
4 chairs of Viennese style	1 leather-covered chair
1 very large upholstered reclining chair	

Or the house might be one of the country seats of a family of
grandees — a huge establishment with exterior walls tinted ochre
and white, a columned gateway, a broad forecourt flanked on
either side by a colonnade, a columned portico, a rotunda (with
more columns, of imitation marble), and a series of apartments
furnished in the brass-clawed mahogany of the Napoleonic Empire and the somewhat more humane accoutrements of earlier and
later times; with rearwards a formal garden set out with graceless
statuary, a great park, and a sweeping view of fields, meadows,
white water and wooded hills.[50]

In such illustrated journals as *Stolitsa i Usadba (Capital and
Country-Seat)* one may still see the pageant of those very far-off
times before the war; but the writer once saw it quite unexpectedly, when in 1926 he found on the desk of a Russian scholar what
appeared to be a field-glass — lifted it, looked, and saw dark ever-

greens, snow, a large sleigh converted somehow into a table and set with dishes and winebottles, and around it a party of men, some in uniform and some in hunting costume, joining in a hunters' banquet. The binocular had bored through time, not space; it was actually a miniature stereoscope fitted with a photograph a few years old, and the picture was one of those vivid bits that memory holds to — one that became all the more vivid, when the writer afterward identified one of the banqueters as the former Marshal of this particular *guberniia* and found him in a little room at the head of a back-stairway, cutting sausage and making tea on a gasoline stove. . . Dogs and hunting-horses, parks and gardens, cars, carriages, and sleighs, the portrait of Catherine II in the library of the Nobles' Club, the portrait of Nicholas II in the ball-room — what else on earth can be so near, and so sidereally far away?

In 1905 there had been an agrarian revolution, and behind this revolution, considered as a "result," there must have been its "causes"; if it is not so, then there is no logic in the motions of history. Since the result was deep and wide, the causes must also have extended widely and deeply into the life of the villages; and unless the situation and the attitude of the peasants had changed in a marked degree since the early years of the century, the causes of revolution were still present in the villages when the Great War came.

This problem of causation is really a double one, since it involves: first, the external and more or less measurable conditions of peasant life, and second, the attitude of the peasantry themselves toward these conditions.

In the external situation, there had been many changes since the outbreak of the Revolution of 1905. The peasants now had more personal freedom and more political power than before — though little enough of either, in all conscience; and what with the expansion of landholding, the improvement in yields, the increase in real wages in agriculture and in industry, and the decline in the death-rate, it seems possible that there had been some improvement in the material condition of a majority of the peasants, though hardly enough to raise any large part of them above a very humble level. For this tentative conclusion as to an improvement in condition, some support is to be found, too, in the later tax returns of the pre-war period: in the year 1911, with its poor harvest, the peasants fell behind in the payment of the taxes laid upon their allotment-lands, but in 1910, and again in 1912, they overpaid the new assessments and reduced substantially the amounts in arrears—and this in spite of the fact that the new levies were increased in each of these two years.[51]

But in the opinion of those who were working to forestall an agrarian revolution, the hope of the future lay not alone in providing the stronger peasants with more land, but in altering the relationship of the peasants with the land that they already had. When the head of the household became the individual proprietor of a consolidated allotment, he would not only prosper materially, but would feel less solidarity with his peasant neighbors, and have more respect for the property-rights of the near-by landlord; such was the theory, and it is remarkable that in putting it into practice, the government infringed quite ruthlessly upon certain existing property-rights — as when it sacrificed the junior members of the household to the senior, and when it gave the commune the right to shift even hereditary holdings at will in the process of a physical consolidation. And yet, in spite of many arbitrary measures, a vast majority of the peasants still held their land in separate strips and were still involved, in greater or less degree, in the old system of common rights and communal control; and even where a separate title gave a *quantitative* fixity, the holder of scattered strips did not know when his holding would be shunted over-hill and down-dale by a communal vote in favor of consolidation. There was no mistaking the *trend* toward individual property and independent farming; yet in any attempt to judge the peasant temper, allowance must be made for the part played by official compulsion in producing this trend, and it must also be remembered that with the system of peasant holding and peasant cultivation still in a violent flux of change, there had been thus far only a limited opportunity for the new ways to become habitual. Still it is possible that by reason of the economic and legal developments which have just been summarized, the likelihood of a general uprising of the peasants against the landlords was diminishing. During the years 1910–1914, the industrial strike-movement in Russia mounted steadily to a strength never before attained, except in the Revolution of 1905; [52] but these same years brought, on the other hand, a marked decline in the number of local agrarian disturbances recorded annually.[53]

And then came the war, altering certain of the material conditions of peasant life (such as the working strength of the household, the wages of labor, the supply and price of goods); inflicting desperate and meaningless sorrow upon hundreds of thousands of peasant homes; bringing confusion, bungling, defeat, and desperation; bringing finally the overthrow of the old government and the weakening of all authority; bringing Opportunity to the peasants to do, for the time being, very much what they pleased.

The war-time fortunes of the peasantry require still a brief accounting, and then must come the history of their part in the revolution. What would they do when the rules were all off, and the bars all down? Were they by this time so comfortable and so full of the sense of private property that they would not fight for the land? Or, if some were in a mood to fight, would others join the landlords and help them to fight back? Suppose the peasants did seize the land, what would they try to do with it — and with the land already in their possession? Would they push on still farther toward a system of petty holding and independent cultivation — or would they build upon what still remained of the old common interests and the old collective practices?

The questions were to have their answer. The great scene, so often rehearsed in part, would be played out this time to the finish.

GLOSSARY

Artel: a group organized for co-operative action in production, in consumption, in the sale of labor, or in some other like activity.

Barshchina: corvée; compulsory labor rendered by a serf to his master, or *barin.*

Desiatina: a measure of land-area, equal to 2.70 acres.

Guberniia: from the eighteenth century until after the Revolution of 1917, a major administrative division of the Empire; "the fifty *guberniias*" covered the area of European Russia excepting Finland, Poland, and the region between the Black Sea and the Caspian from Ekaterinodar and Stavropol southward.

Kopeika: one-hundredth part of a *rubl,* hence about one-half of a cent, U. S.

Obrok: dues in kind or in money.

Pud: a measure of weight, equal to 36.11 pounds avoirdupois.

Rubl: a monetary unit; the gold *rubl* was equal to about 51.5 cents, U. S., and was divided into 100 *kopeikas.*

Step: usually means a treeless plain of great extent.

Uezd: an administrative subdivision of the *guberniia.*

Ukaz: a decree issued by the Tsar, or in his name.

Volost: an all-peasant administrative subdivision of the *uezd;* a *volost* usually included several peasant communes.

Zemskii nachalnik: might possibly be translated "territorial chief"; a petty appointive official with large administrative and judicial powers over the peasants.

Zemstvo: the elective assembly of an *uezd* or *guberniia,* in which all classes were to some extent represented; also the executive organization maintained by such an assembly.

APPENDICES

APPENDIX I

LANDHOLDING IN 49 *GUBERNIIAS* OF EUROPEAN RUSSIA IN 1877 AND IN 1905.[1]

HOLDERS.	HOLDINGS, *in desiatinas.* 1877		1905	
I. Peasants and Other Villagers, excepting Cossacks. (2)				
A. Allotment-Lands	111,629,000 d.	....	123,183,000 d.	
B. Non-Allotment-Lands				
1. Individual Holders .. ⎫	5,788,000 d.	....	⎧ 12,671,000 d.	
2. Associations ⎭			⎩ 7,299,000 d.	
3. Communes ..	765,000 d.	....	3,672,000 d.	
Total of Peasant Lands ..	....	118,181,000 d.	....	146,825,000 d.
II. Nobles, Townsmen, State, Church, etc.				
A. Nobles	73,077,000 d.	....	52,104,000 d.	
B. Clergy (personal property)	186,000 d.	....	322,000 d.	
C. Townsmen	11,699,000 d.	....	16,241,000 d.	
D. Non-Peasant (and mixed) Collectives. (2) (3)...	1,717,000 d.	....	4,350,000 d.	
E. State and Imperial Family ..	157,823,000 d.	....	145,881,000 d.	
F. Municipalities. (4)	1,884,000 d.	....	2,030,000 d.	
G. Churches and Monasteries ..	2,129,000 d.	....	2,579,000 d.	
H. Other Institutions	870,000 d.	....	643,000 d.	
Total for Group II	....	249,385,000 d.	....	224,150,000 d.
III. Holders of Other, or of Unspecified, Classes.				
A. Private Holders.	752,000 d.	....	2,514,000 d.	
B. Allotment Holders	5,092,000 d.			
C. Cossacks. (5)				
Allotments	(unknown)	....	5,420,000 d.	
Reserve Lands ..	3,611,000 d.	....	1,568,000 d.	
Total for Group III	....	9,455,000 d.	....	9,502,000 d.
Grand Total	....	377,020,000 d.	....	380,476,000 d.

NOTES TO APPENDIX I

LANDHOLDING IN 49 *GUBERNIIAS* OF EUROPEAN RUSSIA IN 1877 AND IN 1905

(1) The data are from Tsentralnyi Statisticheskii Komitet, *Statistika zemlevladeniia 1905 g. Svod dannykh*, pp. 11, 117, 129, 131–133; and appendix, pp. iv–x, xix–xx, xxii, xxxvi; and the Committee's *Statistika zemlevladeniia 1905 g.*, Issue X, *Bessarabskaia guberniia*, p. 31.

Area covered: The land-census of 1877 covered European Russia excepting (a) Finland, (b) Poland, (c) the *guberniias* between the Black Sea and the Caspian from Ekaterinodar and Stavropol southward, (d) the Don Region, (e) Izmailskii *uezd* in Bessarabskaia *guberniia;* in other words, this census covered 49 *guberniias*, minus one *uezd*.

The land-census of 1905 covered the same area as the census of 1877, plus (a) the Don Region, (b) Izmailskii *uezd;* that is, this census covered 50 *guberniias*.

However, in order that the data for the two periods may be fully comparable in so far as the territory covered is concerned, the returns for the Don Region and for Izmailskii *uezd* have been eliminated in the above table from every item for the year 1905, and all items for both 1877 and 1905 therefore apply to the same area — that is, to the 49 *guberniias* minus Izmailskii *uezd*. (See Note 5, below.) The *Svod dannykh* (Abstract) of the land-census of 1905 provides data which made it possible to make the necessary eliminations throughout, except in the case of those lands in Izmailskii *uezd* which belonged to holders of the following classes: State, and Imperial Family; Municipalities; Churches and Monasteries; Other Institutions. In this connection it was therefore necessary to employ the special volume (Issue X) of this census-report which deals in detail with Bessarabskaia *guberniia*.

The many shortcomings of Russian statistics on land-ownership are discussed in Sviatlovskii, *Mobilizatsiia zemelnoi sobstvennosti v Rossii*, p. 26 ff., and in Vysochaishe Uchrezhd. Kommissiia, *Materialy*, III, p. 46 ff.

Arrangement of data: In the report of the land-census of 1905 the three major categories are: I. Private Lands; II. Allotment-Lands; III. Lands of the State, the Church, and Other Institutions. In the above table, an attempt has been made to rearrange the data in accordance with the social-economic position of the holders.

(2) The categories employed for peasant holdings in the registrations of 1877 and 1905 do not entirely correspond (see Tsentralnyi Statisticheskii Komitet, *op. cit.*, p. 167; Glavnoe Upravlenie Zemleustroistva i Zemledeliia, *Statisticheskie svedeniia*, p. xiii); the results are therefore not exactly comparable, but may nevertheless be accepted as representing the general trend of change. It is also to be noted that some of the mixed collectives (in Class II, D) included peasant members.

(3) In respect to this group (II, D) of Non-peasant (and mixed) Collectives, the results for 1877 and 1905 are not entirely comparable. See Tsentralnyi Statisticheskii Komitet, *op. cit.*, p. 167; Glavnoe Upravlenie Zemleustroistva, *op. cit.*, p. xiii.

(4) Under this heading (II, F. Municipalities), there are included: first, the lands upon which the cities were actually built (irrespective of the character of the ownership of these lands), and second, the pastures, forests, and farm-lands owned by the municipalities, and in part leased by them to private users.

(5) Among the 50 *guberniias* covered by the land-census of 1905, three included Cossack lands: these were Astrakhan, Orenburg, and the Don Region. For reasons explained in footnote 1, above, none of the returns for the Don Region have been included in the table. In this region, in 1905, the Cossack lands were:

Allotments	9,270,000 *des.*
Reserve lands	1,892,000 *des.*

Tsentralnyi Statisticheskii Komitet, *op. cit.*, pp. 117, 132.

APPENDIX II

LANDHOLDING IN 47 *GUBERNIIAS* OF EUROPEAN RUSSIA IN 1905 AND AT THE END OF 1914.[1]

HOLDERS.	HOLDINGS in desiatinas in 1905. (4)	CHANGE in period 1906–1914 inclusive.	HOLDINGS in desiatinas at end of 1914.
I. *Peasants and Other Villagers, including Cossacks.* (2)			
A. Allotment-Lands	136,284,000 d. }	+ 9,586,000 d. (5)	170,461,000 d. (5)
B. Non-Allotment-Lands	24,591,000 d. }		
Total of Peasant Lands	160,875,000 d.	....	170,461,000 d.
II. *All Other Holders.*			
A. Nobles	49,768,000 d.	− 10,210,000 d. (6)	39,558,000 d.
B. State and Imperial Family	145,233,000 d.	− 1,497,000 d. (7)	143,736,000 d.
C. Peasants' Land Bank	276,000 d.	+ 2,005,000 d.	2,281,000 d. (8)
D. All Others (3)	31,601,000 d.	+ 116,000 d.	31,717,000 d.
Total for Group II	226,878,000 d.	....	217,292,000 d.
Grand Total	387,753,000 d.	....	387,753,000 d.

NOTES TO APPENDIX II

LANDHOLDING IN 47 *GUBERNIIAS* OF EUROPEAN RUSSIA IN 1905 AND AT THE END OF 1914

It MUST be understood that this table may not be regarded as definitive, but is offered simply as an incomplete and not altogether reliable patchwork which was pieced together out of materials from various sources in an effort to give some sort of a general view of landholding in European Russia shortly before the Revolution of 1917.

The writer made a serious attempt to discover some means of utilizing for the purpose just mentioned the data on land-ownership published in the reports of the census of 1917, but with small result. The Great War, the Revolution, and the Civil War, in combination, interfered very materially with the original registration and with the assembling of these data of 1917, and even where the materials are more or less complete, the manner in which they were abstracted defeats the purpose of anyone who wants to learn who owned the land of Russia on the eve of the Revolution. In the *Itogi* or *Abstracts* of this census, there is a partial apportionment of land upon the basis of its ownership between the "establishments of peasant type" and the "establishments of private proprietors," but the categories employed do not correspond with those used in the census-reports of earlier years, and it also appears that a considerable area of land actually owned by peasants and by non-peasant proprietors is not included at all in the columns devoted to land-ownership. The major categories of the census of 1905 (I. Private Lands; II. Allotment-Lands; III. Lands of the State, the Church, and Other Institutions) are preserved, it is true, in certain other tables showing land-ownership in 1917 which appear in the *Sbornik* or *Collection* cited below. During the pre-revolutionary period, the great shift in land-ownership was taking place, however, *within* the first category, through the transfer of private lands from one type of owner to another, and inasmuch as the tables in the *Sbornik* do not make any pertinent distinction within this category (upon the basis either of the size of the holdings, or of the legal-social class of the holder), the major issue is avoided and the most important historical possibilities of the census therefore remain unrealized.

The general returns for the census of 1917 have been published in the two following volumes (and also, with supplementary data, in the third): Tsentralnoe Statisticheskoe Upravlenie, *Pogubernskie itogi Vserossiiskoi selsko-khoziaistvennoi i pozemelnoi perepisi 1917 goda;* Tsent. Stat. Uprav., *Pouezdnye itogi;* Tsent. Stat. Uprav., *Statisticheskii sbornik za 1913–1917 g.g.,* pp. 166–239. The quality of these published materials has been the subject of an extremely acrimonious controversy, and in this connection, the following articles have been consulted by the writer: Spiridonov, *Uchet zemlevladeniia i ugodii Evropeiskoi Rossii po perepisi 1917 goda* (in *Selskoe i lesnoe khoziaistvo,* 1923, book 7 combining Nos. 11–14); Lositskii, *Publikatsiia Tsentralnogo Statisticheskogo Upravleniia o zemlevladenii i ugodiiakh po perepisi 1917 g.* (in the same number of this journal); Khriashcheva, *O kritike statisticheskikh izdanii* (in *Vestnik statistiki,* 1923, book XIII); Lositskii, *Eshche k voprosu o publikatsii Tsent. Stat. Uprav.* (in *Selskoe i lesnoe khoziaistvo,* 1923, book II).

FOOTNOTES TO THE TABLE.

(1) *Area covered:* Most of the data for the period 1906–1914 are available for only forty-seven *guberniias* of European Russia; accordingly the table here presented covers that area only, and does not include the three Baltic *guberniias* of Esthonia, Latvia, and Kurland, which were covered in the table for 1877 and 1905 (Appendix I). On the other hand, the present table *does* cover Izmailskii *uezd* in Bessarabskaia *guberniia,* and also the large Don Region, both of which were omitted from the preceding table (Appendix I). Because of these differences in census-area, the data

271

for 1905 are not identical in the two tables, even where the classes of holders correspond exactly.

(2) In the preceding table, the Cossacks were dealt with separately, but because of the character of the data available for the period after 1905, it has been necessary in the present table to combine the allotment- and non-allotment-lands of the Cossacks with those of the "Peasants and Other Villagers." The *reserve* lands of the Cossack armies here fall, however, in Class II, D.

(3) The lack of data that will permit the subdivision of this large group (II, D) in 1914 is the chief defect of this table. This group (II, D) here includes mixed collectives, some of whose members were peasants. It also includes the holdings of non-peasant collectives, and of townsmen, as well as those of municipalities, churches, monasteries, etc.

(4) The data for 1905 are drawn from Tsentralnyi Statisticheskii Komitet: *Statistika zemlevladeniia 1905 g. Svod dannykh*, pp. 130, 132, and appendix, pp. iv, xxxiii; the one exception is the figure for the holdings of the Peasants' Land Bank in 1905, which is from Ministerstvo Zemledeliia, *Sbornik statistiko-ekonomicheskikh svedenii*, 9th year, p. 600.

(5) Information is lacking as to the granting of any additional allotments to the peasants or the Cossacks during this period, and it is here assumed that no such grants took place.

For the amount of the net change in the non-allotment-holdings of the peasants and Cossacks which resulted from their transactions with members of other classes, one must depend upon the returns of the Department of Direct Taxes. The returns of this Department for purchases and sales have been published only to the end of the year 1910 (Departament Okladnykh Sborov, *Materialy po statistike dvizheniia zemlevladeniia*, XXV, pp. 64–65), but in the preparation of the present table, these returns were supplemented with unpublished materials of the Department for the years 1911–1914 inclusive. During the period 1906–1914, the total net increase in the non-allotment-holdings of the peasants and the Cossacks of the 47 *guberniias*, resulting from transactions with members of other classes, is reported in the above sources as 9,347,000 *desiatinas*. To this must be added a total of 239,000 *desiatinas* purchased by the peasants from the State during the same period and in the same guberniias. (G. U. Z. i Z., *Otchetnye svedeniia*, appendix, p. 90). (Land-purchases made directly from the State were not included in the returns of the Department of Direct Taxes, but any resales of such lands, after they had once become private property, were included.)

There is however another question involved here: the land-law of 1911 (G. U. Z. i Z., *Zemleustroistvo*, p. 5, Statute on land-organization, art. 3) provided that when under certain conditions the allotments and the non-allotment-lands of a given group of peasants were lumped together and subjected to a general physical consolidation and partition into unitary farms, each of these new farms should be regarded, as a whole, as a private *non-allotment* property, unless the individual holder wished the farm in its entirety to have the character of allotment-land. In other words, this law makes possible, under certain conditions, the conversion of allotment-land into non-allotment-land, and *vice versa*. The writer does not know of any data that show the net result of such interchanges, but in any case the *total* amount of property belonging to the peasants and the Cossacks could not have been affected by such transfers.

(6) From the materials, published and unpublished, of the Department of Direct Taxes (see note 5 above).

(7) 1,258,000 *desiatinas* of the lands of the Imperial family were sold to the Peasants' Land Bank (Baturinskii, *Agrarnaiia politika*, p. 104), and 239,000 *desiatinas* of State lands were sold directly to the peasants. An additional 142,000 *desiatinas* of State lands were assigned to peasant purchasers under certain specific conditions, upon the completion of which the transfer of the property was to be fully consummated; but because of the conditional character of this arrangement, these 142,000 *desiatinas* are not subtracted from the holdings of the State, or added to those of the peasants, in the above table. G. U. Z. i Z., *Otchetnye svedeniia o deiatelnosti zemleustroitelnykh komissii na I ianvaria 1915 goda*, pp. 21–22; appendix, pp. 88–91; also G. U. Z. i Z., *Obzor deiatelnosti za 1914 god*, pp. 209–210.

(8) From Ministerstvo Zemledeliia, *Sbornik statistiko-ekonomicheskikh svedenii*, 9th year, p. 600.

NOTES

NOTES TO CHAPTER I

[1] Kliuchevskii, *Kurs*, I, p. 126.

[2] *Ibid.*; Miliukov, *Ocherki*, I, p. 46.

[3] Peisker, *Expansion of the Slavs* (in *Cambridge medieval history*, II), pp. 418–458. The question as to whether or not the Slavs were ever a unitary race with a single center of dispersion is still in dispute.

[4] Kliuchevskii, *op. cit.*, I, p. 127.

[5] Kulisher, *Istoriia russkogo narodnogo khoziaistva*, I, division I, chap. II; Kliuchevskii, *op. cit.*, I, chaps. VII–XV.

[6] Kliuchevskii, *op. cit.*, I, p. 354.

[7] Beazley, *Russia from the Varangians to the Bolsheviks*, p. 47.

[8] Kulisher, *op. cit.*, I, pp. 46, 48, 58; Kliuchevskii, *op. cit.*, I, pp. 348–354.

[9] Kliuchevskii, *op. cit.*, I, p. 360.

[10] Kliuchevskii, *op. cit.*, I, pp. 360–367.

[11] Semevskii, *Krestiane*, I, p. iii; Kliuchevskii, *op. cit.*, I, pp. 382–383; Pokrovskii, *Russkaia istoriia*, I, p. 31; Kulisher, *op. cit.*, I, p. 59; Solovev, *Istoriia Rossii*, I, p. 1533. Cf. Simkhovitch, *Feldgemeinschaft in Russland*, p. 39.

[12] Kliuchevskii, *op. cit.*, I, pp. 383–384; Kulisher, *op. cit.*, I, pp. 49–58.

[13] Pokrovskii, *op. cit.*, I, p. 31; Kulisher, *op. cit.*, I, p. 59; Kliuchevskii, *op. cit.*, I, p. 383.

[14] Kulisher (in *Istoriia khoziaistva*, I, pp. 14–17) and Kliuchevskii (in *Kurs*, I, pp. 136–137) discuss the question of collectivism in Old Kievan Russia. For some account of family collectivism during the feudal and Muscovite periods, see Pokrovskii, *op. cit.*, I, pp. 16–21, 36; Kovalevskii, *Modern customs and ancient laws*, pp. 49–53, 75–76, and his *Rodovoi byt*, issue I, esp. p. 37; Kulisher, *op. cit.*, I, pp. 58–59; Kliuchevskii, *op. cit.*, II, pp. 297–298; Efimenko, *Iuzhnaia Rus*, I, pp. 370–412, and her *Krestianskoe zemlevladenie na krainem severe* (in her *Issledovaniia narodnoi zhizni*, I). On p. 372 of the former work, Efimenko thus characterizes what she believes to have been the typical social-economic group of the far North in early times: ". . . an association of near relatives — uncles, nephews, cousins, who live in a close family union. They perhaps live in a single peasant house (down to the present time there still stand in the North great *izbas*, real palaces as compared, for example, with the peasant houses of the South); or they may have established themselves in different *izbas*, constructed one near the other — but nevertheless they still form a single undivided 'hearth' (*pechishche*). To the end of its era, the 'hearth' conducts a joint economy such as we occasionally see down to the present day in a large Great-Russian family." Based very largely upon original research, Efimenko's studies of patriarchal collectivism in Little Russia and in the northern part of Great Russia are of special interest (see especially her *Iuzhnaia Rus*, I, pp. 371–372, 382–384, 395). However it is hardly possible to write anything whatever upon the general subject discussed above, without becoming involved in questions which are still both obscure and highly controversial.

[15] Efimenko, *Iuzhnaia Rus*, I, pp. 372–375, 383, 392–395, 400, 406, 419; and her *Krestianskoe zemlevladenie na krainem severe* (in her *Issledovaniia narodnoi zhizni*, I), pp. 219, 264.

[16] Kliuchevskii, *op. cit.*, II, pp. 298, 395, 397. Cf. Gote, *Zamoskovnyi krai v XVII veke*, pp. 136–140.

[17] Kliuchevskii, *op. cit.*, II, p. 358; Oganovskii, *Zakonomernost*, II, pp. 120–121; Efimenko, *Iuzhnaia Rus*, I, p. 417; Gote, *op. cit.*, pp. 431, 462; Wilson, *Obiasneniia k khoziaistvenno-statisticheskomu atlasu Evropeiskoi Rossii*, p. 57.

[18] Kulisher, *op. cit.*, I, p. 59; Kovalevskii, *Modern laws and ancient customs*, p. 76; Efimenko, *op. cit.*, I, p. 372, 384, 389, 394, 397–398; Lappo-Danilevskii, *Ocherk istorii*

obrazovaniia glavneishikh razriadov (in Dolgorukov, ed., *Krestianskii stroi*, I), p. 20; Semevskii, *Krestiane*, II, pp. 598–601.

19 Kliuchevskii, *op. cit.*, II, p. 367.

20 *Ibid.*, II, pp. 367–372.

21 *Ibid.*, II, p. 367; Kulisher, *op. cit.*, II, p. 158. A *volost* was a rural administrative district which usually included a number of villages.

22 Bogoslovskii, *Zemskoe samoupravlenie*, II, pp. 1–18; Lappo-Danilevskii, *op. cit.*, p. 28; Ivanov, *Pozemelnye soiuzy i peredely na severe* (in Mosk. Arkheolog. obshchestvo, *Drevnosti*, 1902, vol. II), p. 240; Semevskii, *Krestiane*, II, p. 598 ff.; Simkhovitch, *Feldgemeinschaft in Russland*, pp. 35–36.

23 Kliuchevskii, *op. cit.*, II, p. 368; Kulisher, *op. cit.*, II, pp. 158–161; Miliukov, *Ocherki*, I, p. 206; Lappo-Danilevskii, *op. cit.*, pp. 49–51.

24 The existence among the peasants of certain forms of collectivism has been indicated above, but no attempt has been made to explain how or why these phenomena appeared. In the whole range of Russian history, there is perhaps no subject so obscure and so highly controversial as that of the origin and early history of the peasant land-commune, and especially of the practice of making a periodic redistribution of the land. Among the writers whose work is available in a Western European language, Simkhovitch states very strongly the case for the importance of the influence of the State and the landlords in the establishment of the periodic equalizing redistribution of land among the peasants. — *Feldgemeinschaft*, for example pp. 23–24 and 56–64; also his *Hay and History* (in his *Toward the understanding of Jesus*), pp. 140–165. An interesting summary of the various interpretations advanced during nearly three-quarters of a century of debate will be found in Kulisher, *Istoriia khoziaistva*, II, pp. 147–168. A summary is also offered by A. Miller in his recent *Essai sur l'histoire des institutions agraires de la Russie centrale du XVIe au XVIIIe siècles*, pp. 159–170. As an example of the pronounced differences which have arisen in this connection among the most serious students of Russian peasant history, one may cite Efimenko, *Krestianskoe zemlevladenie na krainem severe* (in her *Issledovaniia narodnoi zhizni*, I), pp. 366–377, and the discussion and partial contradiction of her conclusions in Semevskii, *Krestiane*, II, p. 598 ff.

25 Kulisher, *op. cit.*, I, pp. 58–73; Kliuchevskii, *op. cit.*, II, p. 360; Miliukov, *Ocherki*, I, p. 224; Diakonov, *Ocherki obshchestvennogo i gosudarstvennogo stroia*, p. 247; Simkhovitch, *Feldgemeinschaft in Russland*, pp. 34, 35; Lappo-Danilevskii, *op. cit.*, p. 26; Rozhkov, *Russkaia istoriia*, IV, pp. 66–67. In the North, the State claimed proprietorship of the lands occupied by the peasants, but did not succeed in making its proprietorial claims fully effective until the 18th century (Miliukov, *op. cit.*, I, p. 225). No attempt is made above to distinguish between the lands of State, and those "Court lands" the revenues of which were allotted directly to the support of the Imperial court. In 1775 the court lands with their peasants were placed under the same administration with those of the State; in 1797, they were reclassified as *udel* or appanage property, and placed under the control of a special department bearing this name. Semevskii, *Krestiane*, II, pp. xiv–xv.

26 Platonov, *Uchebnik*, pp. 147–148, and his *Lektsii*, p. 118; Kliuchevskii, *Kurs*, I, pp. 444–445; Diakonov, *op. cit.*, p. 247.

27 Kliuchevskii, *op. cit.*, II, p. 381.

28 Kulisher, *Istoriia khoziaistva*, II, pp. 97–98.

29 Kliuchevskii, *op. cit.*, II, pp. 367–368.

30 *Ibid.*, II, pp. 388, 392, and his *Istoriia soslovii*, p. 96; Diakonov, *Ocherki iz istorii selskogo naseleniia*, pp. 7–13, 147; cf. Platonov, *Ocherki*, p. 177.

31 Kliuchevskii, *Kurs*, II, p. 368.

32 Kulisher, *op. cit.*, II, pp. 53, 66.

33 The use of the word "landlord" is not intended, of course, to imply absolute ownership in the modern sense.

34 Kliuchevskii, *op. cit.*, II, p. 368; Kulisher, *op. cit.*, II, pp. 64–65, 104.

35 Kliuchevskii, *op. cit.*, II, pp. 362–363; Kulisher, *op. cit.*, II, p. 85. Kliuchevskii emphasizes a distinction, apparently continuing to the end of the 16th century, between *dues* (paid for the use of land) and *services* (rendered in payment of interest on, or the principal of, loans).

36 Kliuchevskii, *op. cit.*, II, pp. 373, 376, 381, 398; Kulisher, *op. cit.*, II, p. 115 ff.; Platonov, *op. cit.*, pp. 173–174.

³⁷ When the peasant householder himself could not clear up his obligations, there were two other lawful means through which he might possibly arrange for a removal: he might secure a substitute, who would take over his allotment and assume his debts — but only rarely could such a substitute be found; or, *with the consent of his own landlord*, he might arrange with another landowner for the payment of his obligations, in which case he became bound to the new creditor just as he had formerly been to the old. The difficulties in the way of the removal of a *junior* member of a peasant household were by no means so serious as those which affected the house-father. Kliuchevskii, *op. cit.*, II, pp. 389, 398–399, 402; and his *Proiskhozhdenie krepostnogo prava v Rossii* (in his *Opyty i issledovaniia*) p. 231; Platonov, *op. cit.*, pp. 174–175, 179.

³⁸ Kliuchevskii, *Kurs*, II, pp. 401–402; Kulisher, *op. cit.*, II, p. 40; Platonov, *op. cit.*, p. 178.

³⁹ Miliukov, *Ocherki*, I, p. 55 ff., and map opp. p. 64.

⁴⁰ Kliuchevskii, *op. cit.*, II, pp. 297, 399 ff.; Kulisher, *op. cit.*, II, p. 121 ff.

⁴¹ See soil-map in *Rossiia*, opposite p. 54, and map showing the advance of colonization in Miliukov, *op. cit.*, I, opp. p. 64.

⁴² These changes proceeded haltingly, of course, with many set-backs, and sometimes against furious opposition. See Platonov, *Ocherki po istorii smuty*, pp. 160–163; Pokrovskii, *Russkaia istoriia*, I, chaps. II, V, VI; Pavlov-Silvanskii, *Feodalizm v drevnei Rusi*, pp. 116–125, 134–136; Diakonov, *Ocherki stroia*, pp. 200–232; Kliuchevskii, *Kurs*, I, pp. 447–449; II, p. 264 ff.; III, pp. 200–201; IV, pp. 106–112; Kulisher, *Istoriia khoziaistva*, II, pp. 67–84.

⁴³ Kliuchevskii, *op. cit.*, III, pp. 207–213; Kulisher, *op. cit.*, II, p. 139 ff.

⁴⁴ Platonov, *Lektsii*, p. 509.

⁴⁵ Diakonov, *Ocherki stroia*, p. 295.

⁴⁶ Liubavskii, *Ocherk istorii litovsko-russkogo gosudarstva*, pp. 138–139; Grabenskii, *Istoriia polskogo naroda*, pp. 94–95, 161–164; Kliuchevskii, *op. cit.*, III, p. 118; Efimenko, *Iuzhnaia Rus*, pp. 387–395.

⁴⁷ Kliuchevskii, *op. cit.*, I, p. 352; III, p. 128.

⁴⁸ Kliuchevskii, *op. cit.*, I, pp. 351–354.

⁴⁹ *Ibid.*, II, pp. 399, 406; Kulisher, *op. cit.*, II, p. 121; Platonov, *Lektsii*, p. 430.

⁵⁰ Kliuchevskii, *op. cit.*, I, p. 353; II, p. 397.

⁵¹ Fletcher, *Of the Russe common wealth*, in *Works issued by the Hakluyt Society*, No. 20, p. 61.

⁵² Miliukov, *Ocherki*, I, pp. 56–57, and map opp. p. 64; Iakovlev, *Zasechnaia cherta Moskovskogo gosudarstva*, chap. I.

⁵³ Kliuchevskii, *Kurs*, III, p. 130 ff.; Platonov, *Lektsii*, p. 430.

⁵⁴ Ralston, *Songs of the Russian People*, p. 47.

⁵⁵ The above paragraphs do not attempt to summarize the history of the Time of Troubles, but merely to indicate in a very general way the part played in this history by the peasants and the Cossacks. For the general history of the period, see especially Platonov, *Ocherki po istorii smuty*; also Kliuchevskii, *op. cit.*, III, lectures XLI–XLIV, esp. p. 56 ff.; Pokrovskii, *Russkaia istoriia*, II, chap. VII; Iakovlev, ed., *Pamiatniki istorii Smutnogo vremeni.*

⁵⁶ Kliuchevskii, *op. cit.*, II, p. 402.

⁵⁷ Platonov, *op. cit.*, p. 256 ff.

⁵⁸ *Ibid.*, p. 322 ff. Bolotnikov co-operated in the beginning of the campaign with one of the factions of the nobility.

⁵⁹ Platonov, *op. cit.*, p. 352 ff.

⁶⁰ Kliuchevskii, *op. cit.*, III, p. 58.

⁶¹ The Swedes retained the land around the head of the Gulf of Finland. Platonov, *Lektsii*, pp. 272, 292; and his *Uchebnik*, p. 210.

⁶² Platonov, *Ocherki*, p. 487 ff.

⁶³ Kliuchevskii, *op. cit.*, III, p. 222; Kulisher, *Istoriia khoziaistva*, II, p. 132 ff. Before the Time of Troubles, many of the old noble families had already been decimated or destroyed in their conflict with the Tsar Ivan the Terrible.

⁶⁴ Platonov, *Lektsii*, p. 317.

⁶⁵ Platonov, *Uchebnik*, p. 206.

⁶⁶ Pokrovskii, *Russkaia istoriia*, II, p. 80 ff.

⁶⁷ Kliuchevskii, *op. cit.*, II, pp. 392, 406; III, p. 205; and his *Istoriia soslovii*,

p. 194; Lappo-Danilevskii, *Ocherk istorii* (in Dolgorukov, ed., *Krestianskii stroi*, I), pp. 22–24; Vorms, ed., *Pamiatniki*, p. 70.

[68] Kliuchevskii, *Kurs*, III, pp. 214, 217, 225; and his *Proiskhozhdenie krepostnogo prava v Rossii* (in his *Opyty i issledovaniia*), pp. 266–267; Pokrovskii, *op. cit.*, II, p. 84.

[69] The registrations of 1627–28 and 1646. Kliuchevskii, *Kurs*, III, pp. 218, 225.

[70] Kliuchevskii, *op. cit.*, III, pp. 227–231; the text of chap. XI of the Code of 1649 is quoted in Vorms, ed., *Pamiatniki*, pp. 70–76.

[71] Kliuchevskii, *op. cit.*, III, p. 227.

[72] Kulisher, *op. cit.*, II, p. 136; Kliuchevskii, *op. cit.*, III, p. 224; Pokrovskii, *op. cit.*, II, p. 85.

[73] Kliuchevskii, *op. cit.*, III, p. 224.

[74] *Ibid.*, III, pp. 229, 231.

[75] *Ibid.*, III, p. 233.

[76] Kulisher, *op. cit.*, II, p. 144; Kliuchevskii, *op. cit.*, III, pp. 215–216.

[77] Kliuchevskii, *op. cit.*, III, pp. 235, 292–293; Kulisher, *op. cit.*, II, p. 147.

[78] Kliuchevskii, *op. cit.*, III, p. 385; Platonov, *Lektsii*, p. 377.

[79] Kliuchevskii, *op. cit.*, III, pp. 386, 388.

[80] *Ibid.*, III, p. 386; Platonov, *op. cit.*, p. 379; Miliukov, *Ocherki*, II, pp. 42–43.

[81] Kliuchevskii, *op. cit.*, III, pp. 388, 393; Platonov, *op. cit.*, p. 385. The anathema was launched at a general council of the Eastern Orthodox Church, convened at Moscow in 1666.

[82] Conybeare, *Russian dissenters*, p. 87. Those who refused to accept the revision are referred to in the Russian language both as "Old Ritualists" and as "Old Believers," but the former term seems to express much more accurately than the latter the nature of the controversy.

[83] Miliukov, *op. cit.*, II, p. 142; Platonov, *op. cit.*, p. 838.

[84] Platonov, *op. cit.*, p. 584.

[85] Miliukov, *op. cit.*, I, p. 59 ff., and map opp. p. 64. See also, Iakovlev, *Zasechnaia cherta* (with invaluable maps), and Platonov, *Lektsii*, p. 430.

[86] Semevskii, *Krestiane*, I, p. vii; II, p. 667 ff.

[87] Picheta, *Istoriia krestianskikh volnenii*, p. 30.

[88] Kliuchevskii, *Kurs*, III, pp. 129, 237; Kulisher, *Istoriia khoziaistva*, II, pp. 109, 137.

[89] Platonov, *op. cit.*, p. 365.

[90] Picheta, *op. cit.*, p. 33; Kliuchevskii, *op. cit.*, III, p. 142 ff.; Pokrovskii, *Russkaia istoriia*, II, pp. 144, 149.

[91] Picheta, *op. cit.*, pp. 34–38; Platonov, *op. cit.*, pp. 365–367.

[92] Kliuchevskii, *op. cit.*, III, p. 127 ff.; p. 141 ff.; Platonov, *op. cit.*, pp. 427–429; Firsov, *Krestianskie volneniia do XIX veka* (in Dzhivelegov, ed., *Velikaia reforma*, II), pp. 26–29.

[93] Kliuchevskii, *op. cit.*, III, p. 144; Pokrovskii, *op. cit.*, II, pp. 165, 180; Grushevskii, *Istoriia Ukrainy*, pp. 288 ff., 433–434.

[94] Pokrovskii, *op. cit.*, II, p. 168. The Little Russian townsmen and gentry also played a part in the uprising. Grushevskii, *op. cit.*, pp. 295–297, 434. Some of the Little Russian Orthodox gentry fought on the side of the Cossacks against the Poles; but Miakotin believes that in their own attacks the peasants made small distinction between the Little Russian Orthodox landlords, and those of Polish nationality and Catholic faith. Miakotin, *Ocherki sotsialnoi istorii Ukrainy*, I, part I, pp. 13, 54, 55, 56 (footnote).

[95] Pokrovskii, *op. cit.*, II, p. 172; Grushevskii, *op. cit.*, p. 302. This treaty was signed in 1649.

[96] Pokrovskii, *op. cit.*, II, p. 172; Grushevskii, *op. cit.*, p. 303.

[97] Kliuchevskii, *Kurs*, III, pp. 146–152.

[98] Grushevskii, *op. cit.*, pp. 354, 434.

[99] *Ibid.*, p. 361; Pokrovskii, *op. cit.*, II, p. 191; Efimenko, *Iuzhnaia Rus*, I, pp. 395–396.

[100] Grushevskii, *op. cit.*, pp. 359–365; Pokrovskii, *op. cit.*, II, p. 189 ff.; Efimenko, *op. cit.*, I, pp. 398–399.

[101] Grushevskii, *op. cit.*, p. 360.

NOTES TO CHAPTER II

[1] In this chapter and in others to follow, a great deal will be said of the severe conditions under which the Russian peasantry have lived. To what extent these conditions were peculiar to Russia is a question which involves elaborate comparisons with the situation in other countries. Such a comparative study would be an undertaking of great historic interest and importance, but it is one which extends far beyond the scope of the work here in hand.

[2] Kliuchevskii, *Kurs*, V, p. 118; Platonov, *Lektsii*, pp. 617–628.

[3] In the condition of the villagers on the private estates in the latter half of the eighteenth century, there is much that appears to belong to outright slavery, rather than to serfdom. As will presently be shown, the law gave to the person and the property of these villagers only a very limited protection in theory, and still less in practice. It was legally possible for the landlord to establish that system of production which is ordinarily regarded as characteristic, not of serfdom, but of slavery: the system under which the laborer works continuously under the direction of the master (or of his deputy), produces goods which belong in their entirety to the master, and receives his maintenance from the master. As a matter of fact, comparatively few of the villagers were reduced to such complete dependence; much the greater part of them devoted at least a portion of their time to the self-directed and self-supporting cultivation of a share of the master's estate allotted for their use. When one reads of their being sold off the land, sometimes, like so many cattle, one is tempted to call them slaves, but it is still to be remembered that normally (and by custom only — not by law), they enjoyed the partial economic autonomy of serfdom.

[4] Kliuchevskii, *op. cit.*, IV, p. 95 ff., esp. p. 100; Beliaev, *Krestiane*, pp. 241–242, 276; Romanovich-Slavatinskii, *Dvorianstvo*, pp. 120–121.

[5] Kliuchevskii, *op. cit.*, IV, pp. 103–104.

[6] Kliuchevskii, *op. cit.*, IV, p. 111 ff.; Beliaev, *op. cit.*, p. 273.

[7] Kliuchevskii, *op. cit.*, IV, pp. 415–417; Beliaev, *op. cit.*, p. 283 ff.; Romanovich-Slavatinskii, *op. cit.*, pp. 198–200; Korf, *Dvorianstvo*, pp. 1–6.

[8] Kliuchevskii, *op. cit.*, pp. 115–116.

[9] Platonov, *op. cit.*, pp. 543–638. The privileges of the nobility were confirmed and extended by laws of 1775 and by the Nobles' Charter of 1785.

[10] Kornilov, *Kurs*, I, p. 23; Znamenskii, *Rukovodstvo*, pp. 350–351; Semevskii, *Krestiane*, II, pp. 254–255.

[11] Semevskii, *op. cit.*, I, pp. vii–viii.

[12] Kliuchevskii, *Kurs*, IV, lectures LXIII, LXXII; V, lectures LXXXII–LXXXVII; and his *Istoriia soslovii*, p. 209; Beliaev, *op. cit.*, pp. 234–301; Platonov, *op. cit.*, pp. 509–510.

[13] Semevskii, *op. cit.*, I, p. xxii.

[14] Beliaev, *op. cit.*, p. 240; Semevskii, *op. cit.*, I, p. 127; Kliuchevskii, *Kurs*, V, p. 88.

[15] Semevskii, *op. cit.*, I, p. 128.

[16] Kliuchevskii, *op. cit.*, V, pp. 101, 103.

[17] *Ibid.*, V, pp. 88–89; Semevskii, *op. cit.*, I, pp. xxi, 328–330.

[18] Beliaev, *op. cit.*, pp. 268–270, 272 (note); Picheta, *Istoriia krestianskikh volnenii*, p. 40.

[19] Semevskii, *Krestiane*, I, pp. xii–xiii, 45–46; II, p. iv. In practice, the landlords of Great Russia rarely detached their peasants from the land, in the 18th century; in Little Russia, this was much more frequently done.

[20] Semevskii, *op. cit.*, I, p. 303.

[21] Beliaev, *op. cit.*, pp. 268, 295, 300; Kliuchevskii, *Kurs*, V, p. 106; Semevskii, *op. cit.*, I, pp. xvi–xvii, 165–166; Romanovich-Slavatinskii, *op. cit.*, p. 352; Vorms, *Polozheniia 19 fevralia* (in Dzhivelegov, ed., *Velikaia reforma*, VI), p. 24.

[22] Compare Lappo-Danilevskii, *Ocherk istorii* (in Dolgorukov, ed., *Krestianskii stroi*, I), p. 137; Semevskii, *op. cit.*, I, pp. 52–53; Kliuchevskii, *op. cit.*, V, pp. 101–102. Kliuchevskii makes allowance for the decrease in the value of money, and indicates that the *obrok* approximately doubled; Semevskii estimates that if computed in terms of "quarters" of rye at the prevailing prices, the average *obrok* in the 'sixties would perhaps have amounted to something more than one "quarter" — in the 'nineties, to less than one and one-half "quarters"; but Oganovskii criticizes

unfavorably the statistical basis of Semevskii's estimate; see Oganovskii, *Zakonomernost*, II, p. 328, footnote 1.

[23] Kliuchevskii, *Kurs*, V, pp. 101–102; he makes allowance here also for the depreciation in the value of money.

[24] Ignatovich, *Pomeshchichi krestiane*, p. 34; Semevskii, *op. cit.*, I, pp. xiii–xv, 63, 67; Kliuchevskii, *op. cit.*, V, p. 102. Sometimes the required days of corvée were not fulfilled by all the workers of a given household, but by a smaller number who worked a proportionately longer time.

[25] Semevskii, *op. cit.*, I, pp. xiv–xv; Tugan-Baranovskii, *Russkaia fabrika*, I, pp. 31–32.

[26] Beliaev, *op. cit.*, p. 291; Semevskii, *op. cit.*, I, p. xxiv.

[27] Beliaev, *op. cit.*, pp. 268, 288; Picheta, *Istoriia krestianskikh volnenii*, p. 40; Semevskii, *op. cit.*, I, pp. xvii–xx; Kliuchevskii, *op. cit.*, V, p. 96; Ignatovich, *op. cit.*, p. 52.

[28] Vorms, ed., *Pamiatniki*, pp. 113–114; Kliuchevskii, *op. cit.*, V, p. 89; Beliaev, *op. cit.*, p. 301; Miliukov, *Ocherki*, I, p. 215; Semevskii, *op. cit.*, I, pp. xxiii, 208 ff.

[29] Beliaev, *op. cit.*, pp. 290–292; Kliuchevskii, *op. cit.*, V, p. 105; Semevskii, *op. cit.*, I, p. xxiii.

[30] Semevskii, *Krestiane*, I, pp. xix, 208–216.

[31] Beliaev, *Krestiane*, p. 290; Picheta, *op. cit.*, p. 40; Kliuchevskii, *Kurs*, V, p. 97; Ignatovich, *op. cit.*, p. 45; Semevskii, *op. cit.*, I, pp. xxii–xxiii.

[32] Beliaev, *op. cit.*, pp. 294–299; Semevskii, *op. cit.*, I, p. xxv.

[33] Semevskii, *op. cit.*, II, p. vii; Kliuchevskii, *op. cit.*, V, pp. 85–89, 97.

[34] Kornilov, *Krestianskaia reforma*, p. 3.

[35] No attempt will be made here to differentiate, or even to mention, the numerous minor categories of State peasants. See Lappo-Danilevskii, *op. cit.*, p. 134; Semevskii, *Krestiane*, II, Introduction.

[36] Miliukov, *Ocherki*, I, p. 226.

[37] Vorms, *op. cit.*, pp. 123–128, 138–139; Semevskii, *op. cit.*, II, pp. xxxiii, 625–626; Efimenko, *Issledovaniia*, I, pp. 328–330; Lappo-Danilevskii, *op. cit.*, pp. 134–140.

[38] Lappo-Danilevskii, *op. cit.*, p. 151.

[39] Vorms, *op. cit.*, pp. 110, 123–128, 137; Semevskii, *op. cit.*, I, p. vi; II, pp. 729–736; Liashchenko, *Krestianskoe delo*, I, pp. 333–336; Lappo-Danilevskii, *op. cit.*, pp. 143–145.

[40] Lappo-Danilevskii, *op. cit.*, p. 135.

[41] In 1722–1724 the *obrok* was 40K.; in 1797 it was from 3R. 57K. to 5R. 10K., depending upon various considerations as to locality, etc., etc.; Miliukov, *Krestiane* (in *Entsiklop. slovar*, Brockhaus, XVI), p. 693. In the time of Peter I, the silver *rubl* was equivalent to nine *rubls* of the late nineteenth century; late in the reign of Catherine II, to five. Kornilov, *Kurs*, I, p. 44. In the statement made in the text, above, allowance is made for this depreciation. As to the increase in *obrok*, compare Kliuchevskii, *Kurs*, V, p. 112, and Lappo-Danilevskii, *op. cit.*, pp. 137, 148.

[42] Kliuchevskii, *op. cit.*, IV, p. 411.

[43] Miliukov, *op. cit.*, p. 694; Lappo-Danilevskii, *op. cit.*, pp. 152–153.

[44] Kornilov, *op. cit.*, I, p. 23; Semevskii, *op. cit.*, II, pp. 13–22.

[45] Kornilov, *op. cit.*, I, pp. 23–24; Semevskii, *op. cit.*, II, pp. xviii–xxxi, 295–592; Lappo-Danilevskii, *op. cit.*, pp. 153–154.

[46] Tugan-Baranovskii, *Russkaia fabrika*, I, pp. 15, 42, 73.

[47] Kornilov, *op. cit.*, I, pp. 22–24; Pokrovskii, *Russkaia istoriia*, III, pp. 119–126.

[48] Kornilov, *op. cit.*, I, p. 23; Mavor, *Economic history*, I, pp. 233, 241, 245; Pokrovskii, *op. cit.*, III, p. 138; Znamenskii, *Rukovodstvo*, pp. 349–350.

[49] Kornilov, *op. cit.*, I, p. 58; Kliuchevskii, *Kurs*, V, pp. 94, 158; Romanovich-Slavatinskii, *Dvorianstvo*, p. 170.

[50] Oganovskii, *Zakonomernost*, II, pp. 272–273.

[51] That is, the Cossacks in that part of Ukraina which was annexed to Muscovy.

[52] Platonov, *Uchebnik*, pp. 279–280; Solovev, *Istoriia Rossii*, III, p. 1472; Firsov, *Krestianskie volneniia* (in Dzhivelegov, ed., *Velikaia reforma*, II), pp. 29–30.

[53] Platonov, *op. cit.*, p. 335.

[54] Firsov, *op. cit.*, pp. 30–45; Semevskii, *Krestiane*, I, pp. xxv, 419 ff.

[55] Semevskii, *op. cit.*, II, pp. xxi, xxv, 457–509.

[56] Firsov, *op. cit.*, pp. 30–45; Kliuchevskii, *Kurs*, IV, pp. 409–410; Semevskii, *op. cit.*, I, pp. 394–418.

[57] Platonov, *Uchebnik*, p. 336. On the Old Ritualists in this movement, see Conybeare, *Russian dissenters*, p. 102. On the uprising in general, see Firsov, *op. cit.*, pp. 45–55; Pokrovskii, *Russkaia istoriia*, III, pp. 114–147.

[58] Quoted in Pokrovskii, *op. cit.*, III, p. 143.

[59] *Ibid.*, III, p. 140; Firsov, *op. cit.*, p. 51; also his *Pugachevshchina*, esp. chap. VI; Dubrovin, *Pugachev*, III, p. 111 ff.

[60] Quoted in Pokrovskii, *op. cit.*, III, pp. 139–140.

[61] Pokrovskii, *op. cit.*, III, p. 146; Firsov, *Pugachevshchina*, p. 138.

[62] Platonov, *Uchebnik*, p. 338.

[63] Firsov, *Krestianskie volneniia* (in Dzhivelegov, ed., *Velikaia reforma*, II), pp. 55–56.

[64] Oganovskii, *Zakonomernost*, II, p. 224 ff.; esp. pp. 235–236; Miliukov, *Ocherki*, I, pp. 63–65.

[65] Platonov, *op. cit.*, p. 360.

[66] Pokrovskii, *op. cit.*, II, p. 191; Grushevskii, *Istoriia Ukrainy*, pp. 417–419, 422; Kliuchevskii, *Kurs*, V, p. 95; Semevskii, *Krestiane*, I, p. 408; Miakotin, *Ocherki sotsialnoi istorii*, I, pt. II, pp. 262–263.

[67] Semevskii, *op. cit.*, I, p. xxvi; Lappo-Danilevskii, *Ocherk istorii* (in Dolgorukov, ed., *Krestianskii stroi*, I), p. 77.

[68] Oganovskii, *Zakonomernost*, II, p. 229.

[69] Picheta, *Istoriia krestianskikh volnenii*, pp. 46–66.

NOTES TO CHAPTER III

[1] The reasons for the development of this practice of making a periodic redistribution of the land have long been a subject of controversy among students of the history of agrarian relations in Russia, the debate centering upon the question of the comparative importance of the part played in this development by the peasants themselves on the one hand, and by the landlords and the fiscal system of the State on the other. For references, see Chapter I, footnote 24.

[2] Semevskii, *Krestiane*, I, pp. xiii, 103–104; Ignatovich, *Pomeshchichi krestiane*, p. 106. Cf. Kliuchevskii, *Istoriia soslovii*, pp. 194–195.

[3] Miliukov, *Ocherki*, I, pp. 205, 223–226. Of the *odnodvortsy* on the State lands of the South, about one-half still had separate holdings in the middle of the nineteenth century, while the other half held in communal tenure. *Ibid.*, p. 226. On the general subject of the extension of the practice of periodic redistribution among the State peasants, see also Lappo-Danilevskii, *Ocherk istorii* (in Dolgorukov, ed., *Krestianskii stroi*, I), pp. 141–146; Semevskii, *op. cit.*, II, pp. xxxi–xxxv, 623–659, 745–761; Bogoslovskii, *Zemskoe samoupravlenie*, II, pp. 5, 18; Simkhovitch, *Feldgemeinschaft*, p. 70.

[4] Oganovskii, *Zakonomernost*, II, pp. 343, 345.

[5] Ignatovich, *op. cit.*, pp. 191–192, 223–224; Efimenko, *Iuzhnaia Rus*, I, pp. 406–407.

[6] Vorms, ed., *Pamiatniki*, pp. 138–139; Lappo-Danilevskii, *op. cit.*, p. 139.

[7] Semevskii, *op. cit.*, I, p. xx; Ignatovich, *op. cit.*, pp. 151, 188; Miliukov, *op. cit.*, I, pp. 225–226.

[8] Ignatovich, *op. cit.*, pp. 186–188; Oganovskii, *Zakonomernost*, II, pp. 332–335; Semevskii, *op. cit.*, I, pp. 105–122.

[9] Semevskii, *op. cit.*, I, p. xx; Pokrovskii, *Russkaia istoriia*, IV, pp. 103, 110; Ignatovich, *op. cit.*, p. 188.

[10] Ignatovich, *op. cit.*, pp. 186–187.

[11] *Ibid.*, p. 188.

[12] Semevskii, *Krestiane*, I, pp. xiii, 123–125.

[13] *Ibid.*, I, pp. xix–xx, 128; Ignatovich, *op. cit.*, pp. 151, 188.

[14] Miliukov, *Krestiane* (in *Entsiklop. slovar*, XVI), p. 694; Kliuchevskii, *Kurs*, IV, p. 411; V, p. 265; Kornilov, *Kurs*, I, p. 52; Lappo-Danilevskii, *Ocherk istorii* (in Dolgorukov, ed., *Krestianskii stroi*, I), pp. 149–153.

[15] Liashchenko, *Krestianskoe delo*, I, p. 405.

[16] Kliuchevskii, *op. cit.*, V, pp. 264–265; Kornilov, *op. cit.*, III, pp. 10–11; Ministerstvo Gosudarstvennykh Imushchestv, *Istoricheskoe obozrenie*, part II, division II, pp. 5–21; and appendix, p. iii, table 1. One *desiatina* equals 2.70 acres.

[17] Kornilov, *op. cit.*, III, pp. 11–13.

[18] Semevskii, *Krestiane*, I, Introduction.

[19] Ignatovich, *Pomeshchichi krestiane*, p. 42; Kornilov, *op. cit.*, I, p. 57; Semevskii, *Krestianskii vopros*, I, p. 478.

[20] Kliuchevskii, *op. cit.*, V, pp. 228–229; Kornilov, *op. cit.*, II, p. 46; Ignatovich, *op. cit.*, p. 36.

[21] Vorms, *Polozheniia* 19 *fevralia* (in Dzhivelegov, ed., *Velikaia reforma*, VI), pp. 33–34.

[22] *Ibid.*, pp. 3–4; Ignatovich, *op. cit.*, pp. 193, 202–208, 213–219.

[23] Ignatovich, *op. cit.*, pp. 36–37.

[24] Vorms, *op. cit.*, p. 4.

[25] Kliuchevskii, *op. cit.*, V, p. 229; Kornilov, *op. cit.*, II, pp. 46–47; Ignatovich, *op cit.*, p. 36.

[26] Ignatovich, *op. cit.*, pp. 96, 147.

[27] Semevskii, *Krestiane*, I, pp. 20–37, and table on pp. 584–585; and his *Krestianskii vopros* (in Dolgorukov, ed., *Krestianskii stroi*, I), p. 288; also Ignatovich, *op. cit.*, p. 94, note 4; p. 97, note 1, and pp. 386–389, table 4. Cf. Liashchenko, *Ocherki*, I, tables on p. 134.

[28] Ignatovich, *op. cit.*, pp. 101–104.

[29] Tugan-Baranovskii, *Russkaia fabrika*, I, pp. 171–212; Ignatovich, *op. cit.*, p. 122.

[30] Tugan-Baranovskii, *op. cit.*, I, pp. 77, 172; Ignatovich, *op. cit.*, pp. 51, 121–122.

[31] Ignatovich, *op. cit.*, pp. 119, 173, 212–213; Oganovskii, *Zakonomernost*, II, p. 300.

[32] Semevskii, *Krestianskii vopros*, I, p. 478; Kliuchevskii, *Kurs*, V, pp. 265–266; text of manifesto in Vorms, ed., *Pamiatniki*, p. 160.

[33] Kornilov, *Kurs*, I, p. 57; Pokrovskii, *Russkaia istoriia*, III, p. 152.

[34] Ignatovich, *op. cit.*, p. 35.

[35] *Ibid.*, p. 34; Romanovich-Slavatinskii, *op. cit.*, pp. 305–306.

[36] Ignatovich, *op. cit.*, pp. 162, 175–177, 224, 244.

[37] *Ibid.*, p. 154.

[38] Compare Ignatovich, *op. cit.*, pp. 107–108; Oganovskii, *Zakonomernost*, II, pp. 381–382; Kliuchevskii, *Kurs*, V, pp. 101–102. Due allowance being made for the decline in the value of the *rubl*, the increase in the average *obrok* amounted apparently to some 25–50 per cent; the data are incomplete and the estimates are only rough approximations.

[39] Ignatovich, *Pomeshchichi krestiane*, pp. 72, 280; Kliuchevskii, *op. cit.*, V, pp. 230–231; Semevskii, *Krestiane*, I, pp. xix–xx.

[40] Ignatovich, *op. cit.*, pp. 75–76, and table No. 1, p. 379. Included among the forty-one *guberniias* referred to above is the Don Region.

[41] This circumstance introduces most extraordinary difficulties into the statistics of the subject, which make it uncertain whether or not the *obrok* system was spreading at the expense of the *barshchina* system (as certain statistical estimates, on their face, would indicate). Cf. Ignatovich, *op. cit.*, pp. 71, 73, 112, 335; Oganovskii, *Zakonomernost*, II, pp. 287, 301–302; Liashchenko, *Ocherki*, I, p. 118; Kliuchevskii, *op. cit.*, V, pp. 230–231.

[42] Oganovskii, *op. cit.*, p. 288; Liashchenko, *op. cit.*, I, pp. 132–133; Ignatovich, *op. cit.*, pp. 78, 81, 119. There were several exceptions to this approximate differentiation between the northern forest and the southern *step:* for example, in the Lithuanian *guberniias* and in the northeastern *guberniias* of Viatka and Perm — all well to the north of the *step* frontier, the *barshchina* system predominated, while in the *step guberniia* of Astrakhan, *obrok* prevailed.

[43] Ignatovich, *op. cit.*, pp. 186–192, 211; Oganovskii, *op. cit.*, pp. 324–325.

[44] Ignatovich, *op. cit.*, pp. 105–106, 186.

[45] *Ibid.*, pp. 8–9, 27–28, 102–104, 137–138, 152–153.

[46] Ignatovich, *op. cit.*, pp. 157–159, 224, 229.

[47] *Ibid.*, pp. 182–186. The number on the eve of the emancipation was probably somewhat above sixty thousand. See also Tugan-Baranovskii, *Russkaia fabrika*, I, pp. 88–94.

⁴⁸ Ignatovich, *op. cit.*, pp. 34, 36–37, 121; Tugan-Baranovskii, *op. cit.*, pp. 78–80.
⁴⁹ Ignatovich, *op. cit.*, pp. 37, 186; Oganovskii, *Zakonomernost*, II, p. 299.
⁵⁰ Ignatovich, *op. cit.*, pp. 37, 250 (footnote).
⁵¹ *Ibid.*, pp. 36, 250–251, 391; Liashchenko, *Krestianskoe delo*, I, p. 403; Vorms, *Polozheniia 19 fevralia* (in Dzhivelegov, ed., *Velikaia reforma*, VI), p. 19.
⁵² Kliuchevskii, *Kurs*, V, pp. 228–229.
⁵³ Ignatovich, *op. cit.*, pp. 51, 58; Kliuchevskii, *op. cit.*, V, p. 229.
⁵⁴ Ignatovich, *op. cit.*, p. 50.
⁵⁵ *Ibid.*, p 42; Kliuchevskii, *op. cit.*, V, pp. 228–229. In the time of Peter the Great there had been a law prohibiting these family-dividing sales, but it had become a dead letter.
⁵⁶ Ignatovich, *op. cit.*, p. 43.
⁵⁷ *Ibid.*, pp. 51, 179–180, 252–256.
⁵⁸ *Ibid.*, pp. 52–57.
⁵⁹ *Ibid.*, pp. 56–58, 257–272.
⁶⁰ *Ibid.*, pp. 52, 56–57.
⁶¹ *Ibid.*, pp. 44, 52–54, 56–57.
⁶² Semevskii, *Krestianskii vopros*, II, p. 562.
⁶³ Ignatovich, *op. cit.*, p. 58.
⁶⁴ *Ibid.*, pp. 45–50.
⁶⁵ *Ibid.*, pp. 320–323.
⁶⁶ *Ibid.*, pp. 59–61.
⁶⁷ Kliuchevskii, *Kurs*, V, p. 231.
⁶⁸ Ignatovich, *op. cit.*, pp. 45–46, 57, 63–64; Kliuchevskii, *op. cit.*, V, pp. 229–231.
⁶⁹ Miliukov, *Ocherki*, II, pp. 250, 253, 295–302, 315–329; Semevskii, *Krestiane*, I, p. 287.
⁷⁰ Miliukov, *op. cit.*, II, pp. 333, 372–376. For the extension of education among the State peasants, see Ministerstvo Gosudarstvennykh Imushchestv, *Istoricheskoe obozrenie*, Part II, Division I, pp. 49–70.
⁷¹ Miliukov, *Ocherki*, II, p. 375. For a discussion of such schools in the 18th century, see Semevskii, *Krestiane*, I, pp. 281–287.
⁷² Kots, *Krepostnaia intelligentsiia*, esp. pp. 9–43; Ignatovich, *Pomeshchichi krestiane*, pp. 52, 272–278; Semevskii, *Krestiane*, I, pp. 151–156; Vorms, ed., *Pamiatniki*, p. 183.
⁷³ Leroy-Beaulieu, *The Empire of the Tsars and the Russians*, III, pp. 29–30; Pypin, *Istoriia russkoi literatury*, III, chap. II, esp. pp. 91–96; Vasilev, *Antropomorficheskie predstavleniia* (in *Etnograficheskoe obozrenie*, 1890, No. 1, pp. 87–97, and 1892, No. 4, pp. 157–169); Zapolskii, *Charodeistvo* (ibid., 1890, No. 2), pp. 49–72; Liatskii, *Predstavleniia belorussa o nechistoi sile* (ibid., 1890, No. 4), pp. 25–41; Leger, *La mythologie slave*, pp. 68–69.
⁷⁴ Miliukov, *Ocherki*, II, p. 73; Conybeare, *Russian dissenters*, pp. 101–105, 151–156, 226–234.
⁷⁵ Conybeare, *op. cit.*, pp. 152, 156–158; Miliukov, *op. cit.*, II, pp. 91–92.
⁷⁶ Conybeare, *op. cit.*, pp. 189–213; Miliukov, *op. cit.*, II, pp. 80–87, 91–92.
⁷⁷ Conybeare, *op. cit.*, pp. 215, 222–223.
⁷⁸ *Ibid.*, pp. 264, 268, 304–305, 318, 340, 364.
⁷⁹ *Ibid.*, p. 322.
⁸⁰ Miliukov, *op. cit.*, II, p. 135; Conybeare, *op. cit.*, pp. 269, 327–329.
⁸¹ Conybeare, *op. cit.*, pp. 272, 298–299, 351–352, 367–368.
⁸² Miliukov, *op. cit.*, II, p. 117.
⁸³ Conybeare, *op. cit.*, pp. 283–285.
⁸⁴ *Ibid.*, pp. 283–284, 312, 313; Miliukov, *op. cit.*, II, p. 130.
⁸⁵ Conybeare, *op. cit.*, p. 313.
⁸⁶ *Ibid.*, pp. 293, 302, 314.
⁸⁷ Kornilov, *Kurs*, II, pp. 96–98; Miliukov, *op. cit.*, II, pp. 171–173; Conybeare, *op. cit.*, pp. 239–243. Statistical data and estimates as to the number of dissidents are extremely unreliable, for reasons which these authors explain. The estimates favored by Miliukov and Conybeare are much higher than the one here quoted from Kornilov.
⁸⁸ Conybeare, *op. cit.*, pp. 322–323.
⁸⁹ Dett, *Religious folk-songs of the Negro*, p. 232.

90 Recorded in 1862, and quoted in Shein, *Krepostnoe pravo v narodnykh pesniakh* (in *Russkaia starina*, February, 1886), p. 491. For other examples, see Brodskii, *K vole.*

91 Ignatovich, *Pomeshchichi krestiane*, p. 330.

92 *Ibid.*, p. 296. In Varadinov, *Istoriia Ministerstva Vnutrennikh Del*, many instances of disorders among both private serfs and State peasants are recorded; for instances of the latter, see, for example, part III, book I, pp. 314, 376, 436, 602; see likewise *Materialy dlia istorii krepostnogo prava v Rossii*, esp. table 4.

93 Ignatovich, *op. cit.*, p. 320; and her *Borba*, pp. 9–11; Semevskii, *Krestianskii vopros*, II, pp. 571–573.

94 Ignatovich, *op. cit.*, p. 331; and her *Borba*, pp. 21–22. In an earlier work, by Semevskii (*Krestianskii vopros*, II, p. 595), the total number of disturbances among the serfs for the period 1826–1854 is placed at 554. See also *Materialy dlia istorii krepostnogo prava*, and Romanovich-Slavatinskii, *Dvorianstvo*, pp. 368–376.

95 Ignatovich, *Pomeshchichi krestiane*, p. 331, footnote 1; pp. 336–337.

96 Ignatovich, *Borba*, p. 21.

97 Ignatovich, *Pomeshchichi krestiane*, pp. 331–332.

98 *Ibid.*, pp. 337–341; from his more limited material, Semevskii (*Krestianskii vopros*, II, p. 596) reaches a different conclusion: that a desire for emancipation, or a belief that it had already been granted, was the commonest cause of disturbance.

99 Ignatovich, *op. cit.*, p. 342.

100 *Ibid.*, p. 327; cf. Semevskii, *Krestianskii vopros*, II, pp. 581–583, and Romanovich-Slavatinskii, *Dvorianstvo*, pp. 376–378.

101 Semevskii, *op. cit.*, II, pp. 578–585; Romanovich-Slavatinskii, *op. cit.*, pp. 364–367.

102 Ignatovich, *Borba*, p. 18.

103 Ignatovich, *Pomeshchichi krestiane*, pp. 289–292, 311; and her *Borba*, p. 19.

104 Ignatovich, *Borba*, pp. 18–20; and her *Pomeshchichi krestiane*, pp. 302–318; Oganovskii, *Zakonomernost*, II, p. 229. Cf. Semevskii, *Krestianskii vopros*, II, pp. 596–597.

105 Ignatovich, *Pomeshchichi krestiane*, pp. 328, 343, 345–346.

106 Ignatovich, *Borba*, p. 19.

107 Ignatovich, *Pomeshchichi krestiane*, p. 343; and her *Borba*, p. 19.

108 Ignatovich, *Pomeshchichi krestiane*, pp. 311, 345.

NOTES TO CHAPTER IV

1 Kliuchevskii, *Kurs*, V, pp. 117, 146.

2 *Ibid.*, IV, pp. 100–101.

3 Romanovich-Slavatinskii, *Dvorianstvo*, pp. 119–200.

4 Kliuchevskii, *op. cit.*, V, p. 147.

5 Herzen, *Memoirs*, p. 98.

6 Grabar, *Istoriia russkogo iskusstva*, II, pp. 251–305; Kniazkov, *Ocherki iz istorii*, pp. 579–588.

7 Semevskii, *Krestiane*, I, pp. xv–xvi.

8 Réau, *L'art russe de Pierre le Grand à nos jours*, pp. 84–89.

9 *Ibid.*, p. 85; Kots, *Krepostnaia intelligentsiia*, p. 127, 153–156. The theatre here referred to was at Kuskovo. At Ostankino, in the suburbs of Moscow, is a mansion which belonged to the same family, and included a fine theatre; after the Revolution of 1917, the building was converted into a museum.

10 Masaryk, *Spirit of Russia*, I, p. 73; Pypin, *Istoriia russkoi literatury*, IV, chaps. I–III, esp. pp. 1–10, 109–113.

11 Kliuchevskii, *Kurs*, V, p. 125. It is to be remembered that in treating these cultural influences, we are considering them *only* as they touched the nobility and the peasants; no attempt is made here to deal with their effect upon the clergy or upon the middle and lower classes in the cities.

12 Pypin, *Istoriia russkoi literatury*, III, pp. 108–154; IV, chap. XLIV, esp. p. 460; Masaryk, *Spirit of Russia*, I, pp. 221–293; Radlov, *Ocherk istorii russkoi filosofii*, pp. 30–41; Ivanov-Razumnik, *Istoriia russkoi obshchestvennoi mysli*, I, pp. 48–208, 255–275.

[13] Ignatovich, *Pomeshchichi krestiane*, pp. 338, 361; Oganovskii, *Zakonomernost*, II, pp. 306–313.

[14] Ignatovich, *op. cit.*, p. 362; Oganovskii, *Zakonomernost*, II, pp. 291, 294.

[15] Ignatovich, *op. cit.*, p. 133.

[16] Miliukov, *Ocherki*, I, pp. 81–123; Kornilov, *Kurs*, III, pp. 27–29 (with a criticism of some of Miliukov's statistics); Tugan-Baranovskii, *Russkaia fabrika*, I, pp 53–71.

[17] Kulisher, *Istoriia russkoi torgovli*, pp. 183–188, 208–212, 266–271.

[18] Ignatovich, *op. cit.*, pp. 145, 182–186; Tugan-Baranovskii, *op. cit.*, I, pp. 31–32, 77, 88–89.

[19] Liashchenko, *Ocherki*, I, p. 118; Ignatovich, *op. cit.*, pp. 141–142.

[20] Liashchenko, *op. cit.*, I, pp. 128–129; Ignatovich, *op. cit.*, pp. 141–142.

[21] Romanovich-Slavatinskii, *Dvorianstvo*, pp. 342–345.

[22] Liashchenko, *op. cit.*, I, p. 136; cf. Ignatovich, *op. cit.*, pp. 364–365; Semevskii, *Krestianskii vopros*, II, p. 617; Kornilov, *Kurs*, II, p. 44.

[23] Romanovich-Slavatinskii, *Dvorianstvo*, pp. 345–346.

[24] Oganovskii, *Zakonomernost*, II, p. 303.

[25] Ignatovich, *op. cit.*, pp. 360–362.

[26] Kornilov, *op. cit.*, II, pp. 151–154; Liashchenko, *op. cit.*, I, pp. 131–132; Ignatovich, *op. cit.*, pp. 359–360.

[27] Maslov, *Agrarnyi vopros*, I, p. 376, and tables on pp. 431–432.

[28] Ignatovich, *Pomeshchichi krestiane*, pp. 169–173. That it was legally possible for a given landlord to pass from the one system to the other may easily be shown. He might place his serfs entirely on the dues-paying system, and cultivate the manorial fields with hired labor, or he might completely sever connection with his serfs by selling them, or setting them free. He was of course free to sell serfs with allotments, and normally to reserve to himself the manorial fields which these serfs had formerly tilled for him under the forced labor system. If he wished to keep even the allotments which the serfs had cultivated for themselves, it was possible for him first to convert his peasants into landless men, and then to sell them at will. If he could not find a purchaser, and still wished to be rid of his serfs, he could liberate individuals or single families without land, or whole villages with land, under the laws of 1803 and 1842, to be discussed below; or he could convert the whole population of the village into landless courtyard people, and subsequently liberate them without land.

[29] Romanovich-Slavatinskii, *Dvorianstvo*, pp. 286–293, esp. p. 288.

[30] Tugan-Baranovskii, *Russkaia fabrika*, I, pp. 26, 31, 73, 75.

[31] Peasants bound to factories rather than to individual owners were called "possessional." Vagabonds and beggars were sometimes allotted to these factories in the same way by the authorities, while voluntary ascription also contributed somewhat to this class of bound factory-workers. Tugan-Baranovskii, *op. cit.*, I, pp. 94–95; Ignatovich, *op. cit.*, pp. 352–353; Liashchenko, *Krestianskoe delo*, I, pp. 406–407. Nobles as well as non-nobles enjoyed until 1816 the right to purchase serfs for attachment to their factories, and both classes also profited by ascriptions of State peasants to their manufacturing plants. In the case of the nobles, however, these special sources of bound labor had no great significance, inasmuch as the noble was always free to man his factory with serfs from his estate, or to purchase additional serfs without specification as to their intended use, and to set them to work in industry. Cf. Tugan-Baranovskii, *op. cit.*, I, p. 88, footnote 1.

[32] General statistical data on this subject are lacking for the period from 1825 to the Emancipation. Tugan-Baranovskii's conclusion that the proportion of "free laborers" continued to increase is based in part upon the data for certain particular industries; *op. cit.*, I, pp. 76–77.

[33] Tugan-Baranovskii, *op. cit.*, I, pp. 77–80.

[34] *Ibid.*, I, p. 77.

[35] Even here there was not an altogether free test of the opinion of those who owned serfs of this kind, as to the comparative value of free and factory-bound labor in industry; in the first place, in connection with the liberation, payments might be made by the Government to the owner, and by the owner to the liberated worker, this depending upon the circumstances under which the serf had originally been acquired, and upon the serf's own decision as to his future status — and under these conditions, a given owner might be influenced for or against liberation, ac-

cordingly as he foresaw a debit or a credit balance for himself in connection with these payments. In the second place, with the liberation of the factory-bound serfs, the factories which had possessed such serfs were to be relieved of certain burdensome restrictions peculiar to establishments of this kind — and this was of course an inducement to set the workers free. Tugan-Baranovskii, *op. cit.*, I, pp. 106–115.

³⁶ Tugan-Baranovskii, *op. cit.*, I, p. 380, gives a table for 1866, showing that in seventy-one important branches of production, the factories with not less than one hundred workers each numbered 644, and employed altogether 201,066 workers.

³⁷ Ignatovich, *Pomeshchichi krestiane*, pp. 348–351, 364, 370–372; and her *Borba*, pp. 7–8, 13.

³⁸ Ignatovich, *Pomeshchichi krestiane*, pp. 364–365, 370–371, 378.

³⁹ Engelman, *Istoriia krepostnogo prava*, pp. 210–212, 222; Vorms, ed., *Pamiatniki*, pp. 165–169.

⁴⁰ Cf. Semevskii, *Krestianskii vopros*, I, p. xvi; and Kliuchevskii, *Kurs*, V, p. 266.

⁴¹ Semevskii, *op. cit.*, I, p. 266; II, p. 569. Cf. Romanovich-Slavatinskii, *Dvorianstvo*, pp. 567–568; and Miliukov, *Krestiane* (in *Entsiklop. slovar*, Brockhaus, XVI), p. 698.

⁴² Kornilov, *Kurs*, I, pp. 221–222; Kliuchevskii, *Kurs*, V, pp. 194–195. The regulations required that the landlord should rent a specified portion of his land to the peasants, but under terms to be fixed by the landlord himself.

⁴³ Ignatovich, *Pomeshchichi krestiane*, pp. 374–376; Kliuchevskii, *op. cit.*, V, pp. 267–268; Engelman, *Istoriia*, p. 259; Semevskii, *Krestianskii vopros*, II, p. 569; Vorms, ed., *Pamiatniki*, p. 228.

⁴⁴ Latkin, *Uchebnik istorii russkogo prava*, pp. 211–212; Semevskii, *op. cit.*, II, p. 569; Kornilov, *Kurs*, III, pp. 23–24.

⁴⁵ Oganovskii (*Zakonomernost*, II, pp. 238–240) undertakes to show that this was so, while Kornilov (*op. cit.*, III, p. 24) holds that the decrease was due to liberations alone.

⁴⁶ The first two columns are from Semevskii's *Krestianskii vopros*, II, p. 570, and his statistical note appended to Mavor, *Economic history*, I, pp. 590–592. The statistics of this subject present great difficulties; the first general census of the population of the Russian Empire was not taken until 1897, and the computations based upon the periodic "revisions" of the pre-Emancipation period are frequently in disagreement; cf. Miliukov, *Krestiane* (in *Entsiklop. slovar*, XVI), pp. 685–686, 692–693; and Liashchenko, *Krestianskoe delo*, I, pp. 6–8. In Glavnoe Upravlenie Zemleustroistva i Zemledeliia, *Statisticheskie svedeniia*, the total number of male peasants (*krestiane*) registered in the "revision" of 1858 in forty-nine *guberniias* (European Russia, excluding the Don Region, Finland, Poland, and Pre- and Trans-Caucasia) is given as 22,395,800 (p. 8, and explanatory note, p. viii). In Vysochaishe Uchrezhdennaia Kommissiia, *Materialy*, the total "village population" (*selskoe naselenie*) of both sexes is calculated for the year 1860, for the 50 *guberniias* of European Russia (the Don Region included), as 50,358,089 (part I, p. 16).

⁴⁷ The figures in this column are from *Rossiia*, p. 75.

⁴⁸ Grabenskii, *Istoriia polskogo naroda*, p. 431; Kornilov, *Reforma 19 fevralia 1864 goda v Tsarstve Polskom* (in Dzhivelegov, ed., *Velikaia reforma*, V), p. 289.

⁴⁹ Liashchenko, *Krestianskoe delo*, I, pp. 139–141.

⁵⁰ These are the estimates, claiming only an approximate validity, quoted in Janson, *Opyt statisticheskogo issledovaniia*, p. 2.

NOTES TO CHAPTER V

¹ This account is based upon contemporary newspaper reports, and upon conversations of the writer with certain residents of this neighborhood, held nine years after these events took place.

² The writer has no intention of implying that bark slippers, log houses, wide streets, and the like, have been *everywhere* uniformly characteristic of peasant life.

³ Volkov, ed., *Sbornik*, p. 421.

⁴ Leontev, *Krestianskoe pravo*, pp. 262, 330; Khauke, *Krestianskoe zemelnoe pravo*, pp. 189–197, 203, 220; Rittich, *Zavisimost krestian*, pp. 149–151; Meiendorf, *Krestianskii dvor*, esp. pp. 68–74; Nechaev, *Russkoe krestianskoe obychnoe pravo* (in *Rossiia*), p. 549; Goremykin, ed., *Svod*, I, p. 74 (interpretations of the law

by the Russian Senate); Volkov, ed., *Sbornik*, pp. 421–424 (interpretation by the Ministry of the Interior).

5 *Polnoe sobranie zakonov*, 2d ed., (i. e. second *sobranie* or collection), No. 36657, art. 188; No. 36659, arts. 127, 133.

6 See note 4 above.

7 *P. S. Z.*, 2d ed., No. 36657, arts. 40, 41; Khauke, *op. cit.*, pp. 283–284.

8 *P. S. Z.*, 2d ed., No. 36657, arts. 46–47; Khauke, *op. cit.*, pp. 284–285, 289. Cf. No. 36657, art. 51, annex 2, No. 36662, arts. 113 and 114, and Goremykin, *Svod*, I, pp. 55–56, footnote 1, for vague and inconclusive statements as to the sub-communal groups and assemblies.

9 Khauke, *op. cit.*, pp. 286–287.

10 Tsentralnyi Statisticheskii Komitet. *Statistika pozemelnoi sobstvennosti i naselennykh mest Evropeiskoi Rossii*, I, p. 6.

11 Goremykin, *op. cit.*, I, p. 103, note 21; pp. 55–56, footnote 1; p. 57, note 4; p. 103, note 22; Khauke, *op. cit.*, pp. 289–290; *P. S. Z.*, 3d col. (vol. XIX, p. 805), No. 17286, div. III.

12 *P. S. Z.*, 3d col., No. 28528; No. 33743; No. 35370.

13 *P. S. Z.*, 2d ed., No. 36662, arts. 98, 118; No. 36663, arts. 36, 93; No. 36664, art. 87; No. 36665, art. 81; Khauke, *op. cit.*, p. 12.

14 On the method of original allotment in hereditary tenure, see *P. S. Z.*, 2d ed., No. 36662, arts. 98, 118; No. 36663, arts. 36, 93; No. 36664, art. 87; No. 36665, art. 81; No. 36657, art. 51, par. 18, annex 1; Volkov, *op. cit.*, p. 109, notes 11, 13; Khauke, *op. cit.*, pp. 149–150. On the intermixture of strips, see Pershin, *Uchastkovoe zemlepolzovanie*, p. 14; and his *Zemelnoe ustroistvo*, p. 207; Oganovskii, *Ocherki po ekonomicheskoi geografii*, p. 126. On the land-relations associated with the intermixture of strips, see *P. S. Z.*, 2d ed., No. 36663, art. 100; No. 36664, art. 78; No. 36665, art. 72; Volkov, *op. cit.*, p. 381, note 4; Glavnoe Upravlenie Zemleustroistva i Zemledeliia, *Travaux*, p. 6. On the undivided lands, see *P. S. Z.*, 2d ed., No. 36657, art. 51, par. 7; No. 36663, art. 98; Goremykin, *op. cit.*, I, p. 112, note 6 and footnote 2; Rittich, *op. cit.*, p. 111 On collective redemption and its effect upon hereditary tenure, see *P S. Z.*, 2d ed., No. 36659, arts. 34, 118, 127; Khauke, *op. cit.*, pp. 134–135; Goremykin, *op. cit.*, I, p. 484, note to article 76; p. 503.

15 *P. S. Z.*, 2d ed., No. 36657, art. 51, par. 7; No. 36659, arts. 160, 163; Goremykin, *op. cit.*, I, p. 112, note 6 and footnote 2; Volkov, *op. cit.*, pp. 417, 426; Rittich, *op. cit.*, p. 91; Khauke, *op. cit.*, p. 160; Leontev, *op. cit.*, pp. 315–316.

16 On the renouncement of hereditary allotments before the beginning of redemption, see *P S. Z.*, 2d ed., No. 36663, arts. 109–111, 118; No. 36664, arts. 91, 101; No. 36665, arts. 88, 91. On such renouncements when directly connected with personal separations from the commune, see *ibid.*, No. 36663, arts. 117, 141; No. 36664, arts. 100, 116; No. 36665, arts. 91, 103. On the question of the transfer or retention of hereditary holdings redeemed by the commune as a whole, see Volkov, *op. cit.*, p. 59, note 16; p. 232, notes 2, 3; pp. 415–419, 425; Leontev, *op. cit.*, pp. 44, 318–319; Khauke, *op. cit.*, pp. 134–135, 151; Goremykin, *op. cit.*, I, p. 503; p. 527, art. 116, notes 2 and 3; p. 555, art. 128, note; Rittich, *op. cit.*, pp. 135, 138. Under the General Statute of 1861, the consent of a majority of the communal assembly was required before a household and its property could be divided for the purpose of establishing an additional household and providing it with an allotment. *P. S. Z.*, 2d ed., No. 36657, art. 51, par. 5. However, the Senate subsequently held that this provision was not applicable under hereditary household tenure, but only under the repartitional communal tenure which will be discussed below. Khauke, *op. cit.*, pp. 152–153. On separate redemption by the individual household, and its effect upon salability, see *P. S. Z.*, 2d ed., No. 36659, arts. 34, 131, 165, 169, 175; Volkov, *op. cit.*, p. 59, note 16; Khauke, *op. cit.*, p. 313. On the general character of the hereditary household tenure, see Goremykin, *op. cit.*, I, p. 503; p. 527, art. 116, notes 2 and 3; Rittich, *op. cit.*, pp. 149–150; Leontev, *op. cit.*, pp. 310–321; Khauke, *op. cit.*, pp. 149–150, and esp. pp. 164–169; Tsentralnyi Statisticheskii Komitet, *Statistika pozemelnoi sobstvennosti i naselennykh mest Evropeiskoi Rossii*, (land-census of 1877–78), I, p. 6.

17 On the tenure of house-and-garden plots in repartitional communes, see *P. S. Z.*, 2d ed., No. 36662, arts. 37, 110. On repartition, see *P. S. Z.*, 2d ed., No. 36657, art. 51, pars. 6, 14, and par. 18, annex 1; No. 36662, arts. 113–114; Khauke, *op. cit.*, pp. 108–

112, 143. On the intermixture of strips, see Pershin, *Uchastkovoe zemlepolzovanie,* pp. 14–15; and his *Zemelnoe ustroistvo,* pp. 201, 207; Oganovskii, *Ocherki ekonomicheskoi geografii,* p. 126. On transfers by the commune to outsiders, see *P. S. Z.,* 2d ed., No. 36659, arts. 161–162. On collective redemption, see *ibid.,* 2d ed., No. 36659, arts. 34, 118, 127, 160.

¹⁸ On the dividing of households, see *P. S. Z.,* 2d ed., No. 36657, art. 51, par. 5; Khauke, *op. cit.,* pp. 152–153. On the transfer of allotments by their holders, see *P. S. Z.,* 2d ed., No. 36657, art. 35; No. 36659, art. 164; No. 36662, art. 109; Goremykin, *op. cit.,* I, p. 882, art. 9, annex; Khauke, *op. cit.,* pp. 58–62. On the renunciation of allotments in repartitional communes before the beginning of redemption, see *P. S. Z.,* 2d ed., No. 36662, arts. 125, 128, 129, 140. On separate redemption and renouncement, see *ibid.,* No. 36659, art. 10; No. 36662, art. 130. On the renunciation of allotments in repartitional communes during joint redemption, see Khauke, *op. cit.,* p. 56; *P. S. Z.,* 2d ed., No. 36659, arts. 172–173. On transfers where the commune is free from a State redemption debt, see *ibid.,* No. 36657, art. 130, par. 1; Rittich, *op. cit.,* pp. 133–134.

¹⁹ On the general division of tenure and the general physical consolidation of holdings, see *P. S. Z.,* 2d ed., No. 36657, art. 51, par. 6; art. 54; No. 36662, art. 116; No. 36659, art. 163. On the individual separations of tenure and individual consolidations, when connected with separate pre-redemption, see *ibid.,* 2d ed., No. 36659, art. 165; Khauke, *op. cit.,* pp. 138–139, 308–313; Rittich, *op. cit.,* p. 107; p. 135, footnote 1. On other individual separations and consolidations, see *P. S. Z.,* 2d ed., No. 36657, art. 36; Khauke, *op. cit.,* pp. 65, 68, 178, 304–308.

²⁰ Pershin, *Zemelnoe ustroistvo,* I, p. 172 ff.

²¹ Vorms, *Polozheniia 19 fevralia* (in Dzhivelegov, ed., *Velikaia reforma,* VI), pp. 26–27. It is to be remembered that we are dealing here with the former serfs of the manorial villages, and not with the courtyard people.

²² *P. S. Z.,* 2d ed., No. 36657, arts. 46–70. A large household might send two or more of its members to the assembly, if this accorded with local custom. The law says that when questions having to do with the repartitional lands are dealt with, householders who have no share in these lands are to have no voice in the assembly. A woman who was the head of a household might be admitted to the assembly on an equal footing with the male householders, if this accorded with local peasant custom. Goremykin, ed., *Svod,* I, p. 75. Most questions were decided in the assembly by a simple majority, but in certain cases a vote of two-thirds was required.

²³ *P. S. Z.,* 2d ed., No. 36657, art. 187; art. 51, par. 11; art. 169; art. 177.

²⁴ Vorms, *op. cit.,* VI, pp. 31–32.

²⁵ *P. S. Z.,* 2d ed., No. 36657, art. 188; art. 54, par. 5. The sentence of banishment was required to be submitted to certain officials of the *guberniia* before being put into effect.

²⁶ *Ibid.,* No. 36657, art. 58, par. 10; art. 84, par. 8. Cf. Leontev, *Krestianskoe pravo,* p. 47.

²⁷ *Ibid.,* No. 36657, art. 130, par. 6; No. 36659, art. 176.

²⁸ *Ibid.,* No. 36657, art. 130, par. 3.

²⁹ *Ibid.,* No. 36657, art. 130, par. 9; for exceptions, see arts. 143–145. See also Korkunov, *Gosudarstvennoe pravo,* I, p. 332.

³⁰ *Ibid.,* No. 36657, arts. 42–45.

³¹ *Ibid.,* No. 36657, art. 71; art. 78, par. 1.

³² *Ibid.,* No. 36657, arts. 81, 95, 102.

³³ *Ibid.,* No. 36657, arts. 95–98, 107.

³⁴ Kornilov, *Kurs,* II, pp. 255–256.

³⁵ Kizevetter, *Mestnoe samoupravlenie v Rossii,* pp. 142–152.

³⁶ Vorms, *op. cit.,* p. 31; Kornilov, *Krestianskaia reforma,* pp. 159–160, 180; and his *Kurs,* II, pp. 186–187.

³⁷ *P. S. Z.,* 2d ed., No. 36662, arts. 6–8; No. 36663, arts. 6–7.

³⁸ *Ibid.,* No. 36662, arts. 16, 21. A schedule of the maximal and statutory norms, by *guberniias,* will be found in Glavnoe Upravlenie Zemleustroistva i Zemledeliia, *Statisticheskie svedeniia,* pp. 20–23.

³⁹ *P. S. Z.,* 2d ed., No. 36657, art. 6; No. 36662, arts. 9, 121.

⁴⁰ *Ibid.,* No. 36662, art. 22.

⁴¹ *Ibid.,* No. 36662, arts. 18, 19.

42 *Ibid.*, No. 36662, arts. 17, 29–31.

43 *Ibid.*, No. 36662, art. 20.

44 *Ibid.*, No. 36662, arts. 121, 122; No. 36659, arts. 55–56.

45 *Ibid.*, No. 36659, arts. 2, 8–26, 36; No. 36662, art. 130; No. 36663, art. 119; also footnote 57 below.

46 *Ibid.*, No. 36659, arts. 35, 57–59, 68, 97.

47 *Ibid.*, No. 36662, art. 123; Gote, *Ocherk istorii zemlevladeniia*, p. 181.

48 *Ibid.*, No. 36662, arts. 29–31, 65, 93; Vorms, *op. cit.*, p. 43; Pokrovskii, *Russkaia istoriia*, IV, p. 102; Manuilov, *Arenda zemli* (in Manuilov, ed., *Ocherki*, II), p. 168.

49 *P. S. Z.*, 2d ed., No. 36657, art. 6; Vorms, *op. cit.*, pp. 44–45, 47, 49; Kliuchevskii, *Kurs*, V, p. 269.

50 Vorms, *op. cit.*, pp. 46–48; Pokrovskii, *Russkaia istoriia*, IV, p. 109; Kornilov, *Krestianskaia reforma*, p. 199; Ivaniukov, *Padenie krepostnogo prava*, pp. 288–289; Chernyshev, *Agrarno-krestianskaia politika*, pp. 195–196 (with footnote).

51 Vorms, *op. cit.*, p. 47; Pokrovskii, *Russkaia istoriia*, IV, p. 109.

52 Special provision was made for increasing the dues in little-landed industrial villages in proportion to the industrial earnings of the peasants. *P. S. Z.*, 2d ed., No. 36662, art. 19 (annex).

53 Where labor-dues were in force, the peasants had to shift to the system of current money-payments before they were permitted to begin redemption with State aid. Kornilov, *Kurs*, III, p. 144.

54 *P. S. Z.*, 2d ed., No. 36659, arts. 65–66; Vorms, *op. cit.*, pp. 45–46, 50.

55 Lositskii, *Vykupnaia operatsiia*, pp. 16–19, 38–39. Cf. Kliuchevskii, *Kurs*, V, p. 268. The latter attempts to draw a distinction between the *person* of the serf and the *capital value* of his labor; the former, he says, was liberated unconditionally, while the latter was required to be redeemed.

56 *P. S. Z.*, 2d ed., No. 36659, arts. 4, 27, 64–66. Vorms, *op. cit.*, pp. 50, 52; Kliuchevskii, *Kurs*, V, p. 269; Kaufman, *Agrarnyi vopros*, p. 31.

57 *P. S. Z.*, 2d ed., No. 36659, arts. 35, 56–59, 68, 97; Vorms, *op. cit.*, p. 52. The law seemed to give to the peasant the right to redeem the house-and-garden plot, or *usadba*, without the consent of the landlord, and separately from the remainder of the allotment, but just here the terms of the statute are extremely ambiguous and confusing. *Ibid.*, No. 36659, arts. 2, 10, 23. However, even if the road had been quite clear and open in so far as the law was concerned, there were still important practical obstacles in the path of such a fractional redemption: in the absence of an agreement with the landlord as to price, the official evaluation (always disproportionately high for this part of the allotment) was applied; and inasmuch as the State would not advance a loan for such a fractional redemption, the high price had to be paid in a lump sum. The operation was therefore a difficult one for the peasants. *Ibid.*, No. 36659, arts. 2, 8–26, 36.

After 1870 the peasant who owned an *usadba* separately redeemed might refuse to retain any longer the remainder of the allotment, if a general redemption had not already been enforced by the landlord. If the peasant owned non-allotment-lands nearby, of a certain specified area (usually twice the size of the maximal or statutory allotment for the district), he might refuse after 1870 to continue to hold any part of his original allotment, and might thus escape compulsory redemption. However it is to be remembered that in 1870 the landlords had already had almost a decade in which to enforce the redemption of the legal minimum of land, if they desired to do so. *Ibid.*, No. 36662, arts. 129–131; No. 36663, arts. 118–120.

58 Vorms, *op. cit.*, pp. 3–4, 12, 34, 36, 40.

59 Liashchenko, *Krestianskoe delo*, I, pp. 199–213; Vorms, *op. cit.*, p. 42; Ivaniukov, *op. cit.*, pp. 304–305.

60 Kornilov, *Reforma 19 fevralia 1864 g. v Tsarstve Polskom* (in Dzhivelegov, ed., *Velikaia reforma*, V), pp. 291–295.

61 *Ibid.*, pp. 296–298, 307.

62 Liashchenko, *Krestianskoe delo*, I, pp. 472–474.

63 Quoted in Chernyshev, *Agrarno-krestianskaia politika*, p. 200. See also Pokrovskii, *op. cit.*, IV, p. 96; Kornilov, *Krestianskaia reforma*, pp. 167–168, 175.

64 Chernyshev, *op. cit.*, p. 208.

65 *P. S. Z.*, 3d ed., No. 577; Khodskii, *Zemlia i zemledelets*, II, p. 66; Kornilov, *op. cit.*, p. 218; Kliuchevskii, *Kurs*, V, pp. 271–272.

66 Vorms, *op. cit.*, p. 43; Pokrovskii, *Russkaia istoriia*, IV, p. 102; and esp. Manuilov, *Arenda zemli* (in Manuilov, ed., *Ocherki*, II), p. 168.

67 Anisimov, *Nadely* (in Dzhivelegov, ed., *Velikaia reforma*, VI), table on pp. 92–93 and map on p. 96; Lositskii, *Khoziaistvennye otnosheniia* (in *Obrazovanie*, XV, No. 11, 1906), table on p. 220.

68 These data are drawn from Lositskii, *Vykupnaia operatsiia*, pp. 16–19, and appendix, pp. 38–39. Cf. Shakhovskii, *Vykupnye platezhi* (in Dzhivelegov, ed., *Velikaia reforma*, VI), pp. 114–116.

69 Liashchenko, *Krestianskoe delo*, I, pp. 399–471.

70 *Ibid.*, I, pp. 403–404. The "courtyard people" were given the right to settle if they wished in some village on the estate where they had lived, and to claim a share in the allotment-lands which the village would in any case have received. The village allotment area was not to be increased because of the settlement there of courtyard people, unless the sharing of the land with them reduced the average allotment per soul for the whole village below the minimal level fixed by law. Under the circumstances, the courtyard people were hardly likely to be welcome in the villages.

71 Kornilov, *Krestianskaia reforma*, p. 189.

72 Liashchenko, *op. cit.*, I, pp. 187–198; Shakhovskii, *op. cit.*, p. 114.

73 Liashchenko, *op. cit.*, I, pp. 4, 299–300.

74 Liashchenko, *op. cit.*, I, pp. 301–302, 318–319, 333, 379, *et passim;* Ministerstvo Gosudarstvennykh Imushchestv, *Ocherk piatidesiatiletnei deiatelnosti*, pp. 105–108.

75 *P. S. Z.*, 2d ed., No. 43888, arts. 1, 9–12; Liashchenko, *op. cit.*, I, pp. 318, 328; Ministerstvo Gosudarstvennykh Imushchestv, *op. cit.*, pp. 105–108; Kaufman, *Agrarnyi vopros*, pp. 34–36; Kornilov, *Kurs*, III, p. 13.

76 Kaufman, *op. cit.*, pp. 37–38.

77 *P. S. Z.*, 2d ed., No. 43888, arts. 13–14.

78 *Ibid.*, 3d ed., No. 3807.

79 Shakhovskii, *op. cit.*, p. 114.

80 It will be remembered that the State peasants lived largely in the forest *guberniias*, while the proprietorial peasants predominated in the richer agricultural regions of the center and the South.

81 Liashchenko, *op. cit.*, I, pp. 219–223.

82 Liashchenko, *op. cit.*, I, pp. 570–622.

83 Kornilov, *Reforma 19 fevralia v Tsarstve Polskom* (in Dzhivelegov, ed., *Velikaia reforma*, V), pp. 285–308.

84 Liashchenko, *op. cit.*, I, p. 314; Ministerstvo Gosudarstvennykh Imushchestv, *op. cit.*, p. 103; Strakhovskii, *Krestianskii vopros* (in Dolgorukov, ed., *Krestianskii stroi*, I), p. 388; Korkunov, *Russkoe gosudarstvennoe pravo*, I, p. 330 ff.

85 *P. S. Z.*, 2d ed., No. 42899, esp. arts. 3, 5, 6.

86 This class of "persons of village condition" (*litsa selskogo sostoianiia*) included the former State and proprietary peasants, strictly so called, together with other groups legally assimilated to them. The term is sometimes applied also to the lower rank of the Cossacks, in spite of the fact that the Cossacks of every rank were distinguished from all other villagers by special laws and special forms of organization. Korkunov, *Russkoe gosudarstvennoe pravo*, I, p. 330; Leontev, *Krestianskoe pravo*, pp. 10–12.

87 *P. S. Z.*, 2d ed., No. 43888, esp. arts. 2, 4; Liashchenko, *op. cit.*, I, pp. 317, 319, 327, 583; Strakhovskii, *op. cit.*, p. 386; Kachorovskii, *Russkaia obshchina*, I, pp. 379–380; Chernyshev, *Agrarno-krestianskaia politika*, p. 301; Khauke, *op. cit.*, pp. 15, 65, 69, 136, 284, 313, 318–319. On alienations connected with personal withdrawals from the commune, see *P. S. Z.*, 2d ed., No. 42899, art. 6; No. 36657, art. 130; Goremykin, *op. cit.*, I, p. 251, note 7.

88 Surov, *Kazaki* (in *Entsiklop. slovar*, Brockhaus, XIII), pp. 883–884.

NOTES TO CHAPTER VI

1 The estimate for 1860 is from Vysochaishe Uchrezhd. Kommissiia, *Materialy*, I, p. 16; for a discussion of the difficulties involved in arriving at the estimate, see *Materialy*, III, p. 35. The figures for 1897 are from Tsentralnyi Statisticheskii Komitet, *Obshchii svod*, I, pp. 161–163.

Both totals are for "the 50 *guberniias* of European Russia"; that is, for the European portion of the Empire, exclusive of Finland, Poland, and the *guberniias* between the Black and Caspian Seas, from Ekaterinodar and Stavropol southward. Various difficulties stand in the way of a comparison of the totals for 1860 and 1897. For example, because of the statistical impossibility of a complete elimination, a part of the Cossack population is included in 1860, whereas the Cossacks are entirely excluded here from the total for 1897. The totals for both 1860 and 1897 include the peasants who lived and worked at least a part of their time in the cities. For 1860, the number of these is undetermined; whereas the total for 1897 includes more than five million persons classed as peasants, who were actually found in the cities on the day of the census (28 January). However, as will later be shown, some of these peasants still had allotments of land upon which they worked for a part of the year.

In the 50 *guberniias* on the day of the census of 1897, eighty-one millions of persons of *all* classes (including nobles, merchants, *meshchane* or lesser townsmen, etc.) were actually present in the rural districts, and twelve million persons of all classes in the cities.

2 This figure is no more than a questionable approximation. It is the sum of the known allotment-area in 49 *guberniias* in 1877, increased by the area of the net reduction made in the allotments of the proprietary serfs of 43 *guberniias* at the time of the Emancipation. (See Chap. V above.)

3 Tsentralnyi Statisticheskii Komitet, *Statistika zemlevladeniia* 1905 g., appendix, p. xxxvi. These totals are not for the whole of European Russia, or even for the whole area of "the 50 *guberniias*" (see note 1 at the beginning of this chapter). The land-census of 1877 did not cover the Don Region, or Izmailskii *uezd* in Bessarabskaia *guberniia;* in other words, it covered 49 *guberniias* minus Izmailskii *uezd.* In order that the results for 1877 and 1905 may be fully comparable, in so far as the territory covered is concerned, the Don Region and Izmailskii *uezd* have been eliminated from the returns for 1905, as given above. The Cossack allotments are omitted throughout.

4 *Ibid.,* pp. xxiv–xxvii.

5 This is still conspicuously true, even if there be excluded from the peasant population all those peasants not actually found in the villages on the day of the census of 1897. This means the exclusion of most of the peasants who were engaged all or a part of the year in industrial wage-work; but it must be remembered that many of these absentees were members of allotment-holding families, and were engaged in agriculture for a part of each year. See footnote 42 below.

6 *Ibid.,* pp. 178–179; the averages are for 49 *guberniias* minus Izmailskii *uezd.* Only the households which actually held allotments were taken into account in computing these averages. The number of peasant households without allotments was not recorded in 1877 or in 1905. See also footnote 42 below.

7 Vysochaishe Uchrezhd. Kommissiia, *Materialy,* I, p. 290.

8 Strakhovskii, *Krestianskii vopros* (in Dolgorukov, ed., *Krestianskii stroi,* I), p. 410.

9 Liashchenko, *Ocherki agrarnoi evoliutsii,* p. 137; Kornilov, *Krestianskaia reforma,* p. 194. In 1887, in 50 *guberniias,* 54.5 per cent of the area of the peasant allotments was plow-land, while the corresponding percentage for the private holdings was 33.1. Glavnoe Upravlenie Zemleustroistva, *Statisticheskie svedeniia,* pp. 22, 34.

10 Vysochaishe Uchrezhd. Kommissiia, *op. cit.,* I, p. 291.

11 Kornilov, *op. cit.,* p. 219; Liashchenko, *Krestianskoe delo,* I, p. 647; Departament Okladnykh Sborov, *Otchet o vykupnom dolge . . . za* 1902 g., p. iii.

12 Kornilov, *op. cit.,* p. 222.

13 Liashchenko, *op. cit.,* I, pp. 677–678; Departament Okladnykh Sborov, *op. cit.,* p. iii.

14 Vysochaishe Uchrezhd. Kommissiia, *op. cit.,* I, p. 291.

15 Lositskii, *Vykupnaia operatsiia,* p. 7.

16 Shakhovskii, *Vykupnye platezhi* (in Dzhivelegov, ed., *Velikaia reforma,* VI), pp. 130–131.

17 Peshekhonov, *Ekonomicheskoe polozhenie krestian* (in Dzhivelegov, ed., *Velikaia reforma,* VI) pp. 219–224.

[18] Tsentralnyi Statisticheskii Komitet, *Statistika zemlevladeniia* 1905 g., appendix, p. xxxvi. The data are for 49 *guberniias* minus Izmailskii *uezd*.

[19] *Novyi entsiklopedicheskii slovar*, Brockhaus, XVIII, p. iii (following p. 479).

[20] Oganovskii, *Zakonomernost*, II, p. 442; and his *Ekonomicheskaia geografiia* p. 189.

[21] Rubinow, *Russia's wheat surplus*, pp. 52–53. Cf. Oganovskii, *Zakonomernost*, II, pp. 422–423; Chernyshev, *Agrarno-krestianskaia politika*, p. 277.

[22] Vysochaishe Uchrezhd. Kommissiia, *Materialy*, I, p. 177. A *pud* is 36 pounds. The data are for the 50 *guberniias*. The quality of these statistics is admitted to be distinctly doubtful, and the improvement in the methods of reporting and recording is probably in itself responsible in part for the showing of an increased yield (*Materialy*, III, p. 268).

[23] Ministerstvo Zemledeliia i Gosudarstvennykh Imushchestv, *Atlas kartogramm i diagramm;* the maps in Section 4 show the superior productivity of proprietorial lands as compared with peasant lands.

[24] Rubinow, *Russia's wheat surplus*, pp. 49–50, 26. The average yield per acre for the period 1898–1902 was: for European Russia, 8.8 bushels; for the United States, 13.9 bu.; for the United Kingdom, 35.4.

[25] Vysochaishe Uchrezhd. Kommissiia, *op. cit.*, I, pp. 84–85; III, pp. 161–164, and 262–263.

[26] *Ibid.*, I, p. 89; III, p. 164, and important corrective note on pp. 262–263. The subsistence-norm employed is 20 *puds* per person per year; whereas the norm for the Russian soldier's ration at the time was 29 *puds;* only food-grains and potatoes are included — the latter at only one-third of their actual weight, with the idea of reducing them to some kind of a parity in food-value with the grains.

[27] Manuilov, *Arenda* (in Manuilov, ed., *Ocherki*, II), p. 170.

[28] Manuilov, *op. cit.*, II, p. 168, and tables on pp. 174–187. Professor Manuilov's conclusions are based upon *zemstvo* data for about half the *uezds* of the fifty *guberniias*, relating chiefly to the period of the 'eighties.

[29] Estimates of the amount of non-allotment-land rented by the peasants of European Russia in the 'eighties and 'nineties and at the beginning of the twentieth century, have varied in a fantastic degree, from something more than ten millions of *desiatinas* to nearly five times as much. The official estimate quoted above is that published in the *Materialy* (I, p. 149) of the Vysochaishe Uchrezhd. 16 noiabria 1901 g. Kommissiia (the Commission constituted on 16 November 1901 for the Investigation of the Question of the Change, in the Period 1861–1900, in the Well-being of the Village Population of the Central-Agricultural *Guberniias* as compared with other Parts of European Russia).

In the *Materialy* (III, p. 265) it is stated that the estimate probably shows a considerable measure of error.

Among the various investigations of this question, that of Professor A. A. Manuilov of the University of Moscow (referred to in note 28 above) has had considerable celebrity. Prof. Manuilov concluded that in the *uezds* which he studied, the peasants rented non-allotment-lands (other than pasturage) to the extent of one-fifth of the area of their own allotments. If this estimated proportion were applied throughout the 49 *guberniias*, with the total allotment area taken as that recorded by the land-census of 1877 (111,629,000 *desiatinas*), then the area rented at that time would have amounted to about twenty-two millions of *desiatinas*, or some two and one-half millions of *desiatinas* in excess of the Imperial Commission's estimate for the later period. In the *Materialy* of the Commission (III, p. 191) it is however stated that the renting by peasants of non-allotment-lands, "developing from the time of the liberation of the peasants from bondage, continues year by year to increase."

Writing about a decade after the period of the Imperial Commission's activities, N. P. Oganovskii cites and compares a number of different estimates of the area of peasant non-allotment renting, and finally states that the data available do not permit a definite conclusion as to whether renting by the peasants had increased or decreased since the 'eighties. (See Oganovskii, *Zakonomernost*, II, pp. 446–453; published 1911.)

[30] Manuilov, *op. cit.*, II, pp. 168–170; Prokopovich, *Krestianskoe khoziaistvo*, pp. 45–73.

[31] Manuilov, *op. cit.*, II, p. 131 ff.

[32] Vysochaishe Uchrezhd. Kommissiia, *Materialy*, I, pp. 142, 199; III, p. 98. The estimate of net income is based upon materials for 250 *uezds* in 27 *guberniias*, scattered in every quarter of European Russia; these materials cover time-periods of varying length, falling between the years 1880 and 1901. The average rental rate is based upon incomplete returns from 44 *guberniias*.

[33] Manuilov, *op. cit.*, II, p. 172.

[34] Oganovskii, *Zakonomernost*, II, p. 436.

[35] Skalon, *Krestianskii Bank* (in Manuilov, ed., *Ocherki*, II), p. 1 ff.

[36] Glavnoe Upravlenie Zemleustroistva, *Statisticheskie svedeniia*, p. 35; data for 50 *guberniias*.

[37] Tsentralnyi Statisticheskii Komitet, *Statistika zemlevladeniia 1905 g.*, appendix, pp. v, xx, xxii; data for 49 *guberniias* minus Izmailskii *uezd*. Oganovskii, *Zakonomernost*, II, p. 437.

[38] Departament Okladnykh Sborov, *Materialy po statistike dvizheniia zemlevladeniia*, XXV, pp. 64–65. For a discussion of the character and scope of these data, see Vysochaishe Uchrezhd. Kommissiia, *Materialy*, III, p. 73.

[39] Glavnoe Upravlenie Zemleustroistva, *op. cit.*, p. 41; data for 44 *guberniias*.

[40] *Ibid.*, p. xiii.

[41] Vysochaishe Uchrezhd. Kommissiia, *op. cit.*, I, pp. 110–111; data are for 44 *guberniias*.

[42] In the following table an attempt is made to compare the changes in peasant population and in peasant land-holding:

	Before the Great Reforms	1877	1897	1905
Peasant Lands				
Allotment-Lands	113,000,000 *des.*	111,629,000 *des.*	———	123,183,000 *des.*
Allotment- and Non-Allotment-Lands	———	118,181,000 *des.*	———	146,825,000 *des.*
Peasant Population				
In the Villages		(61,000,000)	73,500,000	(78,000,000)
In Villages and Cities	50,000,000	(63,000,000)	78,600,000	(84,000,000)

Peasant Lands: As to the source and character of these data, see footnotes 2 and 3 at the beginning of this chapter; also the table of land-holdings at the end of this volume with the explanatory notes attached thereto (Appendix I).

Peasant Population: For observations on the data for the pre-Reform period, and for 1897, see footnote 1 at the beginning of this chapter. In order that a direct comparison may be made between population and land-area, the populations for the years of the land-censuses (1877 and 1905) have been calculated very roughly from the known populations for the years 1860 and 1897, with the assumption that the annual increase was constant.

Conclusion: I. It is beyond question that in the period 1877–1905 the increase in the peasant population was more than proportional to the increase in the allotment-lands.

II. When the non-allotment-lands are also included, it still appears that in this same period the increase in population was more than proportional to the increase in land-area (the number of peasants in the villages increased by about three-tenths; the land-area by 24.2 per cent). However, because of the shortcomings of the data, and because of the somewhat arbitrary assumption involved in the calculations (the assumption as to the *constancy* of the annual population-increase), this second conclusion must be regarded as at best only tentative.

[43] Vysochaishe Uchrezhd. Kommissiia, *op. cit.*, I, pp. 184–185; Ministerstvo Zemledeliia, *Sbornik statistiko-ekonomicheskikh svedenii*, ed. of 1916, pp. 476–477.

[44] Departament Zemledeliia, *Selsko-khoziaistvennyi promysel*, pp. 106–112.

45 Liashchenko, *Ocherki agrarnoi evoliutsii*, I, pp. 137, 157, 159, 165, 215. Vysochaishe Uchrezhd. Kommissiia, *op. cit.*, III, p. 276.

46 Peshekhonov, *Ekonomicheskoe polozhenie krestian* (in Dzhivelegov, ed., *Velikaia reforma*, VI), pp. 221–224.

47 Vysochaishe Uchrezhd. Kommissiia, *op. cit.*, I, p. 89; III, pp. 164 and 262–263; Liashchenko, *op. cit.*, I, pp. 248, 250–252.

48 Liashchenko, *op. cit.*, I, pp. 236–243.

49 *Ibid.*, I, p. 235.

50 Vysochaishe Uchrezhd. Kommissiia, *Materialy*, I, p. 210; III, pp. 103–106, 274; Oganovskii, *Zakonomernost*, II, pp. 454, 458, 489. In the southwestern *guberniias*, oxen are much employed as work-animals; but if, in the absence of data on this subject, one add together the *total* numbers of "large horned cattle" and of work-horses, in 1870, and again in 1900, the increase in the number of both together does not keep pace with the increase in the number of peasant households (*dvors*). The data on the subject of the number of domestic animals in the possession of the peasants of European Russia are scattered and incomplete, but the general trend of change seems to be well established.

51 Vysochaishe Uchrezhd. Kommissiia, *op. cit.*, I, pp. 218–219; III, pp. 107–112, 216–223. An attempt is made in the *Materialy* to estimate the number of peasant-workers engaged in the various activities mentioned above; but the method of making up the estimate appears to be more than doubtful.

52 Moratchevsky, *Petites industries rurales, dites de koustari* (in de Kovalevsky, ed., *La Russie à la fin du 19e siècle*), pp. 538–545; Tugan-Baranovskii, *Russkaia fabrika*, I, pp. 360–408. Ministerstvo Zemledeliia i Gosudarstvennykh Imushchestv, *Kustarnye promysly*, gives data on the craft-industries, *guberniia* by *guberniia*, in the middle 'nineties; two other publications of the same ministry (*Otchety i issledovaniia po kustarnoi promyshlennosti v Rossii*, 4 vols., and *Obzor kustarnykh promyslov Rossii*) contain studies of particular regions and industries, with photographs and diagrams illustrating the methods of the craftsmen.

53 Glavnoe Upravlenie Zemleustroistva, *Statisticheskie svedeniia*, p. 17, and explanation on pp. ix–x.

54 Rybnikov, *Zemledelcheskie rabochie* (in *Novyi entsiklop. slovar*, Brockhaus, XVIII), p. 498. See also Vysochaishe Uchrezhd. Kommissiia, *op. cit.*, I, pp. 218–219; III, pp. 216–223.

55 Ministerstvo Zemledeliia, *Sbornik statistiko-ekonomicheskikh svedenii*, 1916, p. 526; for 50 *guberniias*.

56 Vysochaishe Uchrezhd. Kommissiia, *op. cit.*, I, pp. 236–237, 242–243; from incomplete reports for European Russia.

57 Vysochaishe Uchrezhd. Kommissiia, *op. cit.*, I, pp. 242–243 (for 48 *guberniias*); Ministerstvo Zemledeliia, *op. cit.*, 1916, p. 526 (for 50 *guberniias*).

58 Glavnoe Upravlenie Zemleustroistva i Zemledeliia, *Selskokhoziaistvennyi promysel*, thirteen regional graphs on pp. 106–112.

59 Tugan-Baranovskii, *Russkaia fabrika*, I, p. 348 ff.; de Kovalevsky, ed., *La Russie*, pp. 602–616; Prokopovich, *Mestnye liudi o nuzhdakh Rossii*, pp. 219–220.

60 Maslov, *Agrarnyi vopros*, I, p. 407. On the general subject of the cause of these labor-pilgrimages, see also Miliutin, *Rabochii vopros v selskom khoziaistve Rossii*, pp. 34–39; Mints, *Otkhod krestianskogo naseleniia*, pp. 10–13.

61 Vysochaishe Uchrezhd. Kommissiia, *op. cit.*, I, pp. 218–219, 226–227; III, pp. 112, 223–226, 273 (data for 50 *guberniias*); Kirillov, *Otkhozhie promysly* (in *Rossiia*) pp. 264–267; Mints, *op. cit.*, pp. 14–15, 28.

62 Mints, *op. cit.*, pp. 11, 14, 39, and esp. tables on pp. 22–24 and 36. Cf. Kirillov, *op. cit.*, pp. 265–266, 268; Miliutin, *op. cit.*, p. 32; Maslov, *op. cit.*, I, p. 408.

63 Maslov, *op. cit.*, I, pp. 408–415; Mints, *op. cit.*, p. 28; Miliutin, *op. cit.*, p. 50.

64 Tugan-Baranovskii, *Russkaia fabrika*, I, pp. 347–348, 352; Mavor, *Economic history*, II, pp. 397–400; Guchman, *Proizvoditelnost truda* (in Strumilin, ed., *Problemy truda*, I), p. 163.

65 Tsentralnyi Statisticheskii Komitet, *Obshchii svod*, I, p. 161.

66 Mints, *op. cit.*, table on p. 29.

67 Tugan-Baranovskii, *op. cit.*, I, pp. 352–359; Mavor, *op. cit.*, II, pp. 390–397.

68 Maslov, *op. cit.*, I, p. 368. An investigation conducted in Moscow *guberniia* showed that a similar proportion of the factory-workers returned to the country in

the Summer; *ibid.*, p. 372. Cf. Pogozhev, *Uchet chislennosti rabochikh*, pp. 99–102.

[69] Tsentralnyi Statisticheskii Komitet, *Obshchii svod*, I, p. 1; *Rossiia*, p. 75; Oganovskii, *Ocherki po ekonomicheskoi geografii*, p. 61.

[70] Kornilov, *Krestianskaia reforma*, pp. 227–233; Kaufman, *Agrarnyi vopros*, pp. 90–94; Oganovskii, *op. cit.*, p. 81.

[71] Kornilov, *op. cit.*, pp. 249–251. See also Glavnoe Upravlenie Zemleustroistva, *Statisticheskie svedeniia*, pp. 8–9; according to the introductory note (p. viii) these official figures fall somewhat short of the actual strength of the movement.

[72] Vysochaishe Uchrezhd. Kommissiia, *op. cit.*, I, p. 16, 22, 26. Cf. Oganovskii, *op. cit.*, p. 82; Kornilov, *op. cit.*, p. 253.

[73] Evreinov, *Istoriia telesnykh nakazanii*, pp. 196–198; Peshekhonov, *Ekonomicheskoe polozhenie krestian* (Dzhivelegov, ed., *Velikaia reforma*, VI), p. 216.

[74] Oganovskii, *Zakonomernost* (see esp. II, pp. 470–532) may be taken as representative of the *narodnik* school; this author undertakes to show that post-Emancipation history was characterized by a progressive *equalization* of the peasantry.

The case for a progressive *differentiation* of the peasantry into proletariat and bourgeoisie was set out at length by Lenin in *Razvitie kapitalizma v Rossii;* see chap. II, and esp. pp. 141–143.

[75] Rittich, *Zavisimost krestian ot obshchiny i mira*, pp. 72, 73 (with footnote 1); Leontev, *Krestianskoe pravo*, pp. 318–319.

[76] Rittich, *op. cit.*, pp. 144–146; Khauke, *op. cit.*, pp. 58–62; Lokhtin, *Bezzemelnyi proletariat*, esp. pp. 57–58; Goremykin, *Svod*, I, p. 97, note 4. Cf. Goremykin, *Agrarnyi vopros.*

[77] A law of 1893 made this restriction much more severe. Strakhovskii, *Krestianskii vopros* (in Dolgorukov, ed., *Krestianskii stroi*, I), pp. 437–438.

[78] Tsentralnyi Statisticheskii Komitet, *Statistika zemlevladeniia 1905 g.*, p. 177; data for 50 *guberniias*. The communes with hereditary household tenure as well as those with repartitional tenure are covered by these returns.

[79] *Ibid.*, pp. 128–129.

[80] For these and other similar returns, see Svavitskie, *Zemskie podvornye perepisi*, pp. 69–184.

[81] The land-census of 1905 dealt primarily with holdings, rather than with holders, and distributed the holdings of the peasants among three categories: allotment-holdings, collective non-allotment-holdings, and personal non-allotment-holdings. The allotments were classified as to size, not upon the basis of an *individual* record of their actual area, but upon the basis of the *average* amount of allotment-land for each allotment-holding-household in each commune (whether under repartitional or hereditary tenure). In the case of the collective non-allotment-holdings, there is no indication as to how many members shared in a given collective. In the case of the individual non-allotment-holdings, there is always the possibility that several holdings, separately recorded and classified as to size, actually belonged to a single peasant. Thus a given peasant holder might have, first, an allotment; second, a share in one or more collective non-allotment-holdings; third, one or more individual non-allotment-holdings; but these holdings, of three different categories, would figure in three separate tables and would nowhere be assembled into a single unit. In other words, there is no possibility whatever of classifying all peasant holders in a single series in accordance with the *total* extent of their respective holdings of all classes of land taken together.

A minor obstacle to the determination of the amount of non-allotment property in peasant hands, was the existence of certain collectives which included in their composition not only peasants, but members of other classes as well. The number of such mixed collectives, and the extent of their holdings, was, however, inconsiderable.

See Tsentralnyi Statisticheskii Komitet, *Statistika zemlevladeniia 1905 g.*, pp. 12–17, 128–131.

[82] Tsentralnyi Statisticheskii Komitet, *op. cit.*, pp. 130–131.

[83] Baturinskii, *Agrarnaia politika*, table on p. 79; cf. Oganovskii, *Zakonomernost*, II, p. 437.

[84] Oganovskii, *op. cit.*, II, pp. 436–437; Manuilov, *Pozemelnyi vopros* (in Dolgorukov, ed., *Agrarnyi vopros*), pp. 33–34.

85 Tsentralnyi Statisticheskii Komitet, *op. cit.*, p. 78; data for 50 *guberniias*.
86 Tsentralnyi Statisticheskii Komitet, *op. cit.*, pp. 78–79, 128–129.
87 Vysochaishe Uchrezhd. Kommissiia, *op. cit.*, I, pp. 210–211.
88 Vysochaishe Uchrezhd. Kommissiia, *op. cit.*, summary and general conclusions in Vol. III, pp. 265–280.
89 *Ibid.*, I, p. 205.
90 Vysochaishe Uchrezhd. Kommissiia, *Materialy*, I, p. 33; III, p. 125; for 50 *guberniias*.
91 For England and France this is the annual average for the years 1901–1905; for European Russia, for the years 1901–1903. Webb, *New dictionary of statistics*, p. 183; Kaufman, *Agrarnyi vopros*, p. 58.

NOTES TO CHAPTER VII

1 Nechaev, *Russkoe krestianskoe obychnoe pravo* (in *Rossiia*), p. 549.
2 Lisitsyn, *Dvor* (in *Entsiklop. gosudarstva i prava*, I), pp. 774–775.
3 Kaufman, *Agrarnyi vopros*, p. 122; Chernyshev, *Agrarno-krestianskaia politika*, pp. 214–215; Kornilov, *Krestianskaia reforma*, p. 242; Khauke, *Krestianskoe zemelnoe pravo*, pp. 223–224.
4 Efimenko, *Semeinye razdely* (in her *Issledovaniia narodnoi zhizni*, I), p. 124 ff.; Chernyshev, *op. cit.*, p. 281; Kovalevskii, *Rodovoi byt*, I, pp. 41–42.
5 Vysochaishe Uchrezhd. Kommissiia, *Materialy*, I, pp. 16, 210.
6 Kovalevskii, *op. cit.*, I, pp. 30–42; Leontev, *Krestianskoe pravo*, division II, chap. I, esp. p. 330.
7 Chernyshev, *op. cit.*, p. 228; Kornilov, *op. cit.*, p. 244; Strakhovskii, *Krestianskii vopros* (in Dolgorukov. ed., *Krestianskii stroi*, I), pp. 437–438.
8 Chernyshev, *Obshchina*, I, p. viii; Lositskii, *Raspadenie obshchiny* (in Imperatorskoe Volnoe Ekonomicheskoe obshchestvo, *Trudy*, 1912, Nos. 1–2), p. 13; Rittich, *Zavisimost krestian*, pp. 95, 103–118; Khauke, *op. cit.*, pp. 308–314, 319; Witte, *Zapiska*, p. 90.
9 Glavnoe Upravlenie Zemleustroistva i Zemledeliia, *Statisticheskie svedeniia*, p. 23.
10 Tsentralnyi Statisticheskii Komitet, *Statistika zemlevladeniia 1905 g.*, pp. 173–174; Sviatlovskii, *Mobilizatsiia*, p. 51.
11 Tsentralnyi Statisticheskii Komitet, op. cit., pp. 172–175; data for 50 *guberniias*.
12 Chernyshev, *Obshchina*, I, pp. viii–ix; Kachorovskii, *Russkaia obshchina*, I, pp. 79, 254.
13 Chernyshev, *Agrarno-krestianskaia politika*, p. 256.
14 Chernyshev, *op. cit.*, p. 231.
15 *Ibid.*, pp. 231–232; Kornilov, *Krestianskaia reforma*, p. 244.
16 Chernyshev, *op. cit.*, pp. 296–297.
17 Chernyshev, *Obshchina*, I, p. ix; Kaufman, *Agrarnyi vopros*, pp. 123–124; Oganovskii, *Ocherki po ekonomicheskoi geografii*, p. 118; Kachorovskii, *op, cit.*, I, pp. 258–316; Vysochaishe Uchrezhd. Osoboe Soveshchanie, *Svod trudov*, division 2, pp. 46–47. In Barykov, ed., *Sbornik materialov pozemelnoi obshchiny*, I, there will be found information regarding the workings of repartition in certain individual communes, with maps showing the arrangement of the fields and their division into strips.
18 Chernyshev, *op. cit.*, I, p. ix.
19 Chernyshev, *Agrarno-krestianskaia politika*, p. 231; Kachorovskii, *op. cit.*, pp. 396, 399; Kaufman, *Russkaia obshchina*, pp. 416–421.
20 The first estimate above was made by Kachorovskii, on the basis of the *zemstvo* statistics for 191 *uezds*. See his *Biurokraticheskii zakon i krestianskaia obshchina* (in *Russkoe bogatstvo*, July, 1910, No. 7) pp. 133–135.
The second (official) estimate was to the effect that in 1910 3,500,000 peasant households belonged to communes which had not made a fundamental redistribution of their lands since their allotment during the Great Reforms. Chernyshev, *Obshchina*, I, p. xiv; Kaufman, *Agrarnyi vopros*, p. 128. In 1905 the number of peasant households with allotments in repartitional tenure was 9,201,262 in the 50 *guberniias*. Tsentralnyi Statisticheskii Komitet, *Statistika zemlevladeniia 1905 g.*, appendix, table 25b.

21 Chernyshev, *op. cit.*, I, p. xiv.

22 Chernyshev, *Agrarno-krestianskaia politika,* p. 277; Oganovskii, *op. cit.*, pp. 124-126; Vysochaishe Uchrezhd. Osoboe Soveshchanie, *Svod trudov mestnykh komitetov,* division 2, p. 27; Oganovskii, *Ocherki po ekon. geografii,* p. 126; Pershin, *Uchastkovoe zemlepolzovanie,* pp. 14-15; and his *Zemelnoe ustroistvo,* pp. 201, 207; Lositskii, *op. cit.*, p. 13; Rittich, *op. cit.*, pp. 95-97; Sviatlovskii, *op. cit.*, p. 57.

23 Manuilov, *Arenda* (in Manuilov, ed., *Ocherki,* II), p. 168.

24 Manuilov, *op. cit.*, II, pp. 78-85; Vysochaishe Uchrezhd. Kommissiia, *Materialy,* III, p. 175.

25 Tsentralnyi Statisticheskii Komitet, *Statistika zemlevladeniia 1905 g.*, pp. 164-167, appendix, pp. v, xx, xxii. The categories employed in the land-registrations of 1877 and in 1905 did not completely coincide, and the results are therefore not fully comparable. Besides this, in 1905 some peasants were members of collectives not entirely of peasant composition which, because of their mixed character, could not be included in the table above; the holdings of all the mixed collectives amounted, however, to only 60,336 *desiatinas.* The data in the table above are for 49 *guberniias,* minus Izmailskii *uezd* in Bessarabskaia *guberniia.*
The conclusion that collective peasant property was increasing more rapidly than individual peasant property is completely confirmed by the materials of the Department of Direct Taxes. See Kosinskii, *Osnovnye tendentsii v mobilizatsii zemelnoi sobstvennosti,* II, appendix, table xxi.

26 Oganovskii, *Zakonomernost,* II, p. 438.

27 See, for example, Chernyshev's account of the opposing opinions current in official circles during the 'eighties and thereafter. *Agrarno-krestianskaia politika,* pp. 232-384.

28 Quoted in Chernyshev, *Agrarno-krestianskaia politika,* p. 251.

29 Maslov, *Agrarnyi vopros,* I, p. 413.

30 Kaufman, *Agrarnyi vopros,* pp. 95-96.

31 Kheisin, *Istoriia kooperatsii v Rossii,* p. 29.

32 The statistics of the co-operative movement are of doubtful quality, and are to be accepted only as rough approximations. Kheisin, *op. cit.*, pp. 31-36, 158-162; Bubnoff, *Co-operative movement in Russia, passim,* and table 1, p. 161.

33 Pypin, *Istoriia russkoi literatury,* III, pp. 91-96; Liatskii, *Predstavleniia belorussa o nechistoi sile* (in *Etnograficheskoe obozrenie,* 1890, No. 4), pp. 25-41; Leger, *La mythologie slave,* pp. 68-69.

34 Réau, *L'art russe de Pierre le Grand à nos jours,* p. 237 ff.; Holme, ed., *Peasant art in Russia* (special Autumn number of *The studio,* 1912); Voronov, *Krestianskoe iskusstvo;* Nekrasov, *Russkoe narodnoe iskusstvo;* Bobrinskoi, *Narodnye russkie dereviannye izdeliia* (superb portfolios showing examples of craft-work in wood).

35 Conybeare, *Russian dissenters,* p. 332; Miliukov, *Ocherki,* II, p. 135.

36 Kornilov, *Kurs,* III, pp. 305-306.

37 Tsentralnyi Statisticheskii Komitet, *Obshchii svod,* I, p. 206; data for 50 *guberniias.* The Cossacks are here included in the "village population."

38 *Ibid.*

39 Quoted in Kolpenskii, *Iz offitsialnoi zapiski* (in *Arkhiv istorii truda,* II), p. 124. See also Maslov, *Agrarnyi vopros,* I, pp. 45, 48, 59, 104-123.

NOTES TO CHAPTER VIII

1 Kornilov, *Krestianskaia reforma,* p. 192; Liashchenko, *Ocherki,* I, p. 136.

2 Liashchenko, *op. cit.*, p. 136.

3 Oganovskii, *Zakonomernost,* II, p. 451.

4 Kornilov, *op. cit.*, pp. 168-169, 191-192.

5 Kornilov, *Kurs,* III, p. 147.

6 Rubinow, *Russia's wheat surplus,* pp. 26, 49-50.

7 Manuilov, *Arenda* (in Manuilov, ed., *Ocherki,* II), pp. 123-130; cf. Lenin, *Razvitie kapitalizma,* pp. 147-163.

8 Departament Okladnykh Sborov, *Materialy,* XXV, pp. 62-63; data for 47 *guberniias.*

9 Tsentralnyi Statisticheskii Komitet, *Statistika zemlevladeniia 1905 g.*, appendix,

p. iv; data are for 49 *guberniias*, excluding Izmailskii *uezd* in Bessarabskaia *guberniia*.

[10] *Ibid.*, p. 162; for 46 *guberniias*.

[11] Oganovskii, *op. cit.*, p. 458.

[12] Kliuchevskii, *Kurs*, V, p. 271.

[13] Kaufman, *Krestianskii Pozemelnyi Bank* (in *Entsiklop. slovar*, Granat, XXV), p. 566. See also Baturinskii, *Agrarnaia politika* . . . *i Krestianskii Pozemelnyi Bank*, p. 47; Herzenstein, *Krestianskii Bank* (in Dolgorukov, ed., *Agrarnyi vopros*, I), pp. 163–165.

[14] Vysochaishe Uchrezhd. Kommissiia, *Materialy*, I, pp. 306–307; data for 46 *guberniias* for period 1886–1900.

[15] Glavnoe Upravlenie Zemleustroistva, *Statisticheskie svedeniia*, pp. 40–41. Of all the land on mortgage in 1904, 35.8 per cent was pledged to the Nobles' Bank, 11 per cent to the Peasants' Bank, and 53.2 per cent to other institutions; data are for 50 *guberniias*. Of the lands in the latter group, a very considerable proportion undoubtedly belonged to the nobility.

[16] Gosudarstvennyi Dvorianskii Zemelnyi Bank, *Otchet* . . . *za 1903 god*, p. 7.

[17] Krestianskii Pozemelnyi Bank, *Otchet* . . . *za 1903 god*, p. ii.

[18] Gosudarstvennyi Dvorianskii Zemelnyi Bank, *op. cit.*, p. iii. Cf. Vysochaishe Uchrezhd. Kommissiia, *Materialy*, I, pp. 306–307.

[19] Kornilov, *Krestianskaia reforma*, pp. 240–241; Leontev, *Krestianskoe pravo*, p. 145 ff.

[20] Kornilov, *op. cit.*, p. 244.

[21] Kornilov, *Kurs*, III, pp. 300–302; Veselovskii, *Istoriia zemstv*, III, p. 349 ff.

[22] In Russia the clergy were so enormously inferior to the nobility in wealth and power that their personal, economic, and political position in the rural districts hardly seems to demand a detailed treatment. Their personal (non-institutional) property amounted in 1877 to 186,000 *des.*; in 1905 to 322,000 (for 49 *guberniias*, exclusive of Izmailskii *uezd*, in Bessarab. *guberniia*). In 1905 the average size of their properties was 34.3 *des.*, against an average of 26.9 *des.* for the private personal properties of the peasants; and there were only 26 personal properties of the clergy above 1,000 *des.* in size (data for 50 *guberniias*). Tsentralnyi Statisticheskii Komitet, *Statistika zemlevladeniia 1905 g.*, appendix, p. x.

[23] *Ibid.*, appendix, pp. v–vii; data for 49 *guberniias* minus Izmailskii *uezd*.

[24] *Ibid.*, pp. 16–17, 162; in 1905 the average size of their properties was only a little more than half again the average size of the peasant non-allotment-holdings. The term *meshchanin* was officially translated *bourgeois de la ville*, but at the time of the census of 1897, among the 9,945,000 persons of this class counted in the 50 *guberniias*, 4,712,000 were found outside the cities. Tsentralnyi Statisticheskii Komitet, *Obshchii svod*, p. 161.

[25] Tsentralnyi Statisticheskii Komitet, *op. cit.*, pp. 16–17. The number of their individual properties, and the total extent of their holdings for 1877, are for 49 *guberniias* minus Izmailskii *uezd*.

[26] *Ibid.*, p. 162. Data for 46 *guberniias*. This predominance in size of the average merchant holding was not confined to the northern forest *guberniias* but extended to many of the *guberniias* of the South and Southwest.

[27] Oganovskii, *Zakonomernost*, II, p. 435; Departament Okladnykh Sborov, *op. cit.*, XXV, pp. 64–65.

[28] Tsentralnyi Statisticheskii Komitet, *op. cit.*, appendix, pp. v–vii, xix–xxiii; the data are for 49 *guberniias* exclusive of Izmailskii *uezd* in Bessarabskaia *guberniia*.

[29] Oganovskii, *op. cit.*, II, p. 458.

[30] According to Oganovskii, *op. cit.*, II, p. 436.

[31] Tsentralnyi Statisticheskii Komitet, *op. cit.*, p. 78; data are for 50 *guberniias*. The statistics deal not with *holders*, but with *holdings*, and in the case of the non-allotment-lands, several holdings may possibly belong to one holder.

[32] Tsentralnyi Statisticheskii Komitet, *op. cit.*, appendix, pp. iv–vii, xix. The data for the holdings of the townsmen, the non-peasant and mixed collectives, and the nobles, are for 49 *guberniias* exclusive of Izmailskii *uezd*.

[33] This statistical difficulty has already been explained; see above, Notes to Chapter VI, note 81.

[34] *Ibid.*, pp. 129, 162; data for 50 *guberniias*.

35 *Ibid.*, pp. 78–79.

36 Tsentralnyi Statisticheskii Komitet, *op. cit.*, pp. 132–133; also the Committee's *Statistika zemlevladeniia* 1905 g., Issue X, *Bessarabskaia guberniia*, p. 31; the data are for 49 *guberniias* excluding Izmailskii *uezd* in Bessarabskaia *guberniia*. The unpopulated lands of the Church were not secularized in the 18th century, and the subsequent acquisition of lands by the Church was not prohibited. Gote, *Ocherk*, p. 178.

37 Oganovskii, *Zemlevladenie v Rossii* (in *Novyi entsiklop. slovar*, XVIII), p. 481; Chernyshev, *Selskoe khoziaistvo*, p. 43.

38 Leroy-Beaulieu, *Empire of the Tsars*, III, p. 237; Richter, *Skolko zemli*, p. 16.

39 Oganovskii, *op. cit.*, XVIII, p. 481; these data as to the distribution of land among the monasteries are from the Synodal investigation of 1890.

40 Tsentralnyi Statisticheskii Komitet, *op. cit.*, pp. 132–133; also the Committee's *Statistika zemlevladeniia* 1905 g., Issue X, *Bessarabskaia guberniia*, p. 31; the data are for 49 *guberniias* excepting Izmailskii *uezd* in Bessarabskaia *guberniia*; Oganovskii, *op. cit.*, XVIII, p. 481.

41 Tsentralnyi Statisticheskii Komitet, *op. cit.*, pp. 132–133; Glavnoe Upravlenie Zemleustroistva, *Statisticheskie svedeniia*, p. 47; Chernyshev, *Selskoe khoziaistvo*, pp. 42–43; Vysochaishe Uchrezhd. Osoboe Soveshchanie, *Svod trudov*, division 5, pp. 102–103. There were no *udel* lands in Izmailskii *uezd* in Bessarabskaia *guberniia*.

42 Tsentralnyi Statisticheskii Komitet, *op. cit.*, pp. 132–133; also the Committee's *Statistika zemlevladeniia* 1905 g., Issue X, *Bessarabskaia guberniia*, p. 31; the data are for 49 *guberniias* excepting Izmailskii *uezd* in Bessarabskaia *guberniia*.

43 Glavnoe Upravlenie Zemleustroistva, *op. cit.*, p. 46; data for 50 *guberniias*, in 1904. Cf. Vysochaishe Uchrezhd. Kommissiia, *Materialy*, I, pp. 144–145; data for 50 *guberniias*, in 1901. See also Chernyshev, *Selskoe khoziaistvo*, p. 42.

44 Vysochaishe Uchrezhd. Osoboe Soveshchanie, *op. cit.*, division 19, pp. 183–198.

NOTES TO CHAPTER IX

1 Dubrovskii and Grave, *Krestianskoe dvizhenie nakanune revoliutsii 1905 goda* (in Pokrovskii, ed., *1905. Istoriia revoliutsionnogo dvizheniia v otdelnykh ocherkakh*, I), pp. 250–255. Cf. Maslov, *Agrarnyi vopros*, II, pp. 104–140.

2 Veselovskii, ed., *Krestianskoe dvizhenie 1902 goda*, p. 10; Maslov, *op. cit.*, II, pp. 109, 115.

3 Veselovskii, *op. cit.*, pp. 18, 79, 100, and esp. p. 104.

4 Dubrovskii and Grave, *op. cit.*, pp. 311, 313.

5 *Ibid.*, p. 312.

6 Veselovskii, *op. cit.*, p. 109.

7 *Ibid.*, pp. 116–120; Dubrovskii and Grave, *op. cit.*, p. 313; Maslov, *op. cit.*, II, p. 143.

8 Veselovskii, *op. cit.*, pp. 6–7, 19–22.

9 *Ibid.*, pp. 60–63, 64–113.

10 Maslov, *op. cit.*, II, p. 51; Kornilov, *Kurs*, III, pp. 170–172.

11 Maslov, *op. cit.*, II, pp. 52–55, 60–63; Kornilov, *op. cit.*, III, pp. 178–180, 188.

12 Maslov, *op. cit.*, II, pp. 63–67; Kornilov, *op. cit.*, III, pp. 192, 216–220, 238–239, 294 ff., 308.

13 Egorov, *Zarozhdenie politicheskikh partii i ikh deiatelnost* (in Martov, ed., *Obshchestvennoe dvizhenie v Rossii v nachale xx-go veka*, I), pp. 414–415.

14 *Ibid.*, I, pp. 416–418; Ivanov-Razumnik, *Istoriia russkoi obshchestvennoi mysli*, II, pp. 483–488; Masaryk, *Spirit of Russia*, II, pp. 306–308, 362–363. The position of this party on the agrarian question is set out in a manifesto of the Peasants' Union of the Party of Socialist Revolutionaries, addressed "to all workers for revolutionary socialism in Russia." The manifesto was published in April 1902 in the organ of the party, *Revoliutsionnaia Rossiia*, and reprinted in a book published by the party in 1903: *Po voprosam programmy i taktiki*, pp. 23–47.

15 Rossiiskaia Kommunisticheskaia partiia (bolshevikov), *Rossiiskaia Kommunisticheskaia partiia (bolshevikov) v rezoliutsiiakh*, p. 8.

16 Egorov, *op. cit.*, I, p. 407. This writer says: "Of the fifty-five delegates with full

voting-power or with only advisory votes, only four were of the working class."
The specific figure may not be altogether reliable, but whatever allowance may be
made for its inaccuracy, it is clear enough that the leaders were prevailingly of a
non-proletarian character. Two years later there was still "a relative predominance
of intellectuals in the party centers" — or at any rate so states a resolution of the
Bolshevik congress of April–May 1905. Ross. Kom. partiia (bolshevikov), *op. cit.*,
pp. 19–23, 38.

17 For the text of the program, see *ibid.*, pp. 19–23. For Lenin's view of the
mistakes of the agrarian section of the program of 1903, see his *Agrarnaia programma
sotsial-demokratii v pervoi russkoi revoliutsii 1905-7 g.g.*, pp. 48–51; this book was
written in 1907.

18 Ross. Kom. partiia (bolshevikov), *op. cit.*, pp. 19, 29, 55, 77; Rozhkov, *Russkaia
istoriia*, XII, pp. 180–184; Egorov, *op. cit.*, I, pp. 408–409. At the congress held at
Stockholm in 1906, the Mensheviks had 62 votes, the Bolsheviks 46. At the congress
of 1907 in London, the Russian delegation was made up of 105 Bolsheviks, 97 Mensheviks, and 4 non-faction delegates, while the organizations of the Jewish, the
Polish, and the Latvian Social Democrats on Russian territory were also represented, and the control of the congress depended upon the ability of the one
Russian faction or the other to influence the votes of the delegates of these smaller
groups.

19 Egorov, *op. cit.*, I, pp. 409–410.

20 Maslov, *op. cit.*, II, pp. 68–69; Dubrovskii and Grave, *op. cit.*, I, pp. 364–378;
Veselovskii, *op. cit.*, p. 3; Spiridovich, *Partiia Sotsialistov-revoliutsionerov*, pp. 102–
110; Spiridovich, *Istoriia bolshevizma*, p. 51; Veselovskii, *Krestianskii vopros*,
pp. 25–26.

21 Veselovskii, ed., *Krestianskoe dvizhenie*, p. 8.

22 Chernyshev, *Agrarno-krestianskaia politika*, pp. 267–308. For an account of the
work of the Special Conference, see its report to the Tsar: Vysochaishe Uchrezhd.
Osoboe Soveshchanie, *Vsepoddanneishii otchet, 1902–1904*.

23 *Polnoe sobranie zakonov*, 3d col., No. 17286, art. 38; No. 22627.

24 Veselovskii, *Dvizhenie zemlevladeltsev* (in Martov, ed., *op. cit.*, I), pp. 300–301,
307.

25 Korkunov, *Russkoe gosudarstvennoe pravo*, II.

26 Veselovskii, *op. cit.*, I, pp. 293–294, 302–305; Egorov, *op. cit.*, I, pp. 387–392.

27 Ermanskii, *Krupnaia burzhuaziia do 1905 goda* (in Martov, ed., *op. cit.*, I),
pp. 313–317, 347–348.

28 Varzar, *Statistika stachek rabochikh na fabrikakh i zavodakh za trekhletie
1906–1908 g.g.*, p. 3 and diagram opp. p. 4; Koltsov, *Rabochie v 1890–1904 g.g.* (in
Martov, ed., *op. cit.*, I), pp. 224–225; Piontkovskii, *Istoriia rabochego dvizheniia v
Rossii (1870–1917 g.)*, pp. 61–114. The statement made in regard to strikes is based
upon the official data published in Varzar; according to Koltsov, these data are far
from complete.

29 Cherevanin, *Dvizhenie intelligentsii* (in Martov, ed., *op. cit.*, I), pp. 288–290;
Veselovskii, *op. cit.*, I, p. 306; Egorov, *op. cit.*, I, p. 392.

30 Ross. Kom. partiia (bolshevikov), *op. cit.*, pp. 8–9, 23–24, 37; Egorov, *op. cit.*,
I, p. 408.

31 Lenskii, *Natsionalnoe dvizhenie* (in Martov, ed., *op. cit.*, I), pp. 356–371; Berard,
The Russian Empire and Tsarism.

32 Maevskii, *Obshchaia kartina dvizheniia* (in Martov, ed., *op. cit.*, II, pt. I), p. 36.

33 Veselovskii, *Krestianskii vopros*, pp. 27–28; Tolstoi, *Prodovolstvennoe delo* (in
Veselovskii, ed., *1864–1914. Iubileinyi zemskii sbornik*), p. 304.

34 Maevskii, *op. cit.* (in Martov, ed., *op. cit.*, II, pt. I), pp. 38–39; Veselovskii,
Dvizhenie zemlevladeltsev (in Martov, ed., *op. cit.*, I), p. 310; Cherevanin, *Dvizhenie
intelligentsii* (in Martov, ed., *op. cit.*, I), p. 286; Chernyshev, *op. cit.*, p. 268.

35 Pavlovich, *Vneshniaia politika i Russko-iaponskaia voina* (in Martov, ed., *op.
cit.*, II, pt. I), p. 27.

36 Vanag, *9-e ianvaria* (in Pokrovskii, ed., *1905. Istoriia revoliutsionnogo dvizheniia*, II), pp. 22–78; Pokrovskii, *Russkaia istoriia v samom szhatom ocherke*, III,
issue 1, pp. 118–135.

37 Varzar, *op. cit.*, pp. 3–8; Piontkovskii, *op. cit.*, p. 115.

[38] Rozhkov, *op. cit.*, XII, pp. 38–41, 105; Piontkovskii, *op. cit.*, pp. 170–171.

[39] The investigation was conducted by the Imperial Free Economic Society. About 20,000 *questionnaire*-blanks were sent out to some 10,000 addresses in forty-seven *guberniias* (European Russia exclusive of the following regions: Finland, the Baltic *guberniias*, Poland, and the region of the Caucasus). For various reasons — no doubt in part because of the fear that a reply describing the peasant movement in a particular locality might possibly bring on an investigation by the police — only 1,400 correspondents sent in replies. Almost exactly half of these stated that there had been no manifestation of the agrarian movement in their respective localities, while the other half described what happened in some seven hundred different places, scattered over forty-six *guberniias*. It is of course entirely out of the question to accept the proportion between the number of positive and negative answers received, as representing the proportion between districts where the movement did and did not manifest itself. Again, the affirmative answers are so lacking in uniformity that they do not permit of a genuinely statistical treatment; yet the digests of these answers, by *guberniia* and by region, still constitute perhaps the most valuable material that has been published on the subject with which they deal, although these digests must of course be used in connection with the official documents published since the Revolution of 1917. The digests were published in: Imperatorskoe Volnoe Ekonomicheskoe obshchestvo, *Agrarnoe dvizhenie 1905–1906 g.g.*, (2 vols.) (in the *Trudy* of the Society, 1908, Nos. 3–5). The citations of this work below usually refer to the regional digests of the answers to the *questionnaire*.

[40] *Ibid.*, I, pp. 50, 96, 177, 362; II, pp. 35, 291, 424.

[41] *Ibid.*, I, pp. 51, 95, 362; II, p. 21.

[42] *Ibid.*, I, pp. 50, 96, 177; II, p. 291.

[43] Prokopovich, *Agrarnyi krizis*, p. 133.

[44] Imperatorskoe Volnoe Ekonomicheskoe obshchestvo, *op. cit.*, I, p. 177; II, pp. 34, 291.

[45] *Ibid.*, I, pp. 177, 362; II, p. 34.

[46] Vorobev, *Zemelnyi vopros v zaiavleniiakh krestian* (in Dolgorukov, ed., *Agrarnyi vopros*, II), pp. 367, 373–375, 397, 413–414; Kornilov, *Fakticheskie dannye o nastroenii krestian* (in *Pravo*, 21 Aug. 1905, No. 33), p. 2690; Veselovskii, *Krestianskii vopros*, p. 146; Maslov, *op. cit.*, II, pp. 175, 181–183, 194, 279–289; Sivkov, *Krestianskie prigovory 1905 goda* (in *Russkaia mysl*, 1907, No. 4, supplement), p. 38.

[47] Prokopovich, *op. cit.*, p. 61; Tsentralnyi Statisticheskii Komitet, *Statistika zemlevladeniia 1905 g. Svod*, pp. xxxii–xxxiii.

[48] Imperatorskoe Volnoe Ekonomicheskoe obshchestvo, *op. cit.*, I, pp. 49, 174, 363, 364; II, pp. 26, 290, 416, 417, 450, 480, 509.

[49] *Ibid.*, I, pp. 49, 93, 174, 364; II, pp. 25, 290.

[50] *Ibid.*, I, pp. 49, 93, 174, 364; II, pp. 25, 290.

[51] *Ibid.*, II, pp. 34–35.

[52] Departament Politsii, *Dokladnaia zapiska* (in *Krasnyi arkhiv*, 1925, No. 9), pp. 68–69.

[53] Karpov, *Krestianskoe dvizhenie v revoliutsii 1905 goda*, pp. 94–97. See also Dubrovskii, ed., *Agrarnoe dvizhenie 1905–1907 g.g.*, I; citations in his index under heading *rukovoditeli* (leaders).

[54] Vysochaishe Uchrezhd. Kommissiia, *Materialy*, summary and general conclusions in Vol. III, pp. 265–280; Dubrovskii, *Krestianstvo v 1917 g.*, p. 51.

[55] Departament Politsii, *op. cit.*, p. 70; Prokopovich, *op. cit.*, p. 29.

[56] Prokopovich, *op. cit.*, p. 64. Prokopovich's tabulations for 1906 and 1907 cover 47 *guberniias* (including 478 *uezds*); his table for 1905 includes in addition the three Baltic *guberniias*, but in order that the totals for the three years, 1905, 1906, and 1907, may be comparable, the present writer has eliminated from the totals for 1905 the figures for the Baltic provinces. Prokopovich depends upon various sources of information, including the answers to the *questionnaire* of the Imperial Free Economic Society, referred to above, and apparently also the reports printed in various newspapers. In the absence of any statement from Prokopovich as to the verification of the reports of disorders, it certainly can not be supposed that he is always accurate in recording this or that manifestation of the agrarian movement in this or that *uezd*.

Another point to be noted is that Prokopovich's tables show simply the total number of *uezds* or counties in which one or more manifestations of a given type were recorded during a given period; the tables thus show the *extensive*, rather than the *intensive* development of the peasant movement, and the attempt which Prokopovich makes elsewhere in this volume to deal with the question of intensiveness does not appear to the present writer to be successful. See also Dubrovskii, *Krestianstvo v 1917 g.*, table on p. 45.

⁵⁷ Prokopovich, *op. cit.*, pp. 37–38, 43, 51, 64. Cf. Savarenskii, *Ekonomicheskoe dvizhenie krestianstva* (in Gorn, ed., *Borba obshchestvennykh sil v russkoi revoliutsii*, III), pp. 12–16, 57; Maslov, *op. cit.*, II, pp. 145–167.

⁵⁸ Prokopovich, *op. cit.*, pp. 41–43; Lander, *Krestianskoe dvizhenie v Pribaltiiskom krae* (in Maslov, *Agrarnyi vopros*, II, appendix), pp. 57–60.

⁵⁹ Zalevskii, *Agrarnye otnosheniia i krestianskoe dvizhenie v Tsarstve Polskom* (in Maslov, *Agrarnyi vopros*, II, appendix), pp. 110–119.

⁶⁰ Maslov, *op. cit.*, II, pp. 433–439.

⁶¹ Spiridovich, *Revoliutsionnoe dvizhenie v Rossii*, I, pp. 89–93; Martov, *Istoriia russkoi sotsial-demokratii*, pp. 121, 161.

⁶² Ross. Kom. partiia (bolshevikov), *op. cit.*, pp. 34–37.

⁶³ Morokhovets, *Krestianskoe dvizhenie 1905–1907 g.g.* (in *Proletarskaia revoliutsiia*, 1925, No. 7 [42]), pp. 34–35; Lander, *op. cit.*, II, appendix, p. 60.

⁶⁴ Maslov, *op. cit.*, II, pp. 205, 431; Morokhovets, *op. cit.*, 1925, No. 7 [42], pp. 33–34.

⁶⁵ Spiridovich, *op. cit.*, II, pp. 179–182; Maslov, *op. cit.*, II, pp. 214–215; Karpov, *op. cit.*, pp. 45–47 (protocol of conference), pp. 30–34 (text of proclamations).

⁶⁶ Spiridovich, *op. cit.*, II, p. 179.

⁶⁷ Departament Politsii, *Dokladnaia zapiska* (in *Krasnyi arkhiv*, 1925, No. 9), p. 68; Karpov, *op. cit.*, pp. 10–11, 29, 54–55; Mazurenko, ed., *Vserossiiskii Krestianskii soiuz*, p. 15.

⁶⁸ Maslov, *op. cit.*, II, p. 219; Mazurenko, *Krestiane v 1905 godu*, pp. 41–42.

⁶⁹ Vserossiiskii Krestianskii soiuz, *Protokol uchreditelnogo sezda* (in *Osvobozhdenie*, 1905, No. 77), pp. 470–472.

⁷⁰ Shestakov, *Krestianskaia revoliutsiia 1905–1907 g.g.*, p. 65; Mazurenko, *op. cit.*, pp. 50–51; Mazurenko, ed., *Vseros. Krest. soiuz*, p. 5.

⁷¹ Vseros. Krest. soiuz, *Protokol*, pp. 470–472; Mazurenko, *Krestiane*, pp. 50–52; Shestakov, *op. cit.*, pp. 64–67; Mazurenko, ed., *Vseros. Krest. soiuz*, pp. 4, 17, 21.

⁷² Mazurenko, *op. cit.*, p. 15; Karpov, *op. cit.*, pp. 63–64, 67.

⁷³ Vseros. Krest. soiuz, *Protokol;* Karpov, *op. cit.*, p. 62; Groman, *Vseros. Krest. soiuz* (in *Materialy k krestianskomu voprosu*), pp. 16, 19.

⁷⁴ Vseros. Krest. soiuz, *Postanovleniia sezdov*, pp. 1–5.

⁷⁵ Maevskii, *op. cit.*, pp. 57–60, 72; Veselovskii, *Dvizhenie zemlevladeltsev* (in Martov, ed., *Obshchestvenooe dvizhenie*, II, pt. 2), pp. 14–16.

⁷⁶ Mavor, *Economic history of Russia*, II, pp. 476, 601. The official tables are reproduced in Mavor.

⁷⁷ Khrustalev-Nosar, *Istoriia Soveta Rabochikh deputatov*, pp. 55–78.

⁷⁸ Nevskii, *Sovety v 1905 godu* (in Pokrovskii, ed., *1905. Istoriia revoliutsionnogo dvizheniia*, III, pt. 1), pp. 4–72.

⁷⁹ Mavor, *op. cit.*, II, pp. 476, 601.

⁸⁰ Sovet Rabochikh deputatov goroda S.-Peterburga, *Izvestiia S. R. D.*, No. 1, 17 Oct. 1905, p. 1; No. 2, 18 Oct. p. 1. The early numbers of *Izvestiia* are reprinted in full in Nevskii, ed., *1905. Sovetskaia pechat i literatura o sovetakh.*

⁸¹ Maevski, *op. cit.*, pp. 84–85; Khrustalev-Nosar, *op. cit.*, p. 58; Rozhkov, *op. cit.*, XII, p. 72; Shestakov, *Vseobshchaia oktiabrskaia stachka 1905 goda* (in Pokrovskii, ed., *1905. Istoriia*, II), *Pravo*, 31 Oct. 1905, No. 42, pp. 3477–3478.

⁸² P. S. Z., 3d col., No. 26053; Tolstoi, *Prodovolstvennoe delo* (in Veselovskii, ed., *1864–1914. Iubileinyi zemskii sbornik*), p. 304.

⁸³ Pokrovskii, *Mir i reaktsiia* (in Pokrovskii, ed., *1905. Istoriia*, II), pp. 244–249; Rozhkov, *op. cit.*, XII, pp. 59–63; P. S. Z., 3d col., Nos. 26656, 26661, 26662.

⁸⁴ So Witte says in his memoirs; quoted in Veselovskii, ed., *Agrarnyi vopros*, p. 8.

⁸⁵ P. S. Z., 3d col., No. 26803.

⁸⁶ *Ibid.*, Nos. 26871, 26872, 26873; Departament Okladnykh Sborov, *Departament Okladnykh Sborov, 1863–1913*, pp. 166–167.

1 Sovet Rabochikh deputatov, *Izvestiia*, No. 3, 20 Oct. (in Nevskii, ed., *1905. Sovetskaia pechat*).
2 Khrustalev-Nosar, *Istoriia Soveta Rabochikh deputatov*, p. 84.
3 *Ibid.*, pp. 112, 124–125.
4 Mavor, *Economic history of Russia*, II, pp. 476, 601; Varzar, *Statistika stachek rabochikh*, p. 3.
5 Khrustalev-Nosar, *op. cit.*, pp. 170, 197–199.
6 Iaroslavskii, *Dekabrskoe vosstanie* (in Pokrovskii, ed., *1905. Istoriia*, III, pt. II); Maevskii, *Obshchaia kartina dvizheniia* (in Martov, ed., *Obshchestvennoe dvizhenie v Rossii*, II, pt. I), pp. 117–118. An interesting account of the Moscow rising by a foreign eye-witness will be found in Baring, *A year in Russia*, pp. 43–62.
7 Varzar, *op. cit.*, pp. 3, 6–7.
8 Vserossiiskii Krestianskii soiuz, *Otchety sezda* (in *Materialy k krestianskomu voprosu*), p. 33; Groman, *op. cit.*, pp. 4–6; Maslov, *op. cit.*, II, pp. 223–224; Mazurenko, ed., *Vseros. Krest. soiuz*, p. 13; also his *Krestiane v 1905 godu*, pp. 55–56; Shestakov, *op. cit.*, pp. 70–71.
9 Vseros. Krest. soiuz, *Otchety sezda* (in *Materialy k krestianskomu voprosu*), pp. 45, 58, 62; Groman, *op. cit.*, p. 14.
10 Vseros. Krest. soiuz, *Postanovleniia sezdov*, pp. 6–16.
11 Mazurenko, *Krestiane*, p. 60, and his *Vseros. Krest. soiuz*, p. 16.
12 Khrustalev-Nosar, *op. cit.*, pp. 188–190.
13 Karpov, *op. cit.*, p. 95.
14 Gosudarstvennaia Duma, *Stenograficheskie otchety 1906 g.*, *sessiia pervaia*, II, pp. 1347, 1353–1354, 1358, 1361, 1366–1367.
15 Dubrovskii, *Krestianstvo v 1917 g.*, p. 45; Imperatorskoe Volnoe Ekonomicheskoe obshchestvo, *Agrarnoe dvizhenie*, I, pp. 171, 362; II, pp. 289, 400, 525.
16 Prokopovich, *Agrarnyi krizis*, pp. 46–49, 64, 66. Cf. Savarenskii, *Ekonomicheskoe dvizhenie krestian* (in Gorn, ed., *Borba obshchestvennykh sil*, III), pp. 16–20, 57.
17 Vseros. Krest. soiuz, *Otchety sezda* (in *Materialy k krestianskomu voprosu*), pp. 41, 44.
18 Karpov, *op. cit.*, p. 260.
19 Prokopovich, *op. cit.*, p. 61. For a discussion of losses by arson and by other fires in the *guberniias* of Podolsk, Volyn, and Kiev, see Imperatorskoe Ekonomicheskoe obshchestvo, *op. cit.*, II, pp. 271–279; however, the figures there given for the increase in insurance-losses can hardly be very significant in the absence of any data as to the amount of insurance in force.
20 Prokopovich, *op. cit.*, p. 69.
21 *Ibid.*, pp. 71–95; Savarenskii, *op. cit.*, pp. 21, 58.
22 Maslov, *op. cit.*, II, pp. 439–442.
23 Lander, *Krestianskoe dvizhenie v Pribaltiiskom krae* (in Maslov, *Agrarnyi vopros*, III, appendix), pp. 60–89.
24 Pestkovskii and Krasnyi, *Ocherk revoliutsionnogo dvizheniia v Polshe v 1905 g.* (in Pokrovskii, ed., *1905. Istoriia*, III, pt. 1), pp. 260–264.
25 Partiia Sotsialistov-revoliutsionerov, *Protokoly pervogo sezda*, pp. 312–313, 326, 331–333, 338; Veselovskii, *Krestianskii vopros*, p. 133; Prokopovich, *op. cit.*, p. 49.
26 Rossiiskaia Kommunisticheskaia partiia (bolshevikov), *op. cit.*, p. 50; Shestakov, *Krestianskaia revoliutsiia 1905–1907 g.g.*, pp. 73–78, 101–102; Martov, *Istoriia russkoi sotsial-demokratii*, pp. 160–161, 175–177; Morokhovets, *Krestianskoe dvizhenie* (in *Proletarskaia revoliutsiia*, 1925, Nos. 2–8 [37–43]); Dubrovskii, ed., *Agrarnoe dvizhenie*, I, references in index under heading *rukovoditeli* (leaders).
27 Ross. Kom. partiia (bolshevikov), *op. cit.*, pp. 57, 61–63; Lenin, *Agrarnaia programma sotsial-demokratii*, pp. 50–68, 172–177; Kaufman, *Agrarnyi vopros*, pp. 193–202; Mesiatsev, *Zemelnaia i selsko-khoziaistvennaia politika*, pp. 32–37; Rossiiskaia Sotsial-demokrat. rabochaia partiia, *Protokoly obedinitelnogo sezda*, pp. 334–336, 340–341.
28 Maslov, *op. cit.*, II, p. 269; Koltsov, *Rabochie v 1905–1907 g.g.* (in Martov, ed., *op. cit.*, II, pt. I), p. 265; Marev, *Politicheskaia borba* (in Gorn, ed., *Borba*, III), p. 100; Veselovskii, *Agrarnyi vopros*, p. 81.

29 Maslov, *op. cit.*, II, pp. 270–275; Marev, *op. cit.*, III, pp. 101–103.

30 *Pravo*, 25 Oct. 1905, No. 41, pp. 3424–3432; text of the program worked out at the party congress of 12–18 October 1905.

31 *Ibid.*, p. 3405.

32 *Ibid.*, 15 Jan. 1906, No. 2, pp. 154–158; text of resolutions of January congress of party.

33 Marev, *op. cit.*, III, p. 97; *Polnyi sbornik platform vsekh russkikh politicheskikh partii*, pp. 93–103; Ermanskii, *Krupnaia burzhuaziia* (in Martov, ed., *op. cit.*, II, pt. II), p. 127.

34 *Pravo*, 13 Nov. 1905, No. 44, pp. 3602–3603; 20 Nov. 1905, No. 45–46, pp. 3703–3705.

35 Veselovskii, *Dvizhenie zemlevladeltsev* (in Martov, ed., *op. cit.*, II, pt. II), p. 24.

36 *Pravo*, 29 Jan. 1906, No. 4, pp. 330–333.

37 *Ibid.*, 11 June 1906, No. 23, pp. 2061–2063; Chernyshev, *Agrarno-krestianskaia politika*, pp. 310–314.

38 Veselovskii, *Krestianskii vopros*, pp. 102–105; Soiuz Russkogo naroda, *Zagovor protiv Rossii*, pp. 15–16.

39 Mech, *Sily reaktsii* (in Gorn, ed., *Borba obshchestvennykh sil*, I), pp. 65–69, 83–90; Chernovskii, ed., *Soiuz Russkogo naroda*, pp. 3–18, 411–424.

40 Maevskii, *Obshchaia kartina dvizheniia* (in Martov, ed., *op. cit.*, II, pt. 1), pp. 96–104. Maevskii quotes the estimate given by Obninskii in his *Polgoda russkoi revoliutsii*.

41 Semennikov, ed., *Revoliutsiia 1905 goda i samoderzhavie*, pp. 14–16; *Armiia v pervoi revoliutsii*, pp. xi, 374–379.

42 An account of the reception of the deputies will be found in *Pravo*, 4 Dec. 1905, No. 48–49, pp. 3913–3916. For a brief description of the palaces, with illustrations, see Iakovlev, *Kratkii ukazatel po Ekaterininskomu dvortsu-muzeiu*, and his *Okhrana tsarskoi rezidentsii*.

43 Veselovskii, ed., *Agrarnyi vopros*, p. 75; Karpov, ed., *Krestianskoe dvizhenie*, pp. 95, 162.

44 Veselovskii, *op. cit.*, pp. 3–4, 30–48, 76–79. The officer of the government who was later called the Minister of Agriculture was known at this time as the Chief Administrator of Land-Organization and of Agriculture.

45 *Ibid.*, pp. 70–71.

46 *Ibid.*, pp. 72–80.

47 Dubrovskii, ed., *Agrarnoe dvizhenie v 1905–1907 g.g.*, I, pp. 48, 141, 247–248, 310–311, 355, 357, 359, 361; Imperatorskoe Volnoe Ekonomicheskoe obshchestvo, *Agrarnoe dvizhenie v Rossii v 1905–1906 g.g.*, I, pp. 52, 97, 178; II, pp. 36–37, 293, 419–420; Gosudarstvennaia Duma, *Stenograficheskie otchety 1906 g. sessiia pervaia*, II, pp. 1210–1215, 1347–1367; *Pravo*, 12 March 1906, No. 10, pp. 910–915; Maevskii, *Obshchaia kartina* (in Martov, ed., *op. cit.*, II, pt. I), pp. 174–177; Semennikov, ed., *Revoliutsiia 1905 goda*, pp. 16–18, 165–223; *Iskry*, illustrated journal, 1906.

48 Witte, *Vospominaniia*, II, pp. 131–132, 135, 216–218.

49 *Pravo*, 26 Feb. 1906, No. 8, pp. 649–651; *P. S. Z.*, 3d col., Nos. 27423, 27424, 27425.

50 *P. S. Z.*, 3d col., No. 27805, esp. the following sections: 4, 12–14, 17, 44, 72–73.

51 Boiovich, *Chleny Gosudarstvennoi Dumy*; Rozhkov, *op. cit.*, XII, p. 119; Miakotin (in *Entsiklop. slovar*, Granat, XVI), p. 194; Maslov, *op. cit.*, II, pp. 276–278; Obninskii, *Novyi stroi*, I, p. 163; Miliukov, *Vtoraia Duma*, p. 15.

52 Gosudarstvennaia Duma, *Stenograficheskie otchety 1906 g., sessiia pervaia*, I, pp. 239–243.

53 *Ibid.*, I, pp. 321–324.

54 *Ibid.*, I, pp. 248–250, 560–562; II, pp. 1153–1156.

55 *Pravitelstvennyi vestnik*, 20 June 1906, No. 137, p. 1.

56 Veselovskii, ed., *Agrarnoe dvizhenie*, p. 18.

57 Gosudarstvennaia Duma, *Materialy k stenograficheskim otchetam 1906 g.*, pp. 2078–2080; Obninskii, *Novyi stroi*, I, pp. 183–187.

58 *Pravo*, 16 July 1906, No. 28, pp. 2370–2371; *P. S. Z.*, 3d col., Nos. 28102, 28103, 28105.

59 *Ibid.*

60 Rozhkov, *op. cit.*, XII, pp. 135–140; *Pravo*, 16 July 1906, No. 28, pp. 2354–2356.

61 Varzar, *op. cit.*, pp. 6–7; Mavor, *op. cit.*, II, p. 601.

62 Prokopovich, *op. cit.*, pp. 91–95.

63 Partiia Narodnoi svobody, *Vestnik*, 10 Nov. 1906, No. 36, p. 1913; Rozhkov, *op. cit.*, XII, pp. 141, 143; Ross. Kom. partiia (bolshevikov), *op. cit.*, pp. 67, 81; Miliukov, *Vtoraia Duma*, p. 135.

64 Chernyshev, *op. cit.*, pp. 315–318.

65 *Moskovskie vedomosti*, 2 March, 24 March, 3 May, 1907; Mech, *op. cit.*, p. 84 ff.

66 *Pravo*, 13 Aug. 1906, No. 32, p. 2595.

67 *Ibid.*, 27 Aug. 1906, No. 34, pp. 2704–2707.

68 All these figures on executions are taken from *The Terror in Russia*, a book written by Prince P. A. Kropotkin, the celebrated exponent of anarchist theory. The official figures are quoted by him. As to the degree of accuracy of his unofficial tabulations, nothing can be said except that they are based upon reports in newspapers and periodicals. Cf. Pokrovskii, *Russkaia istoriia v samom szhatom ocherke*, III, issue 1, p. 331.

69 *Pravo*, 19 Nov. 1906, No. 46, p. 3612.

70 Baturinskii, *Agrarnaia politika*, pp. 74–76, 98, 109–111.

71 *Ibid.*, p. 99.

72 *Ibid.*, pp. 96–97; Meiendorf, *Krestianskii dvor*, pp. 110–113; *P. S. Z.*, 3d col., Nos. 28315, 28416, 28546.

73 Gosudarstvennaia Duma vtorogo sozyva, *Doklady*, No. 89. This report was brought in on 13 April.

74 Rozhkov, *op. cit.*, XII, pp. 143–145; Miliukov, *op. cit.*, pp. 135–141, 269–270.

75 Ross. Kom. partiia (bolshevikov), *op. cit.*, pp. 80–81.

76 Rozhkov, *op. cit.*, XII, pp. 146–148.

77 *P. S. Z.*, 3d col., No. 29240.

78 *Ibid.*, No. 29242, and tables in appendix; *Pravo*, 17 June, No. 24, pp. 1731–1737; Rozhkov, *op. cit.*, XII, p. 147.

79 Varzar, *op. cit.*, pp. 3, 6–7.

80 Prokopovich, *op. cit.*, pp. 107–111.

81 Gosudarstvennaia Duma, *Prilozheniia k stenograficheskim otchetam Gos. Dumy. Tretii sozyv. Sessiia I. 1907–1908 g.g.*, I, pp. 425–435.

82 Marev, *Politicheskaia borba* (in Gorn, ed., *Borba obshchestvennykh sil*, III), pp. 130–133.

83 Prokopovich, *Agrarnyi krizis*, p. 66; Dubrovskii, ed., *Agrarnoe dvizhenie v 1905–1907 g.g.*, I, pp. 67–68, 87, 120, 302. In the *questionnaire* previously referred to, on the agrarian movement of 1905–07, the correspondents were specifically requested to report whether the agrarian movement was accompanied by the replacement by the peasants of their own officials, but in the replies, such instances are hardly so much as mentioned: Imperatorskoe Volnoe Ekonomicheskoe obshchestvo, *op. cit.*, I, p. xiv.

84 Imperatorskoe Volnoe Ekonomicheskoe obshchestvo, *op. cit.*, I, pp. 8, 92, 163, 173; Drozdov, *Nashe okladnoe oblozhenie* (in *Sovremennyi mir*, 1914, No. 9).

85 Gosudarstvennaia Duma, *Stenograficheskie otchety 1906 g., sessiia pervaia*, I, pp. 560–562.

86 Attempts at such an analysis will be found in Vorobev, *Zemelnyi vopros v zaiavleniiakh krestian* (in Dolgorukov, ed., *Agrarnyi vopros*, II); Kornilov, *Fakticheskie dannye o nastroenii krestian* (in *Pravo*, 21 Aug. 1905, No. 33); Veselovskii, *Krestianskii vopros*, pp. 146–152; Maslov, *op. cit.*, II, pp. 176–181, 279–289, 366–376; Sivkov, *Krestianskie prigovory 1905 goda* (in *Russkaia mysl*, 1907, No. 4, supplement), p. 38.

87 Imperatorskoe Volnoe Ekonomicheskoe obshchestvo, *op. cit.*, II, pp. 13–15: for further testimony of the correspondents as to the objectives of the peasant movement, see I, pp. 92, 96, 97, 170, 363; II, pp. 17, 292, 406, 440.

88 *Ibid.*, I, pp. 94, 175, 364; II, pp. 24, 291.

89 *Ibid.*, I, pp. 50, 94, 175, 364; II, pp. 22–24, 30, 295, 413.

90 *Ibid.*, I, p. 359; II, pp. 11–13, 18, 26, 408–410; Prokopovich, *op. cit.*, pp. 129–134; Morokhovets, *Krestianskoe dvizhenie 1905–1907 g.g.* (in *Proletarskaia revoliutsiia*, 1925, No. 7 [42]), p. 99.

NOTES TO CHAPTER XI

[1] *Polnoe sobranie zakonov*, 3d collection, No. 26871.

[2] *Ibid.*, No. 27478.

[3] *Ibid.*, No. 28392.

[4] *Ibid.*, No. 28528.

[5] *Ibid.*, No. 33743.

[6] *Ibid.*, No. 35370.

[7] *Ibid.*, No. 28392, arts. x, xi, xii; Khauke, *Krestianskoe zemelnoe pravo*, p. 17.

[8] *P. S. Z.*, 3d col., No. 28392, arts. v, vi; Leontev, *Krestianskoe pravo*, p. 58.

[9] *P. S. Z.*, 3d col., No. 28392, art. iv; Volkov, ed., *Sbornik*, p. 340, note 2.

[10] Leontev, *op. cit.*, pp. 53–59.

[11] *P. S. Z.*, 3d col., No. 28528, div. i, arts. 1–5. These provisions were repeated in the law of 14 June 1910 with no important alterations except those mentioned in the body of the text above; *ibid.*, No. 33743, arts. 9–19. The provisions described above, in the text, as applying to the meadow lands, were really applicable to all lands which had been subject to "repartition under special rules" — that is, under rules different from those governing the repartition of the plow-lands. In the great majority of the communes, the meadows were the most important of the lands subject to such special rules.

[12] *P. S. Z.*, 3d col., No. 28528, divs. ii, iii; No. 33743, arts. 47–55; Volkov, ed., *Sbornik*, p. 389, note 11.

[13] Oganovskii, ed., *Statisticheskii spravochnik*, I, p. 26; Chernyshev, *Obshchina*, I, p. xiii. Cf. Dubrovskii, *Stolypinskaia reforma*, pp. 106, 282; Karpov, *Agrarnaia politika*, table opp. p. 202.

[14] Karpov, *op. cit.*, table opp. p. 202; these returns are for thirty-five *guberniias* only. Cf. Lositskii, *Raspadenie obshchiny* (in Imperatorskoe Volnoe Ekonomicheskoe obshchestvo, *Trudy*, 1912, Nos. 1–2), p. 29.

[15] *P. S. Z.*, 3d col., No. 33743, arts. 1–8; the law did not apply where the original allotment had been granted after 1 January 1887.

[16] Lositskii, *op. cit.*, p. 20; Chernyshev, *op. cit.*, I, p. xiv; Oganovskii, *Zemleustroistvo* (in *Novyi entsiklop. slovar*, Brockhaus, XVIII), p. 563.

[17] Oganovskii, ed., *Statisticheskii spravochnik*, I, pp. 26–27.

[18] Oganovskii, *Zemleustroistvo* (in *Novyi entsiklop. slovar*, XVIII), p. 564; Oganovskii, *Revoliutsiia naoborot*, pp. 98–99; also his *Ocherki po ekonomicheskoi geografii*, p. 119.

[19] Glavnoe Upravlenie Zemleustroistva i Zemledeliia, *Zemleustroistvo*, pp. 39–41, notes 15, 23; pp. 121–126 (Statute on land-organization, arts. 121–123); Pershin, *Zemelnoe ustroistvo*, I, p. 108; Lositskii, *op. cit.*, p. 28, footnote. Lositskii says: "By whatever means it was brought about (whether by a general consolidation, or by the extrusion of single holdings, the formation of unitary holdings (*otrubs* and *khutors*) in repartitional communes most certainly constituted separation from the commune, in the most decisive form." However, the law touching this subject is exceedingly complex and obscure; Khauke believes that it was possible, at least theoretically, to assemble the scattered strips into unitary plots without at the same time dissolving the communal title; he says that "consolidated plots not formally separated from the communal property are met with, but only very rarely." *Krestianskoe zemelnoe pravo*, pp. 179–180.

[20] Oganovskii, ed., *Statisticheskii spravochnik*, I, p. 24.

[21] In part, these estimates follow Oganovskii, *Revoliutsiia naoborot*, pp. 98–99. See also his *Ocherki po ekonomicheskoi geografii*, p. 119, and his *Zemleustroistvo* (in *Novyi entsiklop. slovar*, XVIII), pp. 563–564; also Manuilov, *Noveishee zakonodatelstvo o zemelnoi obshchine* (in *Vestnik Evropy*, 1912, No. XI), p. 24 ff.

[22] *P. S. Z.*, 3d col., No. 28528, div. ii; No. 33743, arts. 49–55.

[23] Khauke, *op. cit.*, pp. 143–149; *P. S. Z.*, No. 28528, div. i, art. 16; Volkov, *op. cit.*, pp. 381–382, notes 4–5; p. 405; Lositskii, *op. cit.*, pp. 25–27.

[24] G. U. Z. i Z., *Zemleustroistvo*, p. 50, notes 1–4; Khauke, *op. cit.*, p. 152.

[25] *P. S. Z.*, 3d col., No. 28528, div. iv.

[26] *Ibid.*, No. 33743, art. 45.

[27] G. U. Z. i Z., *Zemleustroistvo*, pp. 55–57 (Statute on land-organization, arts. 44–45).

28 To this rule there was one exception of some importance: in communes where the land had originally been granted in repartitional tenure, and had all been converted thereafter to hereditary tenure by a two-thirds' vote of the assembly, there was no provision in the laws of 1906, 1910, or 1911 for individual physical consolidations upon the demand of single holders and against the opposition of the other holders whose allotments would be displaced in the process. On the other hand, provision *was* made for such individual consolidations for single holders against the opposition of the assembly and of the other holders affected, in communes where the land had originally been granted in repartitional tenure, but had all been converted subsequently to hereditary tenure under the optional provisions of 1906 and 1910, or under the arbitrary dissolution-law of 1910. That is, in the communes where all the titles had been converted under these provisions of 1906 and 1910, any given holder might nevertheless be compelled, under the conditions described in the text, to submit to a physical readjustment of his own holding in order that a consolidated plot might be provided for some single applicant. In this respect, therefore, the holdings converted in tenure in the manner provided in the laws of 1906 and 1910 were not recognized as fully assimilated to the original type of hereditary holding, but here resembled the holdings still under repartitional tenure. In communes where a general conversion of title had been made by a two-thirds' vote, the holdings were more fully assimilated to the basic hereditary form, since, as has been said, the physical readjustments necessary for the establishment of a consolidated holding for a single applicant might be made in such communes only with the consent of every holder whose allotment would be displaced, in whole or in part, by the change. G. U. Z. i Z., *Zemleustroistvo*, pp. 50–51 (Statute on land-organization, as amended in 1912, art. 41; also notes 1–4).

29 *P. S. Z.*, 3d col., No. 28528, div. i, arts. 12–14, 16. If the householder had already secured a separate title to a number of scattered strips, the consolidated holding was to be the equivalent of these strips. If he had not previously secured such a title, the consolidated holding was to have the area of the strips which the household would normally have received in the current repartition.

30 *Ibid.*, No. 33743, arts. 33–34; G. U. Z. i Z., *Zemleustroistvo*, pp. 37–42 (Statute on land-organization, arts. 35–36); p. 187, art. 95.

31 G. U. Z. i Z., *Zemleustroistvo* (Statute on land-organization), p. 39, art. 35, note 15; p. 42, art. 36; p. 48, art. 39; p. 14, art. 8, note 13.

32 *P. S. Z.*, 3d col., No. 28528, div. iv; No. 33745, art. 46.

33 G. U. Z. i Z., *op. cit.*, p. 51, art. 42.

34 *Ibid.*, pp. 55–57, arts. 44–45.

35 *Ibid.*, p. 8, art. 7; p. 14, art. 8, note 13; p. 51, art. 42.

36 But see note 19 above.

37 G. U. Z. i Z., *op. cit.*, p. 6, art. 5; G. U. Z. i Z., *Travaux*, p. 39.

38 G. U. Z. i Z., *Zemleustroistvo*, p. 5, art. 3.

39 *P. S. Z.*, 3d col., No. 33743, art. 39.

40 Volkov, *op. cit.*, p. 381, note 1; G. U. Z. i Z., *op. cit.*, p. 301, art. 19; Khauke, *op. cit.*, pp. 241–245.

41 *P. S. Z.*, 3d col., No. 33743, art. 56. On inheritance, see Volkov, *op. cit.*, pp. 45–47, art. 13 and notes.

42 Volkov, *op. cit.*, pp. 482–493 (Instructions to the Land-Organization Commissions, 19 Sept. 1906, arts. 68–97).

43 G. U. Z. i Z., *Zemleustroistvo*, p. 78 (Statute on land-organization, art. 64 and note); in regard to the possibility of appeal from the decisions of the commissions, see *ibid.*, p. 22, art. 18, and p. 116, art. 114; as to the distribution of cost, see pp. 27–28, art. 22.

44 *P. S. Z.*, 3d col., No. 27478; No. 35370.

45 Volkov, *op. cit.*, p. 378 (Provisional rules on the consolidation and separation of allotment-land, 15 October 1908, arts. 28–29); p. 529 (Technical instructions to land-organization officials, appended to the provisional rules of 19 March 1909); G. U. Z. i Z., *Zemleustroistvo*, pp. 154–156 (Instructions to the Land-Organization Commissions, 19 June 1911, arts. 7–12).

46 G. U. Z. i Z., *op. cit.*, pp. 154–156, arts. 7–12. Important provisions as to roads, water-supply, etc., are to be found on pp. 226–234 (Provisional rules for land-organization technique, arts. 7, 13, 15, 21, 34–36).

306 NOTES TO CHAPTER XI

47 G. U. Z. i Z., *op. cit.*, pp. 3–4 (Statute on land-settlement, art. 2 and notes).
48 *Ibid.*, p. 12, art. 8; p. 6, art. 6.
49 G. U. Z. i Z., *op. cit.*, p. 230 (art. 21 of provisional rules for land-organization technique accompanying the instructions to the Land-Organization Commissions dated 19 June 1911).
50 G. U. Z. i Z., *Otchetnye svedeniia o deiatelnosti zemleustroitelnykh komissii na I ianvaria 1915 goda*, pp. 23–25; G. U. Z. i Z., *Obzor deiatelnosti za 1914 god*, pp. 84–88; G. U. Z. i Z., *1915. Ezhegodnik Departamenta Zemledeliia*, pp. xl–xliii.
51 G. U. Z. i Z., *Zemleustroistvo*, pp. 30–37 (Statute on land-settlement, arts. 23–34).
52 *Ibid.*, p. 33, art. 28; p. 69, art. 54 and notes.
53 *Ibid.*, p. 60, art. 49.
54 Pershin, *Ocherki zemelnoi politiki*, p. 26, footnote. This writer gives the official total as 6,408,707, and says that for the reasons given in the text above, it should be reduced to 4,448,005; his eliminations were made upon the basis of unpublished materials collected by the Ministry of Agriculture in 1917.
55 G. U. Z. i Z., *Otchetnye svedeniia*, p. 4.
56 *Ibid.*, p. 7.
57 *Ibid.*, appendix, p. 3, for official tables carrying the record to the end of 1914. Oganovskii, ed., *Statisticheskii spravochnik*, I, pp. 24–25, continues the record to the end of 1915.
58 Pershin, *Uchastkovoe zemlepolzovanie*, p. 7.
59 P. S. Z., 3d col., No. 28528, art. 11; No. 33743, art. 60; G. U. Z. i Z., *Zemleustroistvo*, p. 299, art. 17³³. The peasants might bring about consolidations in advance of the establishment of the Land-Organization Commission in a given district, and even after the establishment of the local commission they were still free, down to 1911, to act without its aid if they chose. Most Russian writers seem to assume that the reports of the commissions cover every case of consolidation effected on allotment-land during the period. Where the commissions were involved, the complicated labor of surveying was carried out largely at the expense of the State.
60 G. U. Z. i Z., *Otchetnye svedeniia*, p. 20, gives 6.6 per cent, down to the end of 1914; see also pp. 16–17. Pershin, *op. cit.*, p. 16, gives 6.7 per cent, to the end of 1916. See also Khauke, *op. cit.*, pp. 181–182.
61 Pershin, *op. cit.*, p. 16.
62 *Ibid.*, pp. 49, 51, last column of table; see also the table on p. 14. The data on this subject are scattered and incomplete.
63 P. S. Z., 3d col., No. 28528, div. i, art. 2; div. iii; No. 33743, arts. 4, 47; G. U. Z. i Z., *Zemleustroistvo*, pp. 121–126 (Statute on land-organization, arts. 121–123); also p. 41, note 23; Khauke, *op. cit.*, pp. 213–214.
64 P. S. Z., 3d col., No. 28528, div. iii; No. 33743, art. 47; Khauke, *op. cit.*, pp. 208–210, 217–219.
65 See the laws mentioned in the two preceding notes; also Khauke, *op. cit.*, pp. 215–216.
66 Khauke, *op. cit.*, pp. 228–231; P. S. Z., 3d col., No. 28392, div. viii.
67 Leontev, *Krestianskoe pravo*, pp. 351–352.
68 *Ibid.*, p. 59.
69 P. S. Z., 3d col., No. 28392, div. v; Volkov, *op. cit.*, pp. 842–843; Leontev, *op. cit.*, p. 54.
70 P. S. Z., 3d col., No. 28392, div. iv.
71 Baturinskii, *Agrarnaia politika*, p. 97; Bilimovich, *The land settlement* (in Antsiferov, *Russian agriculture during the War*), pp. 319–320.
72 Baturinskii, *op. cit.*, pp. 113–114, 118–120; Ministerstvo Zemledeliia, *Sbornik statistiko-ekonomicheskikh svedenii*, 9th year, p. 601.
73 Between 1897 and 1914 the rural population of the fifty *guberniias* increased from 82,000,000 to 112,000,000; *Rossiia*, p. 76; Ministerstvo Zemledeliia, *op. cit.*, 10th year, p. 5.
74 Ministerstvo Zemledeliia, *op. cit.*, 9th year, pp. 596–598; Oganovskii, ed., *Statisticheskii spravochnik*, I, p. 20.
75 Ministerstvo Zemledeliia, *op. cit.*, 9th year, pp. 602–609; Oganovskii, *op. cit.*, I, pp. 28–29; Baturinskii, *op. cit.*, p. 132.
76 P. S. Z., 3d col., No. 28528, div. i, art. 6; No. 33743, art. 22.
77 Karpov, *op. cit.*, table opp. p. 202. Cf. Dubrovskii, *Stolypinskaia reforma*,

table on pp. 282–283; Chernyshev, *Obshchina*, I, pp. 164–165; II, pp. 136–137.
    78 *P. S. Z.*, 3d col., No. 33743, art. 4.
    79 Oganovskii, *op. cit.*, pp. 26–27.
    80 G. U. Z. i Z., *Otchetnye svedeniia*, pp. 11, 19; Pershin, *Uchastkovoe zemlepolzovanie*, p. 51.
    81 Dubrovskii, *op. cit.*, pp. 264–272; Karpov, *op. cit.*, pp. 95–106; Pershin, *op. cit.*, pp. 12–13.
    82 The results of the inquiry are published in Chernyshev, *Obshchina posle 9 noiabria 1906 g.* (*po ankete Volnogo Ekonomicheskogo obshchestva*), 2 vols. More than two-thirds of the answers were from peasants, while priests and schoolteachers supplied about half of the remainder. The manner in which the original inquiry-sheets were distributed is described in Lositskii, *Raspadenie obshchiny* (in Imperatorskoe Volnoe Ekonomicheskoe obshchestvo, *Trudy*, 1912, Nos. 1–2).
    83 Chernyshev, *op. cit.*, II, p. 127.
    84 Oganovskii, *Zemleustroistvo* (in *Novyi entsiklop. slovar*, XVIII), pp. 557–558, and table opp. p. 559; Dubrovskii, *op. cit.*, p. 107; Tiumenev, *Ot revoliutsii do revoliutsii*, p. 14.
    85 Oganovskii, *op. cit.*, p. 558; Lositskii, *op. cit.*
    86 This evidence is found in the answers to the *questionnaire* referred to above; Chernyshev, *op. cit.*, I, pp. 155, 157; II, pp. 125, 128.
    87 Dubrovskii, *op. cit.*, p. 230; Kosinskii, *Osnovnye tendentsii*, II, p. 235.
    88 Dubrovskii, *op. cit.*, p. 234; Oganovskii, ed., *Statisticheskii spravochnik*, I, pp. 16–17; Kosinskii, *op. cit.*, II, p. 236. For the years 1908–1910, see Departament Okladnykh Sborob, *Materialy*, XXIV, pp. xix, 89, and XXV, p. 77.
    89 Oganovskii, *Zemleustroistvo* (in *Novyi entsiklop. slovar*, XVIII), table II A, following p. 560. Cf. Chernyshev, *Obshchina*, I, pp. 158–159; II, pp. 131–132; also Dubrovskii, *op. cit.*, p. 237.
    90 Kosinskii, *op. cit.*, II, pp. 235–238; Oganovskii, *op. cit.*, p. 563; also his *Individualizatsiia zemlevladeniia*, pp. 37–39; Mozzhukhin, *Agrarnyi vopros*, p. 36; Dubrovskii, *op. cit.*, pp. 229–243; Tiumenev, *op. cit.*, pp. 35–39.
    91 Oganovskii, *Statisticheskii spravochnik*, I, p. 21; Baturinskii, *op. cit.*, pp. 113, 120.
    92 Kosinskii, *op. cit.*, II, pp. 212–213; Oganovskii, *op. cit.*, I, p. 21.
    93 The figures are for 47 *guberniias*. Departament Okladnykh Sborov, *op. cit.*, XXIV, pp. 26–29; XXV, pp. 26–29; Tsentralnyi Statisticheskii Komitet, *Zemlevladeniia 1905 g. Svod dannykh*, p. 130; appendix, p. xxix.
    94 Departament Okladnykh Sborov, *op. cit.*, XXIV, pp. 12–13; XXV, pp. 12–13.
    95 Dubrovskii, *op. cit.*, table on p. 145; Baturinskii, *op. cit.*, pp. 97, 116–117; Pershin, *Uchastkovoe zemlepolzovanie*, p. 8.
    96 Pershin, *Zemelnoe ustroistvo*, I, pp. 102–104, 109, 137–139, 256, 266, 270–271, 367, 371, 384–390; and his *Uchastkovoe zemlepolzovanie*, pp. 19–22; Dubrovskii, *Stolypinskaia reforma*, pp. 131–132, 151–152, 173, 178, 186.
    97 Most of the data (including those in the table) which served as the basis for this discussion of the hiring of labor and the renting-out of land by the peasants, were drawn from Svavitskie, *Zemskie podvornye perepisi 1880–1913*, pp. 186–260. The following were also consulted: Kritsman, ed., *Materialy po istorii agrarnoi revoliutsii v Rossii*, I, and Glavnyi Zemelnyi Komitet, *Trudy komissii po podgotovke zemelnoi reformy*, III.

NOTES TO CHAPTER XII

    1 Weinstein, *Oblozhenie i platezhi krestianstva*, pp. 38–43; Kaufman, *Agrarnyi vopros*, pp. 77–85; Dubrovskii, *op. cit.*, pp. 190–191; Oganovskii, *Individualizatsiia zemlevladeniia*, pp. 48–50. The last-named writer believes that there was some slight tendency toward a decrease in the rented area after 1900. Rents for 1915 and 1916 are given in Ministerstvo Zemledeliia, *Stoimost proizvodstva glavneishikh khlebov v 1916 godu*, pp. i–iv.
    2 On the subject of assistance by the *zemstvos* to the farmers, see Veselovskii, *Istoriia zemstv*, II, pp. 130–230; Polner, *Russian local government during the War and the Union of Zemstvos*, p. 43 ff. For similar activities of the Ministry of Agriculture, see G. U. Z. i Z., *Obzor deiatelnosti za 1914 god*, p. 38 ff.

The apportionment of peasant acreage among the various crops was undoubtedly somewhat changed between 1913 and 1916 by war-conditions — for example by the withdrawal of labor for military service and by the alteration in the character of the grain-market. Also the number of farm-implements and machines in the hands of the peasants certainly could not have been the same in 1917 as it was in 1913, inasmuch as importation had almost stopped, domestic production had declined very heavily, and many implements had of course been worn out or broken, while on the other hand a certain number had been carried off by the peasants from the landlords' estates during the early stages of the Revolution of 1917 and before the census of that year was completed. Nevertheless the data for 1916 and 1917 may properly be accepted as indicating in a broad and general way the backwardness of peasant agriculture.

See Ministerstvo Zemledeliia, *Instruktsiia . . . perepisi . . . 1917 goda*, p. 20; Tsentralnoe Statisticheskoe Upravlenie, *Pogubernskie itogi Vserossiiskoi selsko-khoziaistvennoi i pozemelnoi perepisi 1917 goda*, pp. 56–63; Ministerstvo Zemledeliia, *Sbornik statistiko-ekonomicheskikh svedenii, 1915* (10th year), p. 83; Glavnoe Upravlenie Zemleustroistva i Zemledeliia, *Selsko-khoziaistvennyi promysel v Rossii*, maps on pp. 22–23, with explanatory text; pp. 77–104; Osoboe Soveshchanie dlia obsuzhdeniia i obedineniia meropriiatii po prodovolstvennomu delu, *Predvaritelnye itogi Vserossiiskoi selsko-khoziaistvennoi perepisi 1916 goda*, I, pp. xiii, xx, xxxiii-xxxv; Weinstein, *Evoliutsiia urozhainosti* (in *Planovoe khoziaistvo*, 1927, Nos. 7 and 8); Kondratev, *Rynok khlebov*, pp. 14–17, 212–219; Kaufman, *op. cit.*, pp. 47, 135–137; Chelintsev, *Russkoe selskoe khoziaistvo pered revoliutsiei*, pp. 39–41, 66–67, 192–194; Antsiferov, *Russian agriculture*, pp. 50, 54–57, 84–88, 129–130. An intensive illustrated study of the implements and methods of peasant agriculture in a single village will be found in Fenomenov, *Sovremennaia derevnia*, I, pp. 72–100.

³ Ministerstvo Zemledeliia, *Sbornik statistiko-ekonomicheskikh svedenii*, 9th year, p. 476; Liashchenko, *Zernovoe khoziaistvo*, pp. 122–125; Domosthenov, *Food prices* (in Struve, ed., *Food supply*), p. 241; Koniunkturnyi Institut, Moscow, *Ekonomicheskii biulleten*, 1927, No. 8, p. 9.

⁴ Prokopovich, *Krestianskoe khoziaistvo*, pp. 16–18, 144–145.

⁵ Polferov, *Selsko-khoziaistvennye rabochie ruki v 1913 g.*, p. 38, quoted in Shestakov, *Naemnyi trud v selskom khoziaistve Rossii*, p. 67. Polferov's conclusions are based upon a general *questionnaire*-investigation made by the official *Gazette of trade and industry*.

⁶ Liashchenko, *Istoriia russkogo narodnogo khoziaistva*, p. 440; Varzar, *Factories and workshops* (in Raffalovich, ed., *Russia: its trade and commerce*), p. 107.

⁷ Polferov, *Kustarnaia promyshlennost v Rossii*, p. 32. This report of the investigation bears the imprint of the Ministry of Finance.

⁸ Filippov, ed., *Promysly po obrabotke dereva*, pp. xi, 5. This volume was issued by the Chief Administration of Land-Organization and Agriculture.

⁹ *Ibid.*, p. v; Petrov, *Promyslovaia kooperatsiia i kustar*, I, pp. 13–23, 126–143, and table opp. p. 312; Rybnikov, *Melkaia promyshlennost Rossii*, pp. 7–15, 108–113.

¹⁰ Miliutin, *Rabochii vopros v selskom khoziaistve Rossii*, pp. 50, 52, 65, 67, 71.

¹¹ Glavnoe Upravlenie Zemleustroistva i Zemledeliia, *Selsko-khoziaistvennyi promysel v Rossii*, graphs on pp. 106–112. Cf. Drozdov, *Zarabotnaia plata*, pp. 12–19; on the basis of materials somewhat different in scope from those employed in the official source just mentioned, Drozdov shows the same general tendency for the period from 1906 to 1910.

¹² Ministerstvo Zemledeliia, *Sbornik statistiko-ekonomicheskikh svedenii*, 9th year, pp. 526–527.

¹³ See the tables in Ministerstvo Torgovli i Promyshlennosti, *Svod tovarnykh tsen . . . za 1913 god*, pp. ii-v.

¹⁴ See table of food-prices in Strumilin, *Oplata truda v Rossii* (in *Planovoe khoziaistvo*, 1930, April, No. 4), p. 118; also p. 117, note 4. The prices given by Strumilin are local, rather than general, and they are only very loosely and approximately representative of conditions in the country as a whole.

¹⁵ Tagantsev, ed., *Ustav o nakazaniiakh, nalagaemykh mirovymi sudiami*, edition of 1912, art. 142; also his *Ulozhenie o nakazaniiakh ugolovnykh i ispravitelnykh*, edition of 1912, arts. 1359⁹ and 1359¹⁰; Varzar, *Factories and workshops* (in Raffalovich, *op. cit.*), pp. 153–154.

16 Dubrovskii, *Stolypinskaia reforma*, p. 263; Strumilin, *Naemnyi trud v Rossii i na zapade, 1913–1925*. As late as the year 1917, only a handful of agricultural workers were organized in unions.

17 Liashchenko, *op. cit.*, p. 440; Varzar, *op. cit.*, p. 107.

18 *Rossiia*, p. 82; Ministerstvo Zemledeliia, *Sbornik statistiko-ekon. svedenii*, 10th year, p. 5.

19 Miliutin, *Selsko-khoziaistvennye rabochie i voina*, p. 12.

20 Guchman, *Proizvoditelnost truda i zarabotnaia plata v dovoennoi promyshlennosti Rossii* (in Strumilin, ed., *Problemy truda*, 1926, No. 1), pp. 160–165. Guchman undertakes to show that between 1900 and 1908, and again between 1908 and 1913, there was an increase in the average industrial wage, both nominal and real, but a decrease in the workmen's *share* in the total value of the output of the industries in which they were employed. Writing several years earlier, another statistician said, on the other hand, that the increase in the money-wage between 1900 and 1913 "did not correspond to the increased prices of the necessities of life"; Varzar, *Factories and workshops* (in Raffalovich, *op. cit.*, pub. 1918), p. 162. If (without any attempt to weight the commodities) a comparison be made between the prices of rye flour, wheat flour, beef, sugar, leather, cotton cloth, wool, and kerosene, on the one hand, and the industrial money-wage on the other, in the years 1900, 1908, and 1913, the result seems to be entirely in harmony with Guchman's statement that the real wage increased between 1908 and 1913, but does not appear to support his finding that there was also an increase during the earlier period (that is, between 1900 and 1908). The list of commodities just given is, however, so limited, and the method employed above in comparing prices with wages is so casual, that our comparison can not possibly *disprove* the accuracy of Guchman's results for the earlier period. For prices, see Ministerstvo Torgovli i Promyshlennosti, *Svod tovarnykh tsen . . . za 1913 god*, pp. ii–vii.

21 For wages in Russia, see Guchman, *op. cit.*, pp. 160–163; Strumilin, *Oplata truda v Rossii* (in *Planovoe khoziaistvo*, April 1930, No. 4); Zagorsky, *Wages and regulation of conditions of labor in the U. S. S. R.* (International Labor Office, *Studies and reports*, Series D, No. 19), p. 196. For wages in Germany and the United Kingdom, see International Labor Office, *Wage changes in various countries, 1914–1925* (*Studies and reports*, Series D, No. 16), pp. 76, 85.

22 The price-comparisons are based on wholesale prices as calculated by the Institute of Conjuncture of the Commissariat of Finance in Moscow, and published in the *Ekonomicheskii biulleten* of the Institute, 1927, No. 8, p. 9. For the prices of many individual commodities in Russia and abroad, see Ministerstvo Torgovli i Promyshlennosti, *Svod tovarnykh tsen . . . 1913 god*. For prices on certain specific commodities in 1913, see Strumilin, *op. cit.*, p. 118. For a comparison of real wages in Russia and abroad during the period 1905–1909, see Grinko, *The Five-Year Plan of the Soviet Union*, p. 129.

23 For Russian emigration abroad, see Woytinsky, *Die Welt in Zahlen*, I, p. 115. For emigration to Asiatic Russia, see G. U. Z. i Z., *Obzor deiatelnosti za 1914 god*, tables in appendix, pp. 18–19; Oganovskii, ed., *Selskoe khoziaistvo Rossii*, pp. 30–53; Kaufman, *op. cit.*, pp. 68–72.

24 Prokopovich, *Krestianskoe khoziaistvo po dannym biudzhetnykh issledovanii i dinamicheskikh perepisei*, pp. 21–22, 27–28, 104. The total outlay for personal needs does *not* include either taxes, or the expenditures involved in production (those for seed, fertilizer, and the like). On the general subject of budget investigations in Russia, see Chaianov and Studenskii, *Istoriia biudzhetnykh issledovanii*. The price-comparisons are for wholesale prices in 1913; the tables were calculated by the Institute of Conjuncture of the Commissariat of Finance in Moscow and published in *Ekonomicheskii biulleten*, 1927, No. 8, p. 9. The Russian and foreign prices of many individual commodities will be found in Ministerstvo Torgovli i Promyshlennosti, *op. cit.* Certain data on the *net income* of peasant households seem to indicate that Prokopovich perhaps gives too dark a picture; see Weinstein, *Oblozhenie i platezhi*, table on p. 24, and text, p. 25.

25 Weinstein, *op. cit.*, pp. 24, 47; appendix, table 2. Weinstein's data on direct taxes are drawn from the report for 1912 published by the Minister of Finance (see *ibid.*, p. 28, footnote 2). The calculation of the indirect payments made by the peasants, referred to in the text above, was made by Weinstein. Collections of direct

taxes by the State are reported in Ministerstvo Finansov, *Svod dannykh o postuplenii kazennykh okladnykh sborov po Imperii za 1907–1909 gg.* On *zemstvo* taxation, see Shingarev, *Vopros ob uluchshenii zemskikh finansov* (in Veselovskii, ed., *1864–1914. Iubileinyi zemskii sbornik*), esp. pp. 132–134. On excises and customs duties, see Michelson, *Revenue and expenditure* (in Michelson, Apostol, and Bernatzky, *Russian public finance during the War*), pp. 15, 30–50, 63; Soboleff, *Foreign trade of Russia* (in Raffalovich, *op. cit.*), pp. 308–309.

26 Lubny-Gertsik, *Dvizhenie naseleniia na territorii S. S. S. R.*, pp. 8, 19–20; Woytinsky, *Die Welt in Zahlen*, I, p. 101; Frenkel, *Osnovnoi nerazreshennyi vopros zemskoi meditsiny* (in Veselovskii, *op. cit.*), pp. 412–428; Polner, *Russian local government*, pp. 40–42.

27 Petrov, *op. cit.*, I, pp. 113–118; Kritsman, ed., *Materialy po istorii agrarnoi revoliutsii v Rossii*, I, pp. 160, 202, 244, 296, 542, 594, 636, 718, 760; II, pp. 54, 58, 62, 108, 112, 116, 120.

28 On societies and associations for the promotion of agriculture, see Kheisin, *Istoriia kooperatsii v Rossii*, pp. 158, 194–198, 215; Antsiferov, *Credit and agricultural co-operation* (in Kayden and Antsiferov, *Co-operative movement in Russia during the War*), pp. 355–363. On the co-operative savings and credit associations, see Kheisin, *op. cit.*, pp. 158, 184, 193, 215, 235; Antsiferov, *op. cit.*, pp. 246, 254, 265–266, 277, 279, 286, 289–290.

29 Kheisin, *op. cit.*, pp. 204–207; Antsiferov, *op. cit.*, pp. 377–380.

30 Petrov, *op. cit.*, I, pp. 82–92, 98–131, 282–311; Polferov, *op. cit.*, pp. 23–32; Veselovskii, *Istoriia zemstv*, II, pp. 231–256.

31 Petrov, *op. cit.*, I, pp. 92–98.

32 Kheisin, *op. cit.*, pp. 158, 184–185, 215; Kayden, *Consumers' co-operation* (in Kayden and Antsiferov, *op. cit.*), pp. 14, 38, 40, 45.

33 Odinetz, *Primary and secondary schools* (in Odinetz and Novgorotsev, *Russian schools and universities in the World War*), pp. 3–13.

34 Bogdanov, *Gramotnost* (in *Bolshaia sovetskaia entsiklopediia*, XVIII), p. 776; Woytinsky, *op. cit.*, VII, p. 255.

35 Vorobev and Makarov, *Krestianskie biudzhety po Kostromskoi gubernii*, pp. 1–26. In a very small minority of these cases the literate persons are described as *malogramotnyi* — that is, able to read and write only with difficulty.

36 Vorobev, *op. cit.*, pp. 116–123.

37 Prokopovich, *op. cit.*, p. 104.

38 *Ibid.*, p. 104; Vorobev, *op. cit.*, pp. 116–123.

39 Vorobev, *op. cit.*, pp. 100–107, 116–123. The total expenditures of the 107 families for the budget-year ran in part as follows:

EDUCATION
Schools	11	*rubls* 76 *kopeikas*
Books	34	*rubls* 49 *kopeikas*

RELIGION
Payments to the clergy	588	*rubls* 53 *kopeikas*
Oil, incense, etc.	505	*rubls* 29 *kopeikas*
Gifts to the poor	89	*rubls* 39 *kopeikas*

FUNERALS AND WEDDINGS	693	*rubls* 01 *kopeikas*
Vodka	1,671	*rubls* 57 *kopeikas*

It is not explained what is the nature of the expenditures under the item "Funerals and weddings"; one does not know, for example, whether additional payments to the priests are included under this heading.

40 Prokopovich, *op. cit.*, p. 104.

41 For some of the latest repressive measures touching the schools, see Odinetz, *op. cit.*, pp. 19–27. On the relations of Church and State, see Korkunov, *Russkoe gosudarstvennoe pravo* (rev. ed. of 1914), I, pp. 533–564; Masaryk, *Spirit of Russia*, II, pp. 191–224. On the censorship, see the interesting lists of some of the books and issues of periodicals confiscated, in Vladislavlev, ed., *Sistematicheskii ukazatel literatury*, issues for 1911, 1912, 1913, 1914. Among the items confiscated in 1912, Vladislavlev lists, for example, a number of writings by Tolstoi, and the program published by the Constitutional-Democratic Party (the Cadets) in 1906.

[42] G. U. Z. i. Z., *Russkoe narodnoe iskusstvo na Vtoroi Vserossiiskoi Kustarnoi vystavke v Petrograde v 1913 g.;* Bogoraz and Sternberg, eds., *Materialy po svadbe i semeino-rodovomu stroiu narodov S. S. S. R.;* Fenomenov, *op. cit.,* I, pp. 256–257; II, pp. 44–211.

[43] Vorobev, *op. cit.,* pp. 100–107, 116–123; see note 39 above.

[44] Chaianov, *Opyt razrabotki biudzhetnykh dannykh po sto odnomy khoziaistvu Starobelskogo uezda, Kharkovskoi gubernii,* p. 39.

[45] Vysochaishe Uchrezhd. Kommissiia, *Materialy,* I, pp. 42–43; II, pp. 135–137.

[46] Goldberg, *Traktorskoe khoziaistvo* (in *Selskoe i lesnoe khoziaistvo,* 1923, No. 7); Kaufman, *K voprosy o kulturno-khoziaistvennom znachenii chastnogo zemlevladeniia* (in Dolgorukov, ed., *Agrarnyi vopros,* II), pp. 442–628; Kaufman, *Agrarnyi vopros,* pp. 180–181, 207–212, 218–231; Chelintsev, *Russkoe selskoe khoziaistvo pered revoliutsiei,* pp. 192–215; Glavnyi Zemelnyi Komitet, *Trudy komissii po podgotovke zemelnoi reformy,* I (reports of Kaufman and Chelintsev). Other materials on the subject of proprietorial farming will be found in the works cited in note 2 above. On the question of the amount and proportion of peasant and non-peasant grain which reached the market, see Kondratev, *Rynok khlebov,* pp. 14–17, 212–219.

[47] Ministerstvo Zemledeliia, *Sbornik statistiko-ekonomicheskikh svedenii,* 9th year, pp. 580–581; the data are for 50 guberniias. See also Kosinskii, *Osnovnye tendentsii v mobilizatsii,* I, *Zemelnaia zadolzhennost,* p. 464.

[48] Based upon photographs and an interview.

[49] The inventory, and other materials on this affair, were copied by the writer in the archives of the *guberniia* in question.

[50] Based upon notes made on the spot in 1925. This manor-house had been preserved as a museum.

[51] Departament Okladnykh Sborov, *Svod svedenii o postuplenii i vzimanii kazennykh, zemskikh i obshchestvennykh okladnykh sborov za 1910–1912 g.g.,* pp. vi, viii, 120–121. The data are for 50 *guberniias,* and they cover the levies for compulsory insurance as well as the direct taxes assessed by the State, the *zemstvos,* the *volosts,* and the communes.

[52] Piontkovskii, *Istoriia rabochego dvizheniia v Rossii,* pp. 190, 202; Meller and Pankratov, ed., *Rabochee dvizhenie v 1917 godu,* p. 16.

[53] Dubrovskii, *Stolypinskaia reforma,* pp. 252–275.

BIBLIOGRAPHY

ANALYTICAL LIST OF WORKS CONSULTED

A COMPLETE bibliography of the subjects treated in this book would itself fill volumes. The following list is designed simply to identify immediately and independently each individual article or book, each composite work, and each periodical consulted in the writing of the present volume and cited in the notes appended to the several chapters. The citations in the notes were made as brief as possible, and the burden of providing full titles, and of translating Russian words into English, was left to be carried by this bibliographical list. The list therefore includes an analytical entry for each separate article cited in the notes; and except where an immediate repetition under the same name would result, there is also included an independent general entry for each periodical or composite work containing one or more of the articles which are separately cited.

In naming the place of publication, certain abbreviations have been employed: M. for Moscow; St. P. for St. Petersburg; P. for Petrograd; L. for Leningrad.

Anisimov, V. I. *Nadely (Allotments)*. In: Dzhivelegov, A. K., and others, editors. *Velikaia reforma (The Great Reform)*, v. VI. M., 1911.

Antsiferov, A. N. *Credit and agricultural co-operation*. In: Kayden, E. M., and A. N. Antsiferov. *Co-operative movement in Russia during the War*. New Haven, 1929.

Antsiferov, A. N., and others. *Russian agriculture during the War*. New Haven, 1930.

Arkhiv istorii truda v Rossii (Archive of the history of labor in Russia). P., 1921–1923. 10 v.

Armiia v pervoi revoliutsii (The army in the First Revolution). M., 1927.

Baring, M. *A year in Russia*. London, 1908.

Barykov, F. A., and others, editors. *Sbornik materialov dlia izucheniia selskoi pozemelnoi obshchiny (Collection of materials for the study of the rural land-commune)*, v. I. St. P., 1880.

Baturinskii, D. A. *Agrarnaia politika tsarskogo pravitelstva i Krestianskii Pozemelnyi Bank (The agrarian policy of the tsarist government and the Peasants' Land Bank)*. M., 1925.

Beazley, R. and others. *Russia from the Varangians to the Bolsheviks*. Oxford, 1918.

Beliaev, I. D. *Krestiane na Rusi; issledovanie o postepennom izmenenii znacheniia krestian v russkom obshchestve (The peasants in Russia; a study of the gradual modification of the significance of the peasants in Russian society)*. M., 1903.

Berard, V. *The Russian Empire and tsarism*. London, 1905.

Bilimovich, A. D. *The land settlement in Russia and the War*. In: Antsiferov, A. N., and others. *Russian agriculture during the War*. New Haven, 1930.

Bobrinskoi, A. A. *Narodnye russkie dereviannye izdeliia (Russian folk-craft work in wood)*. M., 1910.

Bogdanov, I. *Gramotnost (Literacy)*. In: *Bolshaia sovetskaia entsiklopediia (The great Soviet encyclopaedia)*, v. XVIII. M., 1930.

Bogoraz, V. G., and L. Ia. Sternberg, editors. *Materialy po svadbe i semeinorodovomu stroiu narodov S. S. S. R. (Materials on marriage and the family organization of the peoples of the U. S. S. R.)*. L., 1926.

Bogoslovskii, M. M. *Zemskoe samoupravlenie na russkom severe v XVII v. (Local self-government in the North of Russia in the 17th century)*. M., 1909–1912. 2 v.

Boiovich, M. M. *Chleny Gosudarstvennoi Dumy (The members of the State Duma)*. St. P., 1906 (?).

BIBLIOGRAPHY 313

Bolshaia entsiklopediia (*The great encyclopaedia*). St. P., 1909 (?) 22 v.
Bolshaia sovetskaia entsiklopediia (*The great Soviet encyclopaedia*). M., 1926 ff.
Brodskii, N. L. *K vole; krepostnoe pravo v narodnoi poezii* (*Toward freedom; serfdom in folk-poetry*). M., 19—— (?)
Bubnoff, J. V. *Co-operative movement in Russia*. Manchester, Eng., 1917.
Cambridge medieval history. New York, 1911 ff.
Chaianov, A. *Opyt razrabotki biudzhetnykh dannykh po sto odnomu khoziaistvu Starobelskogo uezda Kharkovskoi gubernii* (*An experimental study of the budget data on one hundred and one households in Starobelskii uezd, Kharkovskaia guberniia*). Kharkov, 1915.
Chaianov, A., and G. Studenskii. *Istoriia biudzhetnykh issledovanii* (*History of budget investigations*). M., 1922.
Chelintsev, A. *Russkoe selskoe khoziaistvo pered revoliutsiei* (*Russian rural economy before the revolution*). M., 1928.
Cherevanin, N. *Dvizhenie intelligentsii* (*The movement of the intelligentsiia*). In: Martov, L., and others, editors. *Obshchestvennoe dvizhenie v Rossii v nachale XX-go veka* (*The social movement in Russia in the beginning of the 20th century*), v. I. St. P., 1909.
Chernovskii, A., editor. *Soiuz Russkogo naroda* (*The Union of the Russian People*). M., 1929.
Chernyshev, I. V. *Agrarno-krestianskaia politika Rossii za 150 let* (*Agrarian and peasant policy in Russia for 150 years*). P., 1918.
——*Obshchina posle 9 noiabria 1906 g. po ankete Volnogo Ekonomicheskogo obshchestva* (*The land-commune after 9 November 1906 according to the questionnaire-investigation of the Free Economic Society*). P., 1917. 2 v.
——*Selskoe khoziaistvo dovoennoi Rossii i S. S. S. R.* (*Rural economy of pre-war Russia and of the U. S. S. R.*). M., 1926.
Conybeare, F. C. *Russian dissenters*. Cambridge, 1921.
Demosthenov, S. S. *Food prices and the market in foodstuffs*. In: Struve, P. B., editor. *Food supply in Russia during the World War*. New Haven, 1930.
Departament Okladnykh Sborov. *Departament Okladnykh Sborov, 1863–1913* (Department of Direct Taxes. *The Department of Direct Taxes, 1863–1913*). St. P., 1913.
——*Materialy po statistike dvizheniia zemlevladeniia v Rossii* (——*Statistical materials on transfers of the ownership of landed property in Russia*), v. XXIV, XXV. P., 1915, 1917.
——*Otchet o vykupnom dolge i vykupnykh platezhakh vsekh razriadov krestian za 1902 g.* (——*Report on the redemption-debt and the redemption-payments of all categories of the peasants for 1902*). St. P., 1905.
Departament Politsii. *Dokladnaia zapiska* (Department of Police. *A memorandum-report*). In: *Krasnyi arkhiv* (*The red archive*). M., 1925, no. 9.
Departament Zemledeliia. See: Glavnoe Upravlenie Zemleustroistva i Zemledeliia.
Dett, R. N., editor. *Religious folk-songs of the Negro*. Hampton, Va., 1927.
Diakonov, M. A. *Ocherki iz istorii selskogo naseleniia v Moskovskom gosudarstve* (*Sketches of the history of the village population in the Muscovite State*). St. P., 1898.
——*Ocherki obshchestvennogo i gosudarstvennogo stroia v drevnei Rossii* (*Sketches of social and political organization in old Russia*). St. P., 1912.
Direction Générale de l'Organisation agraire et de l'Agriculture. *Les travaux des Commissions Agraires (1907–1911)*. St. P., 1912.
Dolgorukov, P. D., and I. I. Petrunkevich, editors. *Agrarnyi vopros; sbornik statei* (*The agrarian question; a collection of articles*). M., 1906–1907. 2 v.
Dolgorukov, P. D., and S. L. Tolstoi, editors. *Krestianskii stroi* (*Peasant organization*), v. I. St. P., 1905.
Drozdov, I. *Nashe okladnoe oblozhenie* (*Our direct taxation*). In: *Sovremennyi mir* (*The contemporary world*). St. P., 1914, no. 9.
——*Zarabotnaia plata zemledelcheskikh rabochikh v Rossii v sviazi s agrarnym dvizheniem 1905–1906 g.g.* (*The wages of agricultural workers in Russia in connection with the agrarian movement of 1905–1906*). St. P., 1914.
Dubrovin, N. F. *Pugachev i ego soobshchniki* (*Pugachev and his associates*). St. P., 1859. 3 v.

Dubrovskii, S. M. *Agrarnoe dvizhenie 1905-1907 g.g. (The agrarian movement in 1905-1907)*. In: Pokrovskii, M. N., editor. *Raboty seminariev . . . 1921-1922 (Papers of seminars . . . 1921-1922)*. M., 1923.
——*Krestianstvo v 1917 g. (The peasantry in 1917)*. M., 1927.
——*Stolypinskaia reforma (The Stolypin reform)*. L., 1925.
Dubrovskii, S. M., and B. Grave. *Krestianskoe dvizhenie nakanune revoliutsii 1905 goda (The peasant movement on the eve of the Revolution of 1905)*. In: Pokrovskii, M. N., editor. *1905. Istoriia revoliutsionnogo dvizheniia (1905. History of the revolutionary movement)*, v. I. M., 1926.
——editors. *Agrarnoe dvizhenie v 1905-1907 g.g. (The agrarian movement in 1905-1907)*, v. I. M., 1925.
Dzhivelegov, A. K., and others, editors. *Velikaia reforma; russkoe obshchestvo i krestianskii vopros v proshlom i nastoiashchem (The Great Reform; Russian society and the peasant question in past and present)*. M., 1911. 6 v.
Efimenko, A. Ia. *Iuzhnaia Rus (South Russia)*, v. I. St. P., 1905.
——*Krestianskoe zemlevladenie na krainem severe (Peasant land-holding in the extreme North)*. In her: *Issledovaniia narodnoi zhizni (Researches in the life of the people)*, v. I. M., 1884.
——*Semeinye razdely (Partitions of family-property)*. In ibid., v. I. M., 1884.
Egorov, A. *Zarozhdenie politicheskikh partii i ikh deiatelnost (The birth of the political parties, and their activity)*. In: Martov, L., and others, editors. *Obshchestvennoe dvizhenie v Rossii v nachale XX-go veka (The social movement in Russia in the beginning of the 20th century)*, v. I. St. P., 1909.
Ekonomicheskii biulleten (Economic bulletin) (periodical). M.
Engelman, I. *Istoriia krepostnogo prava v Rossii (History of serfdom in Russia)*. M., 1900.
Entsiklopedicheskii slovar, Brockhaus i Efron *(Encyclopaedic dictionary)*. St. P., 1890-1904. 41 v.
Entsiklopedicheskii slovar, Granat *(Encyclopaedic dictionary)*. M., 191--1931. 49 v.
Entsiklopediia gosudarstva i prava (Encyclopaedia of law and the state). M., 1925. 3 v.
Ermanskii, A. *Krupnaia burzhuaziia (The upper bourgeoisie)*. In: Martov, L., and others, editors. *Obshchestvennoe dvizhenie v Rossii v nachale XX-go veka (The social movement in Russia in the beginning of the 20th century)*, v. I, II. St. P., 1909-10.
Etnograficheskoe obozrenie (Ethnographic review) (periodical). M.
Evreinov, N. *Istoriia telesnykh nakazanii v Rossii (The history of corporal punishments in Russia)*. [n. p., n. d.]
Fenomenov, M. Ia. *Sovremennaia derevnia (A contemporary village)*. L., 1925. 2 v.
Filippov, N. A., editor. *Promysly po obrabotke dereva (Wood-working industries)*. St. P., 1913.
Firsov, N. N. *Krestianskie volneniia do XIX veka (Peasant disturbances before the 19th century)*. In: Dzhivelegov, A. K., and others, editors. *Velikaia reforma (The Great Reform)*, v. II. M., 1911.
——*Pugachevshchina (Pugachev's rebellion)*. L., 1925.
Fletcher, Giles. *Of the Russe common wealth*. In: *Works issued by the Hakluyt Society*, no. 20. London, 1856.
Frenkel, Z. G. *Osnovnoi nerazreshennyi vopros zemskoi meditsiny (The basic unsolved question of zemstvo medical work)*. In: Veselovskii, B. B., and Z. G. Frenkel, editors. *1864-1914. Iubileinyi zemskii sbornik (1864-1914. Zemstvo jubilee collection)*. St. P., 1914.
G. U. Z. i Z. See: Glavnoe Upravlenie Zemleustroistva i Zemledeliia.
Gautier, Iu. V. See: Gote, Iu. V.
Glavnoe Upravlenie Zemleustroistva i Zemledeliia. *Obzor deiatelnosti za 1914 god (Chief Administration of Land-Organization and Agriculture. Review of activities for 1914)*. P., 1915.
——*Otchetnye svedeniia o deiatelnosti zemleustroitelnykh komissii na 1 ianvaria 1915 g. (——Report on the activities of the Land-Organization Commissions as of 1 January 1915)*. P., 1915.

——*Russkoe narodnoe iskusstvo na Vtoroi Vserossiiskoi Kustarnoi vystavke v Petrograde 1913 g.* (——*Russian folk art at the Second All-Russian Handicraft Exhibition at Petrograd, 1913*). P., 1914.

——*Selsko-khoziaistvennyi promysel v Rossii* (——*Rural industry in Russia*). P., 1914.

——*Statisticheskie svedeniia po zemelnomu voprosu v Evropeiskoi Rossii* (——*Statistical data on the land question in European Russia*). St. P., 1906.

——*1915. Ezhegodnik Departamenta Zemledeliia* (——*1915. Yearbook of the Department of Agriculture*). P., 1916.

——*Zemleustroistvo. Sbornik zakonov i rasporiazhenii* (——*Land-organization. Collection of laws and orders*). P., 1914.

Glavnyi Zemelnyi Komitet. *Trudy Komissii po podgotovke zemelnoi reformy* (Chief Land Committee. *Transactions of the Commissions for the Preparation of the Land Reform*). P., 1917(?)–1918. 5 v.

Goldberg, Ia. *Traktorskoe khoziaistvo* (*Tractor economy*). In: *Selskoe i lesnoe khoziaistvo* (*Rural and forest economy*). M., 1923, no. 7.

Goremykin, I. L., editor. *Svod uzakonenii i rasporiazhenii pravitelstva ob ustroistve selskogo sostoianiia i uchrezhdenii po krestianskim delam, s vosposledovavshimi po nim raziasneniiami, soderzhashchimisia v resheniiakh Pravitelstvuiushchego Senata i v postanovleniiakh i rasporiazheniiakh vysshikh pravitelstvennykh uchrezhdenii* (*Code of laws and orders of the government on the organization of the village class and of the institutions in charge of peasant affairs, with the ensuing interpretations contained in the decisions of the Governing Senate and in the regulations and dispositions of the higher governmental institutions*). St. P., 1903. 2 v.

Goremykin, M. I. *Agrarnyi vopros; nekotorye dannye k obsuzhdeniiu ego v Gosudarstvennoi Dume* (*The agrarian question; certain data for the consideration of this question in the State Duma*). St. P., 1907.

Gorn, V., and others, editors. *Borba obshchestvennykh sil v russkoi revoliutsii* (*The struggle of social forces in the Russian revolution*). M., 1907. 3 v.

Gosudarstvennaia Duma. *Materialy k stenograficheskim otchetam 1906 g. Korrekturnye ottiski po zasedaniiam 39 i 40, 6 i 7 iiulia* (State Duma. *Materials for the stenographic report, 1906. Proof-sheets for meetings 39 and 40, 6–7 July*). St. P., 1907.

——*Prilozheniia k stenograficheskim otchetam Gos. Dumy. Tretii sozyv. Sessiia I, 1907–1908 g.g.* (——*Supplements to the stenographic report of the Third Duma. Session I, 1907–1908*). St. P., 1910.

——*Stenograficheskie otchety 1906 goda. Sessiia pervaia* (——*Stenographic report, 1906. Session I*). St. P., 1906. 2 v.

——*vtorogo sozyva. Doklady* (——*Second. Reports*). St. P., 1907.

Gosudarstvennyi Dvorianskii Zemelnyi Bank. *Otchet . . . za 1903 god* (Nobles' State Land Bank. *Report . . . for 1903*). St. P., 1905.

Gote, Iu. V. *Ocherk istorii zemlevladeniia v Rossii* (*Outline of the history of land ownership in Russia*). Sergiev Posad, 1915.

——*Zamoskovnyi krai v XVII veke* (*The territory of Old Muscovy in the 17th century*). M., 1906.

Grabar, I., editor. *Istoriia russkogo iskusstva* (*History of Russian art*). M., 1910–(?) 6 v.

Grabenskii, V. *Istoriia polskogo naroda* (*History of the Polish nation*). St. P., 1910.

Grinko, G. T. *The Five-Year Plan of the Soviet Union.* New York, 1930.

Groman, V. *Vserossiiskii Krestianskii soiuz* (*The All-Russian Peasants' Union*). In: *Materialy k krestianskomu voprosu* (*Materials on the peasant question*). Rostov on Don, 1905.

Grushevskii, M. *Illiustrirovannaia istoriia Ukrainy* (*Illustrated history of the Ukraina*). P., [n. d.]

Guchman, B. A. *Proizvoditelnost truda i zarabotnaia plata v dovoennoi promyshlennosti Rossii* (*Productivity of labor, and wages, in the pre-war industry of Russia*). In: Strumilin, S. G., editor. *Problemy truda* (*Problems of labor*), v. I. M., 1926.

Herzen, A. *Memoirs.* Translated by G. D. Duff. New Haven, 1923.
Herzenstein, M. Ia. *Krestianskii Bank (The Peasants' Bank).* In: Dolgorukov, P. D., and I. I. Petrunkevich, editors. *Agrarnyi vopros (The agrarian question),* v. I. M., 1906.
Holme, C., editor. *Peasant art in Russia* (Special Autumn number of *The studio*). London, 1912.
Iakovlev, A. *Zasechnaia cherta Moskovskogo gosudarstva v XVII veke (The frontier-line of the Muscovite State in the 17th century).* M., 1916.
——editor. *Pamiatniki istorii Smutnogo vremeni (Historical documents of the Time of Troubles).* M., 1909.
Iakovlev, V. I. *Kratkii ukazatel po Ekaterininskomu dvortsu-muzeiu (Brief guide to the palace-museum of Catherine).* L., 1926.
——*Okhrana tsarskoi rezidentsii (The protection of the Tsar's residence).* L., 1926.
Iaroslavskii, E. *Dekabrskoe vosstanie (The December revolt).* In: Pokrovskii, M. N., editor. *1905. Istoriia revoliutsionnogo dvizheniia (1905. History of the revolutionary movement),* v. III, pt. 2. M., 1925.
Ignatovich, I. I. *Borba krestian za osvobozhdenie (The struggle of the peasants for emancipation).* L., 1924.
——*Pomeshchichi krestiane nakanune osvobozhdeniia (The landlords' peasants on the eve of the Emancipation).* L., 1925.
Imperatorskoe Volnoe Ekonomicheskoe obshchestvo. *Agrarnoe dvizhenie 1905–1906* g.g. (Imperial Free Economic Society. *The agrarian movement of 1905–1906*), 2 v. In its: *Trudy (Transactions).* St. P., 1908, nos. 3–5.
——*Trudy (*——*Transactions).* St. P.
International Labor Office. *Wage changes in various countries, 1914–1925.* In its: *Studies and reports,* series D, no. 16. Geneva, 1922.
Iskry (The spark) (periodical). St. P.
Istoriia Soveta Rabochikh deputatov g. S.-Peterburga (History of the Soviet of Workers' Deputies of the city of St. Petersburg). St. P., 190–.
Ivaniukov, I. *Padenie krepostnogo prava v Rossii (The fall of bondage right in Russia).* St. P., 1903.
Ivanov, P., *Pozemelnye soiuzy i peredely na severe v XVII v. (Land unions and land partitions in the North in the 17th century).* In: Moskovskoe Arkheologicheskoe obshchestvo. Arkheograf. komissiia. *Drevnosti. Trudy* (Moscow Archaeological Society. Archaeographic Commission. *Antiquities. Transactions).* M., 1902.
Ivanov-Razumnik. *Istoriia russkoi obshchestvennoi mysli (The history of Russian social thought).* St. P., 1907. 2 v.
Kachorovskii, K. R. *Biurokraticheskii zakon i krestianskaia obshchina (The bureaucratic law and the peasant land-commune).* In: *Russkoe bogatstvo (Russian wealth).* St. P., 1910, no. 7.
——*Narodnoe pravo (Folk law).* M., 1906.
——*Russkaia obshchina (The Russian land-commune),* v. I. St. P., 1900.
Karpov, N. *Agrarnaia politika Stolypina (The agrarian policy of Stolypin).* L., 1925.
——editor. *Krestianskoe dvizhenie v revoliutsii 1905 goda v dokumentakh (The peasant movement in the Revolution of 1905, in documents).* L., 1926.
Kaufman, A. A. *Agrarnyi vopros v Rossii (The agrarian question in Russia).* M., 1919.
——*Krestianskii Pozemelnyi Bank (The Peasants' Land Bank).* In: *Entsiklop. slovar,* Granat (*Encyclopaedic dictionary*), v. XXV. M., 1914(?).
——*K voprosu o kulturno-khoziaistvennom znachenii chastnogo zemlevladeniia (On the question of the agricultural and economic significance of private land-ownership).* In: Dolgorukov, P. D., and I. I. Petrunkevich, editors. *Agrarnyi vopros (The agrarian question),* v. II. M., 1907.
——*Russkaia obshchina v protsesse ee zarozhdeniia i rosta (The Russian land-commune in the process of its inception and growth).* M., 1908.
Kayden, E. M. *Consumers' co-operation.* In: Kayden, E. M., and A. N. Antsiferov. *Co-operative movement in Russia during the War.* New Haven, 1929.
Khauke, O. A. *Krestianskoe zemelnoe pravo (Peasant land law).* M., 1914.
Kheisin, M. L. *Istoriia kooperatsii v Rossii (History of the co-operative movement in Russia).* L., 1926.

Khriashcheva, A. I. *O kritike statisticheskikh izdanii (On the criticism of statistical publications).* In: *Vestnik statistiki (Statistical messenger).* M., 1923, no. XIII.

Khrustalev-Nosar, G. *Istoriia Soveta Rabochikh deputatov do 26 noiabria 1905 g. (History of the Soviet of Workers' Deputies up to 26 November 1905).* In: *Istoriia Soveta Rabochikh deputatov g. S.-Peterburga (History of the Soviet of Workers' Deputies of the city of St. Petersburg).* St. P., 190–.

Kirillov, L. *Otkhozhie promysly (Work away from home).* In: *Rossiia, ee nastoiashchee i proshedshee (Russia, her present and past),* pp. 264–274. St. P., 1900.

Kizevetter, A. A. *Mestnoe samoupravlenie v Rossii, IX–XIX st. (Local self-government in Russia from the 9th to the 19th century).* M., 1910.

Kliuchevskii, V. O. *Istoriia soslovii v Rossii (History of the classes in Russia).* M., 1914.

——*Kurs russkoi istorii (Course in Russian history).* M., 1922–23. 5 v.

——*Proiskhozhdenie krepostnogo prava v Rossii (Origin of bondage right in Russia).* In his: *Opyty i issledovaniia (Essays and researches).* P., 1918.

Kniazkov, S. A. *Ocherki iz istorii do-Petrovskoi Rusi (Outlines of the history of pre-Petrine Russia).* St. P., 1917.

Kolpinskii, V. *Iz offitsialnoi zapiski o krestianskikh besporiadkakh v 8o-kh godakh 19-go veka (From an official memorandum on the peasant disorders of the 'eighties of the 19th century).* In: *Arkhiv istorii truda v Rossii (Archive of the history of labor in Russia),* v. II. P., 1921.

Koltsov, D. *Rabochie v 1890–1904 g.g. (The working men in the years 1890–1904).* In: Martov, L., and others, editors. *Obshchestvennoe dvizhenie v Rossii v nachale XX-go veka (The social movement in Russia in the beginning of the 20th century),* v. I. St. P., 1909.

——*Rabochie v 1905–1907 g.g. (The working men in the years 1905–1907).* In: *ibid.,* v. II, pt. 1. St. P., 1910.

Kondratev, N. D. *Rynok khlebov i ego regulirovanie vo vremia voiny i revoliutsii (The grain market and its regulation during the War and the Revolution).* M., 1922.

Korf, S. A. *Dvorianstvo i ego soslovnoe upravlenie za stoletie 1762–1855 g.g. (The nobility and their class administration during the century from 1762 to 1855).* St. P., 1906.

Korkunov, N. M. *Russkoe gosudarstvennoe pravo (Russian public law).* St. P.; v. I, 1914; v. II, 1913.

Kornilov, A. A. *Fakticheskie dannye o nastroenii krestian (Data on the mood of the peasants).* In: *Pravo (Law).* St. P., 21 Aug. 1905, no. 33.

——*Krestianskaia reforma (The peasant reform).* St. P., 1905.

——*Kurs istorii Rossii XIX veka (Course in the history of Russia in the 19th century).* M., 1918. 3 v.

——*Reforma 19 fevralia 1864 g. v Tsarstve Polskom (The Reform of 19 February 1864 in the Kingdom of Poland).* In: Dzhivelegov, A. K., and others, editors. *Velikaia reforma (The Great Reform),* v. V. St. P., 1911.

Kosinskii, V. A. *Osnovnye tendentsii v mobilizatsii zemelnoi sobstvennosti i ikh sotsialno-ekonomicheskie faktory (Fundamental tendencies and social-economic factors in the purchase and sale of landed property).* v. I, Kiev, 1917; v. II, Prague, 1925.

Kots, E. S. *Krepostnaia intelligentsiia (The serf intelligentsiia).* L. 1926.

Kovalevskii, M. *Modern customs and ancient laws of Russia.* London, 1891.

——*Rodovoi byt v nastoiashchem, nedavnem i otdalennom proshlom (Family life at the present time, and in the past, recent and remote).* St. P., 1905. 2 v.

Kovalevsky, W. de, editor. *La Russie à la fin du 19ᵉ siècle.* Paris, 1900.

Krasnyi arkhiv (Red archive) (periodical). M.

Kritsman, L., editor. *Materialy po istorii agrarnoi revoliutsii v Rossii (Materials on the history of the agrarian revolution in Russia),* v. I, II. M., 1928–1929.

Kropotkin, P. A. *The terror in Russia.* London, 1909.

Kulisher, I. M. *Istoriia russkogo narodnogo khoziaistva (History of Russian national economy),* v. I, II. M., 1925.

——*Istoriia russkoi torgovli (The history of Russian trade).* St. P., 1923.

Lander, K. *Krestianskoe dvizhenie v Pribaltiiskom krae (The peasant movement in the Baltic guberniias)*. In: Maslov, P. *Agrarnyi vopros v Rossii (The agrarian question in Russia)*, v. II, appendix. St. P., 1908.

Lappo-Danilevskii, A. S. *Ocherk istorii obrazovaniia glavneishikh razriadov krestianskogo naseleniia v Rossii (Outline of the history of the formation of the chief categories of the peasant population of Russia)*. In: Dolgorukov, P. D., and S. L. Tolstoi, editors. *Krestianskii stroi (Peasant organization)*, v. I. St. P., 1905.

Latkin, V. N. *Uchebnik istorii russkogo prava perioda Imperii (Manual of the history of the Russian law during the period of the Empire)*. St. P., 1909.

Leger, A. *La mythologie slave*. Paris, 1901.

Lenin, V. I. *Agrarnaia programma sotsial-demokratii v pervoi russkoi revoliutsii 1905–7 g.g. (The agrarian program of Social Democracy in the first Russian revolution of 1905–1907)*. P., 1917.

——*Razvitie kapitalizma v Rossii (Development of capitalism in Russia)*. M., 1925.

Lenskii, Z. *Natsionalnoe dvizhenie (The nationalist movement)*. In: Martov, L., and others, editors. *Obshchestvennoe dvizhenie v Rossii v nachale XX-go veka (The social movement in Russia in the beginning of the 20th century)*, v. I. St. P., 1909.

Leontev, A. A. *Krestianskoe pravo; sistematicheskoe izlozhenie (Peasant law; a systematic exposition)*. St. P., 1909.

Leroy-Beaulieu, A. *Empire of the Tsars and the Russians*. New York, 1893–96. 3 v.

Liashchenko, P. I. *Istoriia russkogo narodnogo khoziaistva (History of Russian national economy)*. M., 1927.

——*Krestianskoe delo i poreformennaia zemleustroitelnaia politika (The peasant question and the policy of land-organization after the Reform)*, v. I. St. P., 1913.

——*Ocherki agrarnoi evoliutsii Rossii (Outlines of agrarian evolution in Russia)*. L., 1924.

——*Zernovoe khoziaistvo i khlebotorgovye otnosheniia Rossii i Germanii v sviazi s tamozhennym oblozheniem (Grain economy and the relations between Russia and Germany in the grain trade in connection with the matter of customs-duties)*. P., 1915.

Liatskii, E. A. *Predstavleniia belorussa o nechistoi sile (White Russian ideas of Satan)*. In: *Etnograficheskoe obozrenie (Ethnographic review)*. M., 1890, no. 4.

Lisitsyn, A. *Dvor (The peasant household)*. In: *Entsiklopediia gosudarstva i prava (Encyclopaedia of law and of the state)*, v. I. M., 1925.

Liubavskii, M. K. *Ocherk istorii litovsko-russkogo gosudarstva do Liublinskoi unii vkliuchitelno (Outline of the history of the Lithuanian-Russian State, to the Union of Lublin)*. M., 1910.

Lokhtin, P. *Bezzemelnyi proletariat v Rossii (The landless proletariat of Russia)*. M., 1905.

Lositskii, A. E. *Eshche k voprosu o publikatsii Tsentralnogo Statisticheskogo Upravleniia o zemlevladenii i ugodiiakh po perepisi 1917 g. (Again on the question of the publications of the Central Statistical Administration on land-ownership and the types of land as shown by the census of 1917)*. In: *Selskoe i lesnoe khoziaistvo (Rural and forest economy)*. M., 1923, book XI.

——*Khoziaistvennye otnosheniia pri padenii krepostnogo prava (Economic relations at the time of the fall of bondage right)*. In: *Obrazovanie (Education)*. St. P., 1906, no. 11.

——*Publikatsiia Tsentralnogo Statisticheskogo Upravleniia o zemlevladenii i ugodiiakh po perepisi 1917 g. (Publications of the Central Statistical Administration on land-ownership and the types of land as shown by the census of 1917)*. In: *Selskoe i lesnoe khoziaistvo (Rural and forest economy)*. M., 1923, book VII, nos. 11–14.

——*Raspadenie obshchiny (The breaking-up of the land-commune)*. In: Imperatorskoe Volnoe Ekonomicheskoe obshchestvo. *Trudy* (Imperial Free Economic Society. *Transactions*). St. P., 1912, no. 1–2.

——*Vykupnaia operatsiia (The redemption operation)*. St. P., 1906.

Lubny-Gertsik, L. N. *Dvizhenie naseleniia na territorii S. S. S. R. za vremia Mirovoi voiny i revoliutsii (The movement of population within the territory of the U. S. S. R. during the time of the World War and the Revolution).* M. 1926.

Maevskii, E. *Obshchaia kartina dvizheniia (A general picture of the movement).* In: Martov, L., and others, editors. *Obshchestvennoe dvizhenie v Rossii v nachale XX-go veka (The social movement in Russia in the beginning of the 20th century),* v. II. St. P., 1910.

Makarov, N. *Krestianskoe khoziaistvo i ego evoliutsiia (Peasant economy and its evolution),* v. I. M., 1920.

Manuilov, A. A. *Arenda zemli v Rossii v ekonomicheskom otnoshenii (The economic aspects of land-renting in Russia).* In: Manuilov, A. A., editor. *Ocherki po krestianskomu voprosu (Essays on the peasant question),* v. II. M., 1905.

———*Noveishee zakonodatelstvo o zemelnoi obshchine (The latest legislation concerning the land-commune).* In: *Vestnik Evropy (The messenger of Europe).* St. P., 1912, no. XI.

———*Pozemelnyi vopros v Rossii (The land question in Russia).* In: Dolgorukov, P. D., and I. I. Petrunkevich, editors. *Agrarnyi vopros (The agrarian question),* v. I. M., 1906.

———editor. *Ocherki po krestianskomu voprosu (Essays on the peasant question).* M., 1904–1905. 2 v.

Marev, P. *Politicheskaia borba krestianstva (The political struggle of the peasants).* In: Gorn, V., and others, editors. *Borba obshchestvennykh sil v russkoi revoliutsii (The struggle of social forces in the Russian revolution),* v. III. M., 1907.

Martov, L. *Istoriia russkoi sotsial-demokratii (The history of Russian Social Democracy).* M., 1923.

———and others, editors. *Obshchestvennoe dvizhenie v Rossii v nachale XX-go veka (The social movement in Russia in the beginning of the 20th century).* St. P., 1909–14. 4 v.

Masaryk, T. G. *Spirit of Russia.* New York, 1919. 2 v.

Maslov, P. *Agrarnyi vopros v Rossii (The agrarian question in Russia).* St. P., 1905–08. 2 v.

Materialy . . . dlia istorii krepostnogo prava v Rossii, izvlechennye iz sekretnykh otchetov Ministerstva Vnutrennikh Del, 1836–1856. (Materials . . . on the history of bondage right in Russia, drawn from the secret reports of the Ministry of the Interior, 1836–1856). Berlin, 1878.

Materialy . . . k krestianskomu voprosu (Materials . . . on the peasant question). Rostov on Don, 1905.

Mavor, G. *Economic history of Russia.* New York, 1914. 2 v.

Mazurenko, S. *Krestiane v 1905 godu (The peasants in 1905).* M., 1925.

———editor. *Vserossiiskii Krestianskii soiuz pered sudom istorii (The All-Russian Peasants' Union before the judgment-bar of history).* Poltava, [n. d.]

Mech, V. *Sily reaktsii (The forces of reaction).* In: Gorn, V., and others, editors. *Borba obshchestvennykh sil v russkoi revoliutsii (The struggle of social forces in the Russian revolution),* v. I. M., 1907.

Meiendorf, A. F. *Krestianskii dvor v sisteme russkogo krestianskogo zakonodatelstva i obshchinnogo prava i zatrudnitelnost ego uporiadocheniia (The peasant household in the system of the Russian legislation on the peasantry and of communal law, and the difficulty of its systematization).* St. P., 1909.

Meller, V. L., and A. M. Pankratov, editors. *Rabochee dvizhenie v 1917 godu (The workers' movement in 1917).* M., 1926.

Mesiatsev, P. A. *Zemelnaia i selsko-khoziaistvennaia politika v Rossii (Russian policy respecting rural economy and the land).* M., 1922.

Miakotin, V. A. *Gosudarstvennaia Duma (The State Duma).* In: *Entsiklopedicheskii slovar,* Granat *(Encyclopaedic dictionary),* v. XVI. M., 191–(?).

———*Ocherki sotsialnoi istorii Ukrainy v XVII–XVIII v. (Outlines of the social history of Ukraina in the 17th and 18th centuries).* Prague, 1924.

Michelson, A. M. *Revenue and expenditure.* In: Michelson, A. M., and others. *Russian public finance during the War.* New Haven, 1928.

Miliukov, P. N. *Krestiane (The peasants).* In: *Entsiklopedicheskii slovar,* Brockhaus *(Encyclopaedic dictionary),* v. XVI. St. P., 1895.

——Ocherki po istorii russkoi kultury (Outlines of the history of Russian culture). St. P., 1900–03. 2 v.

——Vtoraia Duma (The Second Duma). St. P., 1908.

Miliutin, V. P. Rabochii vopros v selskom khoziaistve Rossii (The labor question in the rural economy of Russia). P., 1917.

——Selsko-khoziaistvennye rabochie i voina (The agricultural workers and the War). P., 1917.

Miller, A. Essai sur l'histoire des institutions agraires de la Russie centrale du XVI⁰ au XVIII⁰ siècles. Paris, 1926.

Ministerstvo Finansov. Svod dannykh o postuplenii kazennykh okladnykh sborov po Imperii za 1907–1909 g.g. (Ministry of Finance. Digest of the data on the receipt of direct taxes levied by the central government, for the Empire for the period 1907–1909). St. P., 1911.

Ministerstvo Gosudarstvennykh Imushchestv. Istoricheskoe obozrenie piatidesiatiletnei deiatelnosti Ministerstva . . . 1837–1888 (Ministry of the State Domains. Historical survey of the activities of the Ministry for fifty years . . . 1837–1888). St. P., 1888.

——Ocherk piatidesiatiletnei deiatelnosti Ministerstva . . . 1837–1887 (——An outline of the activities of the Ministry for fifty years . . . , 1837–1887). St. P., 1888.

Ministerstvo Torgovli i Promyshlennosti. Svod tovarnykh tsen . . . za 1913 god (Ministry of Trade and Industry. Digest of commodity prices . . . for 1913). P., 1914.

Ministerstvo Vnutrennikh Del. Sbornik uzakonenii i rasporiazhenii pravitelstva o selskom sostoianii (Ministry of the Interior. Collection of laws and orders of the government respecting the village class). P., 1916. [For other similar collections annotated with extracts from the interpretations of the Senate and the instructions of the Ministries, see Goremykin, editor; also Volkov, editor.]

Ministerstvo Zemledeliia. Instruktsiia po proizvodstvu Vserossiiskoi selsko-khoziaistvennoi i pozemelnoi perepisi i Vserossiiskoi gorodskoi perepisi 1917 goda (Ministry of Agriculture. Instructions for the taking of the All-Russian census of land and of rural economy and the All-Russian urban census of 1917). P., 1917.

——Sbornik statistiko-ekonomicheskikh svedenii po selskomu khoziaistvu Rossii i inostrannykh gosudarstv (——Collection of statistico-economic data on the rural economy of Russia and of foreign countries), years 9, 10. P., 1916–17.

——Stoimost proizvodstva glavneishikh khlebov v 1916 godu (——Cost of production of the chief grains in 1916). P., 1917.

Ministerstvo Zemledeliia i Gosudarstvennykh Imushchestv. Atlas kartogramm i diagramm k svodu statisticheskikh svedenii po selskomu khoziaistvu Rossii k kontsu XIX v. (Ministry of Agriculture and State Domains. Atlas of maps and diagrams to accompany the digest of statistical data on the rural economy of Russia at the end of the 19th century). St. P., 1903–05. 3 v.

——Kustarnye promysly: tekushchaia statistika (——The handicraft industries; current statistics). St. P., 1897.

——Obzor kustarnykh promyslov Rossii (——A survey of the handicraft industries of Russia). St. P., 1902.

——Otchety i issledovaniia po kustarnoi promyshlennosti v Rossii (——Reports and studies on handicraft industry in Russia). St. P., 1892–97. 4 v.

Mints, L. E. Otkhod krestianskogo naseleniia na zarabotki v S. S. S. R. (The goingaway of the peasant population for wage-work, in the U. S. S. R.). M., 1926.

Moratchevsky, V. Petites industries rurales, dites de koustari. In: Kovalevsky, W. de, editor. La Russie à la fin du 19⁰ siècle. Paris, 1900.

Morokhovets, E. A. Krestianskoe dvizhenie 1905–1907 g.g. (The peasant movement in 1905–1907). In: Proletarskaia revoliutsiia (The proletarian revolution). M., 1925, nos. 2–8 (37–43).

Moskovskie vedomosti (Moscow gazette) (newspaper). M.

Moskovskoe Arkheologicheskoe obshchestvo. Arkheograficheskaia komissiia. Drevnosti. Trudy (Moscow Archaeological Society. Archaeographic Commission. Antiquities. Transactions). M.

Mozzhukhin, I. *Agrarnyi vopros v tsifrakh i faktakh deistvitelnosti* (*The agrarian question in authentic facts and figures*). M., 1917.
Nechaev, V. *Russkoe krestianskoe obychnoe pravo* (*Peasant customary law in Russia*). In: *Rossiia, ee nastoiashchee i proshedshee* (*Russia, her present and past*), pp. 547–551. St. P., 1900.
Nekrasov, A. I. *Russkoe narodnoe iskusstvo* (*The folk art of Russia*). M., 1924.
Nevskii, V. I. *Sovety v 1905 godu* (*The soviets in 1905*). In: Pokrovskii, M. N., editor. *1905. Istoriia revoliutsionnogo dvizheniia* (*History of the revolutionary movement*), v. III, pt. I. M., 1927.
——editor. *1905. Sovetskaia pechat* (*1905. The soviet press*). M. 1925.
Novyi entsiklopedicheskii slovar, Brockhaus (*New encyclopaedic dictionary*). St. P., 1911 ff. [not completed.]
Obninskii, V. *Novyi stroi* (*The new régime*). M., 1909. 2 v.
Obrazovanie (*Education*) (periodical). St. P.
Odinetz, D. M. *Primary and secondary schools.* In: Odinetz, D. M., and P. J. Novgorotsev. *Russian schools and universities in the World War.* New Haven, 1929.
Oganovskii, N. P. *Individualizatsiia zemlevladeniia v Rossii i ee posledstviia* (*The individualization of land ownership in Russia and its consequences*). M., 1917.
——*Ocherki po ekonomicheskoi geografii Rossii* (*Outlines of the economic geography of Russia*). M., 1924.
——*Revoliutsiia naoborot* (*razrushenie obshchiny*) (*Revolution in reverse; the breaking-up of the land-commune*). M., 1917.
——*Zakonomernost agrarnoi evoliutsii* (*The orderly nature of agrarian evolution*). Saratov, 1909–1911. 2 v.; v. 2 has title: *Ocherki po istorii zemelnykh otnoshenii v Rossii* (*Outlines of the history of land-relations in Russia*).
——*Zemleustroistvo* (*Land-organization*). In: *Novyi entsiklopedicheskii slovar*, Brockhaus (*New encyclopaedic dictionary*), v. XVIII. St. P., 1914 (?)
——*Zemlevladenie v Rossii* (*Land-ownership in Russia*). In: *Novyi entsiklopedicheskii slovar*, Brockhaus (*New encyclopaedic dictionary*), v. XVIII. St. P., 1914 (?)
——editor. *Selskoe khoziaistvo v Rossii v XX veke* (*Rural economy in Russia in the 20th century*). M., 1923.
——and A. V. Chaianov, editors. *Statisticheskii spravochnik po agrarnomu voprosu* (*A statistical reference book on the agrarian question*), v. I. M., 1917.
Osoboe Soveshchanie dlia obsuzhdeniia i obedineniia meropriiatii po prodovolstvennomu delu. *Predvaritelnye itogi Vserossiiskoi selsko-khoziaistvennoi perepisi 1916 goda* (Special Conference to Deliberate upon and to Coordinate Measures Relating to Food Supply. *Preliminary abstract of the All-Russian rural-economic census of 1916*). P., 1916–1917. 3 v.
Osvobozhdenie (*Liberation*) (periodical). Stuttgart, St. P.
P. S. Z. See: *Polnoe sobranie zakonov.*
Partiia Sotsialistov-revoliutsionerov. *Po voprosam programmy i taktiki* (Party of Socialist Revolutionaries. *On questions of program and tactics*), v. I. [n. p.], 1903.
——*Protokoly pervogo sezda partii* (——*Protocols of the first congress of the party*). St. P., 1906.
Pavlov-Silvanskii, N. *Feodalizm v drevnei Rusi* (*Feudalism in old Russia*). L., 1925.
Pavlovich, M. *Vneshniaia politika i Russko-iaponskaia voina* (*Foreign policy and the Russo-Japanese War*). In: Martov, L., and others, editors. *Obshchestvennoe dvizhenie v Rossii v nachale XX-go veka* (*The social movement in Russia in the beginning of the 20th century*), v. II, pt. I. St. P., 1910.
Peisker, T. *Expansion of the Slavs.* In: *Cambridge medieval history*, v. II. New York, 1913.
Pershin, P. N. *Ocherki zemelnoi politiki russkoi revoliutsii* (*Outlines of the agrarian policy of the Russian revolution*). M., 1918.
——*Uchastkovoe zemlepolzovanie v Rossii* (*The use of land in unitary small holdings in Russia*). M., 1922.
——*Zemelnoe ustroistvo dorevoliutsionnoi derevni* (*The land-organization of the pre-revolutionary countryside*). v. I. M., 1928.

Peshekhonov, A. V. *Ekonomicheskoe polozhenie krestian (The economic position of the peasants)*. In: Dzhivelegov, A. K., and others, editors. *Velikaia reforma. (The Great Reform)*, v. VI. M., 1911.

Pestkovskii, S., and Iu. Krasnyi. *Ocherk revoliutsionnogo dvizheniia v Polshe v 1905 g. (A sketch of the revolutionary movement in Poland in 1905)*. In: Pokrovskii, M. N., editor. *1905. Istoriia revoliutsionnogo dvizheniia (1905. History of the revolutionary movement)*, v. III, pt. 1. M., 1927.

Petrov, G. P. *Promyslovaia kooperatsiia i kustar (Co-operation in production and the handicraftsman)*. M., 1917. 2 v.

Picheta, V. I. *Istoriia krestianskikh volnenii v Rossii (History of peasant disturbances in Russia)*. Minsk, 1923.

Piontkovskii, S. *Istoriia rabochego dvizheniia v Rossii, 1870–1917 g. (History of the workers' movement in Russia, 1870–1917)*. L., 1925.

Planovoe khoziaistvo (Planned economy) (periodical). M.

Platonov, S. F. *Lektsii po russkoi istorii (Lectures on Russian history)*. P., 1915.

——*Ocherki po istorii smuty v Moskovskom gosudarstve, XVI–XVII v. v. (Outlines of the history of the Time of Troubles in the Muscovite State in the 16th and 17th centuries)*. St. P., 1899.

——*Uchebnik russkoi istorii (Manual of Russian history)*. Peking, 1919.

Pogozhev, A. V. *Uchet chislennosti i sostava rabochikh v Rossii (An accounting of the number and composition of the working class in Russia)*. St. P., 1906.

Pokrovskii, M. N. *Mir i reaktsiia (Peace and reaction)*. In: Pokrovskii, M. N., editor. *1905. Istoriia revoliutsionnogo dvizheniia (1905. History of the revolutionary movement)*, v. II. M., 1925.

——*Russkaia istoriia s drevneishikh vremen (Russian history from the earliest times)*. L., 1924. 4 v.

——*Russkaia istoriia v samom szhatom ocherke (Russian history in the most condensed outline)*. M., pts. I–II, 1929; pt. III, issue 1, 1931.

——editor. *Raboty seminariev . . . 1921–1922 (Papers of the seminaries . . . 1921–1922)*. M., 1923.

——, ——*1905. Istoriia revoliutsionnogo dvizheniia v otdelnykh ocherkakh (1905. History of the revolutionary movement, in individual essays)*. M., 1925–27. 3 v.

——, ——*1905. Materialy i dokumenty (1905. Materials and documents)*. M., 1925–28. 8 v.

Polferov, Ia. Ia. *Kustarnaia promyshlennost v Rossii (Handicraft industry in Russia)*. St. P., 1913.

Polner, T. J., and others. *Russian local government during the War and the Union of Zemstvos*. New Haven, 1930.

Polnoe sobranie zakonov Rossiiskoi Imperii (Complete collection of laws of the Russian Empire). Sobranie vtoroe (Second collection), 12 Dec. 1825–28 Feb. 1881 (referred to in the notes as "P. S. Z., 2d ed."). St. P., 1830–84. 55 v. and index.

——*Sobranie tretie (Third collection)*, 1 March 1881–31 Dec. 1913 (referred to in the notes as "P. S. Z., 3d col."). St. P., 1885–1916. 33 v.

Polnyi sbornik platform vsekh russkikh politicheskikh partii (A complete collection of platforms of all the political parties of Russia). St. P., 1906.

Pravitelstvennyi vestnik (Messenger of the government) (official gazette). St. P.

Pravo (Law) (periodical). St. P.

Prokopovich, S. N. *Agrarnyi krisis i meropriiatiia pravitelstva (The agrarian crisis and the measures of the government)*. M., 1912.

——*Krestianskoe khoziaistvo po dannym biudzhetnykh issledovanii i dinamicheskikh perepisei (Peasant economy according to the data of budget studies and dynamic censuses)*. Berlin, 1924.

——*Mestnye liudi o nuzhdakh Rossii (Local opinion on the needs of Russia)*. P., 1904.

Proletarskaia revoliutsiia (The proletarian revolution) (periodical). M.

Pypin, A. N. *Istoriia russkoi literatury (History of Russian literature)*. St. P., 1911–1913. 4 v.

Radlov, E. *Ocherk istorii russkoi filosofii (An outline of the history of Russian philosophy)*. P., 1920.

BIBLIOGRAPHY 323

Raffalovich, A., editor. *Russia; its trade and commerce*. London, 1918.
Ralston, W. R. S. *Songs of the Russian people*. London, 1872.
Réau, L. *L'art russe de Pierre le Grand à nos jours*. Paris, 1922.
Richter, D. I. *Skolko zemli v Rossii i kto etoi zemleiu vladeet (How much land there is in Russia, and who owns this land)* P., 1917.
Rittich, A. A. *Zavisimost krestian ot obshchiny i mira (The subjection of the peasants to the land-commune and the village-community)*. St. P., 1902.
Romanovich-Slavatinskii, A. *Dvorianstvo v Rossii ot nachala XVIII veka do otmeny krepostnogo prava (The nobility in Russia from the beginning of the 18th century to the abolition of bondage right)*. Kiev, 1912.
Rossiia, ee nastoiashchee i proshedshee (Russia; her present and past). St. P., 1900.
Rossiiskaia Kommunisticheskaia partiia (bolshevikov). *Rossiiskaia Kommunisticheskaia partiia (bolshevikov) v rezoliutsiiakh ee sezdov i konferentsii (1898–1922 g.g.)* (The Russian Communist Party [the Bolsheviks]). *The Russian Communist Party [the Bolsheviks] in the resolutions of its congresses and conferences, 1898–1922)*. M., 1928.
Rossiiskaia Sotsial-demokraticheskaia Rabochaia partiia. *Protokoly obedinitelnogo sezda . . . v Stokgolme v 1906 g.* (The Russian Social-Democratic Workers' Party. *Protocols of the "unifying" congress . . . at Stockholm in 1906)*. M., 1926.
Rozhkov, N. *Russkaia istoriia (History of Russia)*. M., 1919–26. 12 v.
Rubinow, I. M. *Russia's wheat surplus*. (U. S. Department of Agriculture. Bureau of Statistics. *Bulletin* no. 42.) Washington, 1906.
Russkaia mysl (Russian thought) (periodical). M.
Russkaia starina (The Russian past) (periodical). St. P.
Russkoe bogatstvo (Russian wealth) (periodical). St. P.
Rybnikov, A. A. *Melkaia promyshlennost Rossii (The small-scale industry of Russia)*. M., 1923.
——*Zemledelcheskie rabochie (Agricultural workers)*. In: *Novyi entsiklopedicheskii slovar*, Brockhaus *(New encyclopaedic dictionary)*, v. XVIII. St. P., 1914 (?)
Savarenskii, N. *Ekonomicheskoe dvizhenie krestianstva (The economic movement of the peasantry)*. In: Gorn, V., and others, editors. *Borba obshchestvennykh sil v russkoi revoliutsii (The struggle of social forces in the Russian revolution)*, v. III. M., 1907.
Selskoe i lesnoe khoziaistvo (Rural and forest economy) (periodical). M.
Semennikov, V. P., editor. *Revoliutsiia 1905 goda i samoderzhavie (The Revolution of 1905 and the autocracy)*. M., 1928.
Semevskii, V. I. *Krestiane v tsarstvovanie imperatritsy Ekateriny II (The peasants in the reign of the empress Catherine II)*. St. P., 1901–03. 2 v.
——*Krestianskii vopros v Rossii v XVIII i pervoi polovine XIX veka (The peasant question in Russia in the 18th and the first half of the 19th century)*. St. P., 1888. 2 v.
——*Krestianskii vopros v Rossii vo vtoroi polovine XVIII i pervoi polovine XIX veka (The peasant question in Russia in the latter half of the 18th and the first half of the 19th century)*. In: Dolgorukov, P. D., and S. L. Tolstoi, editors. *Krestianskii stroi (Peasant organization)*, v. I. St. P., 1905.
Shakhovskii, D. I. *Vykupnye platezhi (Redemption payments)*. In: Dzhivelegov, A. K., and others, editors. *Velikaia reforma (The Great Reform)*, v. VI. M., 1911.
Shein, P. V. *Krepostnoe pravo v narodnykh pesniakh (Serfdom in folk songs)*. In: *Russkaia starina (The Russian past)*. St. P., Feb. 1886.
Shestakov, A. V. *Krestianskaia revoliutsiia 1905–1907 g.g. v Rossii (The peasant revolution of 1905–1907 in Russia)*. M., 1926.
——*Ocherki po istorii naemnogo truda v selskom khoziaistve Rossii (Outlines of the history of hired labor in the rural economy of Russia)*, v. I. M., 1924.
——*Vseobshchaia oktiabrskaia stachka 1905 goda (The general strike of October 1905)*. In: Pokrovskii, M. N., editor. *1905. Istoriia revoliutsionnogo dvizheniia (1905. History of the revolutionary movement)*, v. II. M., 1925.
Shingarev, A. I. *Vopros ob uluchshenii zemskikh finansov (The question of the improvement of the zemstvo finances)*. In: Veselovskii, B. B., and Z. G. Frenkel, editors. *1864–1914. Iubileinyi zemskii sbornik (1864–1914. Zemstvo jubilee collection)*. St. P., 1914.

Shotwell, J. T., general editor. *Economic and social history of the World War.* P. Vinogradoff, editor; M. T. Florinsky, associate editor. *Russian series.* New Haven, 1928–31. 11 v.

Simkhovitch, V. G. *Die Feldgemeinschaft in Russland.* Jena, 1898.

——*Hay and history.* In his: *Toward the understanding of Jesus.* New York, 1921.

Sivkov, K. V. *Krestianskie prigovory 1905 goda (Peasant resolutions of the year 1905).* In: *Russkaia mysl (Russian thought).* M., 1907, no. 4, suppl.

Skalon, V. Iu. *Krestianskii Bank i ego nedoimshchiki (The Peasants' Bank and its clients who are in arrears).* In: Manuilov, A. A., editor. *Ocherki po krestianskomu voprosu (Essays on the peasant question),* v. II. M., 1905.

Soboleff, M. *Foreign trade of Russia.* In: Raffalovich, A., editor. *Russia; its trade and commerce.* London, 1918.

Soiuz Russkogo naroda. *Zagovor protiv Rossii* (The Union of the Russian People. *The plot against Russia*). St. P., 1906.

Solovev, S. M. *Istoriia Rossii s drevneishikh vremen (History of Russia from the earliest times).* St. P., 1893–1897. 6 v. and index.

Spiridonov, I. *Uchet zemlevladeniia i ugodii Evropeiskoi Rossii po perepisi 1917 goda (Statistical account of land-ownership and the types of land in European Russia according to the census of 1917).* In: *Selskoe i lesnoe khoziaistvo (Rural and forest economy).* M., 1923, book VII, nos. 11–14.

Spiridovich, A. I. *Istoriia bolshevizma v Rossii ot vozniknoveniia do zakhvata vlasti: 1883–1903–1917 (The history of Bolshevism in Russia from its origin to the seizure of power: 1883–1903–1917).* Paris, 1922.

——*Revoliutsionnoe dvizhenie v Rossii (The revolutionary movement in Russia).* St. P., 1914–18. 2 v.

Strakhovskii, I. M. *Krestianskii vopros v zakonodatelstve i v zakonosoveshchatelnykh komissiiakh posle 1861 goda (The peasant question in legislation and in the commissions formed to deliberate on legislation after 1861).* In: Dolgorukov, P. D., and S. L. Tolstoi, editors. *Krestianskii stroi (Peasant organization),* v. I. St. P., 1905.

Strumilin, S. G. *Oplata truda v Rossii (The wage of labor in Russia).* In: *Planovoe khoziaistvo (Planned economy).* M., 1931, no. 4.

——editor. *Problemy truda (Problems of labor),* v. I. M., 1926.

Struve, P. B., editor. *Food supply in Russia during the World War.* New Haven, 1930.

The studio (periodical). London.

Surov, A. *Kazaki (The Cossacks).* In: *Entsiklopedicheskii slovar,* Brockhaus (*Encyclopaedic dictionary*), v. XIII. St. P., 1894.

Svavitskie, Z. M., and N. A. *Zemskie podvornye perepisi, 1880–1913; pouezdnye itogi (Zemstvo censuses of peasant households, 1880–1913; totals by uezds).* M., 1926.

Sviatlovskii, V. V. *Mobilizatsiia zemelnoi sobstvennosti v Rossii (Changes in the ownership of landed property in Russia).* St. P., 1909.

Tagantsev, N. S., editor. *Ustav o nakazaniiakh, nalagaemykh mirovymi sudiami (Code of laws on punishments which may be imposed by Justices of the Peace).* St. P., 1912.

——, ——*Ulozhenie o nakazaniiakh ugolovnykh i ispravitelnykh (Code of laws on criminal and correctional punishments).* St. P., 1912.

Tiumenev, A. *Ot revoliutsii do revoliutsii (From revolution to revolution).* L., 1925.

Tolstoi, P. *Prodovolstvennoe delo (The matter of food supply).* In: Veselovskii, B. B., and Z. G. Frenkel, editors. *1864–1914. Iubileinyi zemskii sbornik (1864–1914. Zemstvo jubilee collection).* St. P., 1914.

Tsentralnoe Statisticheskoe Upravlenie. *Pogubernskie itogi Vserossiiskoi selskokhoziaistvennoi i pozemelnoi perepisi 1917 goda* (Central Statistical Administration. *Totals by guberniias of the All-Russian census taken in 1917, of rural economy and of land*). M., 1921.

——*Pouezdnye itogi Vserossiiskoi selsko-khoziaistvennoi i pozemelnoi perepisi 1917 goda* (——*Totals by uezds of the All-Russian census taken in 1917, of rural economy and of land*). M., 1923.

——*Statisticheskii sbornik za 1913–1917 g.g.* (——*Collection of statistical data for 1913–1917*). M., 1921.

BIBLIOGRAPHY

Tsentralnyi Statisticheskii Komitet. *Obshchii svod po Imperii rezultatov razrabotki dannykh Pervoi Vseobshchei perepisi naseleniia, proizvedennoi 28 ianvaria 1897 goda* (Central Statistical Committee. *An abstract for the Empire of the results of the study of the data collected in the First All-Russian census of population taken 28 January 1897*). St. P., 1905. 2 v.

——*Statistika pozemelnoi sobstvennosti i naselennykh mest Evropeiskoi Rossii* (——*Statistics on landed property and on the inhabited places of European Russia*). St. P., 1880–1886. 8 v.

——*Statistika zemlevladeniia 1905. g. Svod dannykh po 50 gub. Evropeiskoi Rossii* (——*Statistics on land-ownership in 1905. Abstract of the data for the 50 guberniias of European Russia*). St. P., 1907.

——*Statistika zemlevladeniia 1905 g.* (——*Statistics of land-ownership in 1905*). St. P., 1906–1909. 50 v. [one volume for each of the 50 guberniias of European Russia].

Tugan-Baranovskii, M. I. *Russkaia fabrika v proshlom i nastoiashchem* (*The Russian factory in past and present*), v. I. Kharkov (?), 1926.

Vanag, N. *9-e ianvaria* (*The 9th of January*). In: Pokrovskii, M. N., editor. *1905. Istoriia revoliutsionnogo dvizheniia* (*1905. History of the revolutionary movement*), v. II. M., 1925.

Varadinov, N. *Istoriia Ministerstva Vnutrennikh Del* (*History of the Ministry of the Interior*). St. P., 1858–63. 3 v.

Varzar, V. E. *Factories and workshops.* In: Raffalovich, A., editor. *Russia; its trade and commerce.* London, 1918.

——*Statistika stachek rabochikh na fabrikakh i zavodakh za trekhletie 1906–1908 g.g.* (*Statistics of strikes of the workers in factories and mills for the three years, 1906–1908*). St. P., 1910.

Vasilev, M. K. *Antropomorficheskie predstavleniia v verovaniiakh ukrainskogo naroda* (*Anthropomorphic images in the beliefs of the Ukrainian people*). In: *Etnograficheskoe obozrenie* (*Ethnographic review*). M., 1890, no. 1; 1892, no. 4.

Veselovskii, B. B. *Dvizhenie zemlevladeltsev* (*The movement of the land-owners*). In: Martov, L., and others, editors. *Obshchestvennoe dvizhenie v Rossii v nachale XX-go veka* (*The social movement in Russia in the beginning of the 20th century*), v. I. St. P., 1909.

——*Istoriia zemstv* (*History of the zemstvos*). St. P., 1909–11. 4 v.

——*Krestianskii vopros i krestianskoe dvizhenie v Rossii, 1902–1906 g.g.* (*The peasant question and the peasant movement in Russia, 1902–1906*). St. P., 1907.

——editor. *Krestianskoe dvizhenie 1902 goda* (*The peasant movement of 1902*). M., 1923.

——and Z. G. Frenkel, editors. *1864–1914. Iubileinyi zemskii sbornik* (*1864–1914. Zemstvo jubilee collection*). St. P., 1914.

Vestnik Partii Narodnoi svobody (*Messenger of the Party of the People's Freedom*) (periodical). St. P.

Vestnik statistiki (*Statistical messenger*) (periodical). M.

Vladislavlev, I. V., editor. *Sistematicheskii ukazatel literatury* (*A systematic index of literature*), issues for 1911, 1912, 1913, 1914. M., 1913–15.

Volkov, N. T., editor. *Sbornik polozhenii o selskom sostoianii* (*Collection of laws respecting the village class*) [with interpretations of the Governing Senate, etc., etc.]. M., 1910.

Vorms, A. E. *Polozheniia 19 fevralia* (*The laws of 19 February* [1861]). In: Dzhivelegov, A. K., and others, editors. *Velikaia reforma* (*The Great Reform*), v. VI. M., 1911.

——and others, editors. *Pamiatniki istorii krestian XIV–XIX v. v.* (*Documents on the history of the peasants from the 14th to the 19th century*). M., 1910.

Vorobev, N. I. *Zemelnyi vopros v zaiavleniiakh krestian i drugikh grupp naseleniia* (*The land question [as reflected] in the declarations of the peasants and of other groups of the population*). In: Dolgorukov, P. D., and I. I. Petrunkevich, editors. *Agrarnyi vopros* (*The agrarian question*), v. II. M., 1907.

——and N. P. Makarov. *Krestianskie biudzhety po Kostromskoi gubernii* (*Peasant budgets in the guberniia of Kostroma*). Kostroma, 1924.

Voronov, V. *Krestianskoe iskusstvo* (*Peasant art*). M., 1924.

Vserossiiskii Krestianskii soiuz. *Otchety o zasedaniiakh delegatskogo sezda Vserossii-skogo Krestianskogo soiuza, 6–10 noiabria 1905 g.* (All-Russian Peasants' Union. *Reports of the meetings of the congress of delegates of the All-Russian Peasants' Union, 6–10 November 1905*). In: *Materialy k krestianskomu voprosu (Materials on the peasant question).* Rostov on Don, 1905.

——*Postanovleniia sezdov Krestianskogo soiuza, 31 iiulia–1 avgusta i 6–10 noiabria 1905 g.* (——*Resolutions of the congresses of the Peasants' Union, 31 July–1 August, and 6–10 November, 1905*). St. P., 1905.

——*Protokoly uchreditelnogo sezda* (——*Protocols of the constituent congress).* In: *Osvobozhdenie (Liberation).* Stuttgart, 1905, no. 77.

Vysochaishe Uchrezhdennoe Osoboe Soveshchanie o nuzhdakh selsko-khoziaistvennoi promyshlennosti. *Svod trudov mestnykh komitetov po 49 guberniiam Evropeiskoi Rossii* (Special Conference Formed by His Majesty's Order to Discuss the Needs of Rural Industry. *Digest of the transactions of the local committees of 49 guberniias of European Russia*). St. P., 1903–04. 22 v.

——*Vsepoddanneishii otchet. 1902–1904.* (——*Most humble report for 1902–1904*), St. P., 1904.

——See also Witte, S. Iu.

Vysochaishe Uchrezhdennaia 16 noiabria 1901 g. Kommissiia po issledovaniiu voprosa o dvizhenii s 1861 g. po 1900 g. blagosostoianiia selskogo naseleniia sredne-zemledelcheskikh gubernii sravnitelno s drugimi mestnostiami Evropeiskoi Rossii. *Materialy* (Commission Formed by His Majesty's Order of 16 November 1901 to Investigate the Question of the Change during the Years 1861–1900 in the Well-being of the Village Population of the Central-Agricultural *Guberniias,* as Compared with Other Parts of European Russia. *Materials*). St. P., 1903. 3 v.

Webb, A. D. *New dictionary of statistics.* London, 1911.

Weinstein, A. L. *Evoliutsiia urozhainosti zernovykh khlebov v Rossii do voiny i perspektivy ee razvitiia (The evolution of the yield [per acre] of grain crops in Russia before the War and the prospect of its improvement).* In: *Planovoe khoziaistvo (Planned economy).* M., 1927, nos. 7–8.

——*Oblozhenie i platezhi krestianstva v dovoennoe i revoliutsionnoe vremia (Taxation and payments of the peasants in the pre-war period and during the revolution).* M., 1924.

Wilson, I. *Obiasneniia k khoziaistvenno-statisticheskomu atlasu Evropeiskoi Rossii (Explanatory comments on the economic-statistical atlas of European Russia).* St. P., 1869.

Witte, S. Iu. *Vospominaniia (Reminiscences).* Berlin, 1922. 2 v.

——*Zapiska po krestianskomu delu (Memorandum on the peasant question).* In: Vysochaishe Uchrezhdennoe Osoboe Soveshchanie o nuzhdakh selsko-khoziaistvennoi promyshlennosti. *Materialy* (Special Conference Formed by His Majesty's Order to Discuss the Needs of Rural Industry. *Materials*). St. P., 1904.

Woytinsky, W. *Die Welt in Zahlen.* Berlin, 1925–1928. 7 v.

Zagorsky, S. *Wages and regulation of conditions of labor in the U. S. S. R.* In: International Labor Office. *Studies and reports,* series D, no. 19. Geneva, 1930.

Zapolskii, M. *Charodeistvo v severo-zapadnom krae v XVII–XVIII v. v. (Witchcraft in the northwestern region in the 17th and 18th centuries).* In: *Etnograficheskoe obozrenie (Ethnographic review).* M., 1890, no. 2.

Znamenskii, P. *Rukovodstvo k russkoi tserkovnoi istorii (Manual of Russian Church history).* Kazan, 1888.

INDEX

Each page-citation to the *notes* is enclosed in parentheses, and each such citation follows immediately after the *text*-citation to which it pertains.

A

AGRICULTURAL associations and societies, 126, 254-255.

Agriculture, natural conditions affecting, 4-9;

before the Emancipation: agriculture as conducted by the peasants, 9-11, 34-35 (277, 279), 38-39; and by the nobles, 38-40 (280), 55-59;

between the Emancipation and the Revolution of 1905: agriculture as conducted by the emancipated serfs, 67, 71, 74; and by the State peasants after the reforms of 1866-67, 91; methods and productivity of peasant agriculture, 97-99 (290); agricultural wage-work, 105-107 (292); the strip system, and economic interdependence among the peasants, 122-123; collective production among them, 125; methods and productivity of non-peasant agriculture, 129-130; townsmen as cultivators, 133;

after the Revolution of 1905: the effect upon peasant agriculture of conversion to hereditary tenure, 216-218; and of consolidation into unitary farms, 221, 226, 237-239, diagrams on 217; and of the weakening of personal and property ties within the peasant household, 227-228; the question of "capitalistic" farming by peasants, 239-242; improvement in methods, implements, and productivity of peasant agriculture, 243 (308), 254; and its comparative primitiveness, 244-245; wage-labor and real wages, 246-249 (308-309); collective activities in production, purchasing, marketing, and banking, 254-256; improvement in equipment and productivity of non-peasant agriculture, 260; comparative importance of large-scale and small-scale agriculture, 260-

261. *See also* Animals, domestic; Landholding.

Alcohol, the spirit monopoly of the State, 252; the peasants' consumption of, 252, 259.

Alexander II, 61, 139, 150.

All-Russian Peasants' Union, the, preliminary local congresses, and the first general congress, July-August 1905, 160-164; second general congress, November 1905, and the influence of the Union, 170-174, 179; arrest of its officers, 173, 187; its policy after the dissolution of the First Duma, 196; the objectives of the peasant movement as reflected in the congresses, 204-206.

Allotment-land of the peasants, distinguished from their private non-allotment-land, 99-102, 114 (293), 133-134, 221-222, 228, 236, 268-272. *See also* Landholding of the peasants; Redemption.

Animals, domestic, increasing dearth of among the peasants, 103 (292); loss of work-horses by the nobles and the townsmen, 1888-1906, 131, 133; poor quality of peasants' animals, 245.

Animals, wild, 3-6. *See also* Hunting.

Anti-Semitism, 183-185.

Architecture, *see* Manor-house; Houses, peasant.

Arctic zone, 3-4.

Armenia, nationalism in, 149, 151.

Artels, 266; of wage-workers, 126, 255-256. *See also* Collective activities.

Asia, influence of, 9. *See also* Colonization.

Assemblies, peasant, *see* Commune; *Volost*.

Astrakhan, conquest of the Khanate of, 14.

Attacks of peasants upon landlords, *see* Disturbances.

Autocracy, growth of the, and of serf-

Labor Group in the First, 205; the land laws of the Third, 209; the educational program of the Third, 256.

Dumas, municipal, 147.

Durnovo, P. N., 187, 189.

E

EASTERN Orthodox Church, the; see Orthodox Church.

Education, before the Emancipation, 44-45, 52; expansion of, and peasant literacy in 1897, 127 (295); work of the *zemstvos*, 147; further expansion of, to 1914, 256-257; the quality of peasant literacy, 257-259 (310).

"Emancipation of the nobility," the, 26.

Emancipation, reforms preceding the, 36-39, 41-44; peasant disturbances preceding the, 49-51; motives for emancipation, 57-61; liberations of serfs before 1861, 60-63; the general emancipation of the agricultural serfs, 1861 ff., 64-88; and of the "courtyard people" and the private industrial serfs, 88-89.

Emigration to foreign countries, 250. For emigration from European to Asiatic Russia, see Colonization.

Equalization, of peasant holdings by repartition, see Commune; on the question of a general, progressive, economic equalization or differentiation among the peasants, see Differentiation.

Esthonia, liberation of the serfs in, 62 (284); nationalism in, 149. See also Baltic provinces.

Eunuchs, the, 46.

Eurasian Plain, the, see Great Eurasian Plain.

Europe, the influence of, 25, 40-45, 53-54.

F

FAMILY, the, among the peasants, see Household.

Famines, 7-8, 18, 28, 40, 116; during the Revolution of 1905, 152-153, 174; in 1911, 245.

"Farm advisers," 224, 243.

Farm machinery, see Implements, agricultural.

Farms, unitary, the formation of, out of scattered strips, see Consolidation of strip holdings.

Finland, nationalism in, 149, 151.

Fishing, 3-4, 10, 255.

Flagellants, the, 46.

Flights of peasants in the era of serfdom, 16-20, 22, 31, 33, 49-51, 60, 62.

Folk-lore and folk-songs of the peasants, 17, 45, 48, 259.

Forced labor before the Emancipation, by the peasants of the Court, 30; by the serfs of the lay proprietors, 15, 20, 27-28, 38-41, 59; by the peasants of the Orthodox Church, 13, 15; by the peasants of the State, 30, 36, 59.

Forest zone, the, 4-6; map, 5.

France, the influence of, upon the nobility, 53-54.

Fundamental State Laws, the, 191, 193, 201.

G

GENERAL strike of October 1905, the, 165-167.

Georgia, the nationalist movement in, 151; the Revolution of 1905 in, 157, 159, 176-177, 188, 190; reduction of representation from, in the Duma, 202. See also Transcaucasia.

Goremykin, I. L., 193.

Government, the, of the peasants, see Commune; Volost; Zemskii chief; Zemstvos.

Grand Duchy of Warsaw, the, 63.

Great Commission of Catherine II, the, 25.

Great Eurasian Plain, the, 3-8; map, 5.

Great War, the, 264, 271 (308).

Greek Orthodox Church, the, see Orthodox Church.

Group of Toil, the, see Labor Group.

Guberniia, definition of, 266.

H

HANDICRAFTS, as practiced by the peasants, before the Emancipation, 38, 56-57; between the Emancipation and the Revolution of 1905, 104-105, 126; between the Revolution and the Great War, 246-247 (308); collective activities in production, purchasing, marketing, and banking, 255-256.

Health work of the *zemstvos*, 147. See also Population.

Hereditary tenure of allotment-land, giving place to repartitional tenure before the Emancipation, 12 (274), 34-35 (279); after the Emancipation, 71-78 (285), 91-92, 97, 119-120, 211; after the Revolution of 1905, 199-200, 211-216 (304), 218, 221-222, 227-228, 231-235 (307), 263-265.

Herzen, Alexander, 53.

Holidays of the peasants, 259.

Holy Synod, the, see Most Holy Synod.

N

11, 97-99, 243-245 (308); of non-peasant agriculture, 55, 130, 260.
Proletariat, *see* Working men.
Protectionism, *see* Tariffs.
Pud, definition of, 266.
Pugachev, Emelian, 31-32, 60, 139, 155.
Punishments, *see* Justice.

R

RAILROADS, 103. *See also* Market.
Raskolniks, the, *see* Old Ritualists.
Razin, Stenka or Stepan, 22-23.
Realism in Russian literature, 54.
Redemption of the peasant allotments, 67, 72-77, 80, 83-91 (287-288); taxes, redemption-dues, and arrears, to 1905, 95-96, 110-111, 129; the abolition of joint responsibility for, 146; cancellations of arrears in 1904, 150; the manifesto of 3 November 1905 on the reduction and cancellation of redemption-dues, 167-168; and the revolutionary manifesto of 2 December 1905, 173; effects of the cancellation, 180, 200, 210, 212.
Religion, *see* Catholic Church; *Dukhobortsy; Khlysty; Molokane;* Old Ritualists; Orthodox Church; Paganism; *Shtundisty; Skoptsy.*
Renting of land; renting-out, by the nobles, 130, 260; and by the State, 136; and by the Imperial family, 136; and by the Orthodox Church, 136; and by the peasants, 239; the peasants as tenants, 99-100 (290), 137, 243 (307).
Rents, *see* Renting.
Repartitional tenure of allotment-land, before the Emancipation, 12 (274), 34-35 (279), 46; after the Emancipation, 74-78, 91-92, 97, 112-113 (293), 119-122 (294), 153, 206, 211; after the Revolution of 1905, 199-200, 211-216 (304), 221-222, 227-228, 231-235 (307), 263-265.
Revolts of peasants, *see* Disturbances.
Revolution of 1905, antecedents of the, 128, 138-151; "Bloody Sunday," 9 January 1905, 151; the industrial workers' movement, January–September 1905, 151; causes of the peasant movement of 1905-07, 152-155; the quality of certain materials on the peasant movement of 1905-07, (299-300); development of the peasant movement, February-August 1905, 155-157; the Socialists and the peasant question, 157-160; the first congress of the All-Russian Peasants' Union, 160-164; the liberals before October 1905, 164; dis-

unity of the revolutionary forces, 164; loss of the Russo-Japanese War and its effect, 165; the general strike of October 1905, 165-166; the counter-revolutionary forces slow to organize, 166-167; the October Manifesto and other concessions by the government, 167-168; effect of the concessions on the alignment of forces, 169; the industrial workers' movement, November 1905-June 1906, 169-170; the second peasant congress, 170-174; the peasant movement, September 1905-August 1906, 174-176 (301); the attitude of the Socialists, 176-179; the peasants in the elections to the First Duma, 179-180; the liberals after October, 180-182; the growth of counter-revolutionary tendencies among the nobles, 182-183; the Union of the Russian People, 183-184; counter-revolutionary *pogroms,* 184-185; the army generally obedient, 185-186; the government and the people, 187; the election law of 11 December 1905, 187; measures of repression, 187; official indecision, 187-188 (302); further measures of repression, 189-190; summary of the situation, January-March 1906, 190; the international loan, 190; new limitations upon the powers of the Duma, 191-192; the party composition of the First Duma, 192-193; its conflict with the government, 193-195; its dissolution, 195; the decline of revolutionary direct action, 196; the development of counter-revolutionary forces, 196-197; further repressions, executions, banishments, 197-198 (303); the peasant reforms of 1906, 198-200; the Second Duma, 200-201; the electoral law of 3 June 1907, 202; the end of the revolution, 202-203; summary, 203; importance of the peasant movement, 203; political and economic objectives of the peasants, and divisions of opinion among them, 204-207 (303).
Revolution of 1917, the, 1-2, 64-65, 208, 262, 271 (308); temper of the peasants before, 263-265.
Revolutionary movements among the peasants, *see* Disturbances.
Revolutionists, non-peasant, the question of their influence upon the peasants, from the Time of Troubles to the Revolution of 1905, 139, 144-145; and during the Revolution of 1905, 153-155. *See also* Social-Democratic Party; Socialist Revolutionaries, Party of.

the Revolution of 1905, 204; the law of 1912 on the *volost* courts, 209; the law of 1906 on peasant registration, 210; taxation by, 252; definition of, 266. *See also* Commune; Household.

W

WAGE-WORK,
before the Emancipation, by peasants, 38, 57, 59;
from the Emancipation to the Revolution of 1905: work and wages in agriculture, 105-107 (292); and in industry, 107-109 (292-293); the trend of agricultural wages, 110; labor *artels*, 126; ideational influence of wage-work and urban connections upon the peasants, 127-128; low agricultural wages as a cause of the agrarian movement of 1905-07, 153;
after the Revolution of 1905: the employment of hired labor by peasants, 239-242; wage-work by peasants in agriculture and in industry, 246-250 (308-309); real wages in agriculture and in industry, 247-250 (308-309); urbanization, and the survival of connections with the village, 249; the working day in industry, 250; labor organizations, 249 (309), 255-256. *See also* Working men.

Wages, *see* Wage-work.
Wanderers, the, 45-46.
Warsaw, the Grand Duchy of, 63.
White Russia, the repartition of peasant holdings little practiced in, 35; the serf reform of 1844, 37, 39; economic inequality among the serfs, 40; the Emancipation, 85, 87-88; the reform of the State peasants, 90.
Witte, Sergei, 125, 145-146, 187-188, 190, 192.
Women, their right to vote in the communal assembly, (286).
Working day in industry, shortening of the, 250.
Working men, attitude of the Socialist Revolutionaries toward, 140, 143; and of the Social Democrats, 141-143; the position and opinions of the industrial workers before the Revolution of 1905, 148 (298); their part in the revolution, January-September 1905, 151;

strikes of agricultural workers, through August 1905, 156-157, 190; the Bolsheviks and the "agricultural proletariat," 158; the general strike of October 1905, 165-166; the workers in the revolution after the October Manifesto, 169-170, 183; strikes of agricultural workers, September 1905-August 1906, 174, 176; measures of repression, 190-191; strikes of factory workers, May-December 1906, with totals for 1905 and 1906, 196; the effect of the new electoral law of 3 June 1907, 202; the decline of the factory-workers' movement, 202-203; the non-proletarian character of the peasant movement, 205-207, 243; urbanization, and the survival of connections with the village, 249; labor organizations, 249 (309), 255-256; the increase in industrial strikes, 1910-14, 264. *See also* Wage-work.
World War, the, *see* Great War.

Y

YIELDS of crops, *see* Productivity.

Z

Zemskii chief, the, 119, 121, 132, 179, 204, 209, 231-232, 266.
Zemstvos, the, their establishment, and the representation of the emancipated serfs in, 79; representation of the State peasants in, 91; predominance of the nobility in, under the law of 1890, 132, 147; work of, for education and public health, 147, 254, 256; the "*zemstvo* liberals," 147-148; attitude of the *zemstvo* toward the Russo-Japanese War, 150; their attitude during the Revolution of 1905, before October, 164; the "righting of the *zemstvos*" after October, 181-182; new regulations for peasant representation in, 209; relations of, with the Land-Organization Commissions, 223; the *zemstvos* provide "farm advisers" and model farms, 243; their assistance to agricultural laborers, 247; taxation by the *zemstvos*, 252; their assistance to the handicraft-industries, 255; definition of, 266.
Zones, natural, 3-8; map, 5.